CATHOLIC RECORD SOCIETY PUBLICATIONS

RECORDS SERIES
VOLUME 89

Essay on the Life and Manners of Robert Grosseteste

by Philip Perry

Edited by

JACK P. CUNNINGHAM

PUBLISHED FOR
THE CATHOLIC RECORD SOCIETY
BY
THE BOYDELL PRESS

2022

First published 2022

ISBN 978-0-902832-34-3

A Catholic Record Society publication
published by The Boydell Press
an imprint of Boydell & Brewer Ltd
PO Box 9, Woodbridge, Suffolk IP12 3DF, UK
and of Boydell & Brewer Inc.
668 Mt Hope Avenue, Rochester, NY 14620–2731, USA
website: www.boydellandbrewer.com

A CIP catalogue record for this book is available
from the British Library

This volume is dedicated to Prof. Giles Gasper as a small token of my gratitude. He is a generous colleague, mentor, friend and a constant inspiration. A scholar who has done so much for me personally and Grosseteste studies generally. In the words of the motto of Belfast City,

Pro tanto quid retribuamus?

CONTENTS

ACKNOWLEDGEMENTS

I first came to know of Fr Philip Perry and his work a number of years ago through a telephone conversation with Fr Peter Harris, librarian at St Albans College in Valladolid. It was then that I learnt for the first time of the existence of a biography of Robert Grosseteste, surviving in two manuscript forms, by an eighteenth-century Catholic priest. Getting to know Perry and meeting Grosseteste afresh in this work has given me enormous pleasure and I will always be extremely grateful to Fr Harris for facilitating the encounter. During my time in Valladolid, Dr Pilar Garcés was enormously helpful and generous with her time. Dr Javier Burrieza, librarian at St Albans, has been a tremendous help in putting this work together and his constant good humour was always uplifting during my time in Spain. A huge thank you also to Dr Sigbjørn Sønnesyn for his invaluable help with some very challenging Latin palaeography. In addition, thank you to Dylan Stodard for his help deciphering the sometimes spidery hand of Fr Perry. I would also like to thank the Durham Residential Research Library for awarding me a Holland Fellowship. Without it this volume would scarcely have been possible. My sincerest thanks to Dr Paul Arblaster for all his fine work as editor of this volume.

Lastly, I would like to thank my wife Maureen and my two daughters Sorcha and Caoimhe who are all a constant source of strength to me.

ABBREVIATIONS

Anglia Sacra	Wharton, Henry, *Anglia Sacra, sive collectio historiarum antiquitus scriptarum de Archiepiscopus et Episcopis Angilae*. 2 vols (London, 1691). Full text at: https://archive.org/details/AngliaSacra
An. Burt.	'Annales de Burton', *The Templars: Selected Sources*. Translated by M. Barber and K. Bate (Manchester, 2002).
Annal. Lanercost	*Annales (Chronicon) de Lanercost*. For a modern translation see, *The Chronicle of Lanercost, 1272–1346*. Translated by Herbert Maxwell (Glasgow, 1913). Full text at: https://archive.org/details/chronicleoflaner02maxw
Bardney	Richard of Bardney, '*Vita Roberti Grosthed quondam Episcopi Lincolniensis*', in *Anglia Sacra*. Edited by Henry Wharton, vol. 2, pp. 325–41.
Biblioth. britannico-hibernica	Tanner, Thomas, *Bibliotheca britannico-hibernica, sive de scriptoribus, qui in Anglia, Scotia, et Hiberia ad saeculi XVII initium floruerunt, commentaries*. Edited by David Wilkins (London, 1748). https://archive.org/details/BibliothecaBritannicoHibernicaTanner
Collectanea Anglo-Minoritica	Parkinson, Anthony, *Collectanea Anglo-Minoritica or A Collection of the Antiquities of the English Franciscans* (London, 1726). https://archive.org/details/collectaneaanglo00park
Chroniconica de Henrici Knighton	Knighton, Henry, 'Chronica de eventibus Angliae a tempore Regis Edgari usque mortem Regis Ricardi secondi', in *Henry Knighton's Chronicle, 1337–1396*. Edited and translated by G. H. Martin (Oxford, 1995).

Chron. Maj.	Paris, Matthew, *Chronica Majora*. Edited by H. R. Luard, Rolls Series 57. 7 vols (London, 1872–83; Cambridge, 2012).
De ordine Fratrum	Trivet, Nicholas, *De ordine Fratrum Praedicatorum, Annales.* Edited by Anthony Hall (Oxford, 1719). *F. Nicholai Triveti, de ordine Fratrum Praedicatorum, Annales sex regum Angliae qui a comitibus Andegavensibus originem traxerunt (AD MCXXXVI–MCCCVII) ad fidem codicum manuscriptorum.* Edited by T. Hog (London, 1845). https://archive.org/details/fnicholaitrivet00trivgoog/
Dunstable annals	*Chronicon, sive annals prioratus de Dunstable*. For a modern version see, *The Annals of Dunstable Priory*. Edited by H. R. Webster. Translated by D. Preest (Woodbridge, 2018).
Epist. Grosseteste	*Roberti Grosseteste epistolae episcopi quondam Lincolniensis*. Edited by H. R. Luard (London, 1861; Cambridge, 2012).
Fasciculus	Brown, Edward, *Fasciculus rerum expetendaum ac fugiendarum* (London, 1690).
Fasti: Lincoln	*Fasti Ecclesiae Anglicanae 1300–1541*, vol. I, *Lincoln Diocese*. Edited by H. P. F. King (London, 1962).
Letters of Robert Grosseteste	*The Letters of Robert Grosseteste, Bishop of Lincoln*. Edited and translated by F. A. C. Mantello and J. Goering (Toronto, 2009).
Mon. Ang.	*Monastici Anglicani*. Edited by W. Dugdale and R. Dodsworth (second edition, London, 1661–82). Revised by J. Caley, H. Ellis and B. Bandinel. 6 vols (London, 1817–30, reprinted 1846).
ODNB	*Oxford Dictionary of National Biography*. Edited by H. C. G. Matthew and B. Harrison (Oxford, 2004).

Polychronicon	Higden, Ranulph, 'Polychronicon de Rebus Britannicis & Hibernicis usque ad conquestum, 1327', in *Polychronicon Ranulphi Higden, Monachi Cestrensis: Together with the English translation of John Trevisa and of an unknown Writer of the fifteenth Century*. Edited by C. Babington and J. R. Lumby (Cambridge, 2012).
Thomson, *Writings*	S. Harrison Thomson, *The Writings of Robert Grosseteste* (Cambridge, 1940).
Wilkins	Wilkins, David, *Concilia Magnae Britanniae et Hiberniae*, 4 vols (London, 1737). https://archive.org/details/conciliamagnaebr03wilk
Wykes	Wykes, Thomas, '*Chronicom Thomae Wykes*', in *Historiae Anglicanae scriptores quinque*. Edited by Thomas Gale (London, 1687), pp. 21–128. For a modern version see H. R. Luard, *Annales monastici* IV (London, 1864).

INTRODUCTION

This volume provides the first printed edition of an eighteenth-century study of the life and writings of a renowned thirteenth-century bishop of Lincoln, Robert Grosseteste (*c.*1168–1253). The author of the study is the Catholic priest Philip Perry (1720–74), who obtained a doctorate of theology in Paris and served as rector of the English College in Valladolid. The essay can be seen as a contribution to the eighteenth-century English Catholic endeavour to reclaim the pre-Reformation national past, as well as an indication of how Grosseteste's contested reputation reverberated down the centuries.

The author, Fr Philip Perry

Philip Mark Perry was born to an established recusant family at Bilston, Staffordshire. At the age of twenty, having demonstrated academic promise, he was sent to study philosophy at the English College at Douai, an institution which had recently experienced something of a renaissance under the presidency of Robert Witham.[1] During this two-year course Perry continued to show scholarly potential and in 1742 he was selected to attend St Gregory's English College in Paris, there to join an elect group of scholars who were pursuing the rigorous theological course at the Sorbonne. These studies were interrupted by an illness which forced his return to Staffordshire; though he finally obtained his MA in 1748. Three years later he was ordained priest and after continuing his demanding programme of study he gained his doctorate in theology in 1754.[2]

After this date Fr Perry was in England, where for eight years he was chaplain to Rowland Eyre at Hassop Hall, Bakewell, in Derbyshire. It seems that it was during these years that he wrote his *Essay on the life and manners of Robert Grossetete*. From 1762 he lived at Heythrop Park, Oxfordshire, where he was chaplain to George Talbot, 14th Earl of Shrewsbury. Three years later he was living once more in Staffordshire at Longbirch, with the Vicar Apostolic of the Midlands, the Catholic apologist John Hornyold.[3] Here he accumulated an impressive library, helped in some measure by his friend, the famous hagiographer Alban Butler,

[1] Edwin H. Burton and Edmond Nolan, eds., *The Douay College Diaries: The Seventh Diary, 1715–1778*, Catholic Record Society 28 (London, 1928).

[2] See Michael E. Williams, 'Perry, Philip Mark', in *ODNB*, doi.org/10.1093/ref:odnb/64187.

[3] J. Milner, 'The Rt. Rev. John Hornyold', *Laity's Directory* (Dublin, 1818).

who would procure books for him in London.[4] His own inventory of the books in his library tells us that on the open shelves there were 283 works (426 volumes), with a further 92 volumes on Church History in glass cases. In addition, he acquired 140 miscellaneous works, 39 bound works, 49 unbound works, as well as twelve manuscripts of his own writing.[5] At Longbirch he continued his academic work, writing his *Schools of Medieval British Authors*. This work is typical of Perry's academic concerns which he approached with a missionary zeal, declaring: '... history raises as it were the dead to life and makes the Great Spectacle of all ages, walk in review before our eyes.'[6] In this work, as elsewhere, it is apparent that he considers the discipline of history to be the best means available to him for combatting the Reformed Churches as he sought no less than the recovery of the ancient Roman Catholic tradition in England.

When Perry was 47 years old his life took an abrupt turn as he was appointed by Richard Challoner, Vicar Apostolic of London and effectively leader of the Catholic Church in England, to the position of rector at St Alban's College in Valladolid in Spain. This was an auspicious time in the history of St Alban's since Challoner had drawn up an agreement with the Spanish Court that subsumed the English Colleges of St George at Madrid and St Gregory at Seville into a single institute at Valladolid. These colleges had been run by the Society of Jesus and their amalgamation had been necessitated by King Carlos's expulsion of the Jesuits from the country in 1767. St Alban's was now in the hands of the secular clergy, and it was about to undergo a dramatic transformation. Previously, though nominally English, it had in fact only two home-grown students resident and the Jesuit staff, along with their administrators, had all been Spaniards.[7] The principal intended function of these seminaries had been to send clergy as missionaries to England, yet during the ten years previous to Perry's arrival, Valladolid had produced as few as five priests for the English mission, a situation that had long been regarded as unsatisfactory by the Vicars Apostolic in England.[8] The expulsion of the Jesuits presented an opportunity for them to take direct control of the colleges and they acted with a good deal of alacrity. Three months after the King's decree they approached the Spanish ambassador and negotiations over the future of English seminary training were initiated. The

---

[4] Michael E. Williams, *St Alban's College Valladolid: Four Centuries of English Catholic Presence in Spain* (London, 1986), p. 103.

[5] Michael E. Williams, 'Philip Perry, Rector of the English College, Valladolid (1768–1774)', *Recusant History* 17.1 (1984), 50.

[6] A. Sáez-Hidalgo and R. F. Yaeger, 'Philip Perry's "Schools" Manuscript and the Invention of the Recusant Middle Ages', *Viator: Medieval and Renaissance Studies* 45.2 (2014), 382.

[7] M. E. Williams, 'St Alban's College, Valladolid and the Events of 1767', *Recusant History* 20.1 (1990), 223.

[8] Williams, *St Alban's College*, p. 71.

choice of rector was considered to be of utmost importance and certain stipulations insisted on him being an Englishman, and furthermore, not one who would be prone to attract 'either persecution or jealously from the British government'.[9] In spite of having no experience of the country and no grasp of the language, Perry spent seven weeks in Madrid where he managed the swift sale of the other English Colleges, the removal and transfer of their property, as well as obtaining assurances that financial assistance would be provided to the professors and students.[10] On the feast of St Anselm, 21 April 1768, the new seminary was opened after a solemn Mass. It had just two students.

Perry took up his new role with characteristic gusto. The relaxed discipline of the Jesuits was far from his tastes and he replaced their regime with one that was altogether more ordered. Within a year the number of resident students had been augmented by eight English seminarians from Douai, who arrived along with Fr John Douglass, their professor of Humanities.[11] Such restructuring must have kept the new rector occupied, yet he still managed to find time to continue his writing and during this period his attention turned to researching the life of Bishop John Fisher and the divorce of Catherine of Aragon. His unfinished two-volume manuscript biography of Fisher is still housed in the Scottish Catholic Archives. Fr Perry clearly regarded the proselytisation of Britain as the main priority of the English Church and his personal contribution was two pronged. Firstly, he would provide much needed priests and secondly, as a historian and polemicist, he would help win over the English population by demonstrating that their Church had ever been attached to Rome. In order to facilitate the latter Perry continued his avid collecting of books, working tirelessly to acquire an impressive library for St Alban's, largely from the collections that had been previously housed in Madrid and Seville. The present-day wealth of the rare books and manuscript collections in the College is testimony to his success in this area.[12] Given the Rector's predilection for waging inter-confessional wars of words he no doubt considered himself to be accumulating a considerable arsenal of ammunitions and weaponry.

Philip Perry was Rector of the College for only six years, but in that time he accomplished such a great deal that he might rightly be considered the seminary's second founder. In the heat wave of 1774 Perry was

[9] Williams, 'Philip Perry, Rector', 49.

[10] Ibid., 75.

[11] Ibid., 52. John Douglass went on to be Vicar Apostolic of the London District from 1790 until his death in 1812. See Geoffrey Scott, 'Douglass, John', in *ODNB*, doi.org/10.1093/ref:odnb/7943.

[12] A. Carrera, M. J. Carrera, C. Herrero, P. Garcés, B. Cano, E. González-Cascos, and A. Sáez, *Philip Perry's Sketch of the Ancient British History* (Newcastle, 2009), p. x.

working in Madrid when he caught a fever. He died on 4 September in the Hospice of *San Andrés de la Nación Flamenca* and was buried the following day in the Hospice chapel.

Robert Grosseteste as a pre-Henrician Reformer

Perry's *Essay* on Robert Grosseteste sets out to serve two functions. Ultimately it presents a case for the Bishop of Lincoln's canonisation: an elevation to sainthood that Perry obviously considered to be both entirely necessary and long overdue. However, the principal function of the work was to wrest Grosseteste's reputation from the hands of Protestants, particularly English Protestants, who had been largely successful in casting an image of him as a type of medieval proto-Reformer. That they were able to do this with a thirteenth-century bishop might at first seem somewhat surprising, but in truth certain events of his life, his sermons, letters and some contemporary accounts (admittedly sometimes of questionable historicity), furnished them with substantial material to work with. The usefulness of Robert Grosseteste in this respect would have been obvious to Protestant historians. In the English annals they would have encountered a man who railed against corruption, which he was unafraid of confronting even at the highest level. If the English Church wanted to prove its ecclesiastical pedigree as well as its antiquity, the Bishop of Lincoln would have provided a very useful ancestor. During the centuries of Reformation he was appropriated and presented many times to the English public as a kindred Protestant spirit; and it was from just such an appropriation that Philip Perry set out in his 'essay' to recapture him for the cause of his *Mater Ecclesiae*.

The fountainhead of what has been described as the 'myth of the proto-reformer'[13] can be traced to a contemporary of Grosseteste, the Benedictine historian Matthew Paris (*c*.1200–59) of St Alban's Abbey in Hertfordshire. Paris's *Chronica maiora* is without doubt an important medieval source but modern scholars have long been used to treating some of his accounts as prone to the type of titillation and scandal that characterises some quarters of our contemporary press. Paris wrote under the year 1250 that the Bishop of Lincoln journeyed to the Roman Curia, at that time resident in Lyon. Here Grosseteste was disgusted by the corruption he witnessed and declared, 'Oh money! Money! What power you have, especially in the Roman Curia.' In addition to this, the chronicler reproduced what was to become a famous letter in Reformation England.[14] In 1253 the Pope conferred a canonry at Lincoln on his nephew, a move to

[13] James McEvoy, *Robert Grosseteste* (Oxford, 2000), pp. 62–75.
[14] *Chron. Maj.*, 5: 393.

which Grosseteste took great exception. His Letter 128, taken as written directly to his Holiness, states in no uncertain terms that he looked upon the command as the action of a 'Lucifer' or 'Antichrist'. Consequently, as a loyal servant of the Church he was under an obligation to disobey. This was, according to Paris, but the start of Grosseteste's animosity to the papal court, which reached a peak at the end of his life when the Bishop employed his last words in a lengthy denunciation of ecclesiastical corruption. In spite of not being present, Paris managed to 'record' a deathbed speech in which the Bishop denounced the Pope as a heretic and an Antichrist.[15] As if this was not enough, the St Alban's chronicler credits Grosseteste with the execution of Innocent IV, albeit in a ghostly form. He tells us that Bishop Robert appeared after his death to the Pope as he lay sleeping in bed and attacking him with his crosier he inflicted on him a pleurisy from which he eventually died.[16] Paris is undoubtedly an important historian but his modern readers do well to remember that much of his motivation is political. As McEvoy has pointed out, Paris resolutely disapproved of the centralising policy of the Pope and the curia whom he looked upon as 'rapacious foreigners who drained money out of England'.[17] Grosseteste was a hero to Paris because in him he saw a redoubtable opponent of Rome's overweening control.

In the following century another highly important figure in English ecclesiastical history took much inspiration and garnered a great deal of personal support from the life and writings of the Lincolniensis. John Wyclif (died 1384) arrived in Oxford in the 1350s where he rose to become Master of Balliol College and the greatest logician and realist metaphysician of his generation. Wyclif discovered Grosseteste early in his career as a lecturer in logic and he was first drawn to him as a philosophical kindred spirit. He was familiar with Grosseteste's commentary on Aristotle's *Posterior Analytics*, to which he frequently had recourse in order to support his own views on such points as the reality of universals, the incorruptibility of celestial bodies, the existence of a primary material which was the essence of the universe as well as the possibility of geometry without sense data.[18] Wyclif was so impressed by his predecessor that he included him as the only modern author in a litany of intellectual giants that takes in Pythagoras, Democritus, Plato and Epicurus.[19] Later, this philosophical appreciation was expanded to include theology as he discovered Grosseteste's library in the Franciscan House at Oxford. In the past there was a tendency to underestimate Wyclif's

---

15 *Chron. Maj.*, 5: 400.
16 *Chron. Maj.*, 5: 429.
17 McEvoy, *Grosseteste*, pp. 64–65.
18 *De logica*, 2: 32–33; 3: 2–3, 35, 109, 119.
19 Ibid., 3: 19.

theological use of Grosseteste but as Anne Hudson has pointed out he read and quoted an enormous range of works including at least twenty-seven of the *Dicta*, and his *De mandatis* reproduces most of Grosseteste's *De decem mandatis*.[20] Other references include *Hexaëmeron*, *De Veritate* and *De libero Arbitrio*. This is a remarkable usage and there are obvious affinities that make this association easier to understand. The beginning of the fourteenth century saw a shift in theological practice from the magisterial *Summa* to a more analytically focused treatment of specific theological problems.[21] Most theologians, Wyclif included, approached their subject in this manner and in Grosseteste's work they would have encountered a similar method. In addition to methodological similarities, Wyclif was to find that his own theological understanding concorded with Grosseteste on many issues such as the existence of Truth implying the existence of God and that nature was important for providing analogies concerning the Trinity. Wyclif identified a theological common ground even as far as the idiosyncratic Grossetestian idea that the Incarnation would have had to occur even without the Fall.[22]

However, sometime in the 1370s what had begun as an intellectual appreciation developed into a lionisation that, according to Richard Southern, had a profound effect on the reformer's outlook. During this decade Wycliff discovered and read the versions of Grosseteste's life found in the pages of Ranulf Higden and Matthew Paris. Here he encountered a rebellious counterpart from whom he could draw inspiration. Southern tells us how, for the first time, Wycliffe saw Grosseteste not only as a congenial philosopher and theologian, but also as an uncanonised and unjustly excommunicated saint.[23] Scholars have long regarded the treatise *On Civil Government* (1376) as marking a turning point in Wyclif's life from which time on he became increasingly critical of the papacy, religious orders and ecclesiastical hierarchy. As Southern has pointed out, it was also at this time that he began to quote Paris. From 1376 until his death Wyclif was in the habit of calling on Grosseteste's support on all important matters. Wyclif perceived his own reflection in the life and works of Grosseteste, 'He saw successively a philosopher, theologian, reformer and persecuted Christian in a hostile world, with whom at every stage he could identify himself.'[24]

---

20 Anne Hudson, 'Wyclif and the Grosseteste Legacy at Oxford Greyfriars', in *Robert Grosseteste, His Thought and its Impact*, edited by J. P. Cunningham (Toronto, 2009), p. 202.

21 Stephen Lahey, 'Wyclif and Lollardy', in *The Medieval Theologians*, edited by G. R. Evans (Oxford, 2001), p. 334.

22 Richard Southern, *Robert Grosseteste: The Growth of an English Mind in Medieval Europe* (Oxford, 1986), p. 299.

23 Ibid., p. 300.

24 Ibid., p. 298.

Just as Wyclif thought that he had found a kindred spirit in Grosseteste it is not difficult to appreciate his appeal two centuries later to religious reformers who were keen to establish religious ancestry among the great historical figures of the medieval Church. As the Reformed English Church emerged from the various parliamentary acts and negotiations of the sixteenth and seventeenth centuries it was incumbent upon it to address three most thorny issues. Of prime importance it had to define its own theology. After that it had to settle on an established order, discipline and liturgy; both concerns caused much argument and ultimately the violence that was the Civil Wars. Lastly, but not of least importance, was the question of legitimacy. It was imperative that any ecclesiastical settlement that materialised from the Reformation demonstrate that it was a renascent Church rather than an innovation. After all, a true Church was *Saecula Saeculorum*, forever without end, and there was no question more stinging than 'Where was your Church before Luther?'[25] In addition, Catholic opponents of the Reformation were fond of pointing out that whilst the Roman Church may have had its faults it did have the advantage of being able to demonstrably trace its continuous roots to an Apostolic foundation. Schism was, of course, a grievous ecclesiological crime as it rent the body of Christ, and therefore Protestant historians were as eager to refute such charges as Catholic scholars were keen to substantiate them. In England this historiographical element of the inter-confessional struggle seems to have developed an exaggerated importance. In the 1960s Fred Levy rightly pointed out that compared to the other European Reformations, 'the English was in terms of justification, the most historical'.[26]

John Flood and James McEvoy indicate the particular appeal of Grosseteste for the Reformation cause:

> … in a time characterised by crises in authority, the moral weight of the bishop of Lincoln was something which participants in religious controversy wanted to claim in support of whatever their opinions were: throughout the sixteenth and seventeenth centuries no one placed himself in opposition to *Lincolniensis*.[27]

Any Reformer wishing to recruit Grosseteste to their cause found a rich seam of potentially sympathetic rhetoric associated with the Bishop in the St Alban's chronicles and it is hardly surprising that Letter 128 was

---

[25] S. J. Barnett, 'Where was your Church before Luther? Claims for the Antiquity of Protestantism Examined', *Church History* 68 (1999), 14.

[26] Fred J. Levy, *Tudor Historical Thought* (San Marino, CA, 1967), p. 79.

[27] John Flood and James McEvoy, '*Romanorum malleus et contemptor*: Confessional Identity and the Early Modern Reputation of Robert Grosseteste', in *Robert Grosseteste and His Intellectual Milieu*, edited by J. Flood, J. R. Ginther, and J. W. Goering (Toronto, 2013), p. 320.

continuously reproduced after the Reformation.[28] The deathbed diatribe was also popular, particularly because Matthew Paris has Grosseteste say that the Church will forever be subject to Egyptian bondage until it is liberated by the edge of the sword.[29] For Protestant writers in the early modern period such words elevated Grosseteste beyond a kindred spirit to somebody more akin to a prophet of their cause. Add to these accounts the Bishop of Lincoln's zeal to rid his diocese of corruption, his letter to the Oxford scholars pressing them to make the Bible the foundation text for their studies, his own *ad fontes* efforts to acquire Greek and Hebrew, and the fact that he closed many religious houses: all activities that, when viewed in a particular light, made Grosseteste somebody who might easily be cast in the mould of a godly Reformer. The fact that his life and writings were so much admired by that 'morning star' of the Reformation, John Wyclif, and by his Lollard followers, only served to add further to his proto-Protestant credentials. James McEvoy described the process of adoption:

> With the coming of the Reformation to England and the successive waves of radicalisation which it ushered in, there came the temptation to regard the medieval bishop of Lincoln as a Protestant *avant la lettre*, a 'harbinger' or a '*Vorgänger*' of the Reformation, and a sympathiser with all who suffered or had suffered under the papal yoke.[30]

John Leland (*c.*1503–52), royal chaplain to Henry VIII, was the first of his generation to speak enthusiastically about Grosseteste. He had been given a warrant to search the libraries of monasteries and during his life he had planned a great dictionary of English writers. His *De viris illustribus* was only published in 1709 but its contents were well known prior to publication. Here he presents his readers with a bibliography of Grosseteste (used by Perry). He also betrays an admiration for the bishop as he relates an account of his visit to Lyon and the 'guilty Innocent', adding for good measure that the pope was so incensed by Grosseteste's rebukes that he planned to have his bones disinterred until he was prevented by his own death.[31]

John Bale (1495–1563) converted to Protestantism sometime in the 1530s after an earlier life as a Carmelite friar.[32] After his conversion he dedicated much of his energy to the polemical cause and he became a

---

28 Ibid., p. 324.

29 *Chron. Maj.*, 5: 407.

30 James McEvoy, 'Robertus Grossatesta Lincolniensis: An Essay in Historiography, Medieval and Modern', in *Robert Grosseteste and the Beginnings of a British Theological Tradition*, edited by M. O'Carroll (Rome, 2003), p. 95.

31 John Leland, *De viris illustribus/On Famous Men*, edited and translated by James P. Carley with Caroline Brett (Toronto, 2010), pp. 477–79.

32 Oliver Wort, *John Bale and Religious Conversion in Reformation England* (London, 2013).

highly important figure with regard to presenting Grosseteste to an early modern audience as a solid enemy of Rome. Much of Bale's work is characterised by an apocalyptic schema which regarded the Church's history as one of a fall from original virtue into a corruption that was presided over by a malignant papacy. With regard to the English Church an initial halcyon period of autonomy followed Joseph of Arimathea's planting of the faith, only to have its purity and independence curtailed by the Roman mission of Augustine in the sixth century. Bale described this turn of affairs as an innovation that 'came together from the dust heap of monkery' and he characterised all these events as necessary preliminaries to the advent of the Antichrist who was to ascend to the throne in the year 666 in the form of Boniface III.[33] According to Bale, during the dark centuries after this particular Roman invasion, the flame of the true Church was kept alight in England by such luminaries as Robert Grosseteste. Inspired by his friend Leland, Bale produced two substantial bibliographies of English writers. In 1548 he published his *Illustrium maioris Britanniae scriptorium* and in 1557–59 he published his two volume *Scriptorum illustrium maioris Brytannie*. Another edition of these works, the *Index Britanniae scriptorum*, was not published until as late as the nineteenth century. Perry, however, makes extensive, if largely uncredited, use of it in manuscript form. In these pages and elsewhere in Bale's work we encounter a bishop of Lincoln who was immersed in Latin, Greek and Hebrew learning, thus anticipating both Humanism and the Reformed impulse toward *sola Scriptura*.[34] Grosseteste refuses to admit 'one of the Pope's bastards' to a canonry in his diocese. Here the Bishop of Lincoln appeals over the head of the Pope to the eternal tribunal of Christ and dispatches an angry letter to the Pope for which he is excommunicated and ultimately denied canonisation.[35]

One other way for Reformation apologists to maintain ecclesiological integrity was to argue that there had existed in Europe, outside the corrupted body of the Roman Church, a pure stream of Christianity that formed a link between the ancient Church and the Reformation via certain persecuted groups and individuals. The highly important English Protestant polemicist John Foxe (1516/17–87) in 1554 published a history of the true Church, the *Commentarii rerum in ecclesia gestarum*, in which he stated that his future intention was to bring his work down to Luther. This would then provide an unbroken link from the proto-Protestants he

33 John Bale, *Actes of the Englysh Votaryes* (Antwerp, 1546), pp. 25–26.

34 John Leland and John Bale, *The laboryouse Iourney serche of Iohan Leylande…* (London, 1549), D2v.

35 John Bale, *The Pageant of Popes contayninge the lyves of all the bishops of Rome, from the beginninge of them to the yeare of grace 1555*. Translated by J. Studley (London, 1574), pp. 116–17.

identified in the medieval period to the martyrs of the Reformation.[36] This was an ambition that he ultimately fulfilled, as the *Commentarii* was a progenitor of his more famous *Acts and Monuments* (1563 first edition) in which he claimed, for example, that the Waldensian articles were much the same as those accepted by the majority of Reformed Churches.[37] One other feature of the *Commentarii* that is worth noting is that it provided prophecies made in the Middle Ages that asserted that the Antichrist was present in the Church.[38] By the time we get to the 1563 edition of the *Acts and Monuments*, its author had conducted much research into the medieval chronicles and during the course of his endeavours he had either discovered or been gifted the *Chronica maiora*.[39] His first edition dealt only briefly with Grosseteste, but in an expanded volume in 1570 his research had provided him with material for a more extensive treatment.

When it comes to the Bishop of Lincoln, Foxe makes much use not only of Paris's *Chronica maiora* but also his *Flores historiarum*. In addition, Foxe reproduces a letter from Innocent IV, a copy of which had fallen into his hands, 'by chaunce, yea not by chaunce, but by the opportune sendyng of God', requesting that Grosseteste appoint his 'nephew' to a prebend in the diocese of Lincoln.[40] After this he goes to great lengths to reproduce Letter 128 from Paris along with his own translation, in which the actions of the pope are 'worse then those chief destroyers to wyt Lucifer and Antechrist'.[41] Foxe presents us then with Innocent's reaction to this communication which he clearly regards as illustrative of both his personality and the general nature of the papacy:

> That when this Epistle came to the knowledge of the pope, he fuming and fretyng, with anger and indignation answered with a fierce look & proud mind saying: what doting franticke wretch is this so boldly and rashly to iudge my doyngs? By swete S. Peter & Paule, were it not but that upon our clemency and good nature we are restrained, we would hurle him down to such confusion, that we would make him a fable, a gasing stock, an example, & wonderment to all the world.[42]

---

36 Elizabeth Evenden and Thomas S. Freeman, *Religion and the Book in Early-Modern England: The Making of John Foxe's 'Book of Martyrs'* (Cambridge, 2011), p. 56.
37 *The Unabridged Acts and Monuments Online* or *TAMO* (HRI Online Publications, Sheffield, 2011). 1563, Bk 1, 57. Available at: https://www.dhi.ac.uk/foxe/
38 Evenden and Freeman, *Religion and the Book*, p. 61.
39 It is possible that Foxe came across Paris himself, though his knowledge of the text may have come instead via the munificence of his colleague John Bale who died in 1563 and might possibly have bequeathed his notes to his friend. Ibid., pp. 122–24.
40 Bk 4, 426. https://www.dhi.ac.uk/foxe/
41 Ibid., 427. https://www.dhi.ac.uk/foxe/
42 Ibid., 428. https://www.dhi.ac.uk/foxe/

Interestingly, the 1570 *Acts and Monuments* finishes its account of 'Grosthed' on an ambiguous note. Whilst it goes to some length to relate the familiar ghost story from *Flores historiarum*, Foxe then makes it clear that such fabulous tales are not acceptable to a true Christian conscience. As Grosseteste's phantom appears before Innocent he addresses him in scurrilous terms. 'Oh thou scoursie, lazie, olde blade, lowsie, wretched, doting pope.' After striking him we are told,

> Neither could any phisicke of his cardinals help him. For Robert of Lincoln … did not spare him. And he that would not heare hym gently correcting hym, beyng a lyve, his stripes did he feale when he was dead.[43]

Foxe could clearly not resist the tale but his obvious discomfort betrays itself as he adds that however God deals with a man on earth it is certain that no one can appear between death and Judgement Day, 'with his staffe or without his staffe'.[44]

In spite the un-Reformed nature of some of the medieval accounts, other writers enjoyed much success in projecting back onto the Bishop of Lincoln the theological sympathies of a later age. By the end of the sixteenth century the Grosseteste the English people knew, and for the most part appreciated, was a great Churchman who clung to the basic *sola scriptura* principles of the Reformation, who was a jealous defender of his national Church's freedom from foreign interference, who railed like a prophet of the Reformation against Roman corruption and who, in a period of emerging national identity, was a local hero, a humble English David, unafraid to take on the proud Philistine giant of the papal court. He identified the pope as the Antichrist, both presaging and preparing the Lutheran Reformation to come. Most importantly, he offered proof that the Reformed tradition in England had a lineage that predated the Tudor revolt. As Simonds D'Ewes was to write in the next century:

> … the Protestant Religion flourished here near four hundred years before Augustine the Monk, the first Popish Archbishop of Canterbury, poisoned the purity of God's worship with his burthensome trinkets and ceremonies. Finally, it was from the first plantation preserved amongst the Welsh and Scots, to the days of John Wycliffe, without any interruption, and secretly practised also in England from Henry II's time, at last, to the begun Reformation of King Edward VI.[45]

---

43 Ibid., 431. https://www.dhi.ac.uk/foxe/

44 Ibid.

45 Simonds D'Ewes, *The Primitive Practise for Preserving the Truth* (London, 1645), p. 28.

Robert Grosseteste and seventeenth-century religious conflicts

In the sixteenth century the denominational makeup of those interested in staking a claim to Robert Grosseteste was almost entirely Protestant, and in the next century this largely remained the case. The first of the seventeenth-century authors to continue the tradition was Francis Godwin (1562–1633), who went on to become the bishop of Llandaff. Godwin's fame as an antiquarian rests for the most part on his *A Catalogue of the Bishops of England* (1601) which gave a good deal of space over to Grosseteste.[46] This is in itself significant since the *Catalogue* went on to become the standard reference work on the subject for the following two hundred years. In its pages we discover nothing new, although we encounter a Grosseteste whose actions are indicative of a leader who belonged to a Church that had always maintained a high level of independence. The Bishop of Lincoln, who would 'ne*v*er be i*n*duced to obey any of those monstrous and unreasonable bullies', was to be admired for taking infinite pains with the government of his Church, 'as by the Pope he was not hindered'.[47] Perry makes use of Godwin's work though nowhere does he make direct reference to it.

Protestant perspectives on Grosseteste continued to diverge from their sixteenth-century predecessor with the dean of Gloucester, Henry Field (1561–1616). His line of attack represented a considerable change as *Of the Church, Five Books* (1606, 1628) set out to claim that the Roman Church was in true essence Protestant, though it had fallen into the hands of fanatical papists. Accordingly, he writes of the Bishop of Lincoln and others of his ilk, 'Gerson, Grosthead, and the rest, were members of the Church that was under the Papacie: but that they were not of the papall faction, nor vassals of the man of sin.'[48] Field's work had the virtue of being the first of its kind since Wyclif and the Lollards to take an interest in the thought as opposed to the events in the life of the Bishop. Though this is by no means an extensive feature, he does make tentative attempts to reference, and even quote writings and sermons.

Field's *Of the Church* led to the first of two notable Catholic exceptions to the rule that academic interest in Grosseteste was the domain of Protestants. Theophilus Higgons (1578–1659) began his career as an Anglican clergyman with anti-Catholic tendencies. Under the influence of a Jesuit he converted to Rome and in 1609 set about making amends

---

46 Francis Godwin, *A Catalogue of the bishops of England, since the first planting of Christian religion in this Island together with a briefe history of their liues and memorable actions, to neere as can be gathered out of antiquity* (London, 1601), pp. 240–42.

47 Ibid.

48 Henry Field, *Of the Church: Fiue Bookes*, edited by Nathaniel Field, second edition (Oxford, 1628), p. 808.

for what he clearly regarded as a misspent youth by writing a defence of purgatory, *The first motive of T.H. Maister of Arts*.[49] As an appendix to this work he attached a chapter with the title, 'The name, and authority of Grosthead abused by D. Field to justify the Lutheran (pretended) Reformation'.[50] In order to attack the prevailing consensus among the opposition that Grosseteste was at heart a godly Christian he reaches for his copy of Godwin's *Catalogue*, from which he quotes a conversation between a Cardinal and Innocent IV in which the former insists that for religion Grossteste is 'a CATHOLICK as well, as we'. Higgons' point is that if an Anglican bishop accepts this statement then how might Field contradict him?[51] After this he makes an attempt to take the sting out of the Bishop of Lincoln's conflict with the Pope by maintaining that the issue was legitimately based on concerns that the Italian candidates were merely inappropriate appointments and the difficulty was no more profound than an organisational issue.[52] In the end he adds with a rhetorical flourish that if Grosseteste were alive at that time and knew by whom he was praised he would exclaim, 'what evill have I done, that they should speake well of me?'[53]

The second attempt to salvage the Catholic reputation of Grosseteste came from John Pits (1560–1616), a scholar and priest from a staunchly recusant family. His bibliographical encyclopaedia of English writers, *Relationum historicarum de rebus Anglicis*, published three years after his death, was intended as an alternative to Bale.[54] Here his treatment of Grosseteste switches the focus entirely away from his testy relationship with the papacy, offering instead a laudatory account of his learning and episcopal activities. It might perhaps be the case that Pits's eirenic nature meant that he was little suited for confrontation but when reading his account of Grosseteste it is difficult to avoid the conclusion that his silence on issues that the Reformed writers were able to make so much of is a rather embarrassed one.

Higgons and Pits aside, there seemed scant Catholic resistance to the appropriation of Grosseteste, a situation that changed little throughout the century. On the contrary, testimony to his acceptance as a legitimate ancestor of the English Reformed Church is the not insignificant role a piece of his scholarly output was to play in the religious debates and

---

49 See Antony Charles Ryan, 'Higgons, Theophilus', in *ODNB* https://doi.org/10.1093/ref:odnb/13241.

50 Theophilus Higgons, *The First motive of T.H. Maister of Arts, and lately minister, to suspect the integrity of his Religion…* (Douai, 1609), appendix 31.

51 Ibid., appendix 33.

52 Ibid., appendix 34.

53 Ibid., appendix 33.

54 John Pits, *Relationum historicarum de rebus Anglicis*, edited by W. Bishop (Paris, 1619), pp. 326–27. Also known as *De illustribus Angliae scriptoribus*.

conflicts that ensued within Protestant ranks. The background to this particular literary resurrection was the argument on Church government that took place in the English Church in the seventeenth century, ultimately manifesting itself in the Civil Wars. In its crudest form the difference could be characterised as between two sides. On the one hand were those of a more Calvinistic persuasion, with an inclination to regard episcopal government as a papist innovation and who favoured instead a Presbyterian structure, which they regarded as a purer, more primitive system. On the other side were those members of the English Church, including the Stuart kings, who were largely persuaded that the office of bishop was divinely ordained. As the differences escalated the two sides reached not only for their weapons, but also their polemical arms. Into the latter skirmish rode James Ussher (1581–1656), Archbishop of Armagh, who cut a rather unusual figure in that he was both a devout Calvinist and an ardent royalist. Most importantly however, with regard to present concerns, he also happened to be a first-class scholar.

In 1646 Ussher answered a long-running hermeneutical question concerning the highly important first-century letters of St Ignatius. The writings of this martyr bishop carried a great deal of weight since they are among the oldest extra-canonical writings in the Christian Church. Until the 1640s English scholars had to rely on the 'long recension' of these works which contained spurious and interpolated texts.[55] Ussher discovered a manuscript translation of the middle recension of the Ignatian letters, and presented a persuasive case that identified six of them as genuine.[56] Given that this medieval text was English, given also that Grosseteste was almost unique among his generation for being proficient in the Greek language it was written in, and considering he is the first scholar to quote it, Ussher thought it safe to conclude that it was the work of the Bishop of Lincoln. This discovery was potentially explosive since in these letters Ignatius categorically testifies to the importance of bishops, whom he tells his readers we ought to 'regard as the Lord Himself'. This was in contrast to the presbyters who should be considered as the Apostles. This had the potential to overturn the view that episcopacy was *iure ecclesiastico* (based simply on custom and consent) and offered in its place an older *iure divino* hierarchy.[57] What is interesting with regard to the opposition to this identification is that it was never argued that Ussher's source was undermined by the fact that its author was a Catholic

---

55 Jacqueline Rose, *Godly Kingship in Restoration England: The Politics of Royal Supremacy, 1660–1688* (Cambridge, 2011), pp. 133–34.

56 Allen Brent, 'The Enigma of Ignatius of Antioch', *Journal of Ecclesiastical History* 57.3 (2006), 429–30.

57 Jack P. Cunningham, *James Ussher and John Bramhall: The Theology and Politics of Two Irish Ecclesiastics of the Seventeenth Century* (Aldershot, 2007), p. 148.

bishop. Nor were its supporters in any way apologetic about its medieval provenance. These are significant indicators that the Bishop of Lincoln was accepted as a *bona fide* Churchman by both wings of the English Reformed Church even at one of the most divided periods of its history. Nor was this Grosseteste's last outing on the English religio-political stage, for as the century rolled on he seemed to appeal to all sides. In 1654 he was being lauded by the Presbyterian Provincial Assembly of London as the 'Hammer of the Romans'.[58] Then at the Restoration, Henry Hammond, a stalwart defender of the office of bishops, was able to use Ussher's edition of Grosseteste's Ignatian letters as a foundation on which to build his defence of the importance of the episcopal office in the re-established Anglican Church at the Savoy Conference in 1661.[59]

At the end of the seventeenth century Grosseteste was brought to renewed public attention when Henry Wharton published a two-volume collection of medieval manuscripts chronicling the history of the English Church.[60] The first volume of the *Anglia Sacra* consisted of a collection of monastic histories, but the second was dedicated to the lives of bishops. It was in the latter that he included a verse life of Grosseteste written in 1503 by a monk of Bardney in Lincolnshire, named only as Richard. Despite the fact that Wharton was a High Churchman his antiquarian activities were partly motivated by a desire to oppose what he saw as the irrationality and fanaticism of the Roman Church, which he contrasted with Anglicanism's reasoned piety. Presumably it is for this reason he betrays an initial anxiety with Bardney's work, which he describes as an 'unworthy effort dignified only by its subject matter'. In addition, he frankly acknowledged that he had eliminated some of the poem's grosser fables.[61] Regardless of this, Wharton achieved a good deal by way of countering a prevailing conception that the medieval Church was so blighted by superstition and popery that it was unworthy of serious study. The *Anglia Sacra*, via the Bardney work, did much to keep alive the image of Grosseteste as a pious illustration of an industrious churchman and it is a volume that Perry continually turns to. Bardney's *Life* continued to have its admirers up to the modern era. Sir Richard Southern, one of the most important Grosseteste scholars of the twentieth century, had much praise for it, writing, 'Without making any excessive claims … Richard of Bardney's account must be considered as a serious attempt

58 Provincial Assembly of London, *Jus divinum minsterii evangelici. Or the Divine Right of the Gospel-Ministry…* (London, 1654), p. 54.

59 H. de Quehen, 'Politics and Scholarship in the Ignatian Controversy', *The Seventeenth Century* 13.1 (1998), 73.

60 See the biographical appendix.

61 J. C. Russell, 'Richard of Bardney's Account of Robert Grosseteste's Early and Middle Life', *Medievalia et Humanista* 2 (1944), 45. For the *Life* see, *Anglia Sacra*, 2, pp. 325–41.

to collect all that could be known about one of the most distinguished bishops of Lincoln ....'[62]

The confessional appropriation of Grosseteste took on another dimension at the hands of Edward Brown (died 1698/9), Anglican priest of Sunbridge, Kent, and a Fellow of Clare Hall, Cambridge. This author had the intention of writing a biography of Grosseteste but was eventually prevented by ill health and death. A contemporary described him as '... an excellent scholar, a spirited writer, and singularly well versed in the controversy between the Protestants and Romanists.'[63] In 1690 he entered the inter-confessional fray by republishing *Fasciculus rerum expetendarum ac fugiendarum* (The little collection of things to be sought and things to be avoided), a German work of 1535 by the devout, though reforming, Catholic priest Hardwin von Grätz, or Ortwin von Graes (1475–1542). This work represented a collection of items that set out to 'expose the noxious elements in the [Catholic] Church's organism',[64] and to this Brown added, by way of an appendix, a second work of his own in which the subject of Grosseteste formed a substantial part. This volume presented to its readers writings that had been 'condemned by the Roman Church', including an impressive number of Grosseteste's sermons, his *Dicta* (short discourses on various topics), his *Statuta* (constitutions), and of course his by now famous Letter 128. To these he added his own commentary and what Perry calls 'peevish notes'. In spite of this conceived bias, Brown was in fact more acknowledging of Grosseteste's un-Reformed tendencies and beliefs than his predecessors; however, he admonishes his readership to excuse such blemishes on the grounds that the Bishop could hardly be expected to live in such an age as he did without being entirely unpolluted. His belief in the intercession of angels,[65] no less than in the efficacy of good works,[66] were to be overlooked in light of his manifest greatness and sincerity. Besides, his scolding sermon before the Pope at Lyon, his immense learning and his deathbed denunciations meant that any Englishman who viewed his exemplary life would be more than satisfied.[67] The Bishop of Lincoln as portrayed within the pages of the *Fasciculus rerum* is understandably tainted, and yet Brown takes it for granted that his coreligionists will, like him, discern the beating heart of a sincere Christian and a true patriot beneath the papist veneer. It is

---

62 Southern, *Grosseteste*, p. 76.

63 Samuel Pegge, *The Life and Writing of Robert Grosseteste, the celebrated Bishop of Lincoln* (London, 1793), pp. 3–4.

64 64 Friedrich Wilhelm Bautz, 'Ortwin Gratius (van Graes)', Biographisch-Bibliographisches Kirchenlexikon, 2, pp. 290–91.

65 *Fasciculus*, pp. 305–07.

66 Ibid., pp. 322–23.

67 Ibid., p. 398.

largely to this author and to this book that Philip Perry addresses his *Essay on the Life and Manners of Robert Grossetete*.

Saving Catholic Grosseteste: Fr Perry's *Fidei defensor*

The *Essay* frequently addresses Brown directly and in the first instances Perry appears to be genuinely appreciative of his scholarship and acknowledges the 'greatest help' his *Fasciculus rerum* had been in providing sources for his own work.[68] However, once the gratitude has been dispensed with Fr Perry gets down to the business of pointing out his adversary's errors as well as demonstrating their author's unscrupulous motives. Beginning with the controversy surrounding Grosseteste's episcopal consecration, in which the monks of Canterbury defended against their archbishop their right to have the ceremony take place in their Cathedral,[69] Perry tells us that Brown, 'hauls in' Grosseteste's twelfth letter (which tries to tackle the issue) as evidence that the monastic community at Canterbury opposed the consecration. The implication was that the heart of the established Roman Church in England recognised instantly that the potential Bishop of Lincoln was not cut from their own cloth. Perry's reply is indicative of the generally exasperated tone that he adopts with Brown throughout as he appeals to his audience, '... whereas it's evident to any Reader, that is not stark blind, that the question is not about consecration but *place* of consecration.'[70]

Similarly, elsewhere he takes issue when Brown seizes on one of the statutes of Grosseteste which directs that children of priests who have inherited their father's parish must be forced to resign it. Brown has accepted this as useful proof that some priests had wives and that consequently the obligation to clerical celibacy is a modern innovation, foreign to the historic practice of the English Church. Perry indignantly points out, 'Now if he means that they had them any otherwise than by abuse, and contrary to the disposition of the canons, the inference is doubly wrong.'[71]

In another place, when *Fasciculus rerum* relates that Grosseteste urged the masters of Oxford to have Scriptures as the foundation stone of all their learning, Brown is clearly impressed. Pressing the issue, he adds that this method was not only distinct from the foreign universities, but different to all practice at this time – the clear inference being that Grosseteste anticipated the *sola scriptura* impulse of the Reformation in an age that was throwing over the Word of God in order to pursue

68 Perry, *Essay on the Life and Manners*, p. 6.

69 Francis Seymour Stevenson, *Robert Grosseteste, Bishop of Lincoln* (London, 1899), p. 115.

70 Perry, *Essay on the Life and Manners*, p. 48.

71 Ibid., p. 54.

the scholarship of men. Perry takes the vicar of Sunbridge to task once more, telling him that in this observation, 'he doth not come one whit near his mark'. For good measure he provides a history lesson to debunk what he obviously regards as a common misconception. Perry informs his readership that though Thomas Aquinas and Duns Scotus might be read in private study or in the schools of the religious orders, they would not be found in the universities, which preferred Peter Lombard's *Sentences*.[72] This book, he reminds them, is made up in the first instance of Scripture passages and then the writings of the Church Fathers. In addition, even during that time when the *Sentences* reigned supreme, Biblical studies were far from neglected; indeed, one year of study was given over to the *Baccalaureus Biblicus*, during which the student learnt to explain the Testaments. This arrangement Perry, in true Counter-Reformation style, considers altogether more satisfactory than the present situation, '... when every ignorant Jackpudding or Smattered in Learning is allowed to handle, or rather mangle, the word of God, after their own wild and whimsical fashion.' Nor does Perry regard such historical misinterpretation as merely a mistake. Brown might have known how theology was taught in the medieval schools had he taken the trouble to examine any foreign divines of note, or even Grosseteste's own words, but the discovery of truth was not his main concern. Perry tells us, '... his business was not to seek proofs for his assertions, but to throw dirt in the Church's face'.[73]

On issues of doctrine, their principal disagreement centres on a common point of divergence between Catholics and Protestants. Arriving at the doctrine concerning the invocation of saints and angels, the argument shifts: here Brown is no longer claiming common ground with the Lincolniensis, this being one area in which he is willing to concede that he is unconscionably Roman, and instead setting out to demonstrate that Grosseteste contradicts not only Scripture, but himself. Brown reproduces a sermon in which the Bishop begins by establishing that 'Christ alone can give the robe of justice', seeing the assertion as clearly undermining the practice of seeking divine assistance elsewhere. On this subject Brown had admitted that a preacher may ask his 'auditory' for their prayers in order to make his preaching profitable, but this, he maintains, is a thousand times better 'than begging the prayers of the Virgin' by saying Hail Marys, 'as modest Romanists are wont to do'. Perry chooses this admission as the target for his first attack when he asks how the prayers

[72] The *Sentences* (*Sententiarum libri quattuor*, the four books of sentences) is a collection of important passages from Scripture and the Church Fathers. It was collated by Peter Lombard (*c*.1100–60). After a not uncontroversial beginning it became the standard text of the Middle Ages and it was commented upon by nearly all the theologians of standing. See P. Lombard, *The Sentences, Books 1–4* (Toronto, 2007–10).

[73] Perry, *Essay on the Life and Manners*, p. 99.

of men can be solicited without hurting the prerogative of God, if it is not permissible to supplicate angelic spirits? That Brown cannot see the logic in this seems altogether surprising to Perry and once more he attributes this to the myopia of a mind distorted by its ulterior motive as he adds, 'So blind is prejudice when it is resolved to find fault!'

Brown, it appears, has not given up entirely on the idea of enlisting Grosseteste as an ally on this issue. Within the pages of the Bishop's work on the Ten Commandments (*De decem mandatis*) he detects a kindred spirit whose statements contradict those of the Council of Trent and consequently contemporary Catholicism. Here Grosseteste states that people who give veneration and worship to creatures, or who seek from others the remission of sins, the Kingdom of Heaven, the gift of prophecy or science, 'or any other immediate or inferior goods' do so in vain, since God alone is the 'principal giver' of even the lowest goods. Brown takes this as an indication that Grosseteste is fundamentally sympathetic to Protestantism in one of his most important theological texts, regardless of whatever he went on to say or do later in life. Perry retorts that this passage distinguishes God as the 'principal giver' with the implication there are others. The process can and does involve those who are only the ministerial, instrumental, or occasional givers of Grace. He adds 'And this is all that our Prelate, or the Trent Fathers, attribute to the Saints or Angels when they invoke their assistance.'[74]

On the related topic of invocation of saints, Brown has similarly declared that any such supplication is futile since they can know nothing of the affairs of humanity. Perry reminds him that saints are said to rejoice in the conversion of sinners, from which he concludes that they must know their commission and 'by good consequence their prayers too'. This is a reference to Luke 15:7 and 15:10, where in fact Jesus only describes a general rejoicing and then the joy of angels respectively. Perhaps aware that he is on weak Scriptural ground, Perry draws on a more mundane illustration. It is 'common sense', he tells us, that kings, who have been placed on their thrones by Christ, have been allotted a 'proportionate power' to assist their supplicants. This is safer ground since he takes it as a given that neither Catholic nor Anglican is going to deny the God-given power of the monarch. Based on this assumption, Perry makes a similar point to the one he made above:

> ... then to advance that begging prayers of a mortal and simple auditory is more to the purpose than to beg immortal and holy choirs above, and especially the Queen of the holy spirits made perfect, is assuredly, to say nothing worse, a coarse compliment to the Mother of our Redeemer.[75]

---

[74] Ibid., p. 61.
[75] Ibid., p. 61.

Perry is so convinced of his argument here that he suspects that Brown is fully aware that his position is untenable and he accuses him of 'only pretending' that Grosseteste's views on invocation are at odds with Tridentine doctrine and the word of God. As Perry sees it, Brown, after a tentative assertion, gives up on this issue taking 'no pains to prove [it]'. This being the case, Fr Perry tells his readers, 'so we shall take none to answer him'.[76]

Perry is perhaps keeping his powder dry for what he clearly regards as the biggest point of contention concerning the Bishop of Lincoln, and that is his Letter 128, and his final opposition to Pope Innocent IV. This alone, he writes, is enough for Brown to exonerate the great man from blame for any doctrinal failings. Indeed, as Perry points out, Brown has in the course of his writing made a frank admission that on the articles of the Eucharist, Purgatory, the number of sacraments, the sanctity of the Roman See, the pope's authority, 'and perhaps other articles in which I am less versed', the Bishop of Lincoln 'is entirely against us'. Nevertheless, his final rebellion is enough to redeem him:

> But forsooth, Lincoln's opposing the Pope, is enough with Browne to make him a good Protestant and to purge off all his other dregs of popery, and this one title of the *Hammer of the Romans* is sufficient to make even the rankest popery at least tolerable![77]

Perry's counterblast represents something like a concerted attempt to rescue Grosseteste from his forced Protestant adoption and restore him to what he considers to be the fold of his natural family in the Roman Catholic Church. For this purpose, he sets out to demonstrate that the Bishop of Lincoln not only maintained a loyalty to the See of Peter up until his death, but that it was precisely because of this steadfast loyalty that he dissented. Considering the strong language, the sentiments of despair and the expressions of revolt that are set out in Letter 128, together with the deathbed invectives, Perry faced no easy task. The letter rails against those who make inappropriate appointments to Church livings (in this case the Pope) as people who set loose the murderers of souls, for which they are to be considered worse even than the murderers themselves and more nearly 'allied to Lucifer and to Antichrist'. Grosseteste adds that their guilt is in direct proportion to their position in the hierarchy, 'as their greater and diviner power, which they have received from God for edification and not for destruction, laith them under a more

---

[76] Ibid., p. 62.

[77] Ibid., p. 203. The 'Hammer of the Romans' (*Romanorum malleus*) comes from Matthew Paris's account of Grosseteste's ghostly assault on Innocent IV. It was a term that became a particular favourite with numerous Reformation scholars. Flood and McEvoy, '*Romanorum malleus*', p. 325.

strict obligation'.[78] Finally Grosseteste declares that nobody could be expected to obey such injunctions, 'rather he is obliged to contradict, and rebel against them'.

Before we look at how Fr Perry tackled the issues that surround this letter it is worth pausing on an interesting feature of his discussion. Perry begins with an important observation, though he seems, rather surprisingly, not to recognise just how important it is. The standard view of this letter was that it was addressed to Pope Innocent IV; this was not only the assumption of Brown in the seventeenth century, but it was taken as given even when Henry Richard Luard edited Grosseteste's letters in the nineteenth century. *Epistola* 128 is in fact written to 'Master Innocent', the pope's factotum in England, as well as to the Archbishop of Canterbury. The correction of this misidentification has always been credited to the German theologian Gotthard Victor Lechler in an 1873 book on Wyclif, and it is an amendment that is generally considered to be significant.[79] However, it is clear that Perry is also aware of the correct addressee since he introduces the letter in his text as addressed to 'Innocent the Pope's secretary'. That he does not make capital out of Brown's error almost certainly indicates that he is unaware that he has made such an important revision.

With regard to the polemical points that Brown has made with the letter, Perry is adamant that if there is one article of Catholic faith in which Grosseteste is more explicit than all others it is that which asserts the pope's authority. This is evident in all his writings, not only the first but those written 'in the warmth of opposition' – even in this last letter of disagreement. Perry points out that in his letters to Gregory IX he calls the Pope 'the successor of St Peter, Prince of the Apostles and of the whole world'. In the Lyon sermon, even as he was railing against the abuses rooted in the Curia, he styles the pope as 'chief representative' and 'vicegerent of Christ'. At the same time, he refers to his see as the 'very throne of God' and the 'Sun of the Universe'. Nor were any of these high opinions rescinded later in life, as the letter to Master Innocent bares testimony. Here, just as he 'crieth still louder against promoting unfit subjects' he repeats over and over that in the ecclesiastical hierarchy the pope is the principal representative of Christ, who has delivered all power to the See Apostolic. Such, according to Perry, was Grosseteste's deep devotion to Catholicism and to the papacy in particular.[80]

If Perry is keen to press Grosseteste's high esteem of the papal office, he is just as anxious to demonstrate that such devotion was reciprocated

---

78 Perry, *Essay on the Life and Manners*, p. 188.

79 James McEvoy, 'Robertus Grossatesta', pp. 46–47; Gotthard V. Lechler, *John Wycliffe and His English Precursors*, translated by P. Lorimer (London, 1878), pp. 20–40.

80 Perry, *Essay on the Life and Manners*, p. 203.

by Innocent IV. Once more he finds it necessary to debunk some hoary myths. Perry tells us that the fourteenth-century chronicler Henry Knighton records that after the infamous letter was received, its author was called to Rome where he was laid under excommunication.[81] After Perry has dismissed this account by showing that the Bishop's last journey to Rome had taken place three years earlier, he produces some sterling evidence to prove that the letter was actually well received by the Pope.[82] In doing so Perry has once more made an important observation, and one that we previously thought had first been made centuries later. In 1979 L. E. Boyle wrote an article which is credited today with being the first to take seriously a remarkable papal letter that was written a short time after Grosseteste's own communication.[83] This document, the *Postquam regimini*, was penned *proprio motu*, at the Pope's own instigation, and many copies of it were sent to the bishops of England. In it the Pope admitted that mistakes had been made by him personally regarding the provision of benefices because he had been under pressure from dishonest petitioners. More importantly the letter reasserts the rights of patrons to appoint to benefices and even goes so far as to instruct them to tear up any mandate that undermines this prerogative. The thirteenth-century *Annals of Burton* inform us that this papal initiative was a direct result of Robert Grosseteste's protest.[84] A papal admission that mistakes have been made is a rare occurrence and Fr Boyle deserves much credit for identifying what he himself described as 'a landmark in the history of the papacy'.[85] However, with Perry's *Essay* we now know that he was not the first scholar to realise the important implications of what amounts to little short of an apology on Innocent's behalf. The *Essay* we have before us contains lengthy extracts of his own translation of what Perry calls 'this moderating bull', taken from the *Annals of Burton* and presented here as proof positive that contrary to the given understanding, the Bishop of Lincoln did not end his days in bad odour with the Curia; indeed, so highly was he regarded that his admonishments were sufficient to make a pope not only admit the justice of his cause but to issue a *volte face* on this important area of his policy. Perry tells us that the *Postquam regimini* was

---

81 Ibid., p. 190. See biographical appendix.

82 Ibid., pp. 191–92.

83 L. E. Boyle, 'Robert Grosseteste and the Pastoral Care', *Medieval and Renaissance Studies* 8 (1979), 3–51.

84 *An. Burt.*, 328. The *Annals of Burton* were written in the Benedictine Abbey of Burton-upon-Trent in Staffordshire. They cover the years 1004–1263 and are an important source for Perry. They are preserved in BL, Cotton, Vespasian E. iii. They were also published in H. R. Luard, ed., *Annales Monastici*. 5 vols (London, 1864–69).

85 Boyle 'Grosseteste and the Pastoral Care', 38.

> … the happy fruit from of [*sic*] our vigorous Prelate's letter and shews how far the Pope was from the censures and sayings some attribute to him. But ere this good Bishop of Lincoln was gone to receive in the Church triumphant above the reward of that zeal he had so gloriously exerted in the Church Militant here below, and perhaps this redress might have been not only one reward of his zeal but the effect of his holy prayers.[86]

With this final flourish it is apparent that Fr Perry considered that he had accomplished his inter-confessional rescue mission, having sufficiently destroyed the crux of Brown's thesis that Letter 128 was a clear indicator of Grosseteste's final disillusionment and rebellion against Rome. So confident is he that he has won his case that in his final chapter, where he treats of Grosseteste's death, not only does he present his own translation of the deathbed speech, but he takes no pains to contextualise it. Given the fulsome nature of the denunciations contained in Matthew Paris's version of the diatribe this demonstrates an enormous amount of confidence on Perry's part. Nor does his translation baulk at delivering to his readership the passages that are potentially most damning to his cause. Here Grosseteste's anguish and indignation reach something of a crescendo.

> Christ came into the world in order to save souls. He then who destroys them, is he not justly styled Antichrist? God spent only six days in creating man, but to repair and redeem him he spent thirty years, and those in hard labour. He therefore who labours at their destruction, is he not an enemy to God and Christ Jesus? The present Pope, by his *non obstantes* annuls in a shameless manner all the ordinances of the holy popes his predecessors, which cannot be done but with the manifest contempt of their memory and to the great prejudice of the Church … who then will hereafter observe his decrees and statutes?[87]

After unapologetically producing his translation Perry tells us that the Bishop of Lincoln added a list of several grievances laid upon the English Church and now, and only with regard to this appended list, does he suggest that the chronicler was allowing his own prejudices to get the better of him. These particular facts, says Perry 'seem rather the amplifications of the historian than of the dying Robert'.[88] Before he leaves the subject Perry offers only one other very slight tilt at his Anglican jousting partner. It was easy for Grosseteste's Reformed admirers to regard his death as a type of martyrdom, if he is perceived as a man who fails in health having been crushed in spirit by a tyranny that ultimately overpowered him. Nothing sits more comfortably with the glory of self-sacrifice than

---

[86] Perry, *Essay on the Life and Manners*, p. 192.
[87] Ibid., p. 194.
[88] Ibid., p. 195.

a final prophetic utterance and Paris's version of events did not disappoint. The fact that it was not difficult to make Grosseteste's words fit with the foretelling of the English Reformation meant that they were all the more appropriate for the type of Reformed hagiography that was so popular in England in the early-modern period. Grosseteste departs the world declaring 'The Church shall not be delivered from this Egyptian slavery but by the edge of the sword.'[89] Perry was well-versed in Protestant writings on Grosseteste and he must have been fully aware of the use they made of this quotation, however he does not trouble himself with a response. After reproducing the words he simply opines tentatively that they hinted at further papal exactions, or perhaps the Pope's 'sorrowful' death and the Barons' War.

It is obvious by the time we get to the final chapter of Perry's *Essay* that he considers that the first of his intentions has been accomplished. Grosseteste's doctrinal orthodoxy is incontestable; his disputes with the papacy were those of a loyal son with the deepest of respect for the patriarch, moreover any such disagreements were vindicated by Pope Innocent's response which contained a tacit deference to the integrity of the Bishop of Lincoln's cause. Perry seems content that he has saved his Catholic Grosseteste and all that remains is to stake a final claim for his elevation to sainthood. He lays before his reader and the Church the testimony of a holy life, a profound wisdom and a multitude of miracles that proceeded from his veneration. His ultimate wish is that his 'imperfect, tho faithfull' history would contribute to this cause, which would not be for Grosseteste's benefit, since he has attained his reward, but for the Church in Perry's time, 'as standing in need of being raised up by new and approved examples of Sanctity!'[90]

The canonisation of Robert Grosseteste

The veneration of 'Saint' Robert began almost immediately after his passing.[91] Matthew Paris provides us with the first reference; his account of Grosseteste's death refers to him as 'sanctus Lincolniensis episcopus Robertus secundus'. In addition, he tells us that miracles increased daily at the Bishop's tomb in Lincoln Cathedral and that one night a heavenly voice declared of Grosseteste and Edmund Rich, 'Dilexit Dominus Edmundum in odorem benignitatis, et dilexit Dominus Robertum in odorem

[89] Ibid., p. 195.
[90] Ibid., p. 204.
[91] For a succinct but detailed account of efforts to have Grosseteste declared a saint, see Eric W. Kemp, 'The Attempted Canonization of Robert Grosseteste', in *Robert Grosseteste, Scholar and Bishop*, edited by D. Callus (Oxford, 1955), pp. 241–46.

fidelitatis'.[92] The *Annals of Burton* add that Richard of Cornwall, the King's brother, made a pilgrimage to the tomb of 'St Robert'.[93]
However, the process involved in recognising the saintliness of the Lincolniensis was not as straightforward as the contemporary records suggest. Throughout the Middle Ages and up until the time of Grosseteste the installation of a saint had been on a semi-informal basis. Local veneration had often been considered enough and if official confirmation was looked for it was usually not from the Church hierarchy, but rather from God via endorsing miracles. However, throughout the twelfth century the papacy exerted an ever-increasing hold on the process, as Anthony Perron points out, 'control of sanctity became an important symbolic monopoly in the pope's jurisdictional arsenal'.[94] In 1171/72 Alexander III issued the *Audivimus* which later became the authoritative statement that papal permission was integral to the process of canonisation. Then in 1234 the *Liber extra* of Gregory IX reasserted this statement, though his letter might be interpreted as making this assertion only about 'saints' of dubious moral integrity.[95]

Philip Perry ends his *Essay* on Grosseteste by addressing the subject of the failure to achieve this papal recognition and in doing so he expresses an anxiety that this has cast a shadow over his reputation. The most obvious explanation was that given by the Benedictine historian Ranulph Higden (died 1364) who claimed that the Curia refused Grosseteste's canonisation, despite his obvious sanctity, because he (or more specifically, his ghost) had killed the Pope.[96] Perry quickly dispenses with such a notion as an 'idle and groundless surmise'. He then goes on to confess that he does not know the reason for the lack of success of these various petitions, though he does feel able to boldly assert that it was never because of doubt concerning either his holiness or orthodoxy, 'as some would make the world believe'.[97] He then offers us a full catalogue of wholly Catholic tenets that Grosseteste cleaved to and taught. Included here are several cornerstones of Tridentine doctrine such as the need to find truth not only in Scripture, but in whatever is delivered by the universal Church. The first representative of Christ 'in his body' is the Bishop of Rome. That the faith required for justification is enlivened by charity and that the Eucharist contains the real presence and is a sacrifice as well as a

---

[92] *Chron. Maj.*, 407 and 490. 'The Lord has loved Edmund in odour of sweetness, and Robert in odour of fidelity.'
[93] *An. Burt.*, 336.
[94] A. Perron, 'The Bishops of Rome, 1100–1300', in *The Cambridge History of Christianity*, edited by M. Rubin and W. Simons (Cambridge, 2009), vol. 4, p. 27.
[95] Ibid.
[96] *Polychronicon*, pp. 242–43.
[97] Perry, *Essay on the Life and Manners*, p. 201.

sacrament. This lengthy litany of Catholic orthodoxy finishes with the assertion that 'This was the true character of the Bishop of Lincoln and this God demonstrated His approving him by miracles after death.'[98] After this it remains only for Fr Perry to add that the one thing wanting after such divine affirmation is 'the approbation of the Church or the Church's supreme Pastor' as sufficient warrant for Grosseteste's veneration 'in the publick honours decreed to canonised saints'.[99]

Ultimately, Perry never got to save his Catholic Grosseteste, nor did he advance his cause toward canonisation, as the tide of history ran completely against him. Few people were ever to hear this plea, the two existing manuscripts of his *Essay* lay unpublished and largely forgotten in libraries in Scotland and at Valladolid. Though Perry was unaware of it, his Catholic Grosseteste was offered at precisely the wrong moment in his Church's English history and no amount of sedulous scholarship or arduous defence was ever going to change that situation. In order to understand this, we now have to turn our attention to the political landscape of eighteenth-century England.

The fate of Perry's manuscript

At 9 p.m. on 1 January 1766, the 'Old Pretender', James Francis Edward Stuart, King James III of England and VIII of Scotland, died at the Palazzo Muti (now the Palazzo Balestra) in Rome after a bedridden decade. He was interred in the crypt of St Peter's Basilica and along with him were buried any Catholic hopes of restoring a Stuart to the English throne. Two weeks later Pope Clement XIII, who had refused to accept the claim of Charles Stuart (Bonnie Prince Charlie), made the momentous decision to recognise the Hanoverian dynasty. In truth, the Jacobite cause had suffered its mortal blow in 1746 at the Battle of Culloden; the ensuing decades had witnessed little more than its death throes. Among the London political elite, after the drawn out demise of the Stuarts, there was a palpable sense that there was no longer a need to fear the imminent threat of an old enemy and this was about to be reflected in legislation. However, at this point the historian has to tread carefully. It has been the fashion among twentieth-century historians to characterise the eighteenth century as an age of growing enlightenment and tolerance, and as a consequence markedly less anti-Catholic than previous centuries. R. J. White, for example, regarded the explosion of violence that characterised the 1780 anti-Catholic Gordon Riots in London as 'an incident that came and went with the short, sharp violence of a

[98] Ibid., p. 204.
[99] Ibid., p. 203.

dog's solitary bark in the silence of the night'.[100] Although it might be added here that those who witnessed the estimated 700 deaths might have been forgiven for thinking that the dog was engaged in something more than merely barking. On the other hand, it is just as easy to fall into the opposite trap of exaggerating the straits of Catholics living in England at this time. Historians sympathetic to the Catholic cause have often taken their cue from John Henry Newman's bleak *Second Spring* sermon, with its grim portrait of suffering which seemed to have left an indelible imprint on the collective English Catholic subconscious:

> Such were Catholics in England, found in corners, and alleys, and cellars, and the housetops, or in the recesses of the country; cut off from the populous world around them, and dimly seen, as if through a mist or in twilight, as ghosts flitting to and fro, by the high Protestants, the lords of the earth.[101]

The Catholic historian Eamon Duffy has cautioned against such over-gloomy perceptions warning that a good deal of nonsense has been talked about a 'catacomb' existence.[102] Dismissing such a caricature, however, does not mean that we should also be dismissive of real suffering. Even as late as the 1760s the London Catholic community was thrown into turmoil when a carpenter called William Payne initiated a number of prosecutions against priests and schoolmasters. Payne was initially highly successful when a Fr John Maloney was sentenced to life imprisonment. However, his seems to have been a lone campaign and after his first triumph, though he managed to bring charges against seventeen others, he did not succeed in securing a single further conviction. Lord Chief Justice Mansfield's verdict that the simple evidence of someone performing a priestly function was no evidence of their priesthood was indicative of a lack of appetite for such persecutions.[103] Nevertheless, anti-Catholicism did not evaporate in the eighteenth century, indeed Linda Colley has pointed out that intolerant Protestantism was much more than mere 'thuggishness'. Rather, it was an important cement that glued together England, Scotland and Wales (she might have added parts of Ireland) in a crucial time of national formation.[104]

Without doubt the key figure on the English Catholic scene at this time was Richard Challoner (1691–1781), the Vicar Apostolic of London and the leader of the Catholic Church in England. In 1737 he had taken over the administration of the London diocese, acting as coadjutor to the

---

100 Reginald J. White, *The Age of George III* (London, 1968), p. 186.

101 See The Newman Reader, at http://www.newmanreader.org/works/occasions/sermon10.html

102 Eamon Duffy, ed., *Challoner and His Church* (London, 1981), p. 9.

103 James Oldham, *English Common Law in the Age of Mansfield* (Chapel Hill, NC, 2004), p. 243.

104 Linda Colley, *Britons: Forging the Nation, 1707–1837* (New Haven, 2009), p. 23.

then Vicar Apostolic Benjamin Petre, who was in exile. When Petre died in 1740 his coadjutor was the natural choice to succeed him. Challoner is generally admired rather than lionised by Catholic historians: he does not possess the heroism of a Thomas More or the intellectual abilities of a John Henry Newman. Nevertheless, he is credited with playing an indispensable part in the evolution of English Catholicism. His approach to the political situation was decidedly Fabian; by temperament he was not a confrontational leader and his fundamentally pacific character had led Edward Diccoson, his onetime teacher at Douai, to wearily exclaim, 'I fear, he has too much of the Dove.'[105] With the death of James III, Catholic emancipation was now firmly on the agenda, and Challoner's policy of presenting a reassuring presence, whilst leaving the politicking to the Catholic nobility, became the general policy of the Church hierarchy. This approach is illustrated by a telling incident in 1778 when Sir John Dalrymple, a Baron of the Scottish Exchequer, visited Challoner with the idea of forming a Scottish Catholic regiment. We are told that the Bishop, 'much alarmed at the idea, expressed apprehensions of awakening the jealousy of the Dissenters, and drawing persecution *not only on himself*, but the [Catholic] Body at large'.[106] Such caution was entirely in keeping with papal strategy. Even as early as 1703, when Jacobite hopes were far from extinguished, a papal edict sanctioned English missionaries against making themselves 'odious to the government and becoming involved with anything except the affairs of the spiritual realm'.[107]

Sometime in the 1760s, probably in the same year as James III died, Philip Perry sent Richard Challoner, his friend and mentor, a manuscript copy of his life of Grosseteste. Challoner's opinion would have mattered much to Perry, not only because he was the principal leader of the Church in England, but also because of his own keen interest in hagiography and martyrology. His two-volume *Memoirs of Missionary Priests* (1741) reviewed the post-Reformation history of the English Catholic clergy and his *Britannia sancta* (1745) recalled the past glories of the saints of Britain and Ireland. The timing of the proposed publication, just when papal olive branches were being presented to the English government and talk of relaxing the penal laws was becoming more serious, could not have been less auspicious. Nor would the irenic temperament of the Vicar Apostolic have made him any more inclined toward what Perry was offering. He replied in a short letter to Perry and his response must have been crushingly disappointing:

105 Edwin H. Burton, *The Life and Times of Bishop Challoner* (London, 1909), vol. 1. p. 232.
106 J. A. Stothert, *Scotichronicon*, edited by J. F. Gordon (Glasgow, 1869), p. 146.
107 Gabriel Glickman, *The English Catholic Community, 1688–1745: Politics, Culture and Ideology* (Woodbridge, 2009), p. 171.

> I here return your M[*anuscript*] according to your directions sufficiently convinced, by what you have collected, that your hero was both a very great and a very good man. And yet to be sincere with my friend, I do not think his life, as it here stands will be very edifying to our English Catholicks. The rehearsal of all the particulars of his perpetual contentions with all sorts of people, which makes up so great a part of the work, will appear to them very dry. But they will be more particularly shocked with his contentions with the Pope; and the manifold abuses you expose on that occasion of the supream ecclesiastical power at that time, and with that passionate speech your historian puts in his mouth on his death bed. For such matters as these, when published by ourselves, will give occasion to our adversaries of insulting over our weaker brethren; and of prejudicing them against the authority of the Holy See. Here I should rather cry out, '*Nolite annuntiare in Geth ne forte laetentur filiae Philisthiim,* [ne] *exultent filiae incircumcisorum.*'[108] (On the other hand your hero's notions of the Pope's power in temporals will equally shock both English Protestants and French Catholicks: and what is offered there for the support of that power, were it to appear in France, would scarce escape the animadversion and censure of the Parliament). As to the rest I know you will excuse my freely giving you my thoughts on this subject, and believe me to be sincerely and affectionately, ever yours in Christ.[109]

There were a number of obvious problems with regard to Perry's proposed publication as far as his patron was concerned. The first two difficulties are paradoxical in that Perry is unflinching in his representations of Grosseteste's contentions with the Curia, and then he is as equally unguarded in presenting the Bishop's extreme view on the *plena potestas* belonging to the papacy. The first of these prompts the question, how could Perry, as a Catholic priest, have been so comfortable with his subject's contentions with the papacy, and why was his mentor not equally as sanguine? The answer to this question lies in the complicated relationship that had developed between English Catholic campaigners and the papacy throughout the eighteenth century.

The vision of the Catholic Jacobites at the end of the seventeenth century had been one of an international Catholic alliance, supported by the papacy, that would restore their nations to the Old Faith. Yet even at the outset this dream met with only a lukewarm response. Aside from providing material support for the Stuart household, successive popes demonstrated a marked disinclination to involve themselves in anything political. Faced with such a lack of enthusiasm, disillusionment began to turn the hearts of the Jacobite and English exiles away from the Curia. Taking the Gallican model of an independent Catholic Church as their model they increasingly came to regard themselves as members of the

---

108 Sam. 1:20. 'Tell it not in Gath … lest the daughters of the Philistines rejoice, lest the daughters of the uncircumcised exult.'

109 This letter in pasted into the cover of the Aberdeen Manuscript.

Church and not the Court of Rome. Such inclinations were reflected in the English seminaries at Paris and Douai where scholars began to appeal to chronicles, annals and hagiographies to bolster their claims for independence.[110] Robert Manning, who was for a time professor of Humanities and Philosophy at Douai, wrote *The Case stated between the Church of Rome and the Church of England* (1721) which might be regarded as the clearest clarion on behalf of an English Catholic community staking its claim to a sizeable portion of self-governance within a universal Church. However, such independence of spirit could not be sustained and one of the characteristics of the sea-change inaugurated by Challoner was a renewed deference to Rome. Herein lies one of the difficulties with Perry's Grosseteste. Its author writes like a man who has been steeped in the Church politics of the Douai and Parisian schools to such an extent that he is inured to the difficulties that might attend his portrait of an ultimately defiant English bishop, difficulties that would have been only too apparent to his ultramontane superior.

The second problem with Perry's *Essay* is almost diametrically opposed to the first. Grosseteste was a thirteenth-century product of the immensely important convocation that was the Fourth Lateran Council. As one of his century's most ardent champions of the values promulgated by this council, Grosseteste made bold statements on the issue of papal powers, statements that were unusually assertive even by the standards of his own time. Once more Perry seems to be unaware of the sensitivity of this issue as he unflinchingly translates Grosseteste's Letter 23 in which he makes a number of uncompromising assertions, including the claim that if princes hold any power and dignity they have received it from the Church, and in addition that the bishops hold none of their power from their sovereigns but from God directly. Both the swords of power, spiritual and temporal, belong to Peter, and though they are divided between the ecclesiastical and civil authorities, they belong to the former. After this, Perry can only add that those who believe the powers of the Church to be confined to matters spiritual will 'not easily admit our Prelate's opinion'; however he calls on them to admit that the case Grosseteste advanced for temporal rulers subordinating their laws to the rules of God and the Church are 'ingeniously set forth'.[111] This was categorically not the face of Roman Catholicism that Challoner's Church wanted to present to the English nation. With the first Catholic Relief Act (1778) on the horizon, the leaders of the Church were anxious to dismantle any previous or existing conceptions of them as an international organisation with designs on the secular English establishment. As enthusiastic as

110 Glickman, *English Catholic Community,* p. 168.
111 Perry, *Essay on the Life and Manners*, p. 154.

Challoner was for hagiographical accounts, an unexpurgated treatment of the life and ideas of Robert Grosseteste would have, in his opinion, presented a poor example to his flock and a shocking example to his non-Catholic compatriots.

In the end Perry's *Essay* was never published. His efforts to resurrect the life of Robert Grosseteste from obscurity, his attempt to rescue his reputation from those he regarded as the enemies of the true Church, and his vision of renewing the campaign for his canonisation all foundered on the rocks of political and ecclesiastical sensitivities. Perry spectacularly failed to read the zeitgeist in Hanoverian England in the latter part of the eighteenth century. Had he been successful he would have presented to the public a Grosseteste whose stern management of the diocese of Lincoln would have reminded Protestants of the draconian spirit they had long ascribed to the Roman Church. His 'Hammer of the Romans' portrait would have alarmed Challoner's Catholic hierarchy who were cultivating a newfound devotion to the papacy. In addition, as the Vicar Apostolic pointed out, the Gallican French would not be impressed by the Bishop of Lincoln's views that amounted to a papal hegemony on all temporal power. Lastly, with the Act of 1778 so close to realisation, the Catholic Church in England did not need anyone to rock the boat with an unnecessary polemical contest over the bones of a medieval bishop, no matter how scholarly his mind or how holy his life.

Whatever the reasons, it is a considerable pity that Perry's work was never published and was consequently almost entirely unknown, even among Grosseteste scholars up to our present age. In spite of the political difficulties it might have provoked, and in spite also of its sometimes rather prolix style, Perry's readership would have found much that was worthwhile in his *Essay* on Grosseteste. For these same reasons Perry's work is also important for a modern audience. In addition, there are two particular features of his work that break new ground. In the first place the previous tussle over Grosseteste had almost exclusively focused on his life story, with the result that the thoughts of an important medieval religious thinker were passed over. As Flood and McEvoy have pointed out, with the exception of a single letter 'his voluminous and largely unedited theological writings were largely sidelined'.[112] What we encounter in Perry's *Essay,* for the first time since Wyclif, is an impressively thorough examination of some key texts in which English readers would have been provided with a lively engagement, and in addition some quite extensive translations of his original letters and sermons. With regard to the former, this is something that did not happen again until the twenty-first century. Nor is his discussion of Grosseteste's

[112] Flood and McEvoy, '*Romanorum malleus*', p. 353.

writing eristic or marred by hyperbole: aside from some comparatively tame tilts at his opposing corner, his arguments are both reasoned and measured. For the most part Perry makes intelligent points based on the texts before him. He also displays many traits of a good historian, with his identification of the correct recipient of Letter 128, as well as the importance of the *Postquam regimini*. He is also quite capable of questioning the integrity of his medieval evidence on the basis of legitimate concerns. For example, his suspicion of Paris's ability to reproduce a lengthy deathbed speech in spite of not being present on the occasion is noteworthy.[113] Secondly, he departs from how his Catholic predecessors wrote on Grosseteste by the admirable way he does not duck difficult questions with regard to the Bishop's relations with the papacy. Higgons made a rather pusillanimous attempt to exonerate Grosseteste from the charge of disobeying his pope but only on the issue of obtruding Italians into English benefices, and ultimately he failed to reconcile the disputing parties.[114] Pits fares even worse since he fails to mention any of the disputes at all. In stark contrast, Perry meets the issues head on, discussing all the major disagreements, and in doing so he presents his reader for the first time with a well-argued Catholic defence of Grosseteste as theologically and ecclesiologically loyal to Rome. Given the gravity of some of the instances this is no easy task and it is to Perry's credit that he makes a very decent fist of stating his case.

Perry's *Essay* makes for an interesting comparison with the hagiographies and martyrologies of Challoner and Butler. Challoner renewed English Catholic martyrology with his two-volume *Memoirs of Missionary Priests* (1741–42), which he intended as a riposte to Foxes' *Book of Martyrs*. Later, his *Britannia Sancta* (1745) was his attempt to promote pride in the Catholics of Britain by recalling them to their sacred heritage. In contrast to Perry, both these texts demonstrate an acute awareness of their audience as well as the climate they lived in. Roy Hattersley described Challoner as a realist who grasped that the fundamental reality relating to the promotion of a faith was that it had to be aware of religious and political climates. Whilst eternal truths could in no way be questioned, just how the Church went about its business had to move with the times. 'Perhaps more than any other priest of his era, he appreciated that the Church had to accommodate a new sort of Catholic', including the increasing number that were 'impeccably loyal to the Crown'.[115] At the outset, the *Memoirs* is placatory in tone, assuring its readers, both Catholic and Protestant, that the subjects of the work were devout but

113 Perry, *Essay*, p. 195.
114 Higgons, *First Motive*, appendix 34.
115 Roy Hattersley, *The Catholics* (London, 2017), p. 260.

not treasonable. In addition, there is an assurance from the author that he fully appreciates that the government of his day is of a more benign nature as he writes, 'it is hoped [the book] will give no offence to our present governors, whose milder ways of proceeding with Catholics' will always be gratefully acknowledged.[116] Perry showed no such intuition as he offered an English audience the example of a bishop who had argued that the ultimate source of all temporal power was ecclesiastical.

Even Challoner's most historical works were at heart devotional rather than polemical in nature. Designed primarily to address conceived misrepresentations but also to assist in the cure of Catholic souls who had, for the most part, made their peace with their government. This feature was even more pronounced in Alban Butler's works. He was professor of philosophy and subsequently theology at Douai when he began his great opus the *Lives of the Fathers, Martyrs and Principal Saints* in which he set out his stall in clear terms at the outset. The primary task of this work was to place before its audience models that they would do well to emulate. In the preface he stated, 'The method of forming men to virtue by example is, of all others, the shortest, and the best adapted to all circumstances and dispositions.' Completed in Paris in 1759 he arranged his text to follow the Church's feast days, inserting a homily at the end of the life of the first saint on each day in order that its reading would function as a spiritual exercise. Like Challoner he was profoundly inspired by the spirituality of St Francis de Sales. In *Lives* he draws directly on Salesian spirituality as he commends his readers to 'gather a nosegay' of pious reflections and sentiments. Butler's work was scholarly in that it was based on impressive research, but it was a text that was categorically aimed at the ordinary faithful rather than the educated elite, a feature that was accentuated when Challoner famously got him to remove the copious footnotes in order to render it both more serviceable and affordable. For Challoner and Butler the study of the saints was the art of living well and putting on the spirit of Christ, something that the former called, the 'science of the saints'.[117] In this regard, for Butler, the principal feature of his spirituality was its insistence on mortification. His audience, even in penal times, were unlikely to be called to martyrdom, however all Christians were obligated to follow the example of the great holy men and women by offering their own sacrifice via the ascetic life.

No such nosegays are to be encountered in the pages of Perry. There is no doubt that in his *Essay* we are presented with a saintly protagonist, but nowhere do we find the kind of inspiring piety that we encounter

---

116 Raymond Challoner, *Memoirs of Missionary Priests* (Manchester, 1803), preface.

117 J. A. Hilton, 'The Science of the Saints: The Spirituality of Butler's *Lives of the Saints*', *Recusant History* 15.2 (1979), 189–93.

in the pages of Butler. Nor do we discover a bishop who offers a particular example of pronounced abstinence; certainly he gives up all of his temporal livings but one, but he does not forthwith adopt a life of poverty. It is doubtful in fact that Perry, who recorded in his own diary the consumption of fifty oysters for breakfast in a single sitting, would have had any sympathy with this brand of piety.[118] Perry does not call upon his audience to meditate on the example of Grosseteste, even less are they called to use the reading of the text as a spiritual exercise. He was an academic and his *Essay* is an academic enterprise characterised by precision and accuracy and written for an erudite readership. It has no practical function save an historically correct account of the life and thoughts of a medieval Catholic who ought to be elevated to sainthood. In a significant episode Charles Butler, who wrote Catholic histories in a similar vein to his uncle, was 'favoured with a perusal' of Perry's manuscript by Bishop Cameron of the Lowlands.[119] Afterwards he commented that the text should be consulted if a life of Grosseteste was to be attempted, but beyond that he had nothing to say. What the text doubtless lacked for Charles Butler is what it lacked also for Challoner, and that was a certain spiritual edification and perhaps the whiff of incense.

In spite of the misgivings of his contemporaries, audiences today with an interest in the Catholic history of England at this time would find much of value in Perry's *Essay*. His is far from a dissenting voice in the throng of English Catholics at this important stage in the formation of their identity, but it is a different voice, and it represents one that is often muffled by the more measured tones of those who were steering their Church toward emancipation. They were no doubt the more important party, but Perry is important too because he demonstrates that in spite of the united front, understandings of what constituted English Catholicism at this time were by no means uniform. Perry does not deliver an overt ecclesiological message with his *Essay*, but reading between the lines his Grosseteste is essentially a Roman Catholic with a well-developed sense of national liberties. It is hard to avoid the assumption that in this respect he meets with the approval of his biographer. This was a perspective that anticipated the Cisalpine movement that emerged later in the century which would look to advance the cause of emancipation by developing a certain independence from Rome. In many respects the debate about what it means to be English and Catholic is still a live one and works like Perry's *Essay* provide any such discussion with a crucial historical context.

---

118 Williams, 'Philip Perry, Rector', 51.

119 Charles Butler, *Additions to the Historical Memoirs respecting the English, Irish and Scottish Catholics, from the Reformation to the present time* (London, 1821), vol. III, p. 62.

Lastly, had Perry's work come to light in the eighteenth century his readership would have discovered a portrait of Grosseteste that might not always have charmed them, but would nevertheless have impressed them with the obvious qualities of immense bravery, undauntedness in his opposition to great potentates, and the type of visceral sincerity that characterises a true saint. It must also be said that Perry's work demonstrates a clearer understanding of Grosseteste's ecclesiology, his theological mind and his ecclesiastical motivations, than any treatment of him up until the twentieth century. Fr Perry knows the Catholic mind of Grosseteste because he shares so much it. For our part, as modern readers we discover in the work we have before us a rare window into the mind of an intelligent, well-informed English recusant as he sets before us his understanding of the strong ties that bind his own outlawed Church with one of the major figures of its medieval past.

EDITORIAL CONVENTIONS

My transcription is based on two manuscript autograph copies of Perry's *Essay*. One was brought to Britain by John Geddes (1735–99),[1] whom Perry had helped set up the Scots College in Valladolid. This was until recently the property of the Scottish Catholic Archives in Edinburgh (MS P/5/10), and is now housed in the historic collection at Aberdeen University. The second is in the library of St Alban's College, Valladolid, Spain (MS Henson Legajo 18.1). M. E. Williams was of the opinion that the Valladolid copy is a second version since he regards its preface as a retort to Challoner's reaction to the first (Scottish) recension.[2] This is not the opinion of the present editor. The Valladolid version is longer than the Scottish one and it has the appearance of a first draft that was later redacted. It is also a good deal untidier, with many deletions, illegible writing, unorganised referencing, as well as a general lack of presentation. The version housed at Aberdeen is not only better organised and presented, but there are numerous occasions when its written style represents an improvement. It is also the copy that has the responses of a Fr George Bishop and Challoner pasted into its first pages, suggesting that this is the manuscript that they had read and was intended for publication. These letters are pasted into the cover of the Aberdeen Manuscript. Challoner's letter might be dated to around 5 April 1766, because it is accompanied by Fr Bishop's letter which carries this date. Bishop was in charge of one of the oldest post-Reformation Catholic churches in England, at Brailes in Warwickshire. His letter is more positive than Challoner's, though he also seems anxious to confer with Perry, 'upon some remarks I have made'. Both would certainly have experienced a great deal of difficulty reading the Valladolid manuscript. It is hard to say with any certainty, but it is my conjecture that the Valladolid version is Perry's rough draft for the Scottish version that was produced for publication. In the production of this transcript I have used both manuscripts to produce a single whole *Essay*, complete with material missing from the Scottish version. The missing material that has been added is marked at the beginning and end with ^.

Both manuscripts are bound quires. I have endeavoured to transcribe them as accurately as possible saving the following changes. Spelling has been kept faithful to the original. Names of people and places have

[1] Williams, 'Perry', in *ODNB*.
[2] Williams, 'Philip Perry, Rector', 64–65.

been reproduced as written by Perry, though I have given the modern version in the first instance where it is different. This includes the author's rendering of his subject's name as *Grossetete*, though the now generally accepted version, *Grosseteste*, has been kept for the title of this volume to help with cataloguing and referencing. Punctuation represented a bigger problem. Perry uses semi-colons for full stops and he makes prodigal use of commas. This transcription uses full stops and has used Perry's commas only when they were deemed necessary. Capitalisation remains the same, though it has been standardised where Perry has not used the upper-case consistently. With regard to nouns, lower case has been used for general bodies of people, such as 'popes' and upper case for specific individuals, such as 'Pope Innocent III'. All Perry's footnotes (lettered) have been reproduced as he wrote them. My editorial notes are numbered and presented in the section 'Editor's notes' in order to distinguish them. Any additions I have made to the main text are in square parentheses and italics.

Essay on the life and manners of the venerable Robert Grossetete, Bishop of Lincoln, from his own works and from contemporary Writers.

P. Perry, auctor, dedit Col. S. Albani.

He was Great according to his name, even very Great, for saving the Elect of God, and for overthrowing the enemies, who rose up against them! … Who hath been able to stand before him?

Ecclesiasticus 46:1, 2–4.

THE CONTENT

PREFACE

If they who have excelled in any one virtue, or in any one science, are objects worthy of publick notice and esteem, they must be still more worthy of both who have excelled in all the sciences and virtues together. And they are the most worthy of all, who raised by the excellency of their virtue and learning, to the first dignities in the Church and to the first seat in the temple of fame, owed their reputation, dignities and merit neither to the fortuitous advantages of high birth, nor to the recommendations of powerful friends, but to the sole power of their abilities, and to the superior lustre of their virtues, which forced the world to take notice of them, and to draw them out of their native obscurity, in order to place them on the seats of honour.

One of these extraordinary characters will be here laid before the Reader, in the person of the illustrious Robert Grossetete or Great-head Bishop of Lincoln in the Thirteenth Century, of whose life, a very knowing Protestant and one that has scarce had his fellow in English Ecclesiastical knowledge, assures us that were it drawn at full length, it would exhibit the picture of a perfect Christian Bishop;[a] and we may add, if any thing can be added to so comprehensive a eulogium, that of a perfect scholar, Grossetete being at once an illustrious linguist, poet, orator, philosopher and mathematician, as well as a prime theologist, and eminent prelate. Nevertheless this eminent prelate and scholar, once so renowned in his generation, and so deserving of the remembrance of all generations to come, is fallen into such oblivion among his own countrymen, and the lame notion the few have of him, with whom he still retaineth some part of his fame, has been the occasion of the following compilation the design whereof is to inform the ignorance of the former and to rectify the imperfect notion of the latter. An English work destined to celebrate the worthies of antiquity, and to retrieve their memory from the shade of oblivion, hath no particular article on this most renowned English worthy, and only makes a transient, tho very honourable mention of him, in the life of Doctor Roger Bacon one of his scholars.[b]

Some other writers who have spoke of Grossetete more at large, have in drawing his character imitated the art of painters in profile, with this material difference, that whereas those artists make an harmless use of the profile, in order to hide and keep certain blemishes out of sight, these

---

[a] Wharton, Preface to *Anglia Sacra*, B. 1, p. 12.

[b] *Biographia Britannica*.

profile writers, as I may call them, have on the contrary employed their illaudable skill, to throw a shade upon our Prelate's virtues, and to make his heroic fortitude look like obstinacy and rebellion.

Hence the design of this work is partly to rescue the memory of so great and good a man from oblivion, in favour of such as are not acquainted with him; and partly to rectify the oblique and dubious character drawn of him, by some partial writers, and to give instead of a profile, a full face and picture of him as far as the materials which are left of him will go.

^The compilation itself is made up of various materials scattered up and down in different authors and here reduced to plain and orderly narration. The sources from which the materials here made use of are taken from the *Annals of Lanercost* a house of Austin canons near Carlisle.[a] From Giraldus Cambrensis, Bishop Elect of St Davids, and Grossetete's particular acquaintance. From the petition of the Dean and Chapter of St Pauls, put up to Pope Clement the V for his canonisation in 1307.[b] And lastly from his metrified life by Richard of Bardney, which tho justly styled by Wharton both inelegant and in some places insipid, contains nevertheless some particularities not to be met with elsewhere,^ and therefore thought worthy to be published by that critick in the second volume of his *Anglia Sacra*,[c] as are the rest of the materials just cited. Besides these the author of this essay, hath consulted the history of Matthew Paris, diocesan and contemporary to Bishop Grossetete, the contemporary *Annals of Burton*, the learned and elegant Dominican annalist, Nicholas Trivet, son of Sir Thomas Trivet, Justice of the King's Bench, and Prior of the Dominicans in London, who lived in the age next to Grossetete. ^Consulted likewise, Tanner's *Bibliotheca britannico-hibernica*, in Grossetete, where he cites *Analecta de vita et scriptis Roberti Grossteste,* collected by Tho[*mas*] Barlow, Bishop of Lincoln, from whence Anthony Wood drew all he saith of our Prelate. The original of these analecta was in the possession of Henry Brown and a copy of them is now among the manuscripts of Anthony Wood 8560: 98. It is a thin manuscript of 3 or 4 quarternions of paper, consisting of the testimonies of various authors concerning Bishop Grosseteste and his life and his writings.[2] Oudin,[3] in his supplement to Bellarmine's *Ecclesiastical Writers* remits us for a further account of his prelate's virtues and learning to the history of the University of Paris,[d] which Browne thinks to be that of Du Boulay.[e] ^But the greatest helps have been received from the Bishop's own excellent

a In the Cotton Library, *Claudius*, D. 7.

b In the History of Westminster Abbey. [John Dart, *Westmonasterium*. 2 vols (London, 1723).]

c Tom. 2.

d Oudin, p. 526.

e [C. E. Du] Boulay, *Historia univer[sitatis] Paris[iensis]* [6 vols (Paris, 1665–73)]. B. 13, p. 248.

letters and sermons presented to the public by Edward Browne in his appendix to the *Fasciculus rerum expetendaum*, tho with many peevish notes, which reflect more upon the critick than the criticised.These various sources with some others, we shall have occasion to point out hereafter, furnish us with many curious and interesting points whether of Bishop Grossetete's private or publick life sufficient to justify and support the high reputation he acquired in his life time, and hath left behind him to all succeeding ages. But a compleat history of this most learned, and venerable Doctor of the English Church, such as his merits and glorious actions deserve, can never be expected till all his works are published. Or at least cast from some hand, who hath free access to all his manuscripts as well as his published works. For this reason, the author chooses rather to call this an essay, than the history of Bishop Grossetete and heartily wishes this faithfull sketch may awaken some abler pen, to give it us more at length. Till this comes the author of the essay flatters himself that even this sketch will not be unpleasing to the curious Reader, as the subject is notably interesting in itself, but in some measure new, whether as to the order and totality of the collection, and treated moreover with a fidelity, and sincerity, necessary in all subjects whatever, but never more so, than in setting forth a character conspicuous for those two virtues above all others.

^With regard to some passages of this life, concerning the abuses of the Court of Rome, let the scrupulous remember that they are recorded by all contemporary historians and especially by Matthew Paris, a learned and pious Benedictine monk of St Albans, and so regular and Catholick as to be employed by the Pope in reforming some monasteries of his order in Norway.[4] However there's no reason to take scandal either at the existence or relation of these abuses, for their existence is foretold by Christ. So the relating is justified by the conduct of the sacred writer. Hath not our Redeemer forewarned us that while his servants are asleep, the enemy comes and sows his tares among the good corn, and that this mixture is to be suffered till the time of harvest and the general separation at the last day? Doth not he also teach us by his prophetick actions, as well as parables, that even sometimes the ship of Peter, tho He himself be in it but seemingly asleep, is ready to be overset with waves and storms and is near upon sinking; but that in its greatest perils he is not only in it, but at length rises up and stills both the storm and waves? Now as in this case the tempest, however violent, only served to manifest the power in a more conspicuous and adorable light. So as to fill his timerous disciples with an admiration equal to their first fears. So do all the abuses and commotions which such abuses raise in the Church. For how could His Church subsist and preserve her faith pure amidst so many corruptions, not only of her children but sometimes of her pastors, if her Almighty founder was not with her according to his promise, behold I am with you all days even to the consummation of the World? And altho in certain great trials he seems asleep and even to have deserted her in the eyes of weak and credulous souls, whose faith is either ill-informed of his prediction or too weak to believe his all-subduing power, yet he never fails to awake, rise up and rebuke the storm. First by raising up some zealous pastors to protest against the reigning abuses and to call for remedy, and then by raising up others in due season to procure the remedy desired. The evil therefore is not in opposing open abuses, for how should they be remedied unless laid open? Nor is the evil in relating them, for this is justified by the pen of the inspired writers who relate the misconduct of the ancient and new pontiffs. Moses relates those of his brother Aaron, and St Mark those of his master St Peter. As doth also St Paul. The evil then is in the manner and intention of laying open or relating such abuses. Men of God have done both with a vigorous but humble zeal, with a view to see them corrected, and in this they did a good and necessary work. Others have ripped them up with the intention only to expose the sovereign pastors of the Church. If these deserve the curse of Cham for the shameless derision of their father's nakedness, then others certainly deserve the blessing of Sem and Japhet for covering the same, or only exposing it to their father that he himself might cover it.[5] Which of these characters belongs to our Prelate and to the compiler of his life, the life itself must determine.^

Book I

Chapter I

GENERAL IDEA AND PLAN OF BISHOP GROSSETETE'S LIFE

The sketch of Bishop Grossetete's life and virtues is thus delineated in a few words by Matthew Paris[a] where he styleth him, 'That great Doctor of the Church, thoroughly versed in Latin, Greek and Hebrew. The lover of truth, the diligent searcher into the Holy Scriptures, the protector of the widow and orphan, the instructor of the people, the teacher of the clergy, the patron of scholars, the director of priests, the persecutor of the unchaste, the corrector of monks, the reprover of prelates, the bold and open reprehender of king and pope, and lastly the *Hammer* (alias scourge) and contemner of the Romans.'

These outlines of our prelate's life the Reader will see filled up throughout his whole story. There he will see him, *a Lover of truth* and wisdom, which from his youth he preferred to corporeal satisfactions. A 'diligent searcher of the Holy Scriptures', which he made the foundation of his sacred studies and pressed the same rational method upon his disciples. A 'protector of the widow and orphan', whom he assisted himself and interceded for with others. An 'instructor of the people', to whom he constantly preached to under the distractions of his professorship, and the occupations of the episcopacy. A 'teacher of the clergy', whether in his synods, or ordinations, or visitations. A 'director of priests', not only by wise regulations but by the vigorous and indefatigable execution thereof and by his own example. A 'patron of Scholars', whether in directing the studies of his diocesan University of Oxford, or by promoting to the Church dignities, such as were respectable for their learning and virtue. A 'persecutor of the unchaste', whether among the clergy, religious or laity, more especially among the two first of those three orders, whom when found incorrigible, he deprived of their benefices and expelled from his diocese. A 'corrector of monks', in seeing that they observed the rules of perfection, prescribed to them by their holy founders and by them professed, especially in the articles of poverty and chastity. In reforming the relaxed by wise constitutions, and putting the disorderly under penance. A 'reprover of prelates', whether abbots, rectors, doctors or bishops, sometimes by charitable and eloquent letters, and sometimes

---

[a] *Chron. Maj.*, pp. 872 and 876.

by the censures of the Church. A bold 'reprehender of kings and popes', by remonstrating to them, in a free, yet humble and respectful manner, whenever he found them reprehensible. Lastly the 'hammer and despiser of the Romans', not by denying the pope's authority which he held sacred, and in the opinion of some will seem to stretch to an excess, but by opposing some exactions of the Roman officers, that abused their master's power and especially the undue promotion of unfit foreigners, without fearing their rash and unjust censures, or threats, when he had duty evidently on his side. This with a great deal more, the Reader will see with satisfaction and edification, and in seeing it will easily subscribe to this short, but pithy eulogium, given to Bishop Grossetete by Prior Trivet, 'That he was a Prelate of excellent wisdom and most pure doctrine, and the pattern of every virtue.'[a]

[a] *De ordine Fratrum*, edit. Hall, p. 204.

Chapter II

GROSSETETE'S BIRTH, HIS GRAMMAR AND PHILOSOPHICAL STUDIES AND HIS WORK

This illustrious personage was born according to Bardney,[a] at Stow in Lindsey, whether Stow in Hoyland, or Stow in Lindsey [*sic*] where St Hugh Bishop of Lincoln had a country seat, as we learn from Geraldus Cambrensis.[b] Nevertheless Trivet, and Matthew of Westminster[6] and after them, the curious and indefatigable Leland,[7] bring him into the world at Stradbrook in Suffolk. The time of his birth is more uncertain than the place; but he being a man fit for business and who had completed his study of Arts, Physicks and Law before the year 1200, we may venture to place the epoch of his nativity about the year 1170, towards the end of the reign of King Henry II. All the authors just cited agree, as doth also Doctor Thomas Gascoigne,[c] that Grossetete was of mean extraction according to the world, and we shall see presently that Grossetete himself was not ashamed to confess it. So that there seems but little grounds for Thoresby's opinion who makes him son of Ralph Copley one of the King's officers, by his wife Mary daughter and heiress of Sir Richard Walsingham of Suffolk.[8] I would not however deny but his family name might be Copley for Grossetete's seems an accidental name. But whatever his family name might be it's clear his extraction was low. Nevertheless this lowness of his origin was abundantly compensated by the most exalted gifts of nature, and grace. Gifts ushered in with a peculiar favour of heaven and with one of those prophetick presages, which frequently attend the entrance of Great and Holy men into this lower world. Sometime before his birth his mother, if we believe Bardney,[d] dreamt that she bore in her womb only a great head from which circumstance, verified in the greatness of his soul, and perhaps by that of the organ in which it was lodged, he seems to have derived his name of Grossetete, or Greathead. His pious mother dying while he was but a youth, gave him for last instruction, to seek God and true wisdom even above *meat and drink*. The

---

[a] *Bardney*, C. 5

[b] *Anglia Sacra*, B. 2 p. 431.

[c] [Thomas] Gascoigne, *Diction[arium] Theol[ogicum]* in 'voce peccatum' [sinner's voice].

[d] *Bardney*, CC. 3 and 4.

docil Robert imbibed the lesson with an eagerness and fidelity equal to its excellence and *as long as he lived he made it the rule of his actions and conduct*. He had very soon an occasion to try his dispositions that way. After his mother's death he was reduced to beg his bread.[a] Coming to Lincoln he there became a shepherd, yet so as to continue in his first poverty, and to be sometimes obliged to beg his subsistence. However in this obscure state he gave several happy symptoms of a promising genius and more promising piety.[b] The first spark of his genius shone forth in a great natural facility for English rhyming verse. Those of his piety on the following occasion. Once begging an alms at the Mayor of Lincoln's door the Mayor offered him a capon adding by way of a jest, that the capon was his, on condition he would promise never to be Bishop of Lincoln. Robert, tho hard pressed by hunger and want rejected the offer, esteeming it a base and mean spirited disposition to give up even the chance of so sublime a dignity for so trifling a dainty and so he walked off, unserved. The Mayor reflecting on the seriousness of his refusal called after him, and offered him the boon without any conditions, but Robert calling to mind the most Christian advice of his dying mother to prefer wisdom to all corporeal food, begged of the Mayor, instead of feasting his hungry body, to procure him the means of improving his mind by learning.[c] The Mayor put him to school in the city of Lincoln where young Grossetete out stripped all those of his age in the Grammar Studies, the more, as his understanding naturally quick and comprehensive was purified, elevated and enlarged, by the voluntary mortifications which he practised upon his body from his youth, and which by freeing the mind from the slavery of the senses, purify and strength all its faculties.[d][9] His temperance and application were enhanced by a great gravity and simplicity of manners[e] and by a special devotion to the passion of Christ,[f] and to the compassion of his most holy mother, the which in his letters he often solicited of those to whom they are addressed.

From Lincoln School the hopeful scholar was removed to the University of Cambridge which at this time, as is testified by Peter de Blois, sent forth its streams of learning, and learned doctors, to the great benefit and honour of the whole English Church. ^Cambridge was of a later date and begot likes beggars children in a barn, its existence being owing to Joffridius,[10] Ingulpus's successor in the Abbey Royal, whose monks having obtained a brief for raising acharitable [*illegible*] toward relieving

---

[a] *Bardney*, C. 7.
[b] *Bardney*, CC. 8 and 9.
[c] *Bardney*, C. 10 and 12.
[d] Petitio Paulino.
[e] *Bardney*, C. 5.
[f] *Epist. Grosseteste*, 40 and 41.

their church, preached for that and gave other concessions for a barn or grange hired at Cambridge.[a] ^Here Grossetete ran through his course of Rhetorick and Logick, with such success, and reputation, that he was soon chosen to teach both those Liberal Arts. The *Annals of Lanercost* assure us, that he passed for the most eloquent speaker of the realm of England, which is to be understood in his native English tongue, for his Latin, tho superior to that of the generality of his contemporaries, savours too much of the barbarity of the times in which he lived. Nevertheless as sometimes we meet under the purple of pompous expressions the most clownish, insipid and uneloquent thoughts, so as in Grossetete's works, under the coarse garb of an imperfect Latin, we find the whole soul and spirit of true eloquence, viz a clear and elevated conception, a most exact judgement, an invincible strength of reasoning, with a beautiful method and great perspicuity of diction, as well as deep and universal learning.

From Cambridge Grossetete passed to Oxford, whose studies were both more ancient and more renownd than those of Cambridge and there he finished his philosophic studies[b] under a Professor named John, whether John of Cornwall or any other. Oxford was a noted place of study before the Conquest, as appears from Ingulphus, who removed from the Monastery of Westminster to Oxford, there to study Aristotle and Tullius,[c] and its antiquity perhaps rises as high back as King Alfred.[11] There he turned out so great an adept in all the Liberal Arts and Sciences, not only in the *Trivia* of Grammar, Rhetorick and Logick,[d] but in the *Quadrivia* of Arithmetick, Musick, Geometry and Astronomy that he wrote upon every part of them, especially, sayeth Trivet,[e] and Knighton,[f] upon Logick, Astronomy, and other useful parts of Philosophy. Tanner[g] observes, that Grossetete was the first, that opened the way to the Mathematicks which must be understood of the perfection of that Science. For Tanner himself gives many instances of English Mathematicians, anterior to our Philosopher and these of no small note, yet so inferior to Grossetete that he seemed to be the first introducer of those studies. Hence the 'Miracle of Philosophers'. Roger Bacon makes this declaration, 'Few,' saith he, 'have been perfectly knowing in Philosophy, as Solomon, and after him Aristotle for his time; in our days, Robert late Bishop of Lincoln, and brother Adam de Marisco, for these were men of perfect wisdom.' And again, 'The Bishop of Lincoln, Robert Grossetete and Adam de Marisco,

---

[a] Ibid., p. 14 speciatim.
[b] *Bardney*, C. 18 and 19.
[c] Hist. Croyl. p. 73.
[d] *Chron. Maj*., p. 206, (line 13).
[e] *De ordine Fratrum*, p. 204.
[f] *Chroniconica de Henrici Knighton*, p. 2436.
[g] *Biblioth. britannico-hibernica*, 'Bacon'.

were the greatest clerks in the world, and were compleatly perfect in all wisdom, both divine and human.

We learn from the writings of Bacon himself that he was much indepted to Will Shirwood Chancellor of Lincoln,[12] whose excellence in all kind of knowledge, but chiefly in mathematical learning, he very highly celebrated, but the most remarkable of all his patrons, and he to whom he owed the greatest gratitude was Robert Grossthead, Bishop of Lincoln a man of prodigious learning and of unblemished integrity, from whom in all probability our author received those lights that were of greatest use to him in his studies. Since he [*Bacon*] freely professes in his writings, there was hardly any man in that age, except this Bishop of Lincoln and his disciples who distinguished between real and useful learning and that kind of empty and useless reading, which thro want of good sense and true taste bore the name and carried the reputation of learning[a] and that as we shall have occasion to shew hereafter, to such a degree as to untitle those who turned their thoughts that way, to reputation and dignity, while such as cultivated that sort of science, which was of real benefit to mankind, fell under grevious suspicion, and were treated as persons prone to novelties.

In fine Grossetete's genius penetrated so deep into all parts of natural knowledge that among the vulgar he passed for a Magician, and the story of the brazen head, which spoke and answered questions, and which is commonly fathered on Friar Bacon, is ascribed by Bardney to our Philosopher.[b] As a work framed by him while a Master of Arts in Oxford is the surest evidence of a man's genius, and application are the number, variety and judiciousness of his works, we shall here subjoin the catalogue of his philosophical writings, as drawn up by Leland and Tanner.[13]

Part of Grossetete's philosophic works were published to the world, almost as soon as the press was set up, but the greatest part are only Manuscripts, in the several libraries of England. Those published are as follows, viz:

One book on the Usefulness of the Arts; to which should be added his book, On the difficulties of natural knowledge. MS. One book on the nature of the understanding. 1 book on Truth. 1 book on the truth of propositions. 1 book on Forms, or that God is the first form of all things, addressed to Adam de Marisco. 1 book on the State, Order and Sufficiency of Causes. 1 Book on the impressions of air, or the generation of humid impressions. Opuscula on the generation of sounds.[14]

Tracts on the heat of the Sun. On the generation of the Stars. On corporeal motion, and Light. On the finiteness of Motion and Time. On

---

[a] Biog[raph]. B[rit]., p. 341; *Opus Maj*., p. 64.

[b] *Bardney*, C. 20.

Angles and Figures. On the nature of Place, or Space. On the beginning of Forms. On the first Form. On man's being a little world. On the movement of supercelestial bodies. On the disposition of the *mover* and the body moved in circular motion. On local differences. On the six differences.[15]

Besides these which are printed at Venice in folio an. 1514, there are these following, printed long before in the same city viz: Two books on Aristotle's works called *Posteriorum*, Edit Venet, an. 1497, 1504, 1514, 1537, 1558.[16]

8 books on Aristotle's eight books of Physicks, Edit Venet, 1504 and 1506. 1 book on the *celestial sphere*, or compendium on the Sphere of the world. Edit Venice, an. 1504 and 1518. 1 book on the art of calculating the Ecclesiastick year, commented by his disciple Roger Bacon and in the next age by the celebrated astronomer Simon de Bredon.[17]

Grossetete's MSS works, are these, viz: 1 book of comments on Logick. Comments on Aristotle's *Predicaments*. 2 books of questions on Aristotle's *Elench.* 2 books on the *Priorums* of Aristotle. 10 books on Aristotle's *Ethicks*.[18] 1 book on the powers of the human soul.[19] 5 books on Boetius' *Philosophic Comfort*.[20] 1 book or Summ of Philosophy, treating of the nature of Forms of Light, of colours, of the rainbow, of the advantages of Liberal Arts.[21]

1 book called *Compendium of the Sciences*, partitioned into 20 divisions: 1 On the various divisions of Philosophy. 2 On natural Philosophy. 3 On Mathematicks. 4 On Metaphysics. 5 On Grammar. 6 On Rhetorick. 7 On Logick. 8 On Physick. 9 On Arithmetick. 10 On Musick. 11 On Geometry. 12 On Astronomy. 13 On Opticks. 14 On Astrology. 15 On Astronomy [*repeating 12*]. 16 On the Mathematical Sciences in general. 17 On Politicks. 18 On Economicks. 19 On Ethicks. 20 On Unity and Simplicity.[22]

2 books on Aristotle's *Caelum* and *Mundus*. 2 books on Aristotle's book on *Generation and Corruption*. 4 books on *Aristotle's Meteors*. 1 book on the Rainbow and the Looking Glass. 1 book on Colours. 1 book on Light and Diaphonius [*sic*] bodies. 1 book on the Comets. 1 book of theories on the latitudes of the planets.[23]

One book on practical Geometry.[24] A little book on Physical Lines. 1 book on the Astrolabe.[25] 1 book on the Philosophical Stone. 1 book on necromancy and geomancy. i.e. divining by lines and figures.[26] 1 book on Astrology.[27] 1 book on Squaring the Circle. 1 book on the prognostications of the Seasons. 1 book on the Intempery of the air, and its forboding. 3 books on the human language.[28] 1 book called *Little Cato*, a commentary on Cato's *Disticks*.[29] 1 book on agriculture, digested according to the months of the year, composed by Grossetete in French, and by him turned into English.[30] 1 book on his *own studies*. Cited by Waldensis lib: 4 cap. 77. A mistake of Tanner's for a book taken out [*of*] Lincoln's study or library in the Franciscan college at Oxford.

A Poem on the Civility of Manners.[31] John Fordun in his *Scotichronicon* cites Grossetete several times, in quality of an historian, but no history of his now appears.[32]

All these works were composed by our Philosopher in Latin, except those expressly mentioned to be in French or English, however they do not appear to be all written either at this time, nor in our home universities, but some abroad, especially those in French.

Chapter III

GROSSETETE STUDIES PHYSICK, AND THE CANON LAW, AND BECOMES SECRETARY OR OFFICIAL TO WILLIAM DE VERE, BISHOP OF HEREFORD

After compleating his philosophic studies, Grossetete applied himself to the study of Physick, and the Canon Law, two sciences which taking care of our bodys and estates were then, and are still in so much greater request among men and the more lucrative to the professors as the generality of men are more tenaciously affected to their life and property, and more liberal towards the defenders of either than to any other profession. And this might be one reason why Grossetete being in low circumstances of fortune applied first to those lucrative professions as a means to help himself forward in the more sublime study of Theology. And here Grossetete's universal genius excelled no less than in the other Liberal Arts, and soon introduced him into the family and friendship of the noble William de Vere, Bishop of Hereford from 1186 to 1199.[33] On which occasion the Bishop of Hereford received a letter of compliment from the famous Giraldus Cambrensis then Archdeacon of Brecken, and since Bishop Elect of St Davids.[34] This letter is so short and at the same so honourable to Dr Grossetete, that its worth the Reader's curiosity to read it and our pains to transcribe it. 'He that interceeds for good men', saith Giraldus to the Bishop,

> Shews his own judgement according to Symmachus,[35] as much as he seeks their interest. Hence having lately heard, and that with the highest satisfaction, that Master Robert Grossetete had been admitted into your Lordship's family, and friendship, I have but one thing to beg, which is that your Lordship's favours may equal the merits of the Subject. For I know of a certainty, that his service will be doubly and trebly useful to your Lordship, not only by transacting business and deciding ecclesiastical causes, but by preserving your Lordship's health of body, he being thoroughly skilled in both those sciences. The more, as these talents, which of all others are the most lucrative in our age, are in his person united to, and founded on the knowledge of all the Liberal Arts, as well as an extensive erudition in literature, and supported by a wonderful parity of manners, which illustrate and inhance his other abilities. And whereas the generality of those who are possessed of the forementioned talents are not always endued with equal fidelity, Grossetete's fidelity is equal

> to all his other virtues and shining qualities. In fine, to conclude his eulogium in few words, I know him to be of such a genius, and of such industry, that either I am greatly mistaken, or your Lordship will find him a man, according to your heart's desire, and one in whom you may repose an entire trust.[a]

Giraldus doth not mention the office which Grossetete enjoyed under the Bishop of Hereford, but by the talents commended in his letter it should seem to have been that of secretary or official. One reason that determind Dr Grossetete to the Bishop of Hereford's service may have been the learning and eminence of the Chapter and City of Hereford which at the time was a celebrated school of all the Liberal Arts, as we learn from these verses, in which Simon Ashe, or Fraxinus, a Canon of that Church, invites Giraldus (above mentioned) to come and fix his abode in that seat of the various arts;[36]

> Fons sine fine fluens, flos Cleri, gemma Sophiæ;
> Wallia cui debet, quicquid honoris habet
> Linque tuum natale solum; dolet Anglia dives,
> Quod speculum mundi Wallia pauper habet.
> Sol apud Antipodes
> si lucet, quid juvat? & quid
> Wallia si fuerit lucida luce tua
> Sol aliquid juvat, illa nichil. Sol sæpe relucet
> Lux tua te solo præterunte perit,
> Flos et honor Cleri, nostram te transfer ad urbem,
> Sunt ubi Philosophi; summus habendus ibi.
> Urbs Herefordensis multum tibi competit, in qua
> Proprius est trivii, quadriuiique locus.
> Floruit et floret, et in hac specialiter urbe
> artis Septenæ prædominatur honos.
> Hunc, ubi tot radiant artes, de iure teneris,
> Cum sis artis honos, artis amare locum.[b]

The time of Grossetete's entering, and leaving the service of Bishop Vere is as uncertain as his office under him, but as he entered after 1186, so he must have quitted at least in 1199, in which that prelate died. This service may help to fix the epoch of Grossetete's birth, for he could scarce be less than thirty years of age, that he had run thro the course of all the Liberal Arts, and the study of Physick and the Law.

---

[a] Ex Symbolo Elect. MSS aquad; *Anglia Sacra*, B. 2, p. 344.
[b] Ibid. p. 641.

Chapter IV

GROSSETETE'S THEOLOGICK STUDIES AND LUCUBRATIONS

The death of Grossetete's patron the Bishop of Hereford seems to have been the date of his passing to the study of Theology which he either began or perfected at Paris, the most renowned School of Arts and Sciences then in the Church, especially for Theology, to which Grossetete now aspired. As a necessary preliminary for arriving at the perfection of the sublime and extensive science, he began by making himself master, not only of the Latin usually spoken in the Schools, but also of the Greek and Hebrew, in which are written the Divine books, the first source of all true Theology.[37] But whether he learned the sacred languages at home or abroad is not very certain. Certain however it seems, that he studied Theology in the University of Paris, whose method in assigning the first hours of the day to the Scripture lectures he strongly recommends to the Masters Regent of that faculty in Oxford. And he recommends it as the excellent and exemplar practice of our, 'ancient Masters Regent in Theology of the University of Paris.' He saith elsewhere in his dying speech[a] that he had seen and heard, as his masters and teachers, those eminent doctors and preachers, in France, Eustachius Abbot of Flays a Cistercian, Magister Robertus de Cutcun, James de Vitry, since Archbishop of Plotemais and Cardinal, Stephen the banished Archbishop of Canterbury and a celebrated professor in the University of Paris. And the learned and holy Robert de Curzon, who all flourished in France in the beginning of the 13th age, who had preached the *Caursini usurers* out of France,[38] and he calls them 'Sancti Patres et Doctores Nostri.'[b] Master Grossetete was not only a student, but according to Du Boulay,[c] an Eminent Professor in the University of Paris. Nevertheless he took his degree of DD in that of Oxford, as he himself signifieth, in his sermon on the Levites.[d39]

---

[a] *Chron. Maj.*, p. 875.

[b] Eustachius praedicavit in Anglia pro cruce sumenda 1200. [Eustachius preached in England the Cross taken up], *Chron. Maj.*, p. 201.

[c] 154Boulay, *Historia parisiensis*, B. 3, pp. 154 et 260.

[d] Hearne's note in *Dunstable annals*, p 299.

Grossetete was the first chancellor of Oxford whether at this time or during his professorship doth not appear. Our illustrious Doctor, and Professor Grossetete studied the Theology of the heart as much, if not more, than that of the mind. And we may judge of his great proficiency in both not only by his works and actions but by the most judicious, and excellent method with which he pursued his sacred studies. A method worthy the peculiar notice and imitation of all students whatever.[a] The Earl of Gloucester, having been once entertained by Dr Grossetete with wonderful courtesy and politeness, asked him in private, by what secret he had attained to such a perfection of courtly behaviour, seeing he had not derived it from his birth. 'Nothing, My Lord,' replied our humble doctor. 'Nothing is more true than that I am come of mean parentage. But then from my youth, I have been educated with the greatest patterns of virtue and with those that have ruled the world.' 'How so?' replied the Earl. 'Because,' said Grossetete. 'Ever since I began to read and meditate the Holy Scriptures, I there met thro every age with many noble and heroick worthies conspicuous for their prudence, modesty, liberality, chastity and all other virtues, who were both able and willing to tutor and instruct me by their striking actions and conduct of life. As by so many expressive hints and significations of what they would have me doe, and accordingly, to their exemplary lessons I have always endeavoured to conform my conduct and conversation.'[b40] John de Athon, or Acton, Doctor and Professor of Law, and Canon of Lincoln, relates in his annotations on the constitutions of the Cardinal Legates Otho and Othoboni, the like answer of Doctor Grossetete to King Henry III.[41] This Prince being once in admiration of the polite and courtly manner in which Bishop Grossetete brought up the sons of the nobility in his episcopal palace, asked Grossetete where he had learnt, 'this great art, since he was not descended of noble but plebeian parents.' Grossetete answered that he had learnt it in the palaces of greater kings than the kings of England, because in meditating the Holy Scriptures, he had conversed with those illustrious Kings David, Solomon and others, and had learnt their manner of life. ^Would to God all Schools, especially those of the sublime study of Theology, had sense to understand and follow this admirable method! It is of study, as of conversation, we naturally and insensibly collect the tincture of the manners of persons we converse with especially when they are persons we esteem and love. And so we do of the authors we read, whether we study their thoughts, their sentiments or their actions. And this is done with more profit, and less danger than in studying the

---

[a] *Annal. Lanercost.*

[b] Atho. Glossa in Constantuos Otho et Tital: 28, et in usto Barones aquid fides *Life of Wolsey* [*illegible*] 6 page 23 of [*illegible*] collect.

living. Living examples, whether of learning or virtue, are but few and seldom to be met with, and then the best have their defects, which are more easily learnt than their perfections. But the examples of the dead are both more numerous, as comprising those of every age, and more profitable, as their defects are commonly censured and their virtues more commended by the veneration of past *ages*. But to reap this advantage it were necessary to follow the advice of the greatest masters, which is to begin always by studying the best, and most perfect models whether for writing, or living. This was Grossetete's practice and the success was admirable. The commonality by studying one another or one model contract something of their style and manner of thinking, but great and exclusive geniuses, who study a multitude of writers, and patterns of virtue, contract the good qualities of them all. By perfect attention to the salutary lessons, and examples of such venerable masters, as he found either among the ancient philosophers, or the Patriarchs, Prophets and Apostles, or among the Holy Fathers and Doctors he imbibed deeply all their maxims and sentiments and what is more commendable, all their virtues.^ This is evident from his works, whether of Philosophy or Theology, and even from his epistles, which are studded as I may say, and shine not only with the choicest axioms and principles of the ancients, but with their most virtuous sentiments and dispositions as with so many precious and sparkling diamonds. There with the wisest sayings of the ancient poets and philosophers, with a perfect knowledge of the Divine Scripture and Holy Fathers, me thinks, I read the virtuous qualities of their minds and hearts. The acuteness and clearness of an Aristotle, the natural wisdom and elevation of Plato, the firm faith and hope of the Patriarchs, the burning zeal of the Prophets and Apostles, the vigour of a Cyprian, the firmness and at the same time the address of an Ambrose. The charity, candour and moderation of an Augustine. The justness and sense of a Jerome or Chrysostom, with the sweetness and humility of a Bernard. These qualities of the ancients Doctor Grossetete attained to in a degree superior to any of the School Doctors of his time, which were neither few nor contemptible. The age in which he flourished boasted many illustrious names, whether for Philosophy or Theology. There we find the *Universal Doctor*, Alan of Lile [*Lille*], the *Irrefragable Doctor*, and the *Doctor of Doctors*, Alexander Hales, an English Franciscan (ob. 1245). The *Contemplative Doctor*, St Edmund Riche, Archbishop of Canterbury (ob. c.w.t.). The *Illustrated Doctor*, Adam de Marisco O. S. Fr. (ob. 1258/60). Doctor John the Welchman (ob. 1260) brother Franciscan Professor, styled for his science and eloquence, *The Tree of Life*. Doctor Henry de Susa (ob. 1271), Archbishop of Embrun and Bishop of Ostia and Cardinal, commonly called *Ostiensis*, and surnamed, the *Fountain and Light of the Law*. The *Pious Doctor* Robert of Sorbonne (ob. 1271) founder of the Sorbonne College. The *Angelick Doctor*, St Thomas of

Aquin (ob. 1274), and the *Seraphick Doctor*, St Bonaventure (ob. 1280), the first a Black, the other a Greyfriar. The Great Doctor Albertus Magnus, Bishop of Ratisbonne [*Regensburg*] (ob. 1280), a Dominican friar. The copious holy and the *Most Grounded Doctor*, Richard de Middleton (ob. 1285 [*vere* 1305]), an English Greyfriar. The *Wonderful Doctor*, Roger Bacon (ob. 1292) another English Franciscan and disciple of Grossetete. The *Solemn Doctor*, Henry of Gand [*Ghent*] (ob. 1293). Walter Burley (ob. 1337), the *Plain and Perspicacious Doctor*. Robert Cowton, OSFr.[a] Walter Brinkley, Oxon., *the Good and Ancient Doctor* (ob. 1310).[b42] Hugh de Novocastro [*Newcastle*], *Doctor Scholasticus, Ord. Min. Scoti defensor* (*c*. 1310).[43] And lastly the *Grounded Doctor* [*Fundatus*], William of Ware (ob. 1290) an English Franciscan styled by Pico G. of Mirandola,[44] *the Lamp of the Church*,[c] and the celebrated master of the more celebrated *Subtle Doctor*, John Duns Scotus (ob. 1308). These were all contemporaries to Doctor Grossetete, some in the beginning, some in the middle and some in the end of his course. Yet in the year 1307, the learned Chapter of St Paul's in London, in a petition put up to Pope Clement V, make no scruple to call Dr Grossetete the most eminent, and the most learned of all the Philosophers, or Theologians of his age. Accordingly his authority is often cited in the Schools, under the title of the Doctor of Lincoln, *Lincolniensis*.[d45] But lest we shoul appear to set the Doctor of Lincoln at a higher bench of the schools than his merits deserve, we shall here lay before the Reader a more unequivocal proof of his learning in the ample catalogue of his Theological works; still preserved in our libraries. Partly wrote at this time partly during his professorship and partly during his episcopate.

The Doctor of Lincoln's sacred writings may be distributed into five several classes. Viz: First his comments on Scriptures. Second his comments on or translations, or abridgments of the fathers. Third his scholastic treaties on several parts of Theology. Fourth his Sermons. Fifth his letters.

In the first class are: 1 book on the prologue of the Bible. 1 book on the Hexameron or Six days Creation. 1 book of *Expositions on Genesis* cited by Waldensis in his doctrinal of faith C. 77. Expositions on Leviticus cited by Fisher, Scripto 4th fl. 3 commentaries on Job. *Postils* or short notes on 80 or 100 of the Psalms, *cut* short by his death. Richard Taverner a lay preacher in King Edward VI days, translated into English the *Prayers*

---

[a] *Biblioth. britannico-hibernica, 1340.*

[b] Said by John Bale to be a doctor at Oxford around 1310. Bale MS. [*Bodl.*] Seld. Sup 64, fol. 166.

[c] *Collectanea Anglo-Minoritica*, p. 70.

[d] See, *Biblioth. britannico-hibernica*, Alyngton in 'Carew,' in 'Dymmock,' in 'Fetton.' See also Woodford against Wycliffe; infer hist dogma, p. 165. *Wilkins*, B. 3, p. 325. Col. 1: Woodensis.

of Bishop Grossetete on the Psalms, perhaps the same as his *Comments on the Psalms*. See Tanner in 'Taverner.' Notes on the Lamentations of Jeremy. *Commentary on the 4 Gospels*, also called a moral treatise according to the intentions of the four Evangelists, alias *Four books of homilies on the four Gospels*, the first book containing 78 chapters, the second 59, the third 98, the fourth 64. 1 book of comments on St Luke. 1 book of comments on the Epistle to the Galatians, referred to by Grossetete, in his *Cessation of the Legal Rites*. Comment on the Epistle to the Corinthians, cited by Gascoigne, according to which last author Doctor Grossetete had wrote in his own hand, on the margins of the *Glossa ordinaria*, notes on all St Paul's Epistles. 1 book on the Apocalypse of St John. 1 book of sentences of the Holy Scripture.[46]

The second class of his theologic works comprises: A translation from the Greek and an explication of all the works of St Dennis the Areopagite, collected from all his other interpreters.[47] His comments on St Dennis' *Mystic Theology* is published among that Father's work, edit: Strasbourg, folis an. 1511. A translation from the Greek of *The Testament of the Twelve Patriarchs* published in almost all the Bibliotheca PP.[48] A translation from the Greek of a book called *Suda*, in defence of the virginity of the mother of God.[49] 4 books of annotations on St John Damascen's, *Orthodox Faith*. 1 book of annotations on *Suidas*, cited by Waldensis lib. 5: C. 113. An abridgment of St Augustine's *City of God*.[50]

The third Class, which comprises his scholastick tracts may be subdivided into his dogmaticks, morals and tracts of discipline. Under the dogmatiks come: A Summ of Theology, in one book. 1 book on the names of God. 1 book on the local presence of God. 1 book on man. 1 book on Original Sin. 1 book on the reparation of man after his fall. 1 book on Grace and Justification, published by Browne in his appendix to the *Fasciculus rerum expetendorum*. 1 book on Triple Justification and Grace. 1 book on Freewill. Another on the same subject, but different beginning. 1 book on God's becoming man, *Deum fieri hominem*. 1 book on Science, or knowledge and will. Treatise on true and false prophets or the manner in which God communicates himself to the prophets, published by Browne *ut supra*. 1 book on the Discernment of Spirits. A book in six chapters on the pains of purgatory, or on the remembrance of the 4 last things, in Corpus Christi Coll. Oxon. 155 [ff. 3a–10b XV1 Asc]. 1 book on the resurrection of Christ, and ours hereafter. 1 book on marriage. 1 book on the Cross. 2 books on the Angelick and Ecclesiastick Hierarchy. A discourse on the threefold Hierarchy.[51]

1 book on the *Cessation of the Legal Rites*, published at London in 1652, quarto, and again 1658, octavo by Mathew Hale or by Mr Brun Ryves, but very imperfectly. The compleat copy which is MSS in the library of Trinity Coll. Cambridge [B. 15. 20 cols. 527–674], is near upon

two thirds more ample, than the printed one saith Browne.[a] 'This book', adds Browne, 'is an excellent demonstration of the truth of the Christian religion.' Its divided into five parts. In the first, he debates whether the Mosaick rites, are to be observed or not observed, under the Gospel. In the second, he proves that the prophet predicted by the ancient Patriarchs and Prophets, as the person in whom all nations were to be Blessed, is the very person of Jesus Christ, Son of the Virgin Mary. And this he proves from the Old Testament where he's so often professed and promised. In the third presupposing the Gospel history as a certain truth, he labours to confirm by convincing reasons (drawn from the Gospel), the truths already proved from the old scripture in the second part. In the fourth, he shews that the legal rites ceased to be obligatory the moment Christ expired. In the fifth, he discusses this question whether the moral precepts of the Decalogue are in force under the Law of Grace and how those persons, that were spiritual under the Law of Moses, were tied to the ceremonials of it.[52] Next to this may be placed two books, on the Decalogue and the Creed which Browne observes, to be next to it in the manuscripts, as well as in order of matter. This work is otherwise called a Theological treatise, comprising all the articles of the divinity and humanity of Christ, and in some manuscripts, *The Castle of Love Divine*. And originally written by him in the Romance, or old vulgar French for the instruction of the Laity. Therein he treats of the creation of the world, of its medium, and end. Of the fall of the world by sin, and its restoration by mercy. Of the King of the world, and of his coequal Son, and of his four daughters viz. Mercy, Truth, Justice, and Peace. Of the coming of Christ, and how he entered into a certain castle, viz. the body of the Immaculate Virgin. Of the properties of the said mystick castle. Of the prophecy of Isaiah, *a child is born to us*. Of the world's end, of the day of judgement, of the pains of hell and the joys of heaven.[53]

Among the moral tracts are: A summ of Justice, in ten books. A summ on the Capital Vices, in one book. 1 book in 34 chapters on the Seven Poisons, or deadly sins and their antidotes. The looking glass of the moral eye. Alias *Speculum Concionatorum*, otherwise called, a treatise on the remedies of the moral eye in 15 chapters.[b] 1 book, on the doctrine of the heart published at Naples by F. Aloysius in 1607, but falsely ascribed to Gerard of Liege. An *Enchiridion*, the same perhaps as his *Manuel des peches*. 1 book of meditations. 1 book on nocturnal illusions. 1 book on confession, alias called *Assensions in forma confessionis*, with this beginning, 'because the thoughts of man shall confess etc.' Another book, called Lincoln's doctrine on Confession beginning, 'It is written of the

[a] *Fasciculus*, append: ad fascical: rerus expetend. B. 2, p. 246.

[b] Hearne in *Dunstable annals*, p. 299.

Levites…'. 1 book against Luxury. 1 book on the humility of Christ. 1 book on the reward promised to the Apostles.[54]

The tracts of Discipline, are these: 1 book on the *Pastoral charge*, beginning, 'to those born and educated'. Another treatise of a similar title called the *Pastoral Charge and Authority*, beginning, 'Moses who by the command of God'. This book seems the same as that *Against the negligence of Pastors*, which hath the same beginning. 1 book on the priestly functions. A memorial for parish priests, extracted from diverse doctors. Another memorial called simply *Memorial*, and of a different beginning from the foregoing. *The Sting of Conscience* in 7 books, written in old English rimes, and wrongly fathered upon Richard Hample; see Tanner, in 'Hampolus'. 1 book of Collections on the penitential tracts or anons. 2 books on penance, or directions for enjoining penances beginning, 'Robert to his beloved friend'. A penitential in one book, beginning, 'First let the Priest say etc.'. *Universalities on penance*, or certain general constitutions on penance. A treatise, how the penitent is to be examined. Advice concerning penitents beginning, 'Priests in Confession etc'. Synodical ordinances, 39 in number published by Browne p. 410, beginning, 'Debentes de vobis racionem'. A list of information to be taken by his archdeacons in their archdeaconaries, something like the foregoing, but shorter, and in number 49. These are in the *Annals of Burton*, p. 317– and in Wilkins, *Concilia Magnae*, B. 1, p. 627. Constitutions for the Prior and Convent of Newenham, whether Newhus, a house of Norbertines in Lincolnshire, or more likely Newenham,[a] a convent of Austin canons in Bedfordshire, founded *c.* 1110 by Roisia wife of Pagan de Bellocampo, who came over with the Conqueror. Whence I suspect these constitutions to belong rather to one of his predecessors in that See of Lincoln, named Robert Bloet. A beautiful and elegant Diocesan Register kept not very [*illegible*] in the treasury of Lincoln but now missing; Hearne in the *Annal[es]. Dunst[able]*, p. 50. Certain rules drawn up for the Countess of Lincoln for the government of her land, hospital, house and family.[55]

Statutes of Robert Grossetete of good memory, for the regulation of his own family, in number 17, in the cabinet of Bishop Barlow *vide analecta vitæ ejus et eund: c. finem*. Among the manuscripts of A[*nthony*] Wood in the Museum Ashmolean, 8560: 98, *His method of Visitation,* which is part of a discourse spoken before Pope Innocent IV and his cardinals at Lions in 1250.[b] A large memorial on the causes of the corruptions and abuses in the Church, presented the same year and at the same place to the same holiness in a private consistory, published by Browne, p. 250. These Theologick works of Doctor Grossetete were so esteemed by Dr

[a] Vide, *Mon. Ang.* vol. 2, p. 238. *Epistola monitoria ad priorem et conventum de Newenham.*

[b] *Anglia Sacra*, B. 2, p. 347.

John Felton, the learned and holy vicar of St Mary Magdalens Oxford, *c*. 1440, that he extracted from them his *Alphabetum Theologicum* for the use of poor students. Tanner, in. 'Felton'.[56]

The fourth Class comprises his sermons, which are very numerous, and upon almost all subjects. 1 book of homilies. 1 Sermon on the first Sunday of advent. 3 Sermons on the Annunciation of Our Lord. Sermon on Mary's choosing the better part. Sermon in praise of religious poverty, preached before the friars on St Martin's day. Sermon on the Ladder of Poverty. 3 or 4 others, which by their titles or beginning seem preached before the same religious. Viz. The first begins, 'Being met according to custom for the Collection or conference.' The second, 'Blessed are the poor, because yours is the kingdom of heaven'. Sermon on the Temple of God. 9 sermons, preached in the Cathedral of Lincoln, one of which begins, 'This day, we sing in honour of the Blessed Virgin'. 37 sermons in the Bodley library. Another book of sermons, called *Sermones Elegantes*. Sermon on the assiduity of Prayer. 7 sermons to his clergy, published by Browne in the *Fasciculus rerum expetendarum* etc. 147 Dicta, or short-heads of discourses, thrown out as a help to his memory for extempore discourses which he preached, while teaching in the Schools, whether to the students or people of Oxford.[57]

Several of these have been also published by Browne above. viz. Dicta: Ona good Judge. On true and false Prophets. On Faith and its Articles. On Grace and Justification. On Prayer and its Divisions. On Pride. On Detraction and its mischiefs. 3 on humility, on patience. On the Mercy and Justice of God, shining forth in all his works. A vesperal panegyrick, pronounced at the vesperial act of Doctor Adam de Marisco. Prophecy of Robert Grossetete, among the Digby Manuscripts in the Bodleian Library 196 [fol. 28 (XVa)], princip. *Externi populis dominabitur*.[58]

The fifth and last Class, contains his most sensible and excellent epistles, to the number of 127, the greatest part of which were published by Browne, with a promise to publish also the remaining part. But whether this promise was ever executed I cannot find.[59] Those made publick, are taken from a copy of Dr Simon Patrick, Dean of Peterborough, collated with several others in the libraries of Cambridge. See Browne's appendix to the *Fasciculus* pp. 307 and 245. These and many other theological works, were composed by our Doctor of Lincoln, in such number that Doctor Thomas Gascoigne, twice Chancellor of Oxon in the forepart of the Fifteenth Century assures us of his known knowledge and reading, that they exceeded in quality those of the voluminous Minorite Doctor, Nicholas de Lyra.[60] Bardney asserts that he had wrote no less than 30 volumes on the higher studies.[a] Blunt in his *Censura of Celebrated Writers*,

[a] *Bardney*, C. 28.

adds, citing Fuller's *Worthies*, that Doctor Grossetete had composed to the amount of 300 treatises, the greatest part then lodged in the Westminster Library, and that Doctor John Williams, Bishop of Lincoln, had projected an edition of them in three volumes folio, but was prevented in the execution by the breaking out of the Civil Wars in 1641.[61] It were greatly to be wished, that some of our many learned librarians, who alone can have proper access to his manuscripts, would resume a design so honourable to the nation, as well as to the Lincoln Doctor, and enrich the Republic of Letters with so valuable treasure. His books being left to the Franciscan Library in Oxford,[a] tis among the inheritors of that treasure that many of them may be found tho indeed most of our publick libraries abound with them. Now the mere titles and tendency of the various works we have here exhibited a catalogue of chiefly taken from Tanner, are enough to fortify what is advanced by the Venerable Chapter of St Pauls, concerning the Doctor of Lincoln's superiority over the other doctors of his time. Yet what the same Chapter adds in their petition to the Pope, is still more honourable to his memory, viz. that as much as he surpassed his contemporary theologians in the knowledge of nature and all his contemporary philosophers in the knowledge of God, and things divine, so much also did he surpass them in humility, in holiness, in simplicity, in innocence of manners and purity of intention, living in constant contempt of earthly things, and solely attached to those of Eternity.[b]

---

[a] *De ordine Fratrum.*
[b] Petitio Paulino.

Chapter V

DOCTOR GROSSETETE MADE ARCHDEACON OF SARUM AND DIVINITY PROFESSOR IN OXFORD

A Doctor of Grossetete's uncommon learning, piety and zeal, could not fail of being pursued by honours, how carefully so ever he might endeavour to fly from them. His first promotion, after his Theological studies, seems to have been in the Church of Sarum where in 1220[a] we find him Archdeacon of Wilts, under that holy and learned prelate, the great canonist Richard Poore.[62] By an obscure and almost unintelligible place in Bardney[b] he appears to have made a journey to Rome, while Archdeacon of Wilts.[63]

The same year 1220, or very soon after Doctor Grossetete, was placed upon a higher and more luminant candlestick in the house of God, and called to communicate his light, not only to inferior clergy but to the choicest portion of the national clergy, in the University of Oxford. And not only to the clergy, but to a new settlement of a religious order just sprung up in the Church, and in great odour of sanctity and learning by the many eminent secular scholars that either embraced or patronised it. This new order was that of St Francis of Assisium, commonly called the *Friars Minors*, and in England the *Grey friars* from the colour of their habit. It was but just founded, and the founder was still living, when their colony came over to England in 1219, or the beginning of 1220, under the conduct of the Blessed Agnellus Pisanus. Three of Agnellus' eight companions in his expedition were Englishmen the first of the three was Richard de Ingeworth [*Ingworth*], a learned secular priest and an eminent preacher, who joined Agnellus in France. The two, were Richard of Devonshire, acolythe and William de Esseby, a great student and a perfect religious. Their first establishment was at Canterbury on a spot given them by Alexander, provost of the Poor Priests' hospital. Their chief benefactress there after Alexander was a certain religious Lady, whom Eccleston, calls Domina Inclosa de Bagginton [*Lady Baginton*]. Their next settlement was in London. The third in Oxford, begun before All Saints

---

[a] Register Sarum, in *Wilkins*, B 1, p. 555, where he is by mistake called Richard, instead of Robert.

[b] *Bardney*, C. 17.

of the same year 1220, under the conduct of William de Esseby their first guardian. Such was their edifying deportment that Matthew Paris saith they filled all England on a sudden. In 1258 less than 40 years after their first arrival, they formed seven wards, which in the year 1400 comprised sixty convents, afterwards encreased to ninety. Twelve of which were observantry, neither were they poor and contemptible as they appeared, only joined by the commonality, but by the prime scholars of the age. In 1228[a] came over to them the 'Irrefragable Doctor', the Doctor of Doctors, Alexander Hales a native of Hayles in Gloucestershire, and at this time Chancellor and Archdeacon of Paris. One of the most celebrated professors of Theology of this time, and noted for being master to the Angelick and Seraphick Doctors. This Doctor was followed by several others.[b] By Robert de Hendred, Benedictine Abbot of Abbingdon, in 1230. By John de Romeyn, Austin Abbot of the Black Sepulchrin canons of Osney, in the west suburbs of Oxford in 1235. And lastly by Doctor Ralph de Maydestone, a celebrated Professor in the University of Paris, and actually Bishop of Hereford, when he entered among the Grey Friars of Gloucester in the year 1239.[64] But their greatest encourager, and promoter, and one that set them in the highest repute, was their first Divinity Professor, in Oxford Doctor Grossetete, the very glory of the University of Oxford, as Wood calls him. The eminent secular Doctor, at the request of their first Provincial, Agnellus of Pisa, read lectures in their new school, for the instruction of the young friars, and was so charmed by their holy and austere lives that, as Matthew Paris[c] informs us, he had once thoughts of entering among them and tho for the greater good of the Church he never executed this thought, he ever after preserved a wonderful esteem for them, held a commerce of letters with their generals, if not with their founder St Francis himself, and ever employed them in making missions, when he was raised to the See of Lincoln. His greatest delight was to confer with these and Dominican friars on the Holy Scriptures.[d]

As Doctor Grossetete was their first professor, so without injury to any of his eminent successors whether secular or religious in the Franciscan Chair we may affirm he was the most celebrated whether for his piety, or wisdom, or zeal. His lectures did not hinder him from preaching frequently whether to the friars, or the students of the University, or to the people. We have mentioned above several sermons, preached to the friars, on the evangelical councils. His *Dicta* or heads of sermons, seem to have been preached to the students. And from them it is evident, that our judicious and zealous Professor took as much care to form the heart

---

[a] *Biblioth. britannico-hibernica*, 'Garlandius'.

[b] *Collectanea Anglo-Minoritica*.

[c] *Chron. Maj*., p. 722.

[d] *De ordine Fratrum*, p. 205.

of his scholars to virtue, as their understanding to learning, and to ground them well in the essential virtues of humility, prayer etc. So difficult to ally with, and yet withal so necessary for succeeding in the sciences. A few extracts of some of these dicta, will justify what we advance, and will set the mind and heart of this illustrious Professor in more clear and respectable light.

In speaking of Pride in the students, he thus shews how it hinders their progress and the superiority at which they aim. 'Pride',[a] saith he,

> Is a love of one's own excellence, as when any one desires a higher rank, than is either fitting or due to him, and in consequence of such a desire, places himself higher than he ought. Now this inordinate desire, blinding the eyes of the soul, it frequently happens that such a person imagines himself to be really arrived at the height to which his pride aspires, while in effect he falls as much below it, as he inordinately rises above himself. Thus many skilled in secular learning, being ambitious to be preferred before all others, in point of knowledge, fancy themselves arrived at the rank, at which they grasp, whereas in very truth they are below many others, and by the very blindness of their inordinate desires, deprive themselves of a great part of that knowledge to which they might have attained, as well as others, only for their affection of preference and superiority, which blinds their understanding.

Then having proved from Ecclesiasticus and Toby [*Tobit*], that all perdition took its rise from pride, he adds concerning its occasion and cure.

> The root of pride is the consideration of our own excellence, the comparing of ourselves with others *below us*, and taking therein a certain complacency and delight. Now the axe to cut up this evil root is the consideration of our own weakness, a fervent reflection that the good which is in us is not of our own growth, but the work of God's grace. A just comparing ourselves with such [*as*] are *better than ourselves*. A dread of the fate of the angel who fell by pride from heaven. And lastly above all, of the example of the Son of God who debased himself so as to take upon him the form of a servant.

In another place, he draws this lively picture of envy and detraction in the person of an envious scholar.[b] 'From pride', saith Professor Grossetete,

> Or the love of one's own excellency springs Envy, or the love of depressing others, and from this love, the actual desire and endeavour to depress them, either by words or other signs. Thus when one student is performing the part, either of Respondent or Opponent a fellow student on the benches expresses his envious sentiments, by a laugh or sneer or some other exterior signification, insinuating thereby that the objection or answer is good for naught. At other times by the immobility of his countenance, or by drawing his head

---

[a] *Fasciculus*, p. 285.
[b] *Fasciculus*, p. 287.

deeper under his hood he hints that the objections or answers, are not worth his attending to them.

And a little further describing the mischief of detraction, he saith.

Should we see a man running thro a garden sword in hand, and lopping the most beautiful branches off the trees, with the most promising part of the fruit. Or through a church defacing with his sword the most beautiful images of the Saints, should we not presently esteem him either mad or sacrilegious, and as such worthy to be confined, or expelled the Society? With how much greater reason ought the detractor either to be shut up as a madman, or banished from the Society, as a sacrilegious wretch. He who makes his rounds not indeed thro a garden, or church, but thro a paradise, and with the sharp edge of his detracting tongue endeavours to destroy the most excellent fruit of all the good works, he sees in others, and to cut off the most fruitful branches of virtue. And defaces whatever he finds most beautiful and orderly in the living images of God? Nay is he not so much the more worthy of confinement, or banishment, as the spiritual fruits of virtue and good works, which he endeavours to blast, excel those of material trees, and as the living image of the Trinity is more precious and estimable than a wooden or golden image of his Saints?

^Then he subjoins the remedy.

If you would learn to put this monster to flight, give ear to Solomon, who says, 'The North wind dissipates the rain and a sad countenance the detracting tongue.' He who by a cheerful countenance applaude the detractor, what does he less than throw fuel upon a fiery tongue, already inflamed by Hell itself? But when by a sad countenance, he signifies the detraction to be displeasing to him, then as by a cold blast of the north wind he disperses the clouds of detraction which overcast the virtues of his neighbour. He therefore that does not oppose a sad countenance against detraction, consents thereto, because he does not hinder evil, when he may. And therefore according to the Apostle[a] he is worthy of death eternal, as well as the detractor; and how terrible a reflection must this be, when we consider that among such as are free from detraction, there are so few that fight against it by the severity of their looks?^

On the article of Grace and Free will, he thus proves their necessity and explains their concurrence with each other.[b]

It is God who effects in us both the aversion of the will from evil and the conversion to good and its perseverance therein. Nevertheless our freewill is also cause of the same. As the grain shoots forth *both by an intrinsical germinating virtue, and by (the external) heat of the Sun, mixing with and animating the juices of the Earth* [*Pr. 25:23*]. If we did not turn ourselves from evil and convert ourselves to God we should not be commanded in Scripture so to do; neither should we be praiseworthy in doing it, and if we did these things without God's grace, then were they not to be begged of God.

---

[a] Rom. 1:30.

[b] *Fasciculus*, p. 282.

On the nature, objects and articles of Faith, he saith.

> Faith (in general) is properly speaking, an assent of the mind grounded on some medium, or reason which tho absolutely speaking may, yet is not want to deceive. According to this notion of faith, that which is believed, is not scientifically (or evidently) known by the same person. In this manner are believed as well the things which do not appertain to salvation as those, that do appertain thereto. But then, as one of the mediums producing faith without science is authority, hence the medium which produced the strongest faith is the authority of the Holy Scriptures. So that the things which fall under the object of faith, are *chiefly* those to which we assent on the authority of Holy Writ. Now amongst the points which are to be believed on the authority of Holy Writ those are the *chief* which when believed[a] operate the justification of the believer. And these I take to be those points and articles from which we expect beatitude, and the sight and clear knowledge whereof in our heavenly country constitute eternal life. Now eternal life is this, that they know thee, the true God, and whom thou hast sent, Christ Jesus. Hence the sight of our Creator and Redeemer is what will constitute our eternal life and true felicity. And from their sight, this beatitude is to be expected and hoped for. But there can be no sight of our beatifying Creator and Redeemer where there hath not been first a faith in them. According to what is written, (Is. 7:9) 'Unless ye believe, ye shall not understand.' The Creator therefore and the Redeemer must be believed in, that by this faith we may arrive at their happy vision. And they are to be believed in with a perfect faith *Summe Credenda*. For such a faith, the authority of Holy Writ, principally inculcates, as the foundation of justice and righteousness. For as happiness in the term and end is joy in the vision of our Creator and Redeemer, so righteousness in the way (of this life) consists in an *humble love of the same*. Now there can be no love, of what is neither known by science or by faith. Whence it follows that as here there's no science or vision of our Creator and Redeemer a faith in them is necessary in order to justification. That then is properly called faith, whereby we believe in the Creator, and Redeemer of men. This faith is contained in the Creed, which expresses one Creator in three persons, and Jesus Christ the Son of God, in quality of Redeemer with all those other points, which appertain to our compleat justification. These articles, as hath been already observed, are the foundation of justification. Nevertheless, all things contained in the Canon of Scripture, and those which the *Universal Church believes*, besides the articles contained in the Creed, may be termed the *accidental cause of justification*, in as much as when disbelieved, contrary to the authority of scripture, *or that of the Church*, they are a cause of damnation to the unbeliever.

We shall finish these extracts, by one from a most excellent discourse on Prayer, its object, divisions, and dispositions.

> To pray, is to express the desire we have of any good, with a confidence that He to whom we manifest our desires, will grant our petition … the good,

[a] *Fasciculus*, p. 281.

we are to desire is either that supreme good, which abides for ever, or those intermediate goods which lead to it … To desire these goods of God, with a confidence that he'll grant them, is praying with interior prayer. To manifest our desires and confidence in words is what we call properly *prayer*. But God being the searcher of hearts what necessity of expressing our inward desires in outward words? This is not done to give God information, but to pay him a due and perfect homage (in body, as well as mind) and to confound the Devil. All vehement affections of the soul, break forth of themselves into exterior sounds, as their natural vehicle. Hence sighs and groans in such as suffer; hence exclamations in such as are struck either with terror, or admiration![a] The very brutes express their affections *with* outward signs hence the affection of him that desires eternal goods, being of all affections the most vehement. How should it be dumb, and not shew itself in exterior words? Doth not an affection outwardly expressed, and as it were amplified by the voice, become greater and stronger. Since however outwardly expressed it remains no less interior than before and acquires moreover the additional strength of the expression of the voice? Hence, as the greatest good ought to be sought with the greatest desire, and that desire is greater which is outwardly expressed than that which is only conceived inwardly, it follows, that we ought to beg and solicit for beatitude, and other real goods not only with inward mental prayer, but with that which is outward and vocal. Besides, the Devil being ignorant of men's thoughts and desires, is not moved [*or*] threat[*ened*] when we only pray interiorly, but when our desires are shot forth in words then the Devil knowing them is galled with envy and sorely tormented, because he ambitions above all things to see himself alone adored, and not God. When therefore we unite vocal with mental prayers then God is more honoured, and the Devil more confounded. But words without the interior affection are as branches without sap, and as leaves without fruit … A man, who honours God only with lip-prayer, but hath his heart afar from him, either occupied with sinful or with vain thoughts, is like to a man who having two tongues, one sonorous and gifted with noble language, the other hoarse and croaking out a miserable jargon, should speak with his last to his Prince on matters of life and death, and employ the former in trumpeting forth things ridiculous in themselves and otherwise offensive to his Sovereign, and contrary to his own life. The inward words of the heart are a noble and divine language, common to us and the angels, whereas exterior words compared to the interior, are in the ears of the Almighty, but a hoarse and contemptible croaking. Wherefore in prayer let the interior tongue keep time and pace with the exterior, and as for the laity, who do not understand what they recite in the Lord's Prayer when they pronounce the words (in Latin, to join with the public offices of the Church) they ought to cry up to their heavenly Father with their inward tongue and mouth that he will give both them, and those they pray for, these true goods they petition for in words they do not understand. Thus Singing i.e. with these two tongues, united together, is singing *wisely* and chanting *gloriously*. Sometimes indeed its necessary to pray only with the inward

---

[a] *Fasciculus*, p. 283.

> tongue of the heart, the outward one of the mouth, being otherwise busied, as when we eat or speak or do any work. Whereby the liberty of the tongue is hindered in all these occasions, our interior tongue ought to cry towards heaven by the desire of heavenly things, and thus at least with the interior tongue we ought to pray always, and if while our thoughts are taken up with ordering our temporal affairs, we direct this order of temporal business to the acquisition of eternal goods, then by this manner of ordering our temporals we express our desire of heavenly goods and by this expression of our desires we pray continually. But because vanity, frailty and iniquity are but too apt to break this continuity of our prayer, hence the more frequent such breaks are the more fervently we ought to continue it at other set times, and so make these interruptions of our prayer an occasion of greater assiduity in it hereafter. True goods then are to be begged continually first for ourselves, then for our neighbours, even for our enemies. For a good, which by its communication is noways liable to diminution becomes more satisfactory, the more there are to partake in it. For as many weights bundled together descend with greater velocity,[65] … so many persons united by the bonds of charity and prayer, do with more fealty and with more fervour, raise up their hearts to heaven the force of each one's prayer, helping forward that of his neighbour.
>
> We ought also to fortify our prayer, by fasting, sackcloth and ashes. We lost heaven by intemperance and how can we recover it again if our prayers are clogged with the same vice? … We are to return back into our country, in sackcloth and ashes, i.e. by some voluntary chastisements of the flesh, and the remembrance of our natural frailty. It was for our transgression we were doomed to the sackcloth of affliction, and to the ashes of mortality, and how can we expect forgiveness and pardon, but by a voluntary submission to the deserved punishment? Had the prince for our misdemeanours loaded us with chains, should we dare to cast them off and appear without them when we come to solicit his pardon? Should we not rather be glad to appear in them, the more powerfully to excite his compassion? And if perchance we had flung them off, and that with his knowledge, should we not to expiate this new offence willingly load ourselves with more heavy chains and so appear before him, to appease his just anger? This is our case, for our original prevarication, we have been cursed with the sackcloth of affliction, and with the dust and ashes of mortality. According to this sentence of the Lord, 'The earth accursed in thy work, shall produce thee thorns and brambles.' And this other, 'Dust thou art, and to dust thou shalt return.' Now this first sackcloth and ashes we have thrown off, to the best of our power, as often as forgetting our misery and mortality we have indulged the flesh in its sensual satisfactions. When therefore, we appear before our King in prayer, let us wear with a willing mind, the first sackcloth and ashes to which we stand condemned and seeing we have sometimes cast them off, let us cheerfully add thereunto new sackcloth and new ashes to those we have thrown off in order to appease the justice of God doubly provoked against us.

This extract on prayer is somewhat long, but its excellence will be its apology.

Professor Grossetete's wisdom and zeal exerted themselves no less in his private and extempore answers to the consultations of his scholars, than in his publick lectures and discourses.[a] While he read lectures in the Franciscan School at Oxford one of their novices, a youth of extraordinary piety, fell sick and had received all the rites of the church, when drawing near his end he cried out under the violence of his pains, 'Is it thus My God, thou punishest? Is it thus then strikest? Yes, then strikest in order to spare and then punishest here not to punish hereafter.' The assistants thinking him delirious suggested other sentiments to him of a more comfortable nature, as they imagined. In the mean time his purified soul was released from its suffering prison. The friars having related the affair to their Professor Grossetete and asked his opinion, the wise and religious Robert answered, 'In my opinion, you've acted imprudently. He was reading you a lecture out of the book of life, and had you permitted him to read on, he would have disclosed many secrets to you.' (Concerning the advantage of present sufferings).

Another time being asked by one of the friars, how it could be agreeable to God and meritorious to a confessor for this latter to hear wicked things in Confession, and to have his mind sullied with the images of other men's crimes. Our judicious Professor made this striking reply, 'Should a prince whose palace is all in flames see the officers he hath sent to put out the fire return back some half burnt, and some discoloured with soot and smoke would he think ye esteem them less deserving of his favour, because they have their persons and clothes sullied in labouring by his orders to save his palace?'

^The sufficiency and reputation with which Dr Grossetete filled the first employs occasioned him being called to a Divinity Chair in Oxford, where he was the first theology professor that ever read in the Franciscan schools in that University^ and one of them, and he not the least, in his great work addressed to Pope Clement IV,[b] declares there was scarce any man in that age, except in Lincoln, and his disciples that distinguished betwixt real and useful erudition, and that kind of empty and useless reading, which thro want of true taste, often bore the name and carried the reputation of learning.[66]

^In return, our religious Doctor conceived no small esteem for those religious, then in their first fervour. Such was his veneration for their Institute, and their exactness in conforming to it, that he had some thought of entering among them,[c] as many of the most eminent scholars did about

---

[a] *Annal. Lanercost.*

[b] Bacon, *Opera maj.*, p. 64, in *Biographia Britannica*, p. 341.

[c] *Chron. Maj.*, p. 722.

the same time; into that and St Dominic's Order.[a] And although he never put those thoughts in execution, yet he kept a close correspondence with them and their generals, especially General Jordan,[b] whom he saw at Oxford, and General Elias of the Franciscans, and had always some of them about him, as will been seen hereafter.[67^]

---

[a] *De ordine Fratrum*, p. 178. [*Ralph*] Maidstone, Bishop of Hereford; *Chron. Maj.*, p. 354, Walter de Mauclerk, Bishop of Carlilse; See, *Wykes*, an. 1245; ib Tanner in Manclearcus. Alexander Hales. See, [*Luke*] Wadding, Adnot Minor [*Annales Minorum*] Tom 1, n. 26 ad an. 1222, apud Cornelius a Lapide, [*Commentaria*] in Matth[*aeum*]. p. 149, col. 1.

[b] *Epist. Grosseteste*, 40.

Chapter VI

GROSSETETE RESIGNS HIS CHAIR IN OXFORD, IS MADE ARCHDEACON OF LEICESTER, PREBENDARY AT CLIFTON IN THE CHURCH OF LINCOLN AND RECTOR OF ALBODEL, WHICH LAST HE RESIGNS OUT OF SCRUPLE. HIS ZEAL IN THE OFFICE OF ARCHDEACON

The high reputation with which Doctor Grossetete filled the Divinity chair in Oxford, seems to have been the occasion of his quitting it and of his being promoted to a more weighty office, in the Diocese of Lincoln, whereof Oxford was then a part. Whitlock saith[a] he was first made Archdeacon of Chester, in the Diocese of Coventry and Lichfield but this seems a mistake built on a wrong interpretation of the word *Legecestrensis*, or *Legrecestrensis*, which are sometimes confounded by our ancient historians, or their copyists, and are used to signify sometimes Chester, and sometimes Leicester.[68] His promotion to the Archdeaconary of Leicester was at latest in the year 1223. For in that year, Adam de Marisco, late rector of the noble church of Wiremouth in the Bishopric of Durham, and now a Franciscan Friar, and one of Professor Grossetete's favourite disciples,[b] was called over into Italy by St Francis. Upon which Doctor Grossetete wrote a letter to the provincial Agnellus Pisanus, expressing his regret to see Adam separated from their holy society. And this letter is subscribed by Grossetete, as Archdeacon of Leicester R. *Archidiaconus Leircestriensis, fratri Agnello, ministro patrum minorum et conventui oxoniensi.*[c] This same year 1223, the sixteenth of the pontificate of Bishop Hugh Wells, who had made him his Archdeacon, the same prelate gave him also for the support of his dignity the rectory of Albodesleigh, or Albotel as Grossetete himself calls it.[69] Tanner places Albodesleigh in Nottinghamshire; there's an *Albodel* in Cambridgeshire.[d] Grossetete was

[a] *Anglia Sacra*, B. 1, p. 457.
[b] Tanner ex Epist. MSS Grossetete, num. 23 et aquidathem: Oxon. Lib. 1, p. 72.
[c] *Collectanea Anglo-Minoritica*, p. 25.
[d] *Chron. Maj.*, p. 408.

only deacon when promoved to this rectory, but was thereupon in all probability ordained Priest.[a] In which last quality he had the church of Clifton given him, which was a prebend in the Cathedral of Lincoln. Sometime after his promotion to the Rectory of Albodel, he had a contest with the Abbot [*Adam de Latebury*], and Convent of Reading, which only served to shew both the spirit and pacific temper with which he carried it on. That Abbot and Convent laying claim to some annual dues or rents upon the Rectory of Albodel, the payment thereof by injunction of the ordinary the Bishop of Lincoln, had been suspended under Robert's predecessor, and by Robert himself till such time as the Abbot of Reading could make but their title to the rent in question. However the Abbot and Convent renewed their claim under Rector Grossetete hoping a great deal from his equity and religion. Accordingly our Rector of Albodel did not refuse entering into a negotiation with them and a day was appointed for deciding the matter by a formal trial. Yet our peaceable Rector, chose rather to accommodate the difference by an amicable reference and a day was fixed for a meeting at Durham. But this meeting being prevented by some pressing affairs which obliged him to take a journey abroad about the Epiphany, not to return till about Whitsuntide. Rector Grossetete was obliged to propose another meeting at Sarum, where he should act by a proxy, whom he calls a great and pacifick man. Perhaps St Edmund [*of Canterbury*] treasurer of Sarum. This occasioned the Abbot and Convent of Reading to write him a letter, which tho slender in words seemed big with injuries but which he answered no less mildly than firmly. In his fourth letter, the first of those published in Browne, therein he calls them his well beloved masters; and after refuting their cavils, he tells them nothing touched him more to the quick than their calling him a *man of authority and eminent learning*. 'Whereas,' saith he, 'I do not think myself arrived at that degree, wherein men of authority are during their discipleship; and am ignorant of infinite points of learning. However if I possess any of those advantages which you ascribe to me, He alone is to be praised and honoured for it, to whom we say daily, not to us O Lord, not to us but to Thy name give glory.' He advises them above all things, not to give their confidence to the lawyers, who had drawn up their letter. 'Who,' saith he. 'Sow wind, and reap storms. Who according to St Bernard's remark, intend law suits rather than law, and what wonder he should advise me to plow, who lives by the plow hire? Who if he hath already wherein to subsist, hath an insatiable thirst for more? Such an one will be ingenious enough to find out reasons for persuading me to plow even the sea shore.' After which he concludes thus.

---

[a] *Bardney*, C. 21.

> Now lest you should retort upon me what hath been said, I reply beforehand, and declare that I utterly detest lawsuits and am now ready, as from the beginning. You may remember I professed myself to pay the rent in question, providing any wise and good man, or men, on whom we shall both agree, shall after hearing your objections and my answers determine without further contest that in receiving the said rent you act *bona fide*, upon a just title and true right. Which if it be wanting, you cannot receive what you demand without exposing yourselves to damnation. As on the other hand I should incur the like danger, did I detain from you what I know to be yours. Let therefore my Lord of Durham (the pious and able canonist Richard Poore) be arbiter betwixt us, and let us agree to abide by his decision. Or if it be more agreeable to you to pitch upon any other method of making peace I am ready, barring accidents, to meet you either at Durham or at any other place on this side of the same, where and when you please. For now as to my journey abroad, as it was designed in good and necessary reasons so now on the like motives it is put off by the advice and command of superiors.

This letter must be written betwixt the year 1228, in which Poore was translated from Salisbury to Durham, and the year 1236, when Dr Grossetete was no longer Rector but Bishop.[70] What was the issue of this contest doth not appear. Neither is it now material, the chief point which interesteth the Reader is the spirited, yet pacifick manner in which our pious Rector carried it on.

However he soon rid himself not only of the contest, but also of the living. His prebend of North Clifton having care of souls annexed to it, as well as his other benefice, our rigorous observer of the canons scrupled holding them both together.[a] However he continued for some time a pluralist on the authority of others who pretended that tho two parishes might be incompatible, yet a parish and a prebend even with care of souls were not so. Nevertheless his enlightened and unbiased purety conceiving an entire parity of reasons in the latter, as well as in the former cases, could neither stifle nor resist his scruples. And therefore by a particular friend in the Court of Rome he consulted the Pope himself, and on his Holiness's declaration that even a prebend with care and a parish were incompatible without dispensation, he chose rather to resign his living than sue for a dispensation, which no doubt his great reputation and the good use he made of his revenues might have easily obtained. Neither did he do this reluctantly but quitted it with more satisfaction then he had hitherto held it. This we learn from a very short, but very religious epistle to his sister I[*vette*] a nun.[b]

> In answer to your solicitous enquiries after my health, I reply in few words, that before the feast of All Saints I was confined by a very sharp fever. But

[a] *Epist. Grosseteste*, 74.
[b] *Epist. Grosseteste*, 8.

God having stretched forth His merciful hand to me I am restored again to my usual state. I must also inform you that I have resigned all my revenues, except the prebend in the Church of Lincoln. Neither ought you, who wear the habit of religious and vowed the observance of it, be any ways moved or afflicted at my becoming poorer by choice, in order to become richer in virtue. Nor at my making myself more contemptible in the eyes of men, to become more agreable to those of God and His angels. Nor at my relinquishing temporal goods, for the good of obedience; since without obedience no virtue can merit Heaven. The good you love in yourself you ought also to cherish in me, the more as we are more nearly allied to the ties of the same blood. Since therefore you declare by your profession that you love these and the like good in yourself, do not envy in me some poor endeavours and aims at the same, but rather congratulate with me for having shook off the heaviest part of an uneasy burden and thrown down a load which unless I laid it down would have crushed me under its weight.

If Archdeacon Grossetete got rid of his rectory it was not with a view to lead a more easy and idle life, but rather to apply himself with less destraction to the functions of his weighty office. This he did with such zeal and success as rendered him the[a] favourite of his Bishop Hugh Wells, whose greatest praise is to have been mutually esteemed and commended by this judicious Archdeacon. Archdeacon Grossetete extended his vigilant zeal not only to the inferior clergy, but even to the heads and teachers, if not by the right of his authority at least by the no less sacred rights of charity and friendship; or rather by both. A certain Doctor of Theology and interpreter of Scripture being accused of leading an infamous life our zealous Archdeacon wrote him a pressing letter, which for its vigorous charity and sweetness may vie with those of St Bernard on the subject of fraternal correction. After pointing out the shocking absurdity and contradiction of teaching the divine word with a polluted mouth, and the scandal he gives both to the clergy and people, the Archdeacon urges him in this manner to repentance.[b]

Consider yourself a little I pray, how your body hath nothing in it that can invite to this sin. That it enjoys neither strength nor comeliness, but is broken with labour, age and sickness. That your bald head, and wrinkled face announce your promiscuity to the grave, and by the water of these considerations extinguish the sulphurous and infernal breath of the Evil Spirit that hath kindled these lustful fires in your heart. Add to this the remembrance of your profession; that you are now in holy orders, to which is annexed *the vow of Chastity*. That you are charged with the cure of souls, to whom you owe the example of chastity. That you are a teacher and expounder of the sacred writings, and a preacher of the Cross of Christ, and how incompatible the infamous sin of fornication is with such holy and divine functions. To these motives add

[a] *Epist. Grosseteste*, 44.
[b] *Epist. Grosseteste*, 10.

> also the fear of hell-fire, the desire of heavenly pleasures and with all these put out this stinking fire of lust. You'll perhaps say, I am too credulous in believing reports, and will object no doubt that of the wiseman,[a] 'He that believes hastily, is light of heart.' To this I answer that this fame, or rather this evil fame, is not new, but of long standing. It sounds in my ears, whether I will or no; its spreads thro the whole country, and flying thro the air even reaches up to heaven itself. Were it false, as I wish it were, it could never be so loud, without some appearance at least of Evil to countenance and give credit to it. Whereas it behoves a soul like yours, enriched with such treasures of wisdom, and with so many other great qualities, to abstain not only from Evil, but as the Apostle requires, even from the appearance of Evil. If then this scandalous cry be true, endeavour, I beseech you by Christ crucified, endeavour to wipe off the stain by the future purity of your conduct, so to stop the mouths of evil speakers by the height of your good works and to expel by the good odour of your virtue the evil odour, which is gone forth into the world. If the report be false, which God grant it may be, then I bessech you to cut off the evil appearance that hath given rise to it … I conjure you with all the bowls of charity to drink with charity, and cheerfulness, this bitter but wholesome draught of correction. I who have drunk in the bitterness of heart, and do still drink the bitter cup of those infamous pleasures, of which you stand accused. Do not despise this admonition because it comes from your inferior in point both of station and learning, and perhaps sick of more violent diseases than yourself. For sometimes a less skilfull, and less healthy physician may prescribe a wholesome draught to another more learned and less sick than himself. Neither can that fruit be unwholesome which springs from the root of charity. Swallow then, I conjure you, this bitter draught of correction that I may henceforward drink of the more pleasant cup of joy in hearing your being changed into a new man.

A Doctor of such a pen and heart and such other eminent abilities as we have seen whether of learning or virtues, *deserved* a higher sphere wherein to display his extensive talents with greater advantage and benefit to the publick. This we are going to see in the following book which shall treat of his *Episcopate*, and of some part of his episcopal virtues and conduct.

---

[a] Ecclesiasticus 19:4.

Book II

Chapter I

ARCHDEACON GROSSETETE, IS MADE BISHOP OF LINCOLN. HIS CHRISTIAN ENTRANCE INTO THE EPISCOPATE WITH A SKETCH OF HIS EPISCOPAL VIRTUES

Bardney writes that the King, moved with the great abilities and reputation of Archdeacon Grossetete, took him into his services and made him Keeper of his Privy Seal.[[a]] This civil promotion is nowhere mentioned by any of our ancient historians and seems a mistake of Bardney in confounding Grossetete with Hugh Wells his predecessor in the See of Lincoln, who as we are informed by the *Annals of Worcester*,[b] and by Matthew Paris,[c] was Signifer, i.e. Chancellor to King John. What Bardney adds is much more certain viz that on the death of Bishop Wells in February 1235, King Henry III promoted his Archdeacon Grossetete to that vacancy at the joint petition of the clergy and people of Lincoln.[d] The royal *congé d'élire* was granted the 19 of February,[71] Grossetete was elected on the 27 March. His election admitted by the King the 5 of April, and the temporalities restored the 16 of the same month. But his consecration was put off till June or September, on account of a contest betwixted his consecrator St Edmund Archbishop of Canterbury and his Metropolitical Chapter. The Chapter of Canterbury, as the metropolitical Church was in possession of having the ordinations of suffragens performed in her precincts. St Edmund, being discontented with the monks, refused to perform the ordination in their church but the monks of Canterbury insisting upon it as their right. The elect of Lincoln wrote to St Edmund a most excellent letter to beg his consecration might be performed at Canterbury, rather than occasion strife and scandal. After proposing the example of St Paul, and that of Christ himself, the former of which to avoid scandalising the weak consented never to eat flesh [*1 Cor. 8:13*], the latter paid the Temple tax to which he was no ways obliged. He subjoins,

---

[a] *Bardney, C. 23.*

[b] *Anglia Sacra*, B. 1. ad an. 1209.

[c] *Chron. Maj.*, p. 228.

[d] *Biblioth. britannico-hibernica*, in 'Grossetete'.

> As I verily believe the monks of Canterbury will never consent to my being consecrated in any other church but their own, and if I am there will ensue a grievous and expensive lawsuit, which ought to be avoided by the servants of God. Therefore not to scandalise them, and not to destroy any of the weak for whom Christ died, I humbly beg that since my consecration may be performed there without either sin or scandal so it may be done. Better it is for me to be ordained there, let the charges be never so great, than elsewhere let the expense be ever so little, if my temporal sacring must be attended by the loss of an infirm brother for whom Christ died. Since the voice of truth hath declared, 'Woe to the man by whom scandal comes.' The wise ones of the world will perhaps treat this my persuasion as a weak and silly scruple; but I believe that wisdom, which is from above, will esteem it a point which ought to move every soul that fears God and is fearful of giving scandal. This then I beg may be done, unless there be any secret reasons why my consecration cannot be held at Canterbury without sin.

Browne hauls in this letter as an instance of the monks of Canterbury opposing Bishop Grossetete's consecration, whereas it's evident to any Reader, that is not stark blind, that the question here was not about his consecration but about the place where it should be performed and their insisting on its being held in their Church is a much better proof of their being glad for his promotion than their opposing its being done elsewhere is of their being averse to it. However to avoid suits and contentions, the monks at Canterbury consented to Grossetete being consecrated out of their metropolitick Church; accordingly he was consecrated at Reading in Berkshire.[a] And thus of a son of Lincoln, he became its father and chief. This consecration is variously dated by our historians, and this variety seems to have risen from the delays occasioned by the contests concerning the place of consecration.[b] During which different days might have been fixed for it but altered on the starting of some new difficulty. Matthew Paris places it on the 3rd of June, if there be no mistake in the numbers. Wikes and the *Annals of Wincester*, on the 15 of June.[72] The *Annals of Lanercost*, on St Michael's Day i.e. 29 of September. According to the *Annals of Tewkesbury* he was enthroned in the Cathedral of Lincoln on the Feast of the Purification following, viz. anno 1236, which may be the reason why the *Annals of Peterborough* place his promotion to the See of Lincoln to that year.

This high promotion of a clergyman of low extraction but whose personal qualities raised him above those of higher condition in the world occasioned some to shew their wit on the subject.[c] John Earl of Chester, by way of reflection on the Bishop's birth, said that Grossetete

---

[a] *Chron. Maj*., p. 409.
[b] Petitio Paulino.
[c] *Bardney*, C. 26.

was the first of his family.[a] The Bishop replied it was better being the first of one's family than the last. And the honour of a low family than the disgrace of a high one. Bishop Grossetete was not only the honour of his own house, but of the House of God and his Church by the great virtues and actions by which he supported his spiritual dignity.[b] Matthew Paris gives the abridgement of his episcopal life in three lines. 'He was hospitable,' saith Matthew. 'Liberal, cheerful and affable at the table where he fed his body; but at the table where he nourished his soul, he was full of devotion and compunction, even to the shedding of tears. And in his episcopal functions, venerable, diligent, and indefatigable.'

Bishop Grossetete's hospitality extended to the rich as well as to the poor, but the civility and generosity with which he seasoned his favours gave them a new relish. This appears from one instance preserved by the *Annals of Lanercost*, and the only one that hath survived of those many acts of liberality for which his memory is celebrated by Matthew Paris.[c] Richard de Clare, Earl of Gloucester, dining once with our prelate, the Bishop's officers served up a large fish to their master and a lesser to the Earl. Shocked at the incivility the courteous and humble Bishop offered his own to the Earl. But the Earl refusing to accept it the Bishop ordered his officer to take the great fish from before him and to serve the Earl with one of equal size. But there being none such he commanded the great fish which had been set before him to be carried to the poor and himself to be served like the rest. This politeness in a person of mean extraction and such profound learning, which commonly renders scholars awkward and stiff in behaviour, filled the Earl of Gloucester with so much admiration that in private he could not help asking, the Bishop, whence he had derived his civility seeing he had it not from birth. And we have already seen the Bishop's answer that he had derived this and his other virtues from the great examples he had conversed with in his studious reading and meditating the examples of the worthies of past ages. This civility Bishop Grossetete possessed in so high degree that the nobility of his time were ambitious of placing their sons in his episcopal palace, as the best school in which they could be trained up to a behaviour and sentiments worthy their exalted station in life. We have seen above in the catalogue of his works a poem which he wrote on the same subject, *Of Civility of Manners*. Bishop Grossetete was not only full of devotion and compunction at the altar, as Matthew Paris assures us, the *Annals of Lanercost* adds that he used to spend great part of his nights in watching and praying for his flock in order to appease the anger of God, and to

[a] *Dunstable annals*, pp. 212 and 234.
[b] *Chron. Maj.*, p. 876.
[c] *Annal. Lanercost* in *Anglia Sacra*, B. 2, p.

move him to be reconciled with his people. Thus practising this excellent lesson, which he lays down, in one of his instructions to his clergy.

> The assaults of the Devil are to be repelled from the flock, by humble and fervent prayers of the pastor for them. By singing psalms, and other hymns of praise to God … The spiritual wickednesses in several places are to be repulsed by the good odour of devout prayer. An odour, as agreeable to God, so offensive to the Devil. After the oblation of this good odour, and perfume of devotion we are to shoot forth the darts of hymns, and praise. For the tongue of him who praises God is like a bow that is bent to shoot, and every word from it is a dart of fire that pierces and burns the Devil's breast. How such darts pierce and torment the evil spirits, every envious person may understand, when he hears those praised whom he himself envieth.

After spending part of the night in humble prayer and praising God, our excellent pastor used to consecrate the day to the instruction of his people or clergy. The *Annals of Lanercost* above cited, observe that he preached to the people in the vulgar tongue. This seems observed in opposition to the Norman, or vulgar French, which being the ordinary language of our Norman princes, and of a great number of subjects, was used by such as affected the Court language and favours and not in opposition to the Latin tongue, as if this were commonly spoke by other pastors in their sermons to the people. For such uninstructive way of instructing the people was never in use, either here in England or any other part of the Church Catholick, where all instruction is and ever hath been delivered in the vulgar language of the people, either directly or indirectly. Directly when such as preached understood the vulgar language, and indirectly by interpreters when those who first preached the Gospel were strangers to the mother tongue. This we see in the person of the brave and holy King Oswald, who interpreted into English what St Aidan preached in Irish to his Northumbrian subjects. They who imagine preaching and instruction to have been here before delivered to the common people in an unknown tongue, ground their observation on the decrees of some ancient English Councils, which order the parish priests to teach the people their Creed, the Lord's Prayer, the Hail Mary, and the Commandments in their mother tongue. Now these decrees being the unanimous act of the episcopal body and of the supreme portions of our national Church evidently clears the said pastors from the absurd imputation laid to their charge, and at the worst only supposeth some neglect in the inferior pastors in contenting themselves with teaching their people the Creed etc. in Latin in order to join in the publick liturgy without taking pains to teach 'em the same in English, for their own information and edification. Now I ask, where's the equity in charging the pastors with abuses they condemned and have endeavoured to root out? Nay where's the common sense in citing as proofs against the Church those very decrees which refute the imputation by shewing her care for the due instruction of her Children in their own mother tongue? Bishop Grossetete was no less diligent in instructing, reforming and correcting his clergy, and what is no less estimable, but much more rare, he was ready himself to be corrected. Even by his inferiors, as he declared from the very beginning of his episcopate. While he was only Bishop Elect, he gave a very sound and very round correction to a certain monk for presenting to him a very unfit clerk for a certain church in his diocese. This correction being ill reported to one of Bishop Grossetete's friends, Master Michael Beleth,[a] founder of Wroxton Abbey near Banbury in the county of Oxford, and this same year Grand Butler of England[b] at the marriage of King Henry III.[73] This true friend wrote to the Bishop thereupon, who so far from taking this liberty amiss, gave him thanks and desired him to continue this friendly office in his regard.[c]

'I return you,' saith the Bishop,

> My most affectionate thanks for your compassion, and charity, in reproving, and correcting my reproof and correction, which to many seems to have exceeded the bounds of moderation. For this your fraternal correction, hath proceeded from the root of charity, and no fruit can be evil which springs from so good a root. I moreover beseech you by that charity with which Christ died for us, that as often as you hear any thing of me, either evil or unedifying, you'll endeavour to prune it off with the knife of correction. Neither will your medicinal hand afflict or offend, but rather rejoice and strengthen me. For I know how it is written, 'He that hates correction is a fool, but he that acquiesces to his corrector acquires glory.'

Assuredly a prelate of such humble sentiments, amongst the most exalted episcopal virtues and talents, was of all others, the most proper to undertake and succeed in the correction of others as we are going to see more of at large in the following articles.

---

[a] *Mon. Ang.*, vol. 2, p. 326.

[b] *Chron. Maj.*, p. 421.

[c] *Epist. Grosseteste*, 11.

Chapter II

BISHOP GROSSETETE SOLICITUDE FOR INSTRUCTING HIS CLERGY

The duty and glory of the episcopal office, consisting in the due regulation of inferior pastors, the judicious Bishop of Lincoln turned his principal attention that way, being fully persuaded that a reformation in the heads of any society is the only natural and effectual way to reform the members and subjects of it. For this end, after regulating his own family, by a body of rules in number seventeen,[a] he was exceeding diligent in holding his diocesan synods, or meetings of his clergy, so strongly recommended by the ancient canons and practice of the purest ages.[74] And practised in these latter times with such admirable success by the great St Charles Boromeo. We have still several sermons which Bishop Grossetete preached to his clergy in these assemblies wherein he presses the virtues and duties of pastors in the most solid and most Christian manner. Of this number Browne hath published six in the appendix to the *Fasciculus*, with a seventh delivered at an ordination. As nothing is a more proper specimen of this Prelate's zeal, doctrine and spirit, nor more edifying to the Reader, we shall have to beg leave to lay a few extracts of them before him and leave him to form thereof what judgement he thinks proper.

^The first of these sermons is upon this text of the *Book of Wisdom*, 'A wise king is the Support of his People' (Sap. 6:26). After a short *exordium*, wherein he presses that pastors are kings in a superior sense, and exhorts them not to degenerate from so high a dignity, he thus divides his subject matter according to the three several offices of a good king. The first of which is to defend their subjects by arms against the assaults of spirits, of different vices, and of evil men.^ The second is to improve their subjects' manners. The third is to restrain them by wise and salutary laws. The last office requires them to defend their subjects against the Devil by prayers and the Sacraments. Against vice by inculcating the terror of future judgement and the fear of Hell fire. And against evil men,

[a] Entitled, Statuta famile bone memorie Dompni Rob[*erti*]. Gros[*seteste*]. Lincoln[*iensis*] Epi[*scopi*]. MS in Museo Dom Barlow. It is a short tract in English; containing 17 rules or laws to be kept in his family, *itæ analecta vitæo ejus eper euand*[*em*]. Barlow c. finem.

either by the word of God, or by the Church censures etc after which the Bishop thus concludes this first part.

> By all these means we are to seek and forward the salvation of our subjects not only with the hatred and malediction of men, or with the loss of our temporal goods, but even with the effusion of our blood. For as Christ laid down his life for us, so ought we to lay down ours for our brethren. If the kings of Earth don't fear to expose their lives in fighting for the temporal liberty and safety of their subjects, how much more should we spiritual kings do the like for the spiritual liberty and salvation of our people, seeing that spiritual things are incomparably above temporal? Nay if wild beast and brutes without reason expose themselves to death for saving their young ones, tho they have no reward to expect hereafter, how much more courageously are we obliged to fight for our spiritual children, we that are animated with hopes of another life infinitely above the present? And if we refuse to comply with so reasonable a duty must not we be justly esteemed more cruel than wild beasts, more unreasonable than brutes void of reason, more senseless than the most senseless animal?

On the second office of spiritual kings, which is to adorn and improve their subjects by good manners, he lays it down as a principle that they are to be form and model of their subject, by a *saintly conversation, and sound doctrine*. That of course they are bound to know how to expound the articles of faith and commandments. How to discern grievous sins and what sort of dispositions are requisite in their penitents. That without this knowledge they are as unfit for the government of their subjects as they are to steer a ship who are ignorant of navigation. And more, because a miscarriage in the last case is only attended with the loss of some temporal lives, whereas in the former the consequence is nothing less than an eternal shipwreck both of the soul and body.

On the third office of his spiritual king, which is to correct and amend the subject by salutary laws, he saith he shall supersede speaking because he shall cause to be recited to them certain statutes drawn up for the purpose and for the execution of their third office. The statutes here referred to seem the same as the constitutions for the Parish Priests, published in Browne's appendix p. 410. By the statutes, the Bishop of Lincoln requires, that every pastor know and expound the Ten Commandments, the Seven Deadly Sins, *the Seven Sacraments* of the Church. That such as are priests often expound to the people in the vulgar tongue the form of Baptism and the dispositions necessary for the Sacrament of Confession and Penance. That they learn also to have a competent understanding of the doctrine contained in the Greater and Lesser Creeds in that called *Quicunque vult*,[75] which he saith is sung in the church every day at prime. That the priests frequently teach the people to bow down in a reverent manner when the *Saving Host* is elevated during Mass. As also when the priest carrieth it to the sick, which the priest is to perform in a decent habit, having a white veil under the holy Eucharist, and carrying it both going and coming in an open and honourable manner, with fear and reverence and with a light born before it. 'As knowing it,' saith the Bishop. 'To be the *brightness of Eternal Light*. That a bell be also rung before the adorable host (*veneradam hostam*) of Christ's body, thereby to awaken the people's devotion to a due adoration of so great a mystery. That the priest be always ready to visit the sick, whether by day or night when called upon, lest any of the flock thro his neglect die without confession, the *viaticum* of Our Lord's body,[76] or extreme unction. That in the Church, the divine service be performed with devotion and the full time allowed to each part …' After which saith the Bishop,

> Let every pastor apply himself to private prayer, and to the diligent reading of the Holy Scriptures … thereby to nourish and improve their Spirit of Prayer. Let them also be careful that the children of their respective parishes learn the Lord's Prayer, the Creed, the Salutation of the Blessed Virgin, and to sign themselves properly with the Sign of the Cross. And because such as carry the holy vessels before the Lord are to be holy and pure we injoin all beneficed persons and as many as are in holy orders, to fly all impurity … That none of them take a wife, and if anyone shall have taken a wife before entering into holy orders, he shall not be capable of holding any church or benefice nor of exercising any function of the order he shall have received after such marriage. And seeing there's an obligation of abstaining not only from evilbut also from the appearance thereof, we strictly forbid all of the clergy to frequent the nunneries of women without just and evident cause. As we do also all priests to retain with them under the same roof any woman whatsoever, whether relation or other, that gives occasion to suspicions.

To cut off all occasion of avarice he strictly forbids, not only by his own ordinary authority, but by special authority of the Holy See Apostolic any of the clergy, whether beneficed or in holy orders, to exercise the secular office of sheriffs, justices, bailiffs or stewards, which may render them accountable to the lay court. He also forbids the clergy to assist at plays or farces, or such like diversions. As also to play at dice, or to be present while others play, because tho these things seem light to some, saith the Bishop, yet in the doctrine of the Holy Fathers such as do these things offer sacrifice to the Devil (by their avarice, impatience, and profane and blasphemous oaths). He moreover injoins, by authority of the See Apostolic, that children who have immediately succeeded their fathers in any church shall be forced to resign the same. Browne infers from hence that the ancient clergy of the English Church, at least some of them, had wives. Now if he means that they had them any otherwise than by abuse, and contrary to the disposition of the canons, the inference is doubly wrong. First, because such inference is directly contrary to the statute above which forbids them to marry and disables such as are marry'd, from the enjoyment of their benefice, and from the exercise of their functions. Secondly, because the children here mentioned as succeeding their parents in Church livings might be children born before their parents entered into orders. The Bishop also prohibits priests to impose lucrative penances or to suffer deacons to hear confessions, as some it seems did to spare themselves trouble. By a special authority from the See Apostolic, he obliges all rectors and vicars to reside in their livings, without a just dispensation from residence. The cure of souls being, as he saith, the *Art of Arts*, he strictly orders all pastors, to apply themselves diligently thereto. And to remove one great distraction from them he forbids them to frequent the schools of the Civil Law, whether to read or to hear lectures. The abuse of this unecclesiastick study, and that of promoting the graduate in it to Church livings without any other science, rose to such a pitch at this time[a] that Pope Innocent the IV, by a constitution of the year 1254, was obliged to forbid any such graduates being admitted to prebend etc. Bishop Grossetete also injoins them, by special authority of the Holy See, to abolish the *execrable custom*, as he terms it, which prevailed in some churches of keeping the *Feast of Fools*. That the house of prayer may not be made a house of derision, nor the bitterness of Our Lord's circumcision become an object of ridiculous sport and jokes. By which words, as well as by the Bishop's 32 epistle, it's plain the feast in question was kept on our Lord's circumcision and that in all appearance it was some ludicrous representation or imitation of that mystery of humility and mortification. This custom subsisted in some churches til the Council of Basel, which forbid it in 1435.[77] These statutes are closed by prohibiting a custom, which is not yet rooted out, viz the beastly custom of *Scotales*, or meetings appointed to drink one another drunk. A practice, which owes it origin to the heathen Danes according to Hygden[b] and worthy to be banished back to some heathen country.[78]

The *Second Sermon*[c] of our Prelate to his clergy, is on these words, *I am the good shepherd.* After laying open five several pastures, into which they are to lead their sheep, and distributing the pastoral charge into six different duties he saith,

> The second is to make their voice heard of the flock, not only with the ears of the body, but with those of the heart. Of these ears it is written, 'Thou hast given me perfect ears.' And again, 'he that has ears to hear let him hear.' Now it is not in the power of him who speaks outwardly to manifest the truth he preaches to the understanding. Nor to fix them in the memory, nor to infuse the love of them in the heart; for Christ is the only master that speaks and

---

[a] *Chron. Maj.*, p. 883 et additament p. 190.

[b] *Dani a natura potatores fortissimi hoc unum prædicabile perpetuum reliquerunt anglis, ut jam Anglorum probitas toti praejudicet mundo in calicibus epotandis. Polychronicon*, p. 265 ex. Will.

[c] *Fasciculus*, p. 260.

> works interiorly. How then shall he, who speaks to the ears of the body, make his voice reach the ears of the Soul? Perhaps, by praying to Christ who is the word that speaks inwardly and by soliciting him to infuse into the ears of the heart what we speak outwardly to those of the body …' The fifth, is to walk before the flock in the harsh ways of penance, so to render them more passable and more easy by his example.

The sixth and greatest of all, saith the Bishop,

> Is in case of necessity, to lay down his life for his sheep … neither ought pastors be backward in aspiring to this perfection, because the very last virtue is incomparably better than our corporeal life. For this corporeal life is only a life communicated to the body by the soul, but virtue is a life communicated to the soul by God. Let us suppose that any master give his shepherd a sum of money to be employed to the said master's profit. And that at the same time he entrust him with the care of some favourite sheep whose life is of incomparable higher value than the sum in question. Now should there happen a case where the sheep being in danger the shepherd might save its life, or had reason to think he might save it by laying down the forsaid sum, would he not be esteemed a faithless servant in case he denied so trifling a sum for saving the life of his sheep? … Moreover death is the unavoidable penalty for Sin. What then we are obliged to pay of necessity, and whether we will or no, why should not we make a cheerful offering of it to God, the destroyer of Death and Sin and the author of life? The more, as if we give up our corruptible corporeal life which is but as a *leaden* penny, we shall hereafter receive back this corruptible little life of the body, in a state of incorruption and as a leaden penny, transmuted into a piece of Gold.

The fourth sermon, which is said to be pronounced in a synod, and is upon these words of Genesis ch. 1, 'He place the stars in the firmament of heaven,' is an ingenious comparison of the virtues of pastors with the properties of stars. 'A star,' saith he,

> Is a spherical lightsome body, moving in a circular uniform motion, and ever retaining its fixed order and situation in the firmament. So ought the spiritual stars of the Church to be so perfectly round and even as to have neither sharp and rough protuberances of anger and contention; nor hollow cavities to receive the filth of avarice and intemperance … The vice of intemperance is detestable in all Christians, but more so in pastors. For how dares he, who feasts on the flesh of the Son of God, on the flesh of his Redeemer, which is food giving life eternal to the worthy receiver, how does he glut himself with the flesh of beasts to his own destruction? And he who drinks of the blood of Jesus shed for his redemption, of that wine which inebriates and cheers the heart of Salvation, how is he not overwhelmed with shame at the very thought of drowning his reason in wine, wherein there is lust? … As often therefore as you shall sit down to meat, remember for Christ's sake, whose flesh you have just been eating, and whose blood you have so lately drank of. How indecent it must be for him, who has been regaled with the food of angels, to glut himself with the bread of the children of men? How absurd for him who

> has feasted on the flesh of the Lamb, to lust after the flesh pots of Egypt at the Sepulchres of Concupiscence? How contrary to all sense and reason the soul which has drunk of the delicious water from the Rock, and of the most pure blood of the grape, to thirst after that wine which is a source of luxury and will be one day changed into the gall of dragons and the venom of asps, which nothing will be able to cure? The spiritual star must be lightsome and shining, both within and without. Within by the light of the Catholick faith; without, by the light of good works … It ought to move uniformly, neither too fast by the precipitate correction of sinners; nor too slow, by tepidity, and a neglect of correction. Its motion ought to be circular, returning always to the point where it first set off. Beginning by him who is the Alpha and beginning of all things. And ending in the same, who is the Omega and end of all. From this flows another property which is never to be drawn from their regular and circular movement, either by the levity of aspiring pride or by the gravity and weight of grovelling concupiscence. Which how contrary it must be to the state of priests who *have vowed chastity* we leave you every one to consider. And from this property follows also another, which is to remain in that order and degree wherein the providence of God hath placed them without ambitioning a higher place in the firmament of the Church, than that which God has assigned them.

The 5 sermon, which was preached at an ordination lays before the *ordinandi* two of their principal duties. The first of which is to raise their minds and hearts to God by inward contemplation. The second is to communicate to their flocks by instruction, what they have learnt of God by meditation.

In the sixth sermon to the clergy upon these words of St Paul to Timothy, *be then an example to the faithfull*, he saith,

> The light of your conversation ought as much to outshine that of the commonality of the faithfull as the light and brightness of the eyes excels that of the other parts of the body. For you are the Eyes of the Spouse. Now dust and chaff, which cannot hurt the other parts of the body, are very sensible and painful to the eyes and oblige them to weep. So the dust of venial faults which affect the commonalty but little or nothing at all, ought to appear grievous to you who are the eyes of the spouse and provoke you to grief and shedding of tears.

After speaking largely on chastity, and of the horrible absurdity of souls fed with the virgin flesh of the Son of God, wallowing in the stinking mire of carnality, he adds. 'The porters, that introduce chastity and her virgin train of other virtues are coarse apparel, and sparse diet, and their guardian, humility.'

Bishop Grossetete's seventh and last sermon to his clergy, of those published in Browne, is on these words of the 131, alias 132 Psalm, *Thy Priests shall be clad with justice*. Among many definitions of justice or righteousness our Prelate and Doctor prefers that of a certain Catholick Philosopher who defines it as *likeness with the heavenly substances, or angels*. And this he observes so much the more justly in regard of priests as they are called angels, by the prophet Malachy, and by St John in the Revelations, where he writes to the angels of the Churches. 'A conformity with angels,' saith the Bishop to his Priests,

> Is that justice with which you who are called angels, are to be clad and adorned. Now to understand more fully the beauty of this ornament, let us examin with attention what the angels are and wherein we are to resemble them.
>
> The angels are incorporeal, intellectual beings who contemplate with a fixt and steady eye, the ineffable beauty of the Holy Trinity. And to whom the wisdom and word of the Father, is the Book of Life, and the Looking Glass of Eternity in which they intellectually read, and clearly behold the immense power of the Father, which they adore. The universal wisdom of the Son, by which they are enlightened, the superlative goodness and sweetness of the Holy Ghost, which they embrace. There they also see and read whatever they owe to God their Superior, what to their equals, and what to their inferiors. And besides this they are carried towards Him, who manifests these duties to them with a love superlatively ardent; they live delighted in the sweet love and sight of Him. They direct all their operations exactly according to the rules which they read in the Book of Life. They observe a perfect peace with each other. They rejoice in each others' good and for us, as long as we are in this mortal pilgrimage, they have a solicitous, prudent and vigorous care. Enlightening the darkness of our ignorance with interior instructions, inflaming our affections to good, directing us in all our works, repelling from us the snares and assault both of the powers of the air, and wicked men. Rejoicing at our proficiency in good and not a little grieved with our defects. In these, and many other similar properties, we must learn to resemble the angels if we desire to be united to their society. Its true, the necessities of this mortal life, will not allow us to come up to them by a likeness of equality and perfection, but we ought at least to follow and advance toward them, by a likeness of imitation. The angels exercise their ministry towards us, and at the same time see the face of God, so that their action is no hindrance either to the continuance, or clearness of their contemplation. But as for us, seeing we cannot at once stand in contemplation and move in the administration of exterior things, let us esteem contemplation our most happy and favourite duty, and the administration of exterior things, as a burthen laid upon us. Let us not suffer ourselves to be drawn aside from the sweets of contemplation, except by our own or neighbours' rational necessities, or for some advantage of piety and religion. When one of these two things call us away, then altho' we should like better to rest in the arms of contemplation, let us go forth with promptitude and cheerfulness, taking care to perform them with discretion and vigour, and after the performance, to return back with eagerness to the rest of contemplation. By this method we shall do by turns and successively according to our capacity what the angels do, not successively, but together. Thus by turns we shall be both Mary and Martha. Mary by contemplation, Martha by action. Thus shall we resemble Moses, first speaking to God in the mount then relating to the people below what we have learnt of God.

> Instead of the Book of Life, which we are not allowed to read here below as the angels do above, we have the book of the two Testaments, wherein we are to read the subject of our contemplations and the rule of our actions. From reading this book, and from consulting this looking-glass, let nothing be able to withdraw us, except the duties above specified, viz our own or neighbours' just necessities, or some act of piety. But never let us forget what was said to Ezekiel and to St John, by way of lesson to us. That they *should devour the book* shewn to them and what is devouring the book, but to read it with avidity and to digest its meaning? Let us therefore in imitation of the angels, eagerly thirst after the lecture of the Holy Scriptures and according to the rules there laid down, so direct all our actions. Keep peace with one another, rejoice in the good of our brethren, watch over our subjects with solicitude, prudence and vigour, enlightening their ignorance by the word of God. Inflaming their hearts with the fire thereof. Guiding all their actions according to its prescriptions, repelling from them by their shield of faith, and the sword of the spirit which is the word of God, all the assaults of the powers of the air and of wicked men. Rejoicing at their progress in good and vehemently grieving for their faults.
>
> One great incentive to the diligent execution of these duties, and a great spur to us who bear the name of angels, is the manner in which the angels are described and represented with wings. For what is signified by the wings of the angels but their ardent zeal and readiness to fly to their duty … It is also an incentive to bear with the infirmities of our neighbour and to conform as much as possible to their exterior ways so to allure them to conform with our interior ones. That the angels have frequently appeared in human shape in order by this condescension and familiar conversing with weak men to gain their confidence, and thus raise them to a heavenly conformity with themselves. If thus we become weak with the weak and with the Apostle make ourselves all to all, so to win all, what is this but putting on, as the angels do, the form of our neighbour's frailty and weakness?

The Bishop concludes this sermon by pressing them to the earnest invocation of the holy angels. 'Let us, who are angels (by office) invoke for this end the aid and assistance of the angels.' Here Browne pretends that the Bishop in pressing the invocation of angels is in contradiction either with himself, or with the Scripture. In the beginning of this sermon the Bishop had said that, 'Christ alone can give the robe of justice.' And in another sermon that, 'All grace comes from Christ and is to be asked of him,' whereas now he exhorts his clergy to invoke the assistance of the angels. As if to confess that all grace comes from Christ, and yet to beg the prayers of the angels were two things contradictory. Hence the Doctor desires some invoker of angels to explain to him, how these two assertions hang together, 'that all true good is to be asked of God alone,' and yet the 'assistance of angels is to be invoked?' To which an invoker of angels may reply that those two assertions *hang* together, just as these two others, which the Doctor admits. 'That all grace is to be asked of God alone,'[a] and yet the 'prayers of the auditory may be asked by the Preacher, that his preaching may be profitable to them.' For this last the Doctor allows, and asserts to be a thousand times better than begging the prayers of the Virgin by saying the Hail Mary, as modern Romanists are wont to do. Now I ask, where's the difference, as to the contradictory part betwixt begging the prayers of the auditory and begging those of angels or the Virgin Mother of God? If those of men can be asked without hurting the prerogative of God, as sole author of Grace, why not those of the angelick spirits? For my part, I think there's a much greater contradiction in allowing us to beg the prayers of weak and sinful men like ourselves and in disallowing us to beg those of the Spirits made perfect both in grace and favour with God? So that in reality here, it is the Doctor both contradicts and forgets himself and not the Prelate. What is added by Browne, to shew that the Bishop's notion of the invocation of angels was at least very different from the modern doctrine of the Council of Trent, is an evident proof that it was the same. And a worse proof could not be alleged to support his assertion than the place he alleges on this occasion. So blind is prejudice when it is resolved to find fault! The place cited by Browne, is from an unpublished work of our Prelate, on the Ten Commandments and is this.

> They give to Creatures the veneration and worship due to God alone who by prayers, or sacrifices, or any other homage or service, intend and endeavour to obtain of any other besides God what God alone can give or who offer to another what God hath reserved to be offered to Himself alone. As they for instance who desire of others the remission of sins, whereas God alone can forgive sins. Or they who seek from another the Kingdom of Heaven, whereas God alone can bestow it. Or they who expect the gift of prophecy, or science, or any other intermediate or inferior goods from any other as the *principal giver*. Whereas God alone is the *principal giver and author of all good*, even the very lowest.

Here the mighty objector hath brought forth less than the mountain in labour, not only nothing to the purpose, but all against himself. Here it's as clear as the sun that our Catholick Prelate here distinguishes betwixt the *principal giver* and those who are only ministerial, instrumental, or occasional givers of grace, i.e. who are either obtainers of grace by their prayers, or conveyors of it by their ministry, tho dependently on God the *principal author, and giver*, and on Christ the sole essential mediator. This last way of obtaining grace by prayer, or of conferring it by their ministry, is of the Competence of Creatures. As to the obtaining of grace St James declares the prayer of the just availeth much and thus all men suppose, who pray either for themselves or others. For they only pray

[a] *Fasciculus*, p. 301.

with a view and in hopes of obtaining succour either for themselves or their neighbours, thro the merits of Christ. And as to the conferring it as instruments under God this the Bishop evidently supposes when he saith, as above, that the angels *enlighten the darkness of our minds* and inflame our wills to good. For what is giving grace either principally or instrumentally, but conveying light to the understanding and fire to our wills, either as original or secondary causes? Hence we may justly infer that Bishop Grossetete, in teaching that God is the principal giver of grace, and yet that the angels ought to be invoked as obtainers or minsters of the same is no ways in contradiction with himself.

And this is all that our Prelate, or the Trent Fathers, attribute either to the Saints or Angels, when they invoke their assistance i.e. either a share in their prayers which they offer to God upon the altar of incense in heaven, or a share in their ministerial service and care of men upon Earth. That the angels may be, and actually are the instrumental causes of many graces, the bishop evidently teaches in the sermon, where he saith that they enlighten the darkness of our minds and inflame our wills to good.

Neither is he in contradiction of Scriptures. He only exhorts us to do what the holy prophet and patriarch Jacob did upon his deathbed in these words. 'God, which fed me all my life long … the angel which redeemed me from all evil, bless the heads.' [*Gen. 48:16*]. What is here been said concerning the lawfulness and reasonableness of invoking angels, holds for the saints and much more for the Queen of the Saints, the Virgin Mother of God, and is consequently an answer to another of Browne's notes, where speaking of the Bishop begging the prayers of the auditory. ^If the saints know nothing of our affairs, nor have any power to help us, this reasoning might pass. But if it be enjoined that the angels and saints, who rejoice in the conversion of sinners, must know their commission, and by good consequence, their prayers too. If it be plain that knowing these prayers, they offer them to God upon the altar of incense above, if it be consonant to common sense to believe that those whom Christ placeth with him upon his throne, to whom he hath given power to rule nations, whom he hath made kings and priest to rule upon Earth, have proportionate power to assist their supplicants here below, then to advance that begging prayers of a mortal and simple auditory is more to the purpose than to beg immortal and holy choirs above, and especially the Queen of holy spirits made perfect, is assuredly, to say nothing worse, a coarse compliment to the Mother of our Redeemer and to Christ himself. As if he were more inclined to hear prayers of sinners of imperfect part, than those of his most holy mother. After all, as to our Prelate it can scarce be thought that he who in the end of his sermon allows and praises the invocation of angels, should scruple invoking the Queen of Angels in the *exordium*, had it been the custom of that day, as it is of the present age.^

This indeed Browne is so sensible of that after trying to prove the contrary by the passage, and in the manner above related he fairly gives him up, only pretending that he's at least in contradiction with the word of God. This indeed would be much worse than contradicting himself, but this as the Doctor takes no pains to prove, so we shall take none to answer him, the less, as this being a part of controversy nowadays belonging to our present design which is only historical, we shall remain content to have shewn that Bishop Grossetete is no ways contrary to himself in this article, and so proceed on to the sequel of his life and activities.

Chapter III

BISHOP GROSSETETE ENQUIRIES INTO THE LIVES AND MANNERS OF HIS CLERGY, BY HIS ARCHDEACONS

The zealous Bishop of Lincoln did not content himself with instructing his clergy by his sermons, nor with directing 'em by salutary laws and statutes. He was no less solicitous to see his exhortations and directions put in practice, as far as lay in his power. With this in view he drew up a body of information to be taken by all his archdeacons, in their respective districts and these informations are but a juridical inquest to be made by the archdeacons to see if the parochial and inferior clergy comply with their duties. Which are pretty much the same as those prescribed in his statutes for parish priests, which we have subjoined to the third part of his first sermon to the clergy. These informations or enquiries, may be seen at length in the *Annals of Burton*[a] and in Wilkins[b] who places them, I know not for what reason, to the year 1230. But this is a gross mistake, not only because [*this was*] 5 or 6 years before Grossetete was made Bishop but because it's plain from the contents that they are either of, or after, the year 1237. These enquiries are 49 in number. By the first, the archdeacons are to enquire whether there be any rector, vicar, parish priest, *enormously illiterate*. By 38, whether any of illegitimate birth be admitted either to benefice or orders without a previous dispensation. By the 3, 4, 5, 6 and 32, whether there be any in holy orders that are married or entertain concubines, and who they are that harbour the concubines of such delinquents. By the 7 and 8, whether any of the clergy frequent the churches or monasteries of nuns, without reasonable and necessary cause; or keep with them under the same roof any persons of the sex, whether kinswoman or other that gives occasion to suspicions. By the 17, whether any of the clergy frequent alehouses or taverns, or profess themselves fighters or wrestlers, or assist at shews or gaming. By the 11 and 18, whether any of them act as sheriffs, justices, bailiffs or stewards to the laity, which renders 'em accountable to the Lay-Courts. Or whether any of them bear arms, or neglect to wear the tonsure and habit of their

---

[a] *An. Burt.*, p. 317

[b] *Wilkins*, B. 1, p. 627.

order. By the 28 whether any beneficed person take or give lessons in the Civil Law. By the 29, 23 and 13, whether any priest act as rector, or vicar without receiving institution from the Bishop. Whether any rector or vicar duly instituted neglect to reside in their living. Whether parish priests receive of their rector a competent maintainance, without being obliged to have recourse to unbecoming means for supplying their necessities. By the 26 and 40, whether church yards be kept shut and the churches decently ornamented and dedicated (according to a statute made by the Legate Otho in 1237). Whether the holy vessels be kept under proper custody. Whether the altar-stones be decent, and not made use of *for grinding colours*. By the 22, whether any deacon presume to hear confession, or to administer any other sacrament reserved to priests. By the 2, 21 and 33 whether any priest extort money for administrating the Sacrament of Penance, or others. Or injoin pecuniary penances to his own profit. Whether he neglect the visitation of the sick. Whether he keep the holy Eucharist in a decent manner, and carry it with due reverence to the sick. By the 29, 27, 47 and 49, whether the canon of the Mass be correct, whether any priest celebrate in vinegar,[79] or twice a day (except in cases allowed), or in any unlicensed chapel. By 45 whether priests there are that have been ordained in other dioceses, and by whom they are licensed to celebrate. By the 48, whether any one be professed an anchoress[a] without the bishop's leave.[80] By the 34 and 25, whether the chrismalia (i.e. either chrismal oil, or chrismal clothes) be put to profane uses. Whether markets etc be kept in holy places. By the 44 whether there be a sufficient number of penitentiaries in each archdeaconary, (for the absolution of reserved cases or perhaps for hearing the confessions of the parochial clergy).[b] By the 49, whether any of the laity live in adultery, or any other notorious crimes. The 46 regards the lives of the archdeacons themselves and others of superior clergy, as rural deans etc.

These archidiaconal regulations of our Prelate appeared so well calculated and at the same so necessary that in 1252 they were adopted by Roger Wesham, the pious and learned Bishop of Lichfield, and one of Grossetete's favourite disciples. And what is still more to their honour, they were embraced the year forthcoming by all the bishops of the Realm.[c]

Besides these 49 regulations of Bishop Grosseteste we have two letters of discipline to his archdeacons, which regard some more particular abuses, whether among the people or the clergy, and which seem to have accompanied or followed the regulations above. These two letters, are the 22 and 107. In the first he recommends to his archdeacons, in

---

[a] Thom. p. 2002, *uti archiepiscopus non faciet anchoritas in eccliis S. Augustini Cantuar. sine consensu abbatis*.

[b] *An. Burt.*, p. 325.

[c] *An. Burt.*, pp. 317 and 323.

the most urgent manner, to retrench the abuses in question, not only by preaching in their synods, chapters, or churches, but by inflicting the canonical censures where necessary and expedient. Among the abuses here mentioned are the beastly drinking-clubs, called *scotales*. Also, certain diversions, which he calls the *Elevation of Rams on wood and wheels*, in which there was *contending* for a prize, and which he condemns after St Isidore, as sacrificing to Devils the inventors and authors thereof because of some superstitions or vicious practices attending them. As also of the dissensions and quarrels they occasioned. Thirdly, certain ridiculous or worse customs practised by some on the vigils and the festivals of the saints, which he strictly commands the archdeacons to preach down. 'Lest,' saith he. 'They provoke thereby upon themselves the wrath of the saints whose suffrages they come to implore.' Lastly the avaricious practice crept into some churches, of refusing the Sacrament, and even the Easter Communion, till the Easter dues were paid. 'And this contrary,' saith he. 'To the ordinance, both of the provincial and general council.' The second of the two letters, orders the archdeacons to correct the negligence of certain parish priests, who either omit the canonical hours, or say them in a disedifying manner or at an hour altogether inconvenient for their parishioners. Also the levity of other clerks, who exhibit shews or plays which they call *Miracles* and other diversions, called the *Ushering in of May* and the *Feast of Autumn*. He censures the practice of certain rectors, vicars and priests, who not only refused to hear the sermons of the friars of the two mendicant orders but maliciously hindered their people as much as they could from hearing their instructions or making their confessions to them. Against all which, he orders them like another Mathathias, to exert themselves like Judas Machabeus, and fight the battles of the Lord, against all the enemies of the Divine Laws.[81] He likewise injoins them in the close to hinder with all their might all cohabitation of Christians with the Jews.

Chapter IV

BISHOP GROSSETETE'S PERSONAL VISITATIONS OF HIS FLOCK WHETHER PEOPLE, PRIESTS OR RELIGIOUS

In taking the forementioned informations of the manners of his clergy and people, our vigorous Prelate did not so rely on his archdeacons, tho men of learning and probity, as not to see with his own eyes and act with his own hands as far as lay in the power of a most active and indefatigable zeal. The Diocese of Lincoln was then very extensive and took in what now forms the three Diocese of Lincoln, Peterborough and Oxford, under eight archdeaconries, viz Lincoln, Stow, Northampton, Leicester, Huntingdon, Bedford, Bucks and Oxford. Bishop Grossetete suffered no year to pass, in which he did not visit some part, if not the whole of so wide a district, and[a] gives his reasons for this diligence which were the continual dread of the account he was to give of them and least [*sic*] their blood should be required of his hands.[b]

> From the time, my unworthiness was first promoted to the episcopal charge to the present time I often ruminate, and deeply reflect, that the duty of pastors is to know their sheep, and that the just man has compassion on the souls of his beasts, and that this knowledge cannot be better acquired than by visiting them and enquiring into their lives and manners. And hence according to my poor abilities I have ever made it my great solicitude and labour to visit them and to correct according to the canons whatever interested the salvation of souls, of which I am thoroughly persuaded I may give a most strict account at the rigorous tribunal of God.

The Bishop's method in his visitations was this.[c] Before setting off, notice was sent to the clergy of each rural deanary to meet at such a place on such a day. The like notice was given to the people to come to hear the word of God and confess their sins, and bring their children with them in order to receive Confirmation. When all were met the Bishop generally preached to the clergy himself, and the sermons above extracted seem delivered on these occasions. At the same time, some Dominican

---

[a] *Anglia Sacra*, B. 2, p. 347.
[b] *Epist. Grosseteste*, 77.
[c] *Anglia Sacra*, B. 2, p. 347.

or Franciscan friar instructed the people, after which four of the said religious heard the confessions of the people and injoined them proper penances. Then the Bishop gave Confirmation the same day and the day following. And this being done, the Bishop with his officers made their enquiries of what required correction or reformation whether among the people or among the clergy, according to rules laid down in his archidiaconal ordinances. The first time he made this timely pastoral visit and mission some said, 'My lord, this is a great novelty!' To which he replied, 'Every novelty that instructs, corrects and improves Christians is a most blessed and desirable novelty.'

In the year 1238,[a] Bishop Grossetete made a general visitation of all the monasteries, archdeaconries, and deaneries, and held in each a general chapter, preaching to them, and making regulations for them. Of the monasteries we shall see more anon in a particular article. In this we shall confine ourselves to his conduct towards his clergy with whom he began as the heads of the people. And as receiving his first care and inspection in this visitation of the year 1238 he suspended many rectors of churches. Some he received on clearing themselves, others on their solemn promise not to relapse under penalty of losing their orders and benefices and on their giving the said promise in writing.

About July 1251[b] our Prelate made another severe scrutiny into the lives and manners of his clergy, especially as to the article of chastity of which he himself was so rigorous an observer, that he was once heard to say that for the whole world he would not dwell so much as a single night under the same roof with his sister.[c] And that tho he did not oblige others to that rigorous caution, yet he removed from about them all such women as might be an occasion either of scandal or of evil suspicion. Such of the pastors as he could convict of violating their engagements to purity he deprived them of their livings. Some however who had concubines,[d] contrived to hide them during his visitation but he urged his archdeacons, who residing on the spot had more opportunities to find them out, to *ferret* out those delinquents and defer them to him, especially those who after a first conviction had bound themselves, and that in writing, to resign their dignities in case they relapsed.

This was not the only abuse he had to correct among the beneficed clergy. Some of them neglected to receive the orders annexed to their benefices; and that not out of humility, nor with a view to render themselves more fit for the dread ministry, but thro more sloth and to live

---

[a] *Dunstable annals*, p. 236.

[b] *Chron. Maj.*, p. 825.

[c] *Annal. Lanercost.*

[d] *Epist. Grosseteste*, 107 and 50.

more at large by keeping free from the care of souls.[a] Many of these our persuasive Prelate won to a sense of their duty, partly by prayers and entreaties, partly by the terrors of his eloquent exhortations wherein he layed before them the dangers of their sinful state. And so prevailed on them to amend and proceed in their orders. Some however taxed themselves, in order to send deputies to Rome, where by exposing their case, as they found convenient for themselves they surprised the Pope's leave for deferring their ordination for some years under pretence of continuing their studies, and so eluded the good design of their holy Pastor, to their own ruin. We have observed above that his visitations extended to the monasteries, and of these visitations the monastick writers of the age have preserved us several instances, especially the author of the *Annals of Dunstaple* and the royal historiographer Matthew Paris. In the visitation of the year 1236,[b] which seems his first, he deposed for their irregularities and incapacity, no less than seven abbots and four priors, all or most of the Augustinian Order. Viz the Abbots of Leicester and Owlston [*Owston*] in Leicester, those of Thornton upon Humber and Brunne or Bourn[*e*] in Lincolnshire, those of Nutley [*Notley*], and Missenden both in Bucks, and the Abbot of Dorchester in Oxfordshire. The four Priors were the Prior of Bradwelle or Bradley and Laund[*e*] in the County of Leicester, and those of St Frideswides in Oxford, and of Cold Norton in the same county. The two last of which he substituted two canons of Dunstable, viz William of Gloucester, at St Frideswides and W[*alter*] de Wilton at Cold Norton. He repeated the visitation of the monasteries in 1238[c] and again in 1240,[d] when he forced an oath upon all the canons of Dunstable. On what occasion is not said, nor any other particulars, only that one of the canons named Walter de Gladelle was moved thereby to become a monk at Woburn Convent of Cistercians, exempt I suppose from the jurisdiction of the archdeaconry.[e] In another visitation of the year 1249, Henry de Bilenda a canon of Dunstaple, and Eudo, Prior of the canons Regulars of Caldwell, in Bedfordshire, and this last accused by his own canons and neither being able to clear themselves, and fearing the Bishop's severity, fled and listed among the Cistercians of Myrival [*Merivale*] in the County of Warwick and Diocese of Coventry and Lichfield. The same year[f] William de Hotot, Abbott of Peterborough, was arraigned by his monks of delapidating the temporalities of his convent.[82] But as he refused to stand corrected the monks

[a] *Chron. Maj.*, p. 833.
[b] *Dunstable annals*, p. 230.
[c] Ibid., p. 236.
[d] Ibid., p. 244.
[e] *Dunstable annals*, pp. 284 and 285.
[f] *Chron. Maj.*, p. 769 et *Hist. Peterburg*, 128.

deferred him to our Prelate, his Diocesan. Whereupon the Abbot finding his deposition unavoidable before a judge who, saith Matthew Paris, was always ready to punish disorders, thought fit to resign and had one manor allowed him wherein to live as a hermit and do penance for his past excesses. The last of Bishop Grossetete's visitations of his diocese, specified by our historians was in 1251, when he came[a] to Ramsey, a Benedictine monastery in the fens of Huntingdonshire, he entered the dormitories and making a very strict search in every part whatever he found ornamented contrary to their rule, whether in plate or furniture, he caused it to be broken in pieces. When he came to the nunneries if any were suspected of injuring their vows our most zealous avenger of chastity, zealous of the honour of the spouses of Christ, caused the *breasts* of the suspected to be pressed by other matrons so to have even a physical proof of their crimes or innocence.[83]

The great difficulty he met with was from the Convent of Mynting [*Minting*] an alien priory in Lincolnshire belonging to the Abbey of Fleury sur Loire in France, whither the abbots of that foreign House, used to banish their disorderly members.[84] To remove sick members from contagious situations to others more pure and wholesome is both wise and charitable, but to remove them merely to get rid of the trouble of their cure, and to places where they are more exposed is uncharitable and unjust. Uncharitable to the parties not only in neglecting their cures but exposing them to greater dangers and unjust to the places they are banished to, as it is unjust for any man to throw his evil and poisonous weeds into his neighbour's garden or to send a scathed sheep into his flock. Hence our Prelate wrote[b] three several letters to the Abbot and Convent of Fleury, remonstrating in a very meek and charitable but vigorous manner against this strange practice, as dishonourable to themselves whose reputation was thereby tarnished. The world judging of their other members by these rotten ones and them so disedifying to his flock and diocese that he declares, he will not suffer any monks in his diocese that do not live honourably and regularly according to St Bennet's [*Benedict's*] rule, which he calls a *Rule of Supereminent Sanctity*, adding withall, that he shall do all in his power to take away the evil thing from amidst his people; he was as good as his word and found himself obliged to expell four or five of them who by their notorious impurities, intemperance and disobedience and love of hunting and other sports, even above worldlings themselves, were become the talk and scandal of the country. Among their other disorders he reckons the love of property and their eating meat on Wednesdays. In one of these letters, which concerns the

[a] *Chron Maj*., p. 814.

[b] *Epist. Grosseteste*, 53, 54 and 108.

sending of a new prior, he presses them to present him one who by his knowledge of the rule and his regularity in practising it may be able to walk before his subjects.

While he expelled the incorrigible, he endeavoured to reclaim those who were not come to the depth of iniquity and for this end, contrary to the practice just censored he used to remove them to more regular houses and there keep them till such times as they gave unequivocal proofs of their repentance and amendment, without suffering himself to be softened by human considerations.[a] H. an Austin Canon of Dorchester, in Oxfordshire, had been sent to the Abbey of Leicester, of the same order of St Augustine, to do penance. After some time, the Abbot of Leicester, wrote to the Bishop of Lincoln entreating him to let the Canon return to his own convent and pleading for that end, his infirmities and old age, and his great desire to die among his brethren. But our wise and firm Prelate, no less careful of one soul than of his whole Diocese, wrote to the Abbot of Leicester that he should come soon to those parts and then he would examine the state of the penitent Canon.[85] In the meantime he sends the Abbot a short but divine instruction concerning the necessity of doing a sound and perfect penance, especially under infirmities and old age. 'You endeavour,' saith he,

> To prevail with us to consent to his return because of his age and infirmities and of his longing desire to die in his own convent, among his brethren. But the older and weaker he is in body, the more urgent necessity there is for his doing a sincere penance for his past transgressions, that so his youth may be renewed like that of the eagle. For the very reason therefore that he's old and infirm, the more expedient it is for him to remain with you, that his spirit may be renewed and healed. The compassion you pretend for him, ought if sincere, to afford his weakness and old age greater comforts than what he could meet with in his own convent. Moreover if he hath a desire to be dissolved and be with Christ, as the Apostle had, then it is good for him to be in a place where this desire hath more exercise and more fuel to nourish and strengthen it … But if this desire of dying proceeds of worldly sadness, which operates death, and from a loathing of his penitential state then is he still a greater object of your compassion, and stands in greater need of your consolations, to alleviate this mortal tedium and sadness than of returning to a place where without a great change in his manners, of which we have received as yet no certain proofs, his sloth and tepidity will meet with fresh fuel to entertain it.

The Abbot having taxed the discreet Prelate with too great severity, he returned this reply, no less ingenious, than religious.

---

[a] *Epist. Grosseteste*, 55.

> You accuse us of having a heart of steel and void of compassion. Would to God we had a heart steeled against all the flattery of seducers, a heart so inflexible that no terrors of the wicked could bend it, and so keen and sharp as to cut up every vice! In Ezechiel it is said, that the whole house of Israel had their hearts hardened, viz with the hardness of cruelty and malice, which God forbid we should ever harbour in our breasts and against which God gave his prophet a face stronger than their faces, and a forehead harder than their foreheads, and like unto a flint and to a diamond. Of this hardness communicated to the prophet may he who is the true Rock give us also some little portion. If then we are hardened with malice and cruelty, pray to God for us that He will soften away this hardness by his grace. But if we have only that hardness and inflexibility which God gave to his prophet then beg of him that as long as we live he shall give us a continual increase of it.

To settle and confirm the work of reformation, he drew up in 1254 regulations[a] for all the religious of his diocese, as he had done before for his diocesan clergy. And these regulations, which regarded the religious of both sexes, he inforced with the blessings and curses pronounced by Moses upon the observers and violators of the Law. Among other rules[b] the *History of Peterborough* observes that he forbid all the monks of his diocese to eat flesh except in the infirmary, and in the *Camara Abbatis*. Some of our modern historians would make the world believe that our disciplinarian Prelate was an enemy to monks and their institutes, but what hath been said above is demonstration that he was only an enemy to their disorders and to the violation of their rule, as the founders themselves were and their most religious followers upon whose steps our enlightened Prelate walked in reforming and correcting their children. If anything more were necessary to prove his esteem and veneration for their institutes, we might add his elogium of St Bennet's rule, which he calls a rule of 'Supereminent Sanctity' and full of the spirit of all the saints. The constitutions he drew up for the convent of Newenham and the religious foundations which he himself made, for he founded the Priory of Chetwode[c] in Bucks in a place called the Hermitage, for Austin canons and according to some the nunnery at Grimesby [*Grimsby*] in Lincolnshire.[d86]

The Bishop of Lincoln's zeal for discipline, made him sollictous to reform, not only his clergy and religious, but the laity.[e] As early as the year 1246, or rather at the beginning of his episcopate, he both ordered and caused his archdeacons and deans to make strict enquiry into the

---

[a] *Chron. Maj.*, pp. 815–16.
[b] Hist. Peterburgh. Edition Sparke, p. 10.
[c] *Mon. Ang.*, p. 339.
[d] Dod, *Church History*, vol. 1.
[e] *Chron. Maj.*, p. 716.

lives both of the nobility and commonality to see if any of them lived in adultery or other notorious disorders. Here his zeal was traversed by the King, who opposed his taking informations upon oath, except in matrimonial, and testamentary causes. Upon which our intrepid Prelate did not stick to tell his Majesty that herein he was walking upon the steps of some conspirators in France, who had lately broke out into the same presumptuous opposition against the zeal of their pastors. However our indefatigable Pastor, continued his unabated zeal in defending the sacred rights of purity, and to reprove its violators, of what degree or estate so ever.[a] The Princess Eleanor, sister to King Henry III, and now widow of the Earl of Pembroke, had on her husband's decease made a solemn vow of chastity[b] and received the sacred nuptial ring[c] from St Edmund, Archbishop of Canterbury, tho she had not actually put on the sacred veil. Notwithstanding her vow she suffered herself to be debauched by Simon Monfort, the famous Earl of Leicester, and to save her honour in some measure she was married to him by dispensation. Bishop Grossestete without regard to her royal descent, or the friendship he bore her husband otherwise a nobleman of great worth, foretold her Highness by way of reproof that she should never have joy or comfort of her offspring, 'because she had preferred the nuptials of a mortal man to those of the immortal Son of God.' The event shewed him a prophet for all her Highness's children came to untimely ends. He used the same episcopal liberty with her husband who had taken him for his director. He took care to remind him not to be excessively[d] severe in dealing out vindictive justice and at other times to bear the disgraces and affronts he received from his Prince with a patience and submission.[e] We shall see hereafter how he took the same respectful liberty ever with his Prince, and that without forfeiting his esteem, but rather gaining his admiration.

---

[a] *Chroniconica de Henrici Knighton*, p. 2426.
[b] *Wykes*, p. 40.
[c] *Chroniconica de Henrici Knighton*, p. 2347.
[d] *Epist. Grosseteste*, 48.
[e] *Epist. Grosseteste*, 75; *Chron. Maj.*, p. 879.

Chapter V

BISHOP GROSSETETE'S ZEAL IN REJECTING BAD OR UNFIT PASTORS

The difficulties which our Prelate found in the correction of unfit pastors on the one hand, and on the other his insatiable zeal for the good of his flock, rendered him extremely careful who he admitted to the pastoral charge. Hence that inflexible and scrupulous niceness in observing the canons relative to church promotions from which no considerations of flesh and blood, nor ties of friendship, nor fear of power, could warp him one line during his whole life. So that in his last moments, and just ready to appear before the Searcher of hearts, he called his judge to witness of the purity of his views in all pastoral promotions, tho as a fallible man he might have been often mistaken. His excellent letters furnish us with several edifying instances of his solicitude to reject unfit pastors and to seek out such as were duly qualified for the charge. However he never rejected any, without giving his reason and those the most solid and substantial, nor without softening the refusal with necessary condescension, especially where the presenters, or presentees, were persons to whom he owed a particular regard.

Scarce had Grossetete been elected Bishop when he gave proof of his firmness this way and signified to the world how he intended to conduct himself for the future on the like occasions.[a] A certain monk who had the nomination to a large cure presented for the same, a deacon without tonsure, clad in red, contrary to the canons of the Council,[87] with a ring on his finger. And in the rest of his mean and carriage a mere layman or rather a soldier and by his answers, almost without learning. The very first sight, and much more a near examen of so irregular a subject filled our zealous Prelate with such indignation that he not only rejected the presentee but gave the blind presenter so severe a reprimand that one of the Bishop's friends, viz Dr Michael Beleth, who only heard the report, thought our Prelate had exceeded the bounds of moderation, and thereupon wrote him a friendly remonstrance. For which the humble Bishop gave his friend thanks, and begged him continue his good office of monitor and corrector to him, and then to justify himself gave first a description

---

[a] *Epist. Grosseteste*, 11.

of the presentee as above and then his own words to his presenter, which are worth hearing. 'These,' saith the Bishop.

> Were my words to the monk, as far as I can remember, 'You who are a monk, i.e. one professing perfection both by your habit and vows of religion, and of course obliged to give your temporal life for the salvation of souls, with what face can you present one to take care of them whose very habit and outward mean, evidently bespeak him rather a destroyer than a guardian of the flock? For the pastor according to St Augustine is guilty of as many murders as there are souls that may perish by his evil example, thus you who deliver up the sheep to the wolf, you who are obliged to lay down your life to rescue them from him! Christ poured out his whole precious blood nay he gave up his whole life by the most ignominious and cruel death, for the salvation of all and of every single soul. And you, you seek to deliver up so great a multitude of souls to a traitor, who by his example will murder the souls for which Christ gave not only a part of his blood, but the whole. Not only a part of his life, but his whole and entire life! You would not expose to the wolf a sheep that had cost you but one shilling; and yet you scruple not to expose a soul which Christ bought with the price of his blood, a price incomparably greater than the whole universe put together. Is not therefore a sheep of one shilling value dearer to you than a soul purchased with the blood of Christ? And thus despising Christ, and trampling on his precious blood, are you not posting on in the high road to perdition?' This I confess, was the reproof, I gave the said monk. Now I ask of your discretion, and of all that love Jesus Christ, what there is in this correction that desires reproof? Have I therein insinuated any falsehood, or have I blurted out an unreasonable truth which ought to have been withheld? I that am obliged to lay down my life for every one of those souls, to the care, or rather to the ruin of which the said deacon was presented. Was I not to open my very mouth or say a word for warding off the destruction? I had reason to fear … or was I not to reprove openly one that was an open transgressor, seeing the Apostle saith, 'Them that sin reprove before all, that the rest also may have fear.' But perhaps I should have corrected with gentleness, a fault tending to the destruction of souls; tho of such the same Apostle saith to Titus,'Rebuke them sharpely, that they may be sound in the faith.' And the High priest Heli is condemned for giving his sons too gentle correction.[88] Errors, which do not interest the salvation of souls may be corrected with gentleness and born with patience, but those where the ulcer is mortal, there no able surgeon presses it with a tender hand. I leave it to your prudence to judge whether in the sight of God, or of those who have the zeal of souls, I am so reprehensible, as is pretended?

We are not to imagine, this to have been only a transient fit of zeal, and only with regard to a monk, for here the Bishop of Lincoln knew no distinction between monk or clergy, neither betwixt friend and no friend. But wherever the good of souls required it he could refuse even his best friend. Only in this case he took care to be more explicit in his reasons, and to qualify the refusal by some other act of generosity. Soon after the fact above mentioned, and while he was still a new Bishop, William de

Ralegh, alias Raley, one of the King's Chaplains, Treasurer of Exeter, and judge of the Prerogative Court, recommended to our Prelate one William de Grana to be beneficed in his diocese. But the said William being under age, and not fraught with sufficient learning, the Bishop of Lincoln thought himself obliged to refuse him. As Ralegh resented the denial Bishop Grossetete called God to witness that nothing but the fear of God and the canons of the Church, hindered him from complying with the request.[a] That in thus acting he not only sought the safety of his own conscience, but the salvation of the presentee and his patron and had only done what any careful physician doth in denying his patient cold water in the height of a burning fever. But then, not to be esteemed ungrateful for past favours, he generously offers to create the said youth an yearly pension of ten marks out of his own coffers till he can be provided of a better living. And he very earnestly begs of his friend Ralegh that the presentee may be allowed to receive the said pension which he offers to pass into a contract, in presence of brother Robert Bacon a deacon and brother, Adam de Marisco a Franciscan friar, of Master Robert de Marisco, of Master Thomas the Welshman and of Master John de Basing[*stoke*] Archdeacon of Leicester after which he concludes in this humble and charitable manner. 'Postrate at your feet I beg with all the earnestness I am capable of, that no occasion may ever alienate your heart from the love of your friend. Since by the grace of God neither death, nor life shall ever hinder me from loving you in the Lord.' The words '*novitati mea*' [*new to my office*] used in this letter proves it written in the beginning of his episcopate, as doth the naming of Thomas the Welshman, simply and without any dignity for he was made Archdeacon of Lincoln on the death of Robert de Hayles in 1238.

But perhaps our prelate was more compliant with persons of high rank? Not in the least. On the contrary here he seemed to call up all his firmness not to be overborn by human fears, and at the same time exerted the whole force of his reasoning and eloquence in order to shew the justice of his refusal in a stronger light. Cardinal Otho, the Pope's Legate in England from the year 1225 to 1241,[b] had desired our Prelate to institute to the Church of Rands [*Raunds*] in Northamptonshire, Thomas the son of the Earl of Ferrers, tho under age, and not in holy orders. The Bishop in his answer to the Legate replys, that as the more knowing and more fervent may do certain things without scruple which the weak and timerous could not do without going against their conscience, so he conjours his Eminence to have regard to his weakness, which scruples

[a] *Epist. Grosseteste*, 17.

[b] *Chron. Maj*., p. 325 and 549.

admitting such persons as the presentee, and he gives these bare and palpable reasons for so doing.[a]

> Our timorousness herein proceeds, not only on the authority of the Holy Scriptures and ecclesiastical canons which will not allow those to be rulers of the flock who fall short of the qualifications required in a Ruler, tho there may be otherwise great hopes of their allowing to them. But on many other palpable and cogent reasons, which strike a very deep impression on our mind. For what master of a ship I pray destined to steer a vessal full of passengers through a rocky and tempestuous sea commits the direction of the vessal to an apprentice, either ignorant of navigation or too weak to guide the steerage, or no ways solicitous for the safety of the passengers, tho this apprentice may give hopes of one day turning out an able Pilot? Would not the master by such an indiscreet commission expose those to ruin and shipwreck whom he's obliged to see safe to port? And to comprise many examples in one, what person commissioned to set up able and skilfull artists over every trade would not justly incur the disgrace of his employers if he only appointed such beginners as give but distant hopes and above probability of one day acquiring the required abilities, and who by their very promotion are perhaps rendered more slack in their endeavours to acquire them? No wise farmer entrusts his flock with an ignorant shepherd under pretense that some years hence he may become more knowing in the shepherdly office. Nor doth he yoke calves to his plow because he hopes they may hereafter grow up to be stout oxen. Since by this very conduct he may so weaken them as to hinder their growth and future size. No one laith heavy burthens upon weak subjects under pretense of their growing stronger in process of time, lest their present weakness should sink under the too weighty burthen. Now if no one is guilty of this absurd conduct, in things even of corporeal and temporal concerns how should our timorousness presume to hold it in spirituals where the danger is so much the greater, by how much spiritual things are superior to and more excellent than corporeal ones? According to the declaration of God himself denounced in Exodus, and Ezechial, and explained by St Gregory, a pastor of souls who doth not sound the trumpet by preaching to his flock dieth spiritually himself, and as far as lieth in him, killeth the sheep entrusted to his care. Hence he that sets up such a pastor, who cannot sound the trumpet of preaching till after a long space of time, doth he not during the said space minister occasion or rather become the very cause of death, both to the pastor and flock too? Our Lord Jesus Christ offered up his most precious life and that by the most ignominious of deaths, in order to bring dead souls to life and hath insinuated by this example how they only should be chosen for pastors of his flock who refuse no sufferings to have it. How then shall I dare, wretch that I am, give unto souls redeemed with so great a price, such pastors, as for a long time, must be to them an occasion of death rather than life? How can I think of enriching man with the price of Christ's blood more than of procuring the salvation of souls?

---

[a] *Epist. Grosseteste*, 52.

After these godly and palpable reasons, the humble and timerous Prelate concludes by desiring the Legate either to prevail with the Earl of Ferrers to present some other subject actually fit for the office, or to take the whole upon his own conscience adding withall that he hopes his Eminence will do what is most for the good of souls, and most agreeable to the Supreme Judge who will demand an account of every idle word. He entreats him, that if he needs will present the said Thomas to the church of Rands he would see an able vicar placed in it, tho he rather choses, if the canons will permit it, to have a perpetual pastor set over it and a pension paid off it to the presentee in question, by way of simple benefice or sinecure. So ready was the zealous Bishop to comply with any thing, rather than to endanger the salvation of his sheep!

There are many other instances of Bishop Grossetete's vigilance in this article, especially in his 72 and 87 letters the former to John Roman,[a] Archdeacon of Richmond whose nephew he refused to institute to the Church of Stamford upon Avon. The latter to Boniface, Archbishop of Canterbury Elect, who had presented an unknown subject to the Church of Caistre [*Castor*], which the Bishop therefore leaves to the Archbishop's conscience, as he had done to the Legate's above. Besides the usual reasons set forth in the foregoing and many other letters he adds in that to the Archdeacon of Richmond, that in the sight of the Supreme Judge, he dreads nothing so much, as giving the care of souls to unfit Pastors. But least he should appear unthankful he subjoins this excellent apology, which if deeply weighed would prevent many a human and base compliance. 'I would not be thought ungrateful to you for the favours wherewith you have honoured me. But we ought every one of us, to be incomparably more afraid of being ungrateful to Him, who gave his blood and life for us!'

We shall finish this article of the rejection of unfit pastors by that of a man in great power, viz Hugh de Pateshull;[89] this clergyman, son of Simon de Pateshulle, Chief Justice of England, was himself Lord Treasurer of England and Canon of St Pauls, and had many other benefices. Yet not being satisfied, he sought more and petitioned our Prelate for one in his diocese. But the Bishop instead of the benefice sent him a very frank and strenuous letter where he gives him his reasons for not harkening to his petition.

> Moved by love, and compelled by fear, I cannot but exhort and conjure you with all paternal solicitude to consult the good of your own soul, and not to think of charging your shoulders with a greater burthen of pastoral office than what is already upon them, least the weight thereof oppress and crush your weakness since you do not carry in a manly manner the burthen you

[a] *Chron. Maj.*, p. 921.

are under at present. For you do not, as pastoral office requires, support him that is weak by the ministry of your voice, nor do you reside among your parishioners in order to edify and stir them by the example of a holy life. Whether by compassion you bear all their sins, and endeavour to make atonement for them by your sighs and tears, and earnest and continual prayers, I know not. And yet of your performing this third part of your office there's but too much reason to doubt whether from your continual or too frequent application to secular affairs with which, according to the Apostle no one is a soldier of God;[a] or from your assiduous living amidst the ambitious pomps and pleasures of the world, which are not usually accompanied with the gift of tears. Hence there is too probable, and too manifest a presumption that you do not comply with the pastoral duties, and that you seem rather of the number of those pastors to whom the prophet makes this complaint, 'You ate the milk and you clothed yourself with the wool and you killed that which was fat; but my flock you did not feed. The weak you have not strengthened, and that which was sick you have not healed. That which was broken you have not bound up and that which was driven away you have not brought back. Neither have you sought that which was lost, but you ruled over them with rigour, and with a high hand. And my sheep were scattered because there was no shepherd.'[b]

If then you would escape the chastisements of the mercenary, who seeks the milk and the wool, without watching over the flock, either rid yourself of the concern and care of secular affairs so to apply yourself to the pastoral charges as becomes the good shepherd; or lay aside the pastoral charge and give up the flock, that so you may lawfully apply to secular business, for both together you cannot do. Now if laying aside the temporal affairs you apply yourself, as you ought to the pastoral care, then I am very sure that so far from seeking a greater burhten [*sic*], you'll seek on the contrary to shake off part of that which is already upon you as soon as you are sensible how strict an account you must give of every soul in your flock. Nor will you suffer yourself to be deceived, as many deceive themselves by pretext of having dispensation to possess so many church benefices together, for he abuses this dispensation who makes use of it for any other end than for the greater encrease of faith and charity. Consult therefore with your own conscience, whether you seek new benefices, inorder to augment faith and charity in your flock or to encrease your own wealth out of theirs. Whether in order to feed the flock with a word of God, with good example and with prayers, or to feed yourself with their milk. Examine well, if you can say with St Austin, 'O Lord, thou knowest that I have preacht, thou knowest I have not held my peace, thou knowest I have wept when I spoke and was not heard.' For all this account must be given of the sheep if then you cannot give this weighty account of the flock, already entrusted to your care, with what grace can you ask for another, seeing thereby you oblige yourself to a more extensive account with our most severe Judge who will exact even the very last farthing? This

---

[a] Tm. 2:14.
[b] Ezk. 34:3.

> I have suggested to you with the anxiety of a father and the compassion of a mother; and with the same affection that a mother withholds her refractory child throwing himself down a precipice, so would I withhold you, if I could, even against your will from taking the charge which is offered you to the great danger of your own soul and to that of your desolate sheep. But if you resist, I can only hinder you, as far as the Canon Law hinders according to which all things are judged in the Church militant. But then you aught to examin so much more carefully whether you may not here transgress the divine law according to which you will be judged, or judge in the Church triumphant.

What was the effect of this truly episcopal letter it doth not appear. Browne saith that, notwithstanding this friendly advice, Pateshull's ambition was not content till he was made Bishop of Lichfield; but this is a rash surmise of the peevish doctor, for so far was he from ambitioning this last dignity that Mr Wharton saith it was with much adoe that he received it when offered him by the Chapter of Coventry and Lichfield.[a] So that very probably, our Prelate's letter had a proper effect upon Pateshull, and served to slacken if not to extinguish his ambition.

In fine, of whatever degree, where the presentees or the presenters, the Bishop ever knew what it was to injure his conscience by any weak or unjust compliance. Sir Philip de Kime [*Kyme*], founder of the Austin Priory of Kime in Lincolnshire, having presented to the same a person whom the Bishop found unfit, he not only rejected him, but according to the canons, put in another more fit, without consulting Sir Philip.[90] And when Sir Philip complained of it, the Bishop[b] answered that in like cases he had acted in like manner with the King, and that the King having therein approved his conduct he hoped Sir Philip would not be ashamed to imitate so great an example.[91] (Sir Philip dying in 1242, as Matthew Paris informs us,[c] this letter must be of that year at latest, and perhaps anterior thereto).

---

[a] *Anglia Sacra*, B. 1, p. 439.
[b] *Epist. Grosseteste*, 30.
[c] *Chron. Maj.*, p. 584.

Chapter VI

BISHOP GROSSETETE'S SOLICITUDE FOR SEEKING OUT AND PROMOTING GOOD SUBJECTS. SOME INSTANCES THEREOF

The vigorous, but prudent Bishop of Lincoln, did not think it enough to reject bad subjects, unless he sought out good ones to put in their place; for otherwise his church might have been left destitute of pastors. Neither did he stay till these good ones presented themselves, for thus the worthy seldom or ever do. But whenever he found, or heard of any, conspicuous for their virtue and learning, he could never rest till he had settled them in his diocese. These being some of the most illustrious persons of the age it will not be disagreeable to the reader to say a word of them nor will it be anyways leaving our heroick prelate to make some acquaintance with those about him or in continual relation with him. The chief of these were Nicholas the Grecian, William de Sherwood, John de Basingstoke, Thomas the Welchman [*Wallensis*], Roger Wesham [*Weseham*], Richard de Cornwall, Thomas Archdeacon of Huntingdon, John de Offington [*Offinton*], all secular doctors. And as Leland expreses it, all Peers of the English School in this age.

Nicholas the Grecian was a native of St Albanus and is called by Matthew Paris, Clerk of the Abbot of St Albanus, whether that he owed his education or some promotion to him, he was made Canon and Subdeacon of Lincoln under Bishop Grossetete and Parson of Dachet [*Datchet*] in Bucks on the presentation of the Abbot and Convent of St Albans.[92] Nicholas drew his name of *Grecian* from his skill in the Greek tongue, out of which he helped our prelate to translate the *Testament of the 12 Patriarchs*. He was still living in 1260.[a]

William Sherwood,[b] student of Oxford, and afterwards of Paris, and Treasurer of the Church of Lincoln and Prebendary[c] of the rich prebend of Aylesbury in the said Church is celebrated by Roger Bacon, his contemporary and acquaintance as an universal scholar, deeply read in all the sciences, but especially in the mathematicks.[93] Of him, the said religious doctor, hath this eulogium in his lesser work addressed to Pope

[a] *Biblioth. britannico-hibernica*, 'Nicolaus'.
[b] *Biblioth. britannico-hibernica*, 'Shirewodus'.
[c] S. Pegge, Weseham, p. 26.

Clement IV, 'What I add, may be proved by the most famous Christian philosophers of the present age; of which number is brother Albertus of the order of preaching friars, and Master William de Sherwood treasurer of the Church of Lincoln, far Superior in knowledge to Albertus. For to him none is superior in *communi Philosophia*.' Shirewood was also an eminent theologian and author of lectures upon the Master of Sentences,[94] and some other theological tracts and sermons. In a word he was master to Friar Bacon, who confesses himself much indebted to Sherwood for his mathematical learning.[a] He died in 1262, or 1263.

John de Basing, or of Basingstoke in Hants, and Archdeacon of Leicester, performed his studies first in Oxford then in Paris, and lastly at Athens under a celebrated female Philosopher named Constantina,[95] who under the age of twenty was mistress of the most obstruse sciences. Basing who had scarce his fellow in the several Liberal Arts confesses himself indebted for the chief part of them, to his Athenian Preceptress. He brought with him out of Greece the knowledge of the Greek numerals, said to be till then unknown in England. He likewise brought with him a Greek grammar, called the Greek *Donatus* which he translated out of Greek into Latin and dedicated to his patron, Bishop Grossetete. By Grossetete's 17 letter, written in the very beginning of his Episcopate, it appears that John de Basing, who is mentioned in it as Archdeacon of Leicester, was our Prelate's immediate successor in that archdeaconary, which he held till the year 1252, in which he died Archdeacon of Leicester. As Matthew Paris expressly writes, so that his being Archdeacon of Chester seems another mistake of Whitlock, or rather of John Bale, grounded upon the same mistaken interpretation of the *Legecestrensis* as that concerning our Prelate himself.

Thomas the Welchman, by the pains Bishop Grossetete took to promote him, seems to have been one of his favourite subjects. When Grossetete quitted the Franciscan Chair in Oxford, about the year 1223, his place was filled by one Peter, the same probably as Peter de Ramsey,[b] Bishop of Aberdeen around 1247 to 1256.[96] Peter was succeeded by Roger Wesham who occurs Franciscan Professor and Archdeacon of Oxford, the third year of Grossetete's Pontificate, i.e. 1237. Wesham was succeeded by Thomas the Welchman either the same year or perhaps not till 1240. This Doctor was at Paris in 1238 expecting a Divinity chair when Robert de Hayles, Archdeacon and official of Lincoln,[c] dying Bishop Grossetete wrote over to the Welch Doctor, who was already a canon of Lincoln, to invite him to accept of the vacant archdeaconary.[97] This letter, being

---

[a] Pegge's *Weseham*, p. 27.

[b] *Chron. Marchionis*. Fic. Pegge in *Weseham*, p. 4 or Wood.

[c] *Chron. Maj*., p. 706; *Dunstable annals*, pp. 237 and 212.

at once an eminent testimony both of the inviter and the invited's merit, we shall here present the Reader with it as one of the most excellent of his excellent epistles and as laying open both their characters in a very shinning manner.[a]

> Robert Archdeacon of Lincoln having entered the way of all flesh, to whose soul God be merciful, we have collated you to his archdeaconary and prebend, providing you are disposed to come and reside therein. For we durst not confer so great a charge of souls upon one that is not resolved on personal residence. The charge, as you know well, is not moderately great but exceedingly so, and requires one always present and continually applied to his functions with vigilances, prudence and vigour. One that preaches the word of God opportunely and importunely, who makes himself an example of all kind of good works; who when he gives wholesome advice and it is not heard is grieved to the heart and to the shedding of tears. Who keeps his hands clean from all presents, and when he receives pecuniary mulcts from the delinquent,[98] puts them to pious use that their reception can cast no aspersion of averice upon him. One who is glad to absolve the accused, when it can be done, and when justice obliges him to condemn knows how to compassionate and condole with the sufferer. One whom neither love nor hatred, neither hopes nor fears; neither entreats, nor bribes, nor acception of persons, can warp from his integrity in judging, nor the opinion of the *many* make him retract what he has once judged right. One whose delights are sobriety and abstinance, whose rest is labour and watching, whose sole passion is to forward the salvation of souls. One who looks upon superiority as a burthen and load, yet submits to it with humility, and bears it with courage for the good of others. Now it is because we have greater hopes of finding these qualifications in you than in any other we can recollect that we have resolved to lay this burthen upon you. And God is our witness, that had any other occurred to us, whom we could have judged fitter for the office in hand we should most certainly have preferred him. Whence you may be sure, that in calling you to share of our pastoral care, our intentions are not to enrich you, but to benefit our flock. If then you love the salvation of souls, or rather him who said to Peter, and in him to us, 'If you love me, feed my lambs.' Don't refuse the trouble of feeding his sheep, nor be tired with the charge when once undertaken. For such weariness only proceeds from sloth. Whereas zeal for the good of souls which is stronger than death cannot esteem or feel any thing tiresome that is for their advantage. But perhaps you may think it a hardship, to relinquish the schools and not to ascend the Doctoral Chair, in order to teach the Holy Scriptures, and many doubtless will cry out to you not to exchange wisdom for riches nor the good you may do by teaching, for honours and dignities. They may even call you an interested and ambitious soul, as if you quitted the good of the mind for those of the body, and spiritual for temporal advantages. Nay we ourselves, must own it a sensible mortification to us to call you out of the schools when we consider how great good you are capable of doing thro

[a] *Epist. Grosseteste*, 51.

the divine graces by your learned lessons. But after all who can entertain the least doubt but what little and uncertain good ought to give way to such as are greater and more certain? And who again can doubt whether the humble and solliticous discharge of so great a cure of souls be not a far greater good than to deal out the most learned lessons from the doctoral pulpit? Assuredly were it not so the Son of God, who is the supreme wisdom, would have only sat in the chair of Doctrine and there given out his wise lessons. And he would not have travelled thro towns and villages to cure the sick and preach to the people this humble lesson, *do penance, for the Kingdom of God is at hand*. Neither would it in this supposition be a greater good to practise than to preach; nor better to give good example than good instruction. Besides it is much more certain that you may, if you will, perform this office of the cure of souls than that you will be able to teach the Holy Scriptures from the Chair. For the first is a thing not near at hand, but even in hand if you please to accept it, whereas the latter is yet at a distance, and you may be excluded from it either by infirmity or by other accidents, which are numberless.

Moreover, if for the sake of teaching a few scholars at Paris in wisdom, and sublimity of speech you refuse to instruct a multitude of Christ's sheep in a more humble but more powerful style by preaching to them Jesus Christ, and him crucified, it's greatly to be feared that you may be punished with the loss of both offices and that you be neither permitted to feed scholars with solid food from the pulpit, nor the simple sheep of Christ with the milk of plain instructions. Shun then every danger and fly from the wrath of Christ. Embrace the greater and more certain good; and with these considerations render the difficulty of quitting the schools more easy to yourself and to us, as to the persuasions of many, who are against your exchanging wisdom for riches, and the advantage of teaching for dignities. It is nowadays necessary to argue the case, with one of your penetration, since by the grace of Christ, you are not about to do any thing like it. For God willing, you shall not lay aside your learning, but find an infinitely more extensive use and exercise for it than in the schools. Neither shall you with unlawful affection cling to the riches annexed to the spirituality nor to any such transitory dignity. God forbid, a soul beautified with the light of wisdom should ever stretch forth its arms to embrace dung and filth! Neither can you be taxed with ambition or interest for undertaking a spiritual office which hath temporalities annexed to it. Should you indeed embrace the temporalities as the principal and the spirituality only as a burthen annexed to them, then you would be justly obnoxious to censure. But this censure none can press upon you, but he who is the Searcher of hearts, and who alone can discover the secret views and intentions with which such employments are undertaken. But after all, if by the mouth of envious persons the ancient enemy should let fly his darts at you for undertaking the work of God to which you are called, you may assure yourself, that he'll find others as keen to shoot at you, tho you refuse it. For it will be said of you, and this aloud, that you impudently and foolishly prefer the breath of vainglory to a work so good, so holy, and so acceptable to God. Wherefore arming yourself with the buckles [*sic*] of faith, learn wisely and valiantly to repel every dart of the enemy. And without any other view than that of the glory of God and the salvation of souls, humbly bend your neck to the yoke and carry it on with courage, discretion and perseverance, seeing that whatever God should command us, be it ever so abject, ever so obnoxious to reproach, ever so difficult and grevious we ought to obey with cheerfulness. Not only by forsaking the schools, and all scholastick honours, but all dignities, pleasure, and conveniences of life. And we conjure you by our Lord and Saviour Jesus Christ, so to behave therein, as not to bely the good opinion we have conceived of you, lest you become, which heaven avert, a castaway before God and render us an object of confusion in the sight of men. Rather on the contrary, so execute the charge laid on you and so accomplish the work of God, not negligently or fraudulently but diligently, faithfully and prudently, that according to that of Paul to Timothy, 'No man may despise thy youth.' Farewell.

By these last words, it appears that this Doctor in so high repute for learning and conduct in the estimation of so nice a judge as an enlightened Prelate, was nevertheless but young. This letter had with him all the weight it deserved and he accepted the archdeaconry of Lincoln, probably this same year 1238, or 1239. For by the 90 letter of Bishop Grossetete, written about the year 1240 or 1241, Thomas was then Archdeacon of Lincoln. Roger Wesham, Franciscan professor as well as Archdeacon of Oxford, being promoted to the deanery of Lincoln, our Welch doctor now Archdeacon of Lincoln, seems to have succeeded him in the Franciscan School the same year and not before, but without relinquishing his archdeaconary. Archdeacon Thomas supported his former reputation in such manner, whether in his professorship or in his archdeaconary, that in 1247 he was elected to the see of St David, and accepted of it, tho a very poor one and half ruined by the wars betwixt Wales and England, merely to comfort his distressed countrymen. He sat till the year 1253 in which he died.[a]

Roger Wesham, one of Grossetete's most favourite subjects, as appears by his care to promote him, was Archdeacon of Oxford, c. 1235 or 6, and at the same time Professor of Theology in the Franciscan School. In 1239 or 40 Grossetete got him made Dean of Lincoln ^and in 1245, Bishop of Litchfield and Coventry.^ He took him to the Council of Lion and there procured his promotion to the see of Coventry and Lichfield.[99] This doctor and prelate, was a person of uncommon learning and merit for which he was in high favour with Bishop Grossetete, and in his episcopate walked on the steps of his patron the Bishop of Lincoln. He adopted his statutes for regulation of his clergy and wrote himself several tracts for the instruction either of his clergy or people, especially *A Brief explication of the Articles of Faith*. Bishop Wesham[b] also founded three prebends in the Church of Lichfield, viz Ructon [*Ryton*] and Bobenhal [*Bubbenhall*]

[a] *Chron. Maj*., p. 739; *Biblioth. britannico-hibernica*, 'Walleus'.
[b] Pegge, *Weseham*, p. 37; *Chron. Maj*., pp. 666 and 706.

in the county of Warwick, and Bolton in Lanchashire. Having governed the see of Lichfield with great edification for the space of eleven years, he resigned it in December 1256 with the permission of Pope Alexander IV, and died the year following at his palace of Brewode [*Brewood*], of a palsy under which he had lingered for some years.

Richard de Cornulia, i.e. of Cornwall, seems to have travelled abroad, and to have enjoyed some post in the Court of Rome. He was recommended to Bishop Grossetete by the illustrious Spanish Cardinal Giles, Cardinal Deacon of SS. Cosmas and Damian, with whom Grossetete had been acquainted during his archdeaconship.[a] However the Bishop did not take him upon the lone recommendation, even of so illustrious prelate, but on the account of Richard's *own eminent merit.* He had already promoted him, or at least one of his name,[b] while only Subdeacon to the Church of Skremby in the archdeaconary of Lincoln anno 5th *Pontificatus* c. 1239.[100] Now he promotes him to the Church of St Martin in Dernestall, a prebend with cure of souls in the Church of Lincoln. But then[c] in his letter to the foresaid Eminence, Bishop Grossetete begs, 'that as the tree drops there its leaves and fruit where it draws its nourishment, so Richard would come and reside in his living; so to edify by his preaching and good example those from whom he is to receive his temporal subsistence. That Richard ought not to think it hard to come over from Rome to England to feed a flock, for the ransom of which the Son of God came down from the throne of his Father's glory even to the ignomy of the Cross.'[d] In his letter to Richard himself the Bishop assures him, 'that from his eminent learning, and laudable manners', he hopes for great advantages to his flock. He desires him not to condemn the smallness of the prebend, lest he should seem rather to seek himself, than Christ, but to come over and labour at the salvation of his flock by the light of his instructions, by the example of his holy life, and by the fervour of his prayers. Which three duties, not being compliable with by the absent, he presses him to come and reside, for fear he should not be able to give in a just account of his talents to God.[e] The Presentee, was not to receive any revenues of his living, till the next St Martin, our generous Prelate, invites Richard to come and be with him till the said term. This clergyman seems different from another Richard of Cornwall, surnamed Rufus a Franciscan friar and a celebrated philosopher who was already entered among the Franciscans in 1230 as will appear by the sequel.

[a] *Epist. Grosseteste*, 36, 46, 47.

[b] *Biblioth. britannico-hibernica*, 'Richard Rufus'.

[c] *Epist. Grosseteste*, 46.

[d] *Epist. Grosseteste*, 47.

[e] *Epist. Grosseteste*, 46.

Thomas of Huntington [*Huntingdon*], is here so called, because we know not his surname, and he seems to have been Archdeacon of Huntington. This excellent clergyman had been already invited by Bishop Grossetete to accept of the prebend of Gretton,[a] but had excused himself because of the Bishop and Chapters being at variance.[101] As soon as this contest was at an end, which was in 1245 and in all appearance on the decease or promotion of William, who *occurs* Archdeacon of Hants in 1241, our Prelate, who could never rest till he had settled good men in his diocese,[b] wrote him a second invitation to accept of the Archdeaconry of Huntington, with the prebend of Bugden, adding withall this reason so honourable to the invited that he hath not now the same excuse as heretofore since by the blessing of God peace and harmony is now restored betwixt him and his Chapter of Lincoln.[102] Hence this letter must be of the year 1245, or later. The Bishop presses Thomas to bend his shoulders to the charge, as a proof of his zeal for the salvation of souls, which he was esteemed to profess and than which no sacrifice saith the Bishop, is more acceptable to God. If this humble and pacifick clergyman accepted the offered dignity, he did not hold it beyond the year 1260, in which we find Roger de Raveningham in possession of it.[c]

The last of Grossetete's favourite subjects, whom Leland calls the 'Peers of the English School' in that age, was John de Offington, of whom Matthew Paris writes, and his judgement is confirmed by that of our Prelate, that all England had not a more celebrated clerk. This Doctor, was a native either of Uffington, alias Offington in Berks, or more probably of Uffington in Lincolnshire. His merit had precured him the honour of Domestick Chaplain to Pope Gregory the IX or Innocent the IV, and it was our zealous Prelate who as I may say made a present of him to his own country, as there's no article in which the Bishop of Lincoln shines more to advantage than in his ardent and ingenious and eloquent zeal for the good of souls. We shall here insert his letter to this celebrated clerk, which with those to Thomas Archdeacon of Lincoln, and Thomas Archdeacon ofHuntington,[103] are powerful exhortations to learned but backward spirits to employ their talents in working at the salvation of souls. The Bishop's letter to Offington is wrote in his own name and that of the pious and eminent Franciscan Doctor Adam de Marisco.[d]

> I and Adam de Marisco, who loves you greatly in the Lord, are exceedingly desirous of seeing you return to England, there to stay and labour in the ministry of Jesus Christ, and in the salvation of souls for which he shed his blood. For

[a] Praefatio Hearnii in Otterbourne et Tanner ut supra.
[b] *Epist. Grosseteste*, 118.
[c] *Dunstable annals*, p. 346.
[d] *Epist. Grosseteste*, 120.

> this admirable lover of souls hath entrusted you with the *pure and approved* talent of the sacred ministry and with powers for executing the same. Not that you might wrap it up in the napkin and throw it aside, but that you might traffick therewith till he comes and by your industry improve and produce the interests of it, which without all doubt is nothing else but the salvation of souls against the day of his coming. Now the day of his coming for each of us is most certainly the day of our departure hence, which when it will come is uncertain; but that this will be soon is most certain. As also, that he who by a solitcitous, unwearied and faithfull traffick, has not his talents to present with their improvements and interests, will have his talents taken from him and by the sentence of the Judge will be cast hand and foot bound into utter darkness, where shall be weeping and gnashing of teeth. All this being clearer than the day itself, as certified by the mouth of the world's Redeemer, how can your wisdom stand out against our solicitations when thus compelled by the interest of your own salvation, and by the dread of our most terrible and exact Judge? Sure I am, that if you weigh these motives they will compel you to yield and break thro all your ties, as thro so many cobwebs. Many other cogent arguments might be gathered from Scripture and philosophy to work you into our persuasion; but these suffice for so noble a soul. Neither do I write thus to instruct you but only to rouse and fan the great fire which burns in your breast, and to make it flame out so as to enlighten and warm all that are in the house, and he who searches the heart is our witness that there's no secular clerk in the world for whose salvation and advancement I, and the foresaid brother Adam, are so solicitous, and so desirous, as yours.

Offington answered so godly a desire of two such friends and came over to England, where he died in 1251, a Canon of Salisbury.[a] Besides these eminent secular clerks patronised by the learned and holy Bishop of Lincoln there were also several religious doctors, noways inferior to the former, whether Franciscans or Dominicans, whom the Bishop retained near his person and who laboured with him in the vineyard without any other reward other than what they expected in the life to come. We have spoke above of Bishop Grossetete's connexion with and esteem for the Franciscans, whose first Professor he was in Oxford, and their perpetual patron. He had the like esteem for disciples of St Dominick, who came to England one year after the Franciscans, viz in 1221. And this esteem was no less grounded in their regard than in regard of the Franciscans, both orders being animated with the spirit of their holy founders, and the latter also enhanced as well as the former, by illustrious secular doctors and bishops. Among which were Doctor Robert Bacon, of whom more anon and Walter Mauclerk,[b] Bishop of Carlisle, who resigned his Bishoprick which he had governed 23 years, without requiring any pension, and entering among the Dominicans at Oxford in 1246 there made a holy end

---

[a] *Chron. Maj.*, p. 817.

[b] [*Perry's footnote is missing*].

in 1248. The religious of these two orders were our Prelate's coadjutors, counsellors and ordinary preachers, especially to the people during his visitations; and his esteem for them was so great that writing to Pope Innocent the IV, to give strong sides and supports i.e. godly as well as able counsellors and monitors to Boniface, Archbishop of Canterbury he adds that such counsellors can only be found among the brethren of the two mendicant orders. We have still several letters of our Prelate which he wrote to the generals or other great men of both orders. His 37 letter to Raymond of Pennerfort [*Penaforte*], of the friar preachers, Grand Penitentiary to Pope Gregory IX, and the celebrated collector of the *Decretals*. The 40 letter is to the venerable Brother Jordan, General of the Dominicans from 1222 to 1237, whom Grossetete had seen and conversed with at Oxford[a] probably in 1230, when the Dominicans there held their first English provincial chapter.[b] The 41 is to the famous brother Elias, the worldly Minister General of the Franciscans. Of General Jordan, he sollicits for a certain English Dominican, of whom more presently. Of General Elias he desires two or four brothers of his order, and declares both to the one and to the other, that in his pastoral labours he had no more efficacious and comforting assistants than the brethren of their two orders. He not only begged this of the two generals but obtained of the Pope a priviledge for the same end, i.e. to demand two Dominicans, and two Franciscans. The most renowned of these religious auxiliaries were Doctor Robert Bacon, Dr Richard Fissakre [*Fishacre*] and Doctor John of St Giles, all three Dominicans. Doctor Adam de Marisco, Peter of Tewkesbury and Doctor Roger Bacon, of the order of St Francis.

Robert Bacon was the first English Doctor among the Dominicans.[c] He had been fellow student with St Edmund, Archbishop of Canterbury, and was a celebrated Master Regent in Theology at Oxford, when the Dominicans coming first to that University in 1221 he entered among them and continued his lectures to them in the School of St Edward and had, first for scholar and then for fellow professor, Richard de Fissakre, the first doctor *in* the English Dominican province as Bacon was the first *of* it. Bacon was not only an eminent Divine, but also an illustrious and intrepid preacher.[d] In 1233, when King Henry III was at variance with his barons, Bacon in a sermon preached before his Majesty at Oxford, declared publically that there would never be peace betwixt the King and his barons, till Peter de Rupibus [*Roches*], Bishop of Winchester, and his relation Peter de Rivallx [*Rivaux*], were expelled the King's Counsel. This Doctor, was one of the most early companions of Bishop Grossetete, as

---

[a] *Epist. Grosseteste*, 40.
[b] *De ordine Fratrum*, p. 183.
[c] *De ordine Fratrum*, p. 193.
[d] *Chron. Maj*., p. 386.

appears by a letter written in the beginning of his episcopate, wherein Bacon is cited as present with the Bishop and Adam de Marisco. He's said to have wrote the life of St Edmund Archbishop of Canterbury.[a] Its certain from Matthew Paris that he supplied the said Matthew with memoirs for writing that life. Bacon died in 1248,[b] with the reputation of one of the most learned and most zealous doctors in England.

Richard de Fissakre whom Leland numbers among those patronised by Bishop Grossetete was of the Diocese of Exeter, and a student of Great University Hall before he entered the order of St Dominick, there he was a disciple of Robert Bacon, but a disciple that even outstripped so great a master. Fissakre was not only the first who took his doctor's degree in the English Dominican province but also, which is no less worth remarking, the *first English Domincian Doctor, that Commented the Master of Sentences*. And that in a very useful manner as Trivet observes. He likewise commented the *Psalter*, as far as the 70th Psalm, in postils or short notes, equally elegant and full of morality and devotion: as also the *Proverbs of Solomon*. He died in 1248 and was buried in the convent of his order in Oxford, leaving behind him a reputation equal or superior to Bacon for his learning, zeal and regularity. Of him and his master Bacon, Matthew Paris[c] writes, that in theology, and other sciences, they were thought not to have any superior, and scarce any equals, and that they were equally renowned for their theological lectures and zealous preaching the word of God.

But the most intimate of all Bishop Grossetete's Dominican coadjutors, was Doctor John of St Giles, a native of St Albans. After his philosophick studies, John St Giles entered upon that of physick, of which he became Doctor and Professor, both at Paris and Montpellier; and was sometime physician to Philip the French King. On his return from Montpellier to Paris, he applied himself to Divinity with the same success and reputation as he had done to his former studies. Once preaching to the clergy, in the Church of the Dominicans on the article of voluntary poverty, he suddenly and in the middle of his sermon came down from the pulpit and put on the Dominican habit, so to confirm his word by his own example and then went up again and finished his sermon. At the request of his scholars he continued his theological lectures among the Dominicans with such reputation of piety and wisdom that in consideration of him the Dominicans had leave from the University to hold two schools within their own precincts. His theological lectures and books were full of morality and piety, as his physical ones were of admirable cures and

[a] *Chron. Maj.*, p. 864.
[b] *Chron. Maj.*, p. 747.
[c] *Chron. Maj.*, p. 747.

prognostications.[a] For he wrote upon those subjects. On physicks, a book *De remedia*, another on *Prognostications* or symptoms of diseases. A third on the *Formation of the Human Body*. And on theology, several learned tracts and homilies. After professing sometime among the French Dominicans he returned to his native country, and according to Matthew Paris became of the Privy Council to King Henry III, but without prejudice to his religious functions. Bishop Grossetete found so much comfort in the conversation and ministry of this venerable Doctor not only in his body, which he once delivered from poison, but much more in his mind that he wrote to his General brother Jordan begging him not only to permit, but to command John to be with him. As in effect he was, even to the Bishop's death. In the same letter he saith of John that, 'he had no more efficacious helper in his episcopal labours than brother John of St Giles, and that he was the prop of his weakness, the supplement of his incapacity, the exciter of his tepidity, and his lifter up and comforter in all his adversities.'[[b]]

If any of the Bishop's religious assistants surpassed John of St Giles, it was the illuminated Franciscan Doctor Adam de Marisco. Adam was born in Somersetshire, brought up in Oxford, and as should seem under Professor Grossetete who on Adam's taking his degree of D.D., presided over the act, and pronounced his *vesperial encomium*.[104] This doctor was first of the secular clergy, and had been three years Rector of the noble and ancient church of Wiremouth [*Wearmouth*] in the Bishoprick of Durham, when the Franciscans coming to England he joined them, as did many other emminent clergymen, about the year 1221.[c] In 1223, Adam was sent for over to Italy by St Francis himself, on which Agnellus their provincial received a letter from Grossetete, then Archdeacon of Leicester, expressing his sorrow to see Adam separated from their holy society. While abroad, Adam was instructed in mystical theology by the famous Benedictine Abbot of St Andrew's of Vercelli, John Gersen, author of the golden book of the imitation of Christ.[105] He returned in 1226. He was in so great a reputation, whether for his piety and learning in which Roger Bacon ranks him with Grossetete, that in 1230 he was dispatched to Rome in company with two other eminent English Franciscans,[d] doctors Haymo de Faversham and Richard Rufus, there to support the original severe poverty of St Francis's rule against the mitigating General Brother Elias, and by joining with St Anthony of Padua procured Elias's deposition by Gregory the IX. Adam attended our Prelate, from the very beginning of his episcopate and was esteemed by him as his right hand. In 1244 the

---

[a] *De ordine Fratrum*, p. 178.
[b] *Chron. Maj*., p. 518.
[c] *Collectanea Anglo-Minoritica*, p. 18.
[d] *Collectanea Anglo-Minoritica*, Ubi Supra, p. 31 and 35.

Bishop took Dr Adam with him to the Council of Lions, but had like to have lost him in his return. The irrefragable Doctor Alexander Hales, dying at Paris in 1245, just as the Bishop and Adam were returning home, Adam was greatly talked of and desired for his successor in the Chair of Theology, but our Prelate prevented it by hurrying him away to England where Adam was, some time after, made guardian of his order in London. Grossetete's affection for the illustrated Doctor was so great that in his consideration, he left [*the*] great part of his library to the Franciscan convent in Oxford. And Adam honoured his Patron with an encomium written just after his death to the Venerable Sewal, Archbishop of York.[106] In 1257[a] Adam was named by King Henry and Archbishop Boniface to the See of Ely, but the nomination did not take place, Hugo Balsham, Superior of Ely, and since founder of Peterhouse in the University of Cambridge, being preferred by the Pope. About the same time Dr Adam was one of the commissaries deputed by Alexander the IV for enquiring into the life and miracle of St Richard, Bishop of Chichester, inorder to his canonisation.[107] Soon after which Adam died 5 November 1258, or 1260 and would be buried near his most dear friend and patron Bishop Grossetete, in the Cathedral of Lincoln. Besides some commentaries on the Scriptures, he wrote several letters to our Prelate, which are MSS in the Cotton Library (*Vitellius*) c. viii. 5:6:7; and one on him, to Sewal, Archbishop of York.[108] This Doctor is remarkable among other things, for the being the first Religious Professor in the Franciscan School at Oxford, after the four secular ones already named, who were all four Bishops, viz Grossetete Bishop of Lincoln, Peter Bishop of Aberdeen, Roger Wesham Bishop of Lichfield and Coventry, and Thomas Gwallensius, Bishop of St Davids.

Peter of Tewkesbury[b] was expressly desired of the English Provincial by our Prelate in 1245, when John, companion to Adam de Marisco, falling sick at Monte on their return from the Council of Lions, Bishop Grossetete wrote for Peter to supply to John's place, and to remain near his person with Doctor Adam.[109] He became afterward the fifth provincial of the English province of his order, *ab anno* 1255 to 1256, and the third English provincial after Haymo de Faversham and William of Nottingham, the two first Agnellus and Albertus of Pisa, being foreigners.[c] Eccleston in his history of the first entrance of the friars minor into England gives the following curious anecdote of this Brother Peter de Tewkesbury, that he not only travelled over many provinces in the service of his order, but was a very pleasant judicious, as well as religious man. And that

[a] *De ordine Fratrum*, p. 205.

[b] *Epist. Grosseteste*, 114.

[c] Hearne, preface to *Ottersbourne* p. 99. *Collectanea Anglo-Minoritica* [*missing*].

he once enjoined to a melancholick person for penance to drink a glass of the most generous wine, adding that a repetition of such penances was the properest way to quiet his conscience. An act and saying which proved Peter to be a good physician, as well as divine. Such melancholy dispositions often arise from poorness of blood and low spirits, and of course the remedy for a sinking jade is good and moderate keeping. This coadjutor of our Prelate seems to have died soon after him, his provincialship only enduring for one year from 1255 to 1256.

The most renouned of all our Prelate's disciples, among the Franciscans, was the *Wonderful Doctor* Roger Bacon, more commonly known by the appellation of Friar Bacon. Roger Bacon, born near Ilchester in Devonshire [*sc. Somerset*], anno 1214 was brought up to Oxford, but not in Merton College, which was not founded till Bacon was far advanced in age. In 1233 Bacon was a junior clerk in the Court of King Henry the III, when his relation Robert Bacon of the Black Friars, preached before that Prince at Oxford in 1233, against Peter de Rupibus Bishop of Winchester. Young Bacon seeing his Majesty in good humour, put him this punning question, alluding to the name and surname of Peter de Rupibus,[a] which signifieth Rock and Shelves. What is it, and please your Majesty, that terrifieth and wrecks those who run the Sees? They know best, saith the King, who run the same. With your Majesty's leave, I'll tell it. It is Rocks and Shelves, *Petrae et Rupes* i.e. Peter de Rupibus. It was at the persuasion of our Prelate, that he entered among the Friars Minors of Oxford.[b] He was doctor of Divinity, both of Oxford and Paris, and the wonder of his age in all kind of knowledge, especially the Mathematicks, for which he owns himself indebted to William Sherewood, Treasurer of Lincoln, and to our Prelate. He is thought to have invented the telescope, which the Italians attribute to Galileo. He first pointed out the defects of the ancient calender, which was reformed three centuries after by Pope Gregory the XIII. He also gives a sufficient hint too of the invention of gunpowder, when he saith that by *Salpetre and fire, a body may be thrown to any distance*. Bacon was also deeply skilled in the sacred languages for learning of which he composed a Greek and Hebrew Grammar and wrote an express treatise, to recommend the study of those and all the other learned languages. Among many other philosophical and theological lucubrations Bacon wrote comments on Bishop Grossetete's ecclesiastical *Computation*. Several books on the means of keeping off old age and preserving the senses in their natural vigour to the last. And two others, more useful and remarkable, one on the defect of the theological studies of the Latins, another in praise of the Holy

---

[a] *Chron. Maj*., p. 388.

[b] *Collectanea Anglo-Minoritica*, p. 37.

Scriptures, both addressed to Pope Clement the IV. In fine his insights into all the sciences, especially into the secrets of nature, was so quick and extensive, that in the eyes of the ignorant he passed for a magician, as well as his master Grossetete.[110] This ingenius Doctor died an. 1292, on the feast of Barnabus in the 78 year of his age and was buried in his conventual church of Oxford. Before we dismiss this article of the Bishop of Lincoln's religious assistants we cannot help taking notice of a piece of judicious advice, which he gives in a letter[a] to M[*atthew*] Provincial and to the diffinitors[111] of the provincial chapter of preaching friars in England which is, 'that for the good of souls, they would not so often change his companions of their order, as they had hitherto done. For that new comers having less experience and less use of the ministry, are not likely to do so much good, as those of older standing.'

The Bishop of Lincoln's zeal, whether for promoting or employing able subjects did not confine itself to those of the second order, but extended even to those of the first. It was by his advice and zealous industry that the two great bishopricks of Durham and Winchester were filled with able pastors, the first by Dr Nicholas de Farnham, the latter by William de Raley or Ralegher.[b112] The first of the two was a scholar of consummate knowledge and of great virtue who had been Master Regent in Arts at Paris for the space of 28 years, and was the second of the five English Professors who quitted that University in 1229 on a dissension betwixt the clergy and city of Paris.[113] Having applied himself to the study of Physick and Divinity at Bologna and collected a very curious library, he returned to England and was made Privy Counsellor to King Henry III, as also Physician Corporal and Spiritual to the same Prince and his Consort Queen Eleanor.[c] In 1239 the Chapter of Coventry elected him their Bishop, while the Chapter of Lichfield chose their dean William of Manchester. But this latter no sooner saw so great a scholar as Farnham chosen but he immediately renounced his election in his favour, but Farnham could never be brought to give his consent, thro dread of the rigorous account to be given of the multitude of souls under the episcopal charge. In 1241, he was offered the Bishoprick of Durham, but refused it with the same humility and firmness as that of Lichfield; nor could he be prevailed on to accept it till our Prelate, who had already promoted him in his Diocese, determind him by this short and pathetick speech.

> Behold the monks of Durham, and their widow Church, with tears beg you for their Pastor, and will you thus canonically elected refuse their offer? By the *aspersion* of Christ's sacred blood I conjure you to take this charge upon

---

[a] *Epist. Grosseteste*, 100.

[b] *Chron. Maj*., p. 206, 354, 489, 549, 550, 565, 573, 628, 759: et *Anglia Sacra*, B. 1.

[c] M. Paris ut Supri; *Anglia Sacra*, B. 1, p. 439.

> you, seeing the King while in his wits, can never except against you. And should you stand off by his intrigues he'll thrust in some foreigner to the dishonour and prejudice both of the Church and the State. As the Bishoprick of Durham lieth on the Scottish Borders and the two castles of Durham and Norham, are the two bulwarks of England against the Scots.

Thereupon Nicholas said, but with a deep sigh, 'I am [*sic*] embrace the virtue of obedience. It was by your diocese, and by your favour, I obtained the benefices I enjoy; and therefore I acquiesce to your paternal advice.'

Accordingly he was consecrated to the see of Durham, but to shew with what spirit and reluctancy he had submitted to the burthen, when he had governed the see eight years with great edification he, with much greater, resigned it and retired in order to prepare himself by more undisturbed prayer and contemplation for the great day of eternity. He still lived eight or nine years, and went to God in the year 1257.

William de Raley or Ralegher, the other prelate whose promotion the Bishop of Lincoln forwarded was chaplain to King Henry III, Treasurer of Exeter, and Judge of the Prerogative Court. To Raley, while in the last office, our Prelate hath two or three letters. In 1239 being chosen to two sees at once, viz that of Lichfield, and that of Norwich, he preferred the latter and was consecrated the same year by St Edmund Archbishop of Canterbury.[a] In 1242 his translation was petitioned for by the monks of Winchester but the King having his eye upon that see for some of his creatures refused his consent, and raised a persecution against Raley. Our Prelate jealous of the honour of the episcopal body, and of the freedom of canonical elections, was the first to intercede for his persecuted friend and fellow Bishop. Attended by the Bishops of Hereford and Worcester, Peter de Egueblank [*d'Aigueblanche*] and Walter de Cantilupe, Grossetete repaired to the King at Reading.[b] But the King retired on their approach, for fear of being wrought upon by our Prelate. The Bishops pursued him, but could not move him. On the contrary the King sent his deputies to Rome with great presents in order to break Raley's election. In the mean time, the three prelates repaired to his Majesty a third time at Westminster, and after reproaching him with the tyrannick persecution of their brother bishop and begging him over and over to be reconciled to him they threatened in case of refusal to interdict his Chapel Royal. The King demanded a truce till the return of his deputies from Rome, hoping their presents would compass his design. On *the contrary hopes* the bishops yielded to the petition. But Raley seeing that thereby his deliverance was put off for some time he took shipping privately and withdrew to Abbeville in Picardy, where by orders of St Lewis,[114] he

---

[a] *Chron. Maj.*, p. 614; *Dunstable annals*, p. 262.

[b] *Chron. Maj.*, p. 617. *See, biographical appendix.*

met with a kind reception from the Mayor of that city,[a] from the month of February 1244 till that of April, when he was restored to the King's favour and to his see, partly at the Pope's interposition, partly by that of Boniface Elect of Canterbury, whom our Prelate had solicited by letter to employ his interest with the Queen his niece, and the Queen with his Majesty.[b] Among other reasons, which he suggests for inclining the King to consent to this election, and to the Pope's approbation and desire of it, he gave this remarkable one which shews how staunch and thorough [*a*] *popesman* our Prelate was: 'Should his Majesty persist,' saith he, 'in this refusal, he might, which God forbid, hurt himself, and his kingdom, since in so doing he openly resists and rebels against the Pope to whom besides the obedience due in common with all other Christian princes his Majesty owes a special fidelity by the charter and oath of his father, the late King John of famous memory, *illustrious memory*, and that as your Grace well knows, under a very grevious penalty.'

---

a *Chron. Maj.*, pp. 634 and 638.

b [*Perry's footnote is missing.*]

Chapter VII

BISHOP GROSSETETE'S WISDOM IN REGULATING THE THEOLOGICAL STUDIES OF HIS DIOCESAN UNIVERSITY OF OXFORD

It is the gift and glory of the great physicians to search into and discover the root of the disease, and they who have the greatest quickness in discerning the causes and the greatest dexterity in applying the proper remedies, not only to assage but to eradicate the evil, are justly esteemed to bear away the laurel and take the lead among those of the profession. The same holds good with regard to the ecclesiasticks as well as to the natural body and this we see exemplified in the most wise and penetrating Bishop of Lincoln. Taught by long experience and observation how difficult it is to correct evil pastors, and how much more difficult to find out good ones, he sought out the roots and causes of so pernicious an evil, and having found that the disorders of ecclesiasticks are often owing either to the ill regulation, or ill performance of their studies, he carrieth his wise and piercing views into the seats of clerical education and laboured hard to bring the theological studies of his University of Oxford to a more rational and more useful method, or rather to prevent their forsaking the ancient method which it seems began to faulter. The primitive and ancient method of teaching theology was to explain the *Divine Books* by the rule of Catholick tradition and by the comments of preceeding doctors. This we see in all the ancient fathers and doctors of the first ages, whether in their commentaries on Scripture or in their polemick works. Their first proofs of the truth they explain, or defend, are taken from the Scriptures. The second, from ecclesiastick doctors, and third sort often from natural reasons where the subject will allow it. This also is the method of the most ancient school doctors and of many eminent modern theologians who have wrote since the revival of good studies. With this difference betwixt the scholastick doctors and the ancient fathers; that these latter wrote in a more prolix and oratorial style, and with all the charms of eloquence of which several of the ancient fathers were the greatest masters of the age. A style indeed more agreeable and attractive to the Reader, and very applicable to particular tracts, but not to the body of Theology which such a style would swell not only beyond the patience of the generality of students, but likewise beyond their purse. Whereas the Doctors of the School, write and that necessarily, in a more concise and consequently less agreeable yet often times more instructive, at least a more speedily instructing style. Among the ancient Fathers some have explored in books of Scripture, some have wrote against one heresy, some against another, and all were confined to write only against such as rose up either before or in their days. Every age since hath produced fresh errors, and hath consequently enlarged the circle of theologick studies. Again, some of the fathers explained one book of Scripture, some another; few have explained the whole, so that a compleat body of Divinity composed of the works of the ancients, would be an immense and expensive library. The business of School Doctors consists in reducing these immense materials into a narrower compass and in digesting the several parts into distinct and methodical treatises for the more speedy perusal and more easy retention of so many various and extensive subjects. And who doth not on the very exposition perceive the necessity and utility of so judicious an undertaking? In these abridged codes of religion, as I may call them, the Holy Scriptures walk first, then follows the explications of the Fathers, afterwards succeed arguments drawn from natural reason, but the whole in a more concise, and tho less agreeable, yet more clear and retainable style than in large oratorial tracts. The method used in writing was also followed in the universities where various chairs were founded. Some for explaining the holy books, some for moral, some for polemic theology and some for explaining the Holy Fathers. Now at Court and elsewhere the most noble peers claim a right to precedence, so it was decent and just that the most noble lectures should walk foremost and first of all the *peerless* lectures on the Divine books. This was the judicious practice of the University of Paris, which has ever held the first rank in the Church. And this our judicious Prelate, who was an alumnus and professor of that foreign University, endeavoured to introduce into or pursue in his diocesan University of Oxford, which seem to have swerved, or at least to be now swerving from it. Nothing being more pious, nor at the same time more sensible, than his letter on this article to the Masters Regents in Theology of Oxford. We shall here lay it before the Reader, who will only be sorry that it is not longer.[a]

> Robert by the grace of God Bishop of Lincoln, to his beloved sons in Christ, the Masters Regents in Theology at Oxford, health, grace, and benediction. Wise architects are very careful to see that every stone laid in the foundations of the building, be truly a foundation stone i.e. able to support the weight of the superstructure which is to be raised upon it. Now you yourselves are the

---

[a] *Epist. Grosseteste*, 123.

> architects and builders up of the house of God, which you are to erect upon the foundation of the Apostles and Prophets, Christ Jesus ever remaining the corner-stone. Hence the foundation stones of the building you have to rear, besides which none can find out or lay any other, are first the books of the Prophets, of which number we are of necessity and practice to reckon the lawgiver Moses. Secondly those of the Apostles and Evangelists. These fundamental stories you lay in the groundwork of the building when with the gift of discretion and wisdom you expound the said books to your disciples, according to the sense and intention of their authors. All possible care therefore is to be taken by you not to lay among the foundation stones such stones as are not truly fundamental, least the inability of these non-fundamental stones to bear the superstructure leave the edifice raised upon them first liable to crack and then to fall in ruins.
>
> Now the most proper time for laying the said foundation stones (for there's a time for laying the foundations, as well for erecting the building) is the morning hour at which you give your ordinary lectures (*qua ordinarie legitis*) it is then but reasonable that your lectures, of that hour especially, should be upon the Old and New Testaments. Lest otherwise, instead of foundation stones, or at least among them, you lay some that are not so, thus running counter to the direction of the Holy Scriptures and to the order of right reason whose prescription is to give everything its proper time; and manifestly departing from the footsteps of our fathers and ancients, and from a due conformity with the Masters Regents in Theology of the University of Paris. Wherefore from the earnest desire that all things be done according to the Apostle, with order and decorum, we beg with all affection and devotion, we admonish you in our Lord Jesus Christ, and we exhort your wisdom, that your ordinary lectures of the morning hour be all taken from the Old and New Testaments, that so you may resemble or rather that you may be the very masters of the family producing out your storehouses both new and old fruits, and not others of a middle kind, not even the doctrines and comments of the Holy Fathers on the Scriptures, which may have another more proper hour assigned them. Farewell.

Thus did our skilfull architect, or rather director of the architects and builders of the house of God, endeavour not only to keep theological studies upon their proper and primary foundation, the sacred and heavenly books, but to preserve for the divine oracles their due preference, even as to the hour of the day in which they are to be taught. This excellent prescription was founded on the just and sublime notion he had imbided of the sacred volumes, of which in another place he has this short, but pithy eulogium. 'The holy Scriptures,' saith he.[a] 'Are the storehouse of the Holy Ghost, supplying us with excellent ointments for every sore, salutary antidotes against every disease and wholesome lenitives for every pain, according to that saying of Chrysostom. "In the Holy Scriptures, the

---

[a] Tract, *De oculo morali*, in Biblioth, Lambeth, c: 44. In auctoris. Whestoni ad Usser. de Sacris vernacularibus, p. 417.

ignorant find instruction, the disobedient terrors, the industrious, reward, and the dejected consolation."' ^Browne's note concerning the difference of the method here presented by our wise Doctor, from the method of the foreign universities in reading Aquinas, Scotus etc. shows his ignorance in the studies of foreign universities.^ For tho Aquinas and Scotus might be read in private studies, or in the conventual schools of their respective orders, and their sentiments followed by their respective clans of Thomists or Scotists, yet the publick university lectures were never read out of either of those two doctors but of the *Master of Sentences*, which is made up first of books of Scripture and then citations of the Fathers of which Aquinas and Scotus are only commentators. Nay the Master of Sentences, tho followed as to the general order of the matter, is no longer either universally or even generally explained in foreign schools, but the professors after his example give their own *dictates* in which, as well as in the Master, the first proofs are taken from Scripture according to the substance of Lincoln's prescription. The second from tradition and this any one that has eyes, may convince themselves of by only looking into any foreign divine of note. Even while the *Master* reigned in the schools, the Scripture lectures were so far from being neglected that besides his text being made up chiefly and primarily of Scripture texts there was one year fixed for every Batchelor to explain the Bible, whence he was styled *Baccalaureus Biblicus* or Bible-Batchelor. As while he explained the Master, he was called *Baccalaureus Sententiorius*, or Sentence-Batchelor. It's true the explaining of the Bible was reserved to one of the last years of his course, nor were the Batchelors admitted into the sanctuary of the divine oracles for explaining therein to others till they had first learnt and understood them themselves by meditating the Sacred text and the best interpreters, nor was it then, as it is now, when every ignorant Jackpudding or Smattered in Learning is allowed to handle, or rather to mangle the word of God, after their own wild and whimsical fashion. ^This Browne might have known if he had ever looked into any foreign divine of note, or even alluded to our Prelate's words, that were under his eye and the object of his note, since the method here prescribed is proposed and pressed, as conformable to the method of the Masters Regent in Divinity at the University of Paris. But his business was not to seek proofs for his assertions, but to throw dirt in the Church's face, or rather the eyes, for so universities be justly termed. I don't know whether he's more lucky in his inference than in his note, for this advice to the university infers that Bishop Grossetete was Chancellor thereof, and the inference might have been possible at least had not he been diocesan Bishop of Oxford and otherwise a doctor of great note and authority in the schools. Which might give him a certain right to direct them without being their Chancellor.[115] Perhaps the terms '*rogamos, monemus* [et] *exhortamur*', [*We ask, warn and exhort*] are not in the style of a Chancellor, but rather a doctor. So that in reality the veracity of Browne's peevish reflexion on foreign universities may be easily decided by looking into the records of the University.[a]^

[a] Pegge, [*Weseham*] p. 4, speaking of his professorship saith he held the seat of Chancellorship.

Book III

Chapter I

GENERAL IDEA OF HIS OPPOSING ABUSE IN ALL STATES OF MEN

^We have seen Bishop Grossetete hitherto instructing and directing the clergy, and carrying his care and forecast into the sources of clerical education. We shall now see him correcting and reducing those, by authority, who would not conform to these directions. Being absolutely bent on correcting abuses, and these being almost without number, he was obliged to make such continual opposition against them that Matthew Paris compares the zelous Bishop of Lincoln to Ishmael,[a] 'Whose hand was set against all his brethren, and all his brethren's hands against him.'[116] There was however this essential difference betwixt our zealous Prelate and the wild father of the arabs,^ that the opposition of our strenuous Prelate was always against evil, or what he apprehended to be so. If in some particular cases he should seem impetuous, the same historian who taxes him with it in certain points regarding the privileges of his own secular, or other religious chapters, ^takes care to excuse him, acknowledging it to have been the effect of his ardent and indefatigable zeal for the salvation of the souls committed to his care.^ For which reason he adds, 'let none be moved to an ill opinion of his sanctity by certain excesses, which are related in this history, one of which was his vexatious and expensive suit with his canons of Lincoln in his attempt to visit them. The same Robert was also wont to thunder and lighten in a terrible manner against religious men and more so against religious women, fired with a good zeal but perhaps not altogether according to science. Nevertheless I boldly assert, that his virtues were pleasing to God, tho certain excesses were displeasing.'[b] Others less warm for priviledges than our pious but censorious and ardent Albanian[c] historiographer would Christen the pretended excesses in question by a more soft and honourable name. So far is incontrovertibly certain, that in most of these excesses as they are termed, and namely his controversy with his secular Chapter of Lincoln and some other religious chapters here censored by Matthew, the Bishop of Lincoln was empowered thereto by

---

[a] *Chron. Maj.*, p. 688.

[b] *Chron. Maj.*, pp. 816 and 880.

[c] *Albanian, as in of St Albans.*

the religious Pope Gregory the IX before the opposition, and after the opposition was supported in them by the decision of Innocent the IV. However we do not pretend our heroe to be either impeccable or infallible, nor exempt from oversights of humanity which the most holy are liable to in this life without forfeiting their justice. But we shall desire more unequivocal proofs than those produced by our most eminent and judicious yet warm, and sometimes sarcastical historian above mentioned. As to faults, Bishop Grossetete was the last man in the world to pretend an exemption from them. Twas with the contrary spirit that he desired his friend Beleth to be free and open in exposing his faults to him and enjoining him correction; and that he thanked him for that he had already given, tho ill grounded. With the same spirit,[a] having once interdicted the secular churches of Hertford, which dependency on the Abbey of St Alban, were all exempt from the ordinary, he made no difficulty of recalling the censure on the admonition of the Pope's Legate Cardinal Otho. These acts of humility shewed that in all his oppositions he had only duty in view. He was so far from having the least liking for contests that his aversion to them made him bewail the loss of time and the distraction which he suffered thereby in the necessary duties of his ministry. Which saith he, 'Remand me entirely, tho I could multiply myself into many thousands of persons.' And therefore he begged of his Metropolitan Primate, Edmund to contrive some remedy to rescue him from these vexatious suits.[b]

---

[a] *Chron. Maj.*, p. 879.

[b] *Epist. Grosseteste*, 26 to S. Edmund A[*rchbishop*] C[*anterbury*].

Chapter II

BISHOP GROSSETETE'S CONTROVERSY WITH HIS SECULAR CHAPTER OF LINCOLN

The first considerable opposition our Prelate met with from any body of men was that from his own secular Chapter of Lincoln, as the first care of his impartial and prudent zeal was to visit and reform them, the more surely to compass the reformation of others. This opposition of the Chapter of Lincoln was against the Bishop's attempts to visit them and their dependent churches. This affair which began in 1239[a] lasted until 1246. i.e. the space of 7 years. A duration which would have tired any other but the vigorous Bishop of Lincoln, whom Matthew Paris justly styles, 'Indefatigable in his Episcopal office'.

This undertaking to visit the Chapter of Lincoln, being likely to raise contradiction, the wise Prelate took the precaution to arm himself, not only with his ordinary episcopal powers, but with an extraordinary delegation from his Holiness Pope Gregory IX. Thus doubly commissioned[b] on the eve of the nativity of the Blessed Virgin he gave notice to the Dean and Chapter of Lincoln that in virtue of an apostolick mandate, as well as by his own ordinary jurisdiction, he intended to visit them on the Thursday after St Luke, immediately after the forementioned feast of Our Lady. The Bishop began his visitation of some of the prebends on St Faith's day, (the 6 of October in the Sarum Calendar), the Dean and Chapter being assembled consulted on the affair of the visitation and on the following Sunday they from the pulpit bespoke the people, as it were for their approbation, to apply to the Pope against the injury done them, they said, by their Bishop.

Upon this as it were declaration of war, the Bishop wrote to William the Dean[117] and to the Chapter his 71 letter, full of affection and humility, complaining that in their appeal to the Pope against the pretended injuries he had done them, they had violated the respect due to him as their father and bishop, and that if he had really done them any injury they ought first to have exposed it to him in private and not to the publick. He also

[a] *Dunstable annals*, p. 239 and 250.

[b] *Epist. Grosseteste*, 80.

exhorted them to lay aside all selflove and only to seek the truth, which if they did an agreement would soon follow. As to himself he makes this humble and affectionate protestation.

> Tho' I am a contemptible man, as being infirm of body and more so in mind, yet I have a double relation to you, one as your brother in Christianity, the other as your Father by your own election and the disposition of God. And as far as my conscience covered with darkness can judge of itself, I verily believe and trust in God that I have for you all, and for every one, as much as a sinner can have, a most sincere and pure affection … I also hope and confide in our Lord Jesus Christ, who is the eternal truth that he has kindled in my soul, sinful as it is, some spark of the love of truth and in consequence thereof, has endued me with a readiness to quit every evil as soon as it shall be made appear to me to be such and to repair all injuries, which I may have done to any one, especially to you. And he that searches his heart knows that in this exercise of my episcopal jurisdiction I have not the least intention either to injure or bring a yoke upon any one, or to abolish any good and laudable customs, but only to labour according to my duty and capacity in delivering the souls entrusted to me from the snares and yoke of the Devil.

He also wrote them a second letter which is the 73 addressed to the Dean Will and the Chapter, to lay before them the ill consequences which, not only in his opinion but in that of prudent and godly persons, seemed to follow from their pretensions. Viz that abuses among them must become incorrigible and the pastor oblidged tamely to see his sheep perish without being able to assist them, tho he might and ought to do it.

The Chapter paid but little attention to this paternal advice. They went so far in their publick sermons as to reproach the Bishop with his low extraction and to express their regret for having chosen him their Bishop. One of the canons, after declaiming against him in the church added, 'that if he were silent the very stones would cry out against the Bishop'. How loud the stones would have cried out against the Bishop in case of the Canon's silence I know not, but as he was not silent it is very certain the stones in some measure cried out against him and for the Bishop. For Matthew Paris,[a] tho' an adversary to the Bishop's conduct in this affair, and the *Annals of Dunstable* relate, that while the vehement Canon pronounced the above invective part of the *New Tower* fell down near the Choir, just behind the Dean's Stall and crushed to death three several persons that happened to be on the spot. This sudden accident was esteemed by the wise a supernatural interposition of Providence, and was regarded as an ill omen for the success of the Chapter's cause. Our most meek Prelate far from returning injury for injury endeavoured to overcome evil with good. He generously set his hand to work and

---

[a] *Chron. Maj.*, pp. 485 and 522; *Dunstable annals*, p. 239.

repaired the fallen tower at his own expence. But neither this exemplary generosity, nor the seeming intervention of heaven could hinder the Dean and Chapter from pursuing their appeal in opposition to his visitation.

The Chapter endeavoured moreover to stir up the people against their spiritual father, and dispatched both their letters and deputies to the several chapters in the Realm, in order to form as it were a general league and combination against him. Hence the Bishop received two several letters, one from the Pope's Legatee Otho, the other from the Dean and Chapter of Sarum both soliciting him to be easy in making peace with his Chapter. These Bishop Grossetete answered in a very civil yet firm and judicious manner.[a] That he desires nothing so much as peace; but such a peace saith he,

> wherein things are in their due order; wherein subjects are under their superiors, and not superiors under their inferiors. For such a peace as this last is noways to be suffered, neither was it such a peace as this that Christ [*was*] brought into the world, but he rather unsheathed the sword against it. For this kind of peace, is only resting in the dreggs of vice, and of this we know you to be an enemy. As far as our slender capacity can judge, we do not seek to exercise any power either over them or their subjects, but what the Divine and Canon Laws have annexed to the episcopal office and which in the present case is enforced by a special commission from the See Apostolick, a commission we cannot give up, without risking the salvation of souls. If through ignorance we have attempted any thing against the canons we are ready by God's assistance to desist as soon as the same shall be made known to us and even to repair it by proper satisfaction. This we have more than once signified to our Dean and Chapter, both by word of mouth and in writing, and have begged them to shew us our mistakes, not by general and vague assertions, but by solid reasons, or from the canons of the Church. But this they have never vouchsafed to comply with; nor so much as to return any answer to our reasons against them.

Hence the Bishop likewise pushed his point. On the day and hour appointed for the visitation, he went to the Chapter House but found no Chapter to receive him. On the contrary the Dean William de Tournay, the Precentor, the Chancellor, the Treasurer and several of the canons, after appealing as above and issuing forth an injunction to their vicars etcetera not to obey the Bishop in the article of the visitation, were set off for the Court of Rome. Whereupon the Bishop wrote his 77 letter addressed to Pope Gregory the IX, begging of his Holiness not to give them letters against him to any judges in England till such time as he had received from him by special messanger a true state of the contest. This special messanger seems to have been Walter de Hemingburgh, the same probably as the famous Canon of Gisburne, and author of the excellent history from

[a] *Epist. Grosseteste*, 79 and 93.

the Conquest to King Edward I.[118] Or the person signified by the initial letter R and recommended in his 78 letter, to the celebrated and learned William Bishop of Paris. After this precautionary letter, the Bishop set out for London whither he had been summoned by St Edmund, Archbishop of Canterbury to consult on the affairs of that Church in the day after All Souls. Hearing of the Bishop's coming to town, the Dean and Chapter waited his arrival to see if an accommodation could not take place. Several conferences were held for that purpose but to no other effect than protracting the business.

The Bishop, who had already suspended the Dean, Subdean and Precentor for not revoking their prohibitory injunctions to their vicars etcetera, and was now tempted to excommunicate them and others of the Chapter. But being his truly Christian and episcopal custom not to come to any important resolution without mature deliberations and advising with the descreet and such as feared God, he weighed first all the consequences of the step he now proposed and specially these three. First, that this proceeding being unusual among the English prelates it might raise the clamours of the whole nation against him, and even scandalise many as he had felt already what he had hitherto done having put many into a ferment both among the little and the great ones. Second, that if any of the above mentioned capitulars, some of which were advanced in years and little used to fatigue should die in the passage to Rome, as was probable or rather almost certain they would, he should then be reputed the murderer of so many venerable personages. Third, that if for a vain shadow of liberty they should thus rashly expose their lives in taking so long and painful a journey, which several of them seemed resolved upon rather than yield, and which however they could not do but with danger to their own souls as well as bodies, then he should never be easy with himself to think he had been even the innocent occasion of them risking their salvation, for which he thought himself bound to suffer all temporal evils whatever. But then he considered on the other hand that it were better scandal should happen than truth and justice perish and that we are not to abstain from defending truth and seeking the salvation of souls for fear of incurring the reproaches of the people, or even of the wise ones of the world; seeing our Lord declares, that we are blessed, when men shall speak ill of us falsely on his account, and that he himself for the good of souls suffered the reproaches and ignominies of the Cross. The Bishop likewise considered that it were a more tolerable inconvenience to leave some to expose themselves to dangers of their own seeking than to let many more perish for want of standing up for the necessary discipline of the Church.

In these opposite straits, our judicious Prelate cast about for some salutary expedient which might ward off the dangers that threatened on both sides. The expedient he pitched upon was to refer the cause of the contested visitation to some upright and inflexible judge whose sentence might pass into a formal decision. From hence he flattered himself with two advantages, the first that as no custom can obstruct the episcopal visitation, against which there is no prescription or demur in law but from an exemption granted by the See Apostolick, the sentence of the judge must be that where this exemption doth intervene there the Bishop proceeds of full right in his office of visitation. Secondly, that such an authentick and general decision in favour of the right of visitation would both enable and excite all other bishops in the realm to visit their respective chapters, whereas by his private censures he could only expect at most to reduce his own single one, but still the main difficulty remained which was to find a knowing and proper judge. In this view three several expedients were proposed by the Bishop, the third of which the Chapter agreed to and this was that both parties should betwixt then and Christmas send over their deputies to the Pope and desire his Holiness to commit the examen and decision of the affair to Walter de Cantilupe, Lord Bishop of Worcester, uncle to St Thomas of Hereford, in conjunction with the Archdeacons of Worcester[a] and Sudbury in Norfolk. The Archdeacon of Sudbury, was Doctor Alan de Bleccles [*Beccles*], a famous English professor in the University of Paris, when he quitted that city in 1229.[119] The name of the Archdeacon of Worcester is not specified but this was perhaps Doctor Richard de Kirkham who as will appear afterwards was one of the judges of this affair, tho at that time in service of the Bishop of Ely.[120] But if these delegates could not decide the cause to the satisfaction of the parties then it should be free for either side to appeal to the Pope in person, both the Bishop *and the Dean* ceasing in the interim their visitations, which as Matthew Paris observes was already one advantage gained by the Bishop over the Dean.

This Convention is dated from the Bishop of London's Chambers in the Old Temple, Saturday after All Souls in the thirteenth year of Pope Gregory the IX i.e. anno 1239, and not in 1240, or 1241, as Browne pretends who mistakes the time of the progress of this affair mentioned by Matthew Paris[b] under the year 1241 for its beginning mentioned by the same[c] historian under the year 1239. Gregory the IX was chosen the 18th of March[d] in the beginning of 1227, so that his thirteenth year falls *on* the year 1239. Immediately after this convention, the Bishop of Lincoln sent it to the Pope's Legate Otho with his 82 letter desiring his opinion thereupon, for he was fearful lest he should be thought to have condescended too far and appear to his Holiness to have given up the cause

---

[a] *Epist. Grosseteste*, 80; *Chron Maj*., pp. 485 and 536; *Dunstable annals*, p. 239.
[b] *Chron. Maj*., p. 571.
[c] *Chron. Maj*., p. 485.
[d] *Chron. Maj*., p. 336

of the visitation. The Legate seems to have approved the convention for our Prelate sent the form of it to his agent at the Court of Rome, named Simon de Ardern,[121] together with his 80 letter giving a succinct account of the whole affair as above described out of the same letter, with orders to the said Simon to act according to this form of convention without minding that he had sent him by W[*alter*] de Hemingburgh. The Bishop wrote at the same time to the Pope himself,[a] imploring his assistance in this weighty business undertaken by his Holiness's special authority, and for the salvation of souls. His Holiness approved of the Convention and granted them the judges they had demanded.

This convention however received some alteration by another drawn up at Thame[b] in Oxfordshire, where as should seem the Dean and Chapter demanded for Judge Richard de Kirkham instead of the Archdeacon of Worcester if so be that they are two different persons and not one and the same.[122] But this new judge found it necessary to suspend or excommunicate some of the Chapter for their illegal and obstinate proceedings. Upon which the Chapter complained in an address to the Pope, that the said Doctor Richard de Kirkham, who had laid their members under censures, had no jurisdiction over the censured Capitulars. To which in his 90 letter, the Bishop replied in a very sharp but paternal manner; that herein they are guilty of a notorious and wilfull untruth, since they themselves had solicited and by their deputies had obtained him for judge. He adds, that it could not be sufficient excuse for them to have recourse to distinctions and quibbles by replying that their present process against the said Doctor is not the act of the capitular body, but only of some particulars; for that the defects of the members affect the body when the body having it in its power to remedy them refuses to do it. 'Neither will it serve to their justification,' saith he again,

> But rather to the aggravation of their guilt to pretend that the said Doctor had jurisdiction over the whole community, but not over the particulars separately taken. For that in punishing some particulars he intends to punish the whole body, as he who puts a man in irons, tho' he only load his hands and feet, in order to spare him as much as possible, yet intends to secure and chastise the whole person. If then Richard did this in order to spare the rest of Chapter, as we are sure both he and his fellow judges did, is it neither justice or humanity in you to persecute him because he spared you?

Then the Bishop reproves them, not only for raising this persecution against Richard but for giving it out that they had done it by way of revenge. 'Revenge,' saith our Prelate, 'is a spear in the hand of a madman, who runs himself thro the body with it in order to pierce the coat of him

---

[a] *Epist. Grosseteste*, 81.
[b] *Epist. Grosseteste*, 91 and 92.

who stands behind him. For none can hurt another but in his external good, or in those of the body, whereas by the very desire of revenge he wounds his own soul.' He also reproaches them with seeking the revenge in question by low underhand dealings. 'Who is Richard de Kirkham,' saith the Bishop, 'in comparison of your mightiness?'

> Is he not as a poor little fly, and you in comparison as an Eagle? It is vulgarly said, 'the Eagle doth not catch at flies; neither indeed is such a prey glorious to the Eagle.' Yet the same is glorious to the spider tho he cannot obtain it but by his invisible and treacherous webs. Such snares I hear you have laid for the Doctor in question. You do not proceed against him in the fair and open way of justice, but by the secret and insidious machinations of fraud and deceit, which our beloved son Thomas Archdeacon of Lincoln and John de Crachale can further explain to you.[123]

The Bishop concludes by exhorting them in a very tender and affectionate manner to detest and shun such low methods and so unbecoming men of their wisdom and reputation. In this and all the other letters on this affair, tho justice obliges the Bishop to give them sharp reproofs, yet the whole is mixed and sweetened with a wonderful charity and humility. He declares that his heart bears him witness that he hath a sincere affection for them all, and that baring some sudden and rugged expressions to some of their body, nothing in this whole proceeding could convict him of not having given them every demonstration possible of this his hearty love for them.

In 1241 the Chapter of Lincoln[a] being among other papers obliged to shew their original Charter granted by King William Rufus, whereby faults uncorrected by the Dean were to be carried to the Bishop, and from him to the King's Majesty, the King began to interfere in the cause betwixt the Chapter and their Prelate and issued forth the royal prohibition[b] to the ecclesiastick judges, not to go on with the cause in *Foro Ecclesiastico* [*ecclesiastical court*]. The King even assigned the parties a day for appearing before him in order to reconcile them. Grossetete knowing this prohibition could not be revoked, unless answered in some measure, procured the Chapter to be cited by the King to prosecute the prohibition. And altho they needed not to appear, such citations being only in the present case a formality of Law necessary for obtaining the suspension or revocation of the Royal prohibition, yet they appeared in Court but protested at the same time in the presence of the King and Bishop that it was not their intention to prosecute the prohibition in the King's Court. This they said because such prohibition of trying Ecclesiastick affairs in the Ecclesiastick Court being contrary to the canons

---

[a] *Chron. Maj.*, pp. 571 and 572.
[b] *Epist. Grosseteste*, 91.

as well as to the dictates of reason, the prosecution thereof would have rendered the Chapter obnoxious to the censures of the Church. Nevertheless our Prelate, accusing them of going against their own protestation by prosecuting in effect and in the eyes of the world what they protested against in words. Nay in his 91 letter, he charges them with being ever the contrivers of the Royal prohibition, only to ward off decision of the cause, and this in contradiction to the two conventions they had agreed to and to the letters which had passed on both sides for fixing a certain time for a final determination of the affair. And in his 92 letter he greviously suspects that their assiduous hovering about the Court was only to hinder the prohibition from being revoked, and that of course they were the occasion of the Lay-court's hindering ecclesiastical causes being tried in the ecclesiastical tribunal. Which if true, he declares to them, that they have incurred the sentence of excommunication fulminated by the Council of Oxford against the infringers of the Church's liberties. And had moreover violated the oath they had at Thame to stand sincerely to the convention there made.

In the mean time, the Bishop of Lincoln found himself obliged to excommunicate Nicholas the Chapter's Proctor.[124] On the Chapter's complaining thereof he tells them in his 94 letter, that this complaint very ill became them. They who had presumed to excommunicate his Dean, tho' noways under their jurisdiction (this must be the Dean of Christianity of Lincoln, and not the Dean of the Chapter, who with his capitulars was the excommunicator of the Dean in question). He adds moreover that if, as they seemed to threaten, they made application to the Chapter of Canterbury, (which during a vacancy of the See of Rome and Canterbury pretended to the reception of appeals made to Rome) they will only saddle themselves with a rider they will never be able get rid of. And thereupon he makes this sensible and religious expostulation with them.

> What hath kindled in the hearts of such wise men, this rage of opposing their father who only seeks, or at least believes he only seeks the salvation of his children, that for putting out one of his eyes, or perhaps not even one, they are bent upon putting out both their own? Would you rather be slaves to such as will Lord it over you, than children of a father who loves you? And will you drench yourself with poison only to make your father sup a few bitter drops, which tho bitter will be wholesome to him? For what can the monks of Canterbury do but only create us trouble and vexation in our defense of the common cause? Now such vexation how bitter soever shall be to us a wholesome potion, the cure of our infirmities, the improvement of our health, the clearing of our sight, the strengthener of our weakness and the perfecting of our imperfections. Whereas the same if administered to us by your contrivance, must have quite contrary effects in your regard. That then, which you threaten us with as your remedy, is so far from being any terror to us that it is our consolation. But as such a remedy cannot but be

> hurtful to you, whom we love as our children, we abhor the very thought of it and to hinder you from poisoning yourselves therewith we protest to you that in case you procure any sentence from the said monks, or by their authority attempt any thing against any of ours, we will most certainly cause you to be publickly denounced as excommunicates thro' our whole diocese.

This vigorous declaration deterred the Chapter from executing their threats of applying to that of Canterbury. And the Bishop of Worcester, the chief of the judges, having got off the Royal prohibition, the cause took its course in the ecclesiastick court and a day was fixed for a final hearing at Westminster.[a]

Before the appointed day came on, the Chapter or some of their abettors, had recourse to other threats so violent that Kirkham one of the judges, and the same who had been obliged to excommunicate some of their members, was afraid to appear. Upon which our Prelate wrote a pressing letter[b] to his friend Hugh Norwold [*Northwold*], the monastic Bishop of Ely in whose service Kirkham then was to send the said Doctor to him lest the cause of the salvation of souls, for which he had laboured so long, should now miscarry for want of one of the judges being present. He also wrote[c] to Kirkham himself, who had excused his presence for fear of ambushes either laid or threatened. To which the Bishop answers, that this rumor of ambushes was but an idle report set on foot to frighten him from appearing and that the authors of it durst not for ten thousand pounds offer to execute their threats. The Bishop sent him a safe-conduct as far as Daintree [*Daventry*] where he promised to meet him and take him up with himself to London. At the same time, our active Prelate, dispatcht another letter to the Bishop of Worcester exhorting him to put on the fortitude, as well as the meekness, of Moses and as he was going to sit as judge by delegation of the sovereign Pontiff, now to execute justice upon his refractory children and chastise them in a suitable manner for proving false to their conventions and oaths, as likewise for their illegal appeals and cavils. To this act of justice he urges Cantilupe so much the more pressingly as his delegateion expired after the day for this hearing at Westminster.

What the issue was at Westminster doth not now appear in our historical records; but in all appearance the Chapter was lost, and of course not being satisfied with the sentence appealed, as had been agreed, to the Pope in person. At least the Bishop of Lincoln, as did the new Dean Roger Wesham [*Weseham*], and some of the Chapter crossed the seas in 1244,[d] the Bishop within the octive of St Martin, i.e. in November, the

---

[a] *Epist. Grosseteste*, 98.
[b] *Epist. Grosseteste*, 96.
[c] *Epist. Grosseteste*, 97.
[d] *Chron. Maj*., p. 649.

Dean and capitulars soon after, according to Matthew Paris or a little before according to the *Annals of Dunstable*,[a] who adds that the Dean arrived before the Bishop at Lions, where the new Pope Innocent IV was also just arrived. However the Dean's cause was not the forwarder for his coming first. On the contrary, after a due hearing of the matter the Bishop obtained a sentence which recompensed him for all his labours and was so much the more acceptable to his ardent and extensive zeal as it decided not only his cause but of consequence, that of all the Bishops with regard to their several chapters. Hence in a letter addressed to the minister provincial of the English Franciscans, 'Blessed be God,' saith he, 'for that in the affair of the visitation sentence has been pronounced not only for us but consequently for all the prelates!'[b] In consequence of this decision his Holiness issued forth a bull, dated Lions the 24 of August in 1245,[c] which empowered the Bishop of Lincoln to visit the Dean and Chapter of Lincoln with all the churches depending on them, whether prebendal or parochial. And this visitation the Bishop executed the year following without any opposition.[d]

Besides the decree in favour of the visitation, the Bishop of Lincoln had a fair opportunity of cutting up the evil by one of its master-roots. Neither did he let it escape him. The present Dean, Roger Wesham being a scholar of singular merit and erudition, and notwithstanding the contest a particular favourite of Bishop Grossetete, the Bishop procured his promotion to the vacant see of Lichfield during his stay at Lions and accordingly Roger was consecrated by the Pope, together with Dr Richard de Wiche named to the see of Chichester, sometime in Lent 1245.[125] The vigilent Bishop of Lincoln profited of this vacancy of the deanery to detatch from it the rich prebend of Aislesbury, worth upwards of 400 marks,[e] which rendered the Dean too powerfull. He gave it to Robert de Mariscos,[f] his Archdeacon of Oxford, and official,[126] who was succeeded in it by that great philosopher William de Sherwode. This ended the Bishop's contest with his secular Chapter of Lincoln, which however his charity cherished ever after as much as if they had never given him any molestation so perfectly was peace and harmony restored betwixt them!

[a] *Dunstable annals*, pp. 266–67.
[b] *Epist. Grosseteste*, 114.
[c] *Chron. Maj.*, p. 688.
[d] *Dunstable annals*, p. 274.
[e] *Dunstable annals*, p. 398.
[f] *Chron. Maj.*, p. 661.

Chapter III

BISHOP GROSSETETE'S CONTROVERSY AND VICTORY OVER THE REGULAR CHAPTER OF CANTERBURY

While Bishop Grossetete's suit with his Chapter was carrying on another started up, which tho begun later, was sooner terminated. This second controversy, was with W. Abbot of Bardney,[127] one of the ancientist monasteries in the Kingdom, on the River Witham a little below Lincoln and incidently with the monastick Chapter of Canterbury. The Abbot of Bardney being in contest with Doctor Thomas the Welchman, Archdeacon of Lincoln, who[a] in 1234 [or] 2[b] endeavoured to make the said Abbot pay a debt of his predecessor's, the cause was brought by the Archdeacon before the Bishop. Thereupon the Abbot interjected an appeal, but the Bishop laid him under an excommunication, and Matthew Paris saith he did it in great wrath, as being an enemy to the privileges of regulars. But as the Bishop of Lincoln allowed of the just and authentick privileges, soe he was an enemy to pretended ones, and this as we have just seen as well in his own secular as in regular chapters. However the excommunicated Abbot appealed to the Chapter of Canterbury, which as Metropolitical Chapter pretended to a power of receiving appeals, *a gravamina*,[128] during the double vacancy of the sees of Canterbury and Rome. This pretension was opposed not only by the Bishop of Lincoln but by all the bishops of the realm who leagued themselves against the Kentish Chapter. Hence our Prelate, after appealing to the Holy See against the Abbot's appeal to Canterbury, deposed the refractory appealing Abbot. In the meantime, the Chapter of Canterbury received the Abbot of Bardney's appeal, and presumed even to excommunicate the Bishop of Lincoln with his fellow Bishop and quondam school-fellow Richard de Wendover, Doctor[c] of Theology of the University of Paris and now Bishop of Rochester.[129] On this sentence of the Chapter being notified to our Prelate, he took the paper and tramped it under his feet adding withal, if we believe Matthew Paris, these words. 'May these monks never pray for me any otherwise

---

[a] *Chron. Maj.*, p. 601.
[b] *Dunstable annals*, Hic.
[c] Bulaeus, *Historia Universitatis Parisiensis* (Paris, 1665).

(than by their excommunications).'[a] A saying more agreeable to Matthew's warm and satyrical temper, who makes the Bishop sometimes speak as himself would do in like occasion rather than to the character of our meek tho firm Prelate. However this be, the Bishop of Lincoln tho he thought himself noways tied[b] by this phantom of excommunication, and therefore[c] went on with his functions as usual, yet for fear some weak souls might be affrighted with it and the fruit of his ministry be frustrated, he applied to the Pope for remedy. The Pope in consequence transmitted his letters to the Chapter of Canterbury, whereby he declared that the reception of the appeals in question to belong immediately to the Holy See, and enjoined them *ad Cautelam* [*as a precaution*] to relax the sentence they had fulminated against our Prelate. The Pope's letter is dated from Anagnia [*Anagni*], the 23 of July in the first year of his Pontificate i.e. an. 1243. However favourable this letter was, yet as the order for the Chapter of Canterbury to relax the sentence *ad Cautelam* might leave room to think the Chapter capable at least of such a power, our penetrating Prelate demurred an admitting this seemingly ambiguous remedy and therefore wrote to a friend the late legate Otho, now with the Pope, his 110 letter in which he conjours him to sollicit of his Holiness some other remedy, more safe and more honourable to the episcopal character. In this letter to Cardinal Otho the judicious Lincoln represents in very strong terms the indiginity of the Chapter of Canterbury's pretensions, in assuming a jurisdiction over suffragans *sede vacante*, and presuming in consequence to suspend and excommunicate not only him but several of his fellow bishops. And how much such a pretention of the monks i.e. of persons by their state inferior to the least subdeacon in the Church must tend to vilify the episcopal order, if thus suffered to be exercised over them. Then he asserts, that altho the jurisdiction of the Archbishop of Canterbury, as bishop of his peculiar diocese might devolve upon the Chapter as his next and immediate members, which however saith he the Archdeacon of Canterbury will scarce allow, yet his jurisdiction as Archbishop, seeing he is Archbishop with regard to his suffragans, should rather devolve upon these last, if so be that it could descend to any inferior, and not rather return to the Holy See, to which all the suffragans are known to be immediately subject, and to receive their confirmation from it during the vacancy of the metropolictical see. Hence the learned Lincoln takes occasion to dilate upon the supereminency of the episcopal character and on the necessity of supporting it, adding that Christ himself made use of no greater power while upon Earth than

[a] *Dunstable annals*, pp. 258–59.

[b] *Epist. Grosseteste*, 110.

[c] *Chron. Maj.*, p. 602.

the episcopal and that the sovereign Pontiff hath no others, tho he be placed on the pinnacle of it and so enjoys the *plentitude of jurisdiction*, that from him all others receive the portion they possess. After which he subjoins this almost prophetick declaration and warning, 'Seeing the Episcopal authority here is not only tottering but almost threatened with ruin whether by the open assaults of the secular power and rebellion of the subject, or by the tumultuous and insidious machinations of such as endeavour to undermine it, there is just reason to fear that unless some solid stay be applied to underprop it the whole edifice of the English Church, which rests on the episcopal order as on its proper basis, must soon be exposed to some violent convulsion.' This seems a prophetick insight into the ecclesiastical revolution which happened three centuries after; when the episcopal body so long hampered in their jurisdiction by the excessive privileges of the regulars and impoverished by their numerous impropriations having lost all authority over them the religious grew in a manner incorrigible, and becoming obnoxious were crushed by the secular power. And the fall of this part of the church drew the whole edifice after it and so the whole fabrick fell because the basis of episcopal power, as our Prelate foresaw, was moved out of its place and almost annilated.

We hear no more of this incident controversy of our Prelate and his brother bishops with the Chapter of Canterbury, nor of the principal one with the Abbot of Bardney, whose appeal had given occasion to it, only that the King [*Henry III*], for a while at least, seemed to support the deposed Abbot. His majesty wrote to William de Compton, his guardian of the temporalities of the vacant Abbey of Bardeny, to treat the deposed Abbot, and his adherents, with more favour than his opponents and even to permit him, tho excommunicated by his Diocesan, free regress and ingress to the Church. Upon which the Bishop of Lincoln, dispatcht to the King his 102 letter, in which he shews both the generous liberty and the respectful address of an Ambrose, in writing like a person who knew the world and how to present disagreeable remonstrances in the most inoffensive manner. He tells the King he can scarely believe his Majesty can have given such an order, 'to treat rebels better than the obedient subjects, and because it might be objected that the former had justly rebelled against him their father and bishop he adds, that this ought not be lightly presumed till such time as the cause should be decided in the Ecclesiastick Court. That no power, which is not ecclesiastical, ought to think of opening the Church doors when shut by ecclesiastick authority and that such an act however coloured with the pretext of piety, was nothing better than the rashness of Oza presuming to support the falling Ark.'[130] He therefore concludes by begging, 'that if his Majesty's piety hath been surprised into this order, he would take care to see it speedily revoked.'

It may be presumed that so just a remonstrance had its proper weight with a Prince of Henry's good and religious dispositions, and who had moreover a great respect for the venerable and renouned writer of it.

Chapter IV

BISHOP GROSSETETE'S CONTROVERSY WITH SEVERAL OTHER RELIGIOUS ORDERS, CONCERNING PAROCHIAL CHURCHES BY THEM POSSESSED

The double victory which the knowing Prelate of Lincoln had gained over his own secular Chapter of Lincoln and the monastick Chapter of Canterbury encouraged him to labour in reducing under his jurisdiction all the churches of his diocese possessed by Regulars, whose possession and title thereunto was not confirmed as the canons require by the consent of his Cathedral Chapter, and that consent authenticated by proper instruments. On a complaint,[a] which he lodged to Pope Innocent IV, that some religious houses enjoyed the revenues and tithes of certain churches without having the Chapter of Lincoln's consent, his Holiness by a bull dated from Lions, the 14 of May, in the sixth year of his Pontificate i.e. in 1249, authorised him to recover all such churches and tithes and to compell by censures all such as opposed their recovery. On the reception of this bull, Bishop Grossetete issued forth an order to all religious of his Diocese, to meet him in three different places,[b] some at Stamford, some at Leicester and some at Oxford in order to hear the lecture of the Pope's bull and to comply with it by shewing their charters of foundation, the bishop's confirmation and the pope's priviledges. They met in the beginning of 1250 and he took copies of the whole in order to consult with the Pope about the contents; this was done the day after Ash Wednesday. While the generality submitted, some as the Templars, Hospitalers, and others found means to elude his zeal by appealing to the Pope as exempt, and backed their appeal, saith Matthew Paris,[c] with large presents, so little confidence had they in the cause itself! These the Bishop of Lincoln pursued to the Court of Innocent then at Lions about the middle of Lent following, but with little success as will be seen hereafter. This disappointment was however compensated in some measure by success in another attempt akin to this.

---

[a] *Chron. Maj.*, p. 772 et in additament p. 179.
[b] *Dunstable annals*, p. 287.
[c] *Chron. Maj.*, p. 773.

Not content with recovering such churches as were possessed by the regulars without an authentick title, he was moreover careful to make them discharge the obligations annexed to such as they were justly possessed of, and here he was supported by the same Pope who by a bull dated at Lions the 25 of September in the 8th year of his Popedom i.e. an. 1251, and received by Bishop Grossetete the next year,[a] empowered him to augment the vicarages of several parishes, which being appropriated either to collegiate or monastick churches had no fixed, at least no competent stipend, and so of course were but very ill served. This augmentation was taken off the revenues of the said colleges or monasteries, and so this wise regulation continued as long as our Prelate lived, tho' after his death some found means to get it reversed.[b] Matthew Paris saith, the Bishop of Lincoln was thought to have obtained this regulation more out of hatred to the regulars than out of love for the poor vicars; but the equity of the project, necessary for the due care of the churches in question, and for the good of the parishioners' souls, as well as the holy Bishop's character, are more than sufficient reasons for rejecting this injurious suspicion, rather related than confirmed by our censorious historian. After all if there were any ill will in the affair the curtailed regulars were more than up with him, if credit may be given to some historians who advance, upon what grounds I know not, that the Bishop was poisoned by them. Matthew Paris[c] indeed writes that our Prelate was once poisoned and only recovered by the help of the Dominican doctor, John de St Giles, but he doth not so much as hint who he was poisoned by, much less that he was poisoned by his religious adversaries and perhaps this is only a rash surmise of the Centuriators, or rather of him they often copy in their account of English affairs.[131] I mean John Bale, the apostate Carmelite, and one always ready to judge and believe any thing of religious, as thinking all others as bad as himself.

---

[a] *Chron. Maj.*, p. 840

[b] *Dunstable annals*, p. 312.

[c] *Chron. Maj.*, p. 974.

Book IV

Chapter I

BISHOP GROSSETETE'S CONTROVERSIES WITH THE KING AND POPE. GENERAL NOTION OF THESE CONTROVERSIES AND THEIR CAUSES

Hitherto we have viewed the Bishop of Lincoln confined as it were to his own Diocese. Now we are going to consider him in a larger field, and extending his zeal to the opposing of abuses, not only of his own church, but of the whole national Church of England. An opposition so much the more nice and difficult as the persons he had to struggle with were of the first and most formidable rank. I mean his two sovereigns, that of the state and that of the *Church*. But with all so much the more glorious to the opposer that in resisting he never exceeded the bounds of respect which he owed to their authority and thereby preserved their esteem, and confidence to the very last, even while he opposed their measures.

The expensive broils of the popes with the Emperor Frederick, and the no less expensive crusades for recovering of the holy land on the one hand, and on the other the lavish conduct and heavy wars of King [*Henry*] the III, had rendered the two powers, to use Matthew Paris's expression, like two heavy millstones, which ground the clergy and religious almost to nothing by the frequent and ample subsidies which their hard circumstances obliged them to raise.[a] Subsidies, which would appear incredible if not testified by the joint voices of our most faithfull monastick historians. Now these two millstones running frequently, if not continually one with the other it is almost impossible to separate the two articles which relate to the Crown and Tiara, especially in their general transactions. However there are some more private and particular controversies between the King and our strenuous and patriot Prelate, which are worth peculiar notice, and which we shall therefore premise before the general ones in which both potentates were jointly concerned.

These separable controversies of the Bishop of Lincoln with his Prince may be reduced to about six in number, viz the Legitimation of Special Bastards, the freedom of Canonical elections and promotions to Church benefices, the preservation of Ecclesiastick immunities, general

---

[a] *Chron. Maj.*, p. 709.

remonstrances against their violation and thereupon a withholding of subsidies. All points of no little moment, and therefore managed by our Prelate with a zeal and activity proportioned to their interesting nature, as we are going to see under so many distinct articles in the ensuing Chapter.

Chapter II

BISHOP GROSSETETE'S PARTICULAR CONTESTS WITH THE KING OR CROWN

The first controversy of the Bishop of Lincoln with the Crown was that regarding the *Legitimation of Special Bastards* i.e. of such children whose parents intermarry after the birth of the said Children.[132] Marriage being a mutual contract of the two sexes for an undivided society of life in order to the production, generation and education of the children. All conjunction of the two sexes without such contract is illicit and offspring of such conjunctions illegitimate, i.e. incapable of inheriting from their parents and of being admitted to holy orders or benefice without dispensation. But this incapacity, whether civil or sacred, being only a positive constitution either of the state or church, the Civil and Canon Laws take it away when the parents of such bastards intermarry, tho it be after the children's birth and restores the said children to their full right of inheriting etc. as much as if born in lawfull wedlock. And this the Canon and Civil Laws allow, not to encourage unlawful conjunctions, which the Church takes care to punish by her canons and penances, but only to make the best of an evil they would but cannot always prevent, *by* encouraging the delinquent parties to intermarry so to prevent the evil effects of their crime, whether upon their harmless offspring which without any fault of its own would suffer the penalty of disinherison, or upon the parties themselves, especially the woman whose dishonour might otherwise hinder her from being an useful and honest mother to the society and hurry her into worse crimes. Or finally upon the contract of marriage of which such hasty anticipation of marriage rites are, or ought to be, deemed an intentional pledge; but a pledge whose effect remains suspended if the contract be not allowed and encouraged to follow, at least where it ought to have proceeded. In opposition to this prudent disposition of the Civil and Canon Laws the laudable Municipal, or Customary Laws of England, more attentive to preserve the purity and holiness of Christian matrimony unstained than to prevent the ill effects of its violation, would not allow of the legitimation approved by the Imperial and Pontifical Laws, but left such bastards whose parents married after their birth in the same state of illegitimacy as they were in before the subsequent marriage of their parents. In consequence of this Customary Law or practice of England our Prelate before he was well seated in his episcopal chair, received as did the other prelates a royal brevet ordering the bishops to signify to the Court whether such and such persons were born before or after the marriage contract of their parents and supposing withall that the children born before the contract were in a state of illegitimacy, whether as to Civil or Ecclesiastick effects. William de Raley, Treasurer of Exeter, and Bishop Grossetete's special friend, being then Judge of the Prerogative Court where such causes were tried, the Bishop of Lincoln addressed to him his 23 letter, asserting that the subsequent contract of marriage has the force and power of legitimating children, not only conceived, but even born before the marriage contract and that of course, the judges who disinherit them as illegitimate act unjustly. And it must be confessed that the Doctor of Lincoln argues for his assertion with great strength, or at least plausibility of reason, whether from the Divine, Canon, or Civil Laws; or from the more ancient custom of the realm. From the Divine Law laid down in the Old Testament, he reasons thus.

> The present and mutual consent of Jacob and his wives Rachel and Liah who had given their handmaids to their husbands rendered the children of the handmaids legitimate, so as to inherit with those of his wives. Now if the present consent of Jacob and his wives could legitimate the children of another womb, why may not subsequent contract of intermarrying parents legitimate the fruit of their own proper wombs? Nay, and which is less than mutual consent of the parties even the marital affections of Thamar, and her right to children from Judah's third son, rendered legitimate the fruit conceived unlawfully of her father-in-law Judah, and her two sons, Pheres and Zara, inherited as lawfull sons of Judah, in the division of the promised land.[133] Now if even such marital affection and right had the force of legitimating incestuous children, how much more hath the mutual subsequent consent of the intermarrying parents a like force upon children conceived in a less criminal manner? Moreover, by virtue of the marriage contract between the blessed Virgin and St Joseph, St Joseph was lawfull spouse of the Virgin, and lawful father of Jesus, tho not in a carnel sense. Yet in a true sense, in as much as Jesus was born of his lawful wife in a lawful manner, and Jesus of course was lawful heir to Joseph, had Joseph had anything heritable to leave. If then the mutual consent of the parties legitimated a son, noways begotten by his lawful father, why should not a subsequent contract have a like force to legitimate children naturally begotten? Here then we see a present consent asserting its force as I may say collaterally upon the fruit of another womb and upon the fruit formed by another parent. Why hath not the like consent of the parties a similiar power to retract upon its own natural offspring?

After this reasoning upon those scripture-facts, and some other physical reasons drawn from natural history, he proves the same from Canon and Civil Laws, which being well known he's short upon that article, and then adds for a last proof from the more ancient customs of the Realm. According to which, as the Bishop saith he had learnt from the testimony of his ancients, the children of such parents as intermarried after their birth were used at their parents' subsequent marriages to be put under the cloak, or veil, which covered their parts during the marriage ceremony as a sign of their now being reputed their lawful offspring.[a134]

From all this the Bishop concludes, that the opposite practice of his time was contrary to all laws and that princes adhering to it, contrary to all laws of the Church, separate themselves from the Church, and what is still more observable he adds that they forfeit even their temporal authority, which he pretends that kings receive and hold of the Church. For this last opinion, Dr Browne declares that Lincoln hath more to say than all the school doctors that have come after him. Without adopting this opinion of Lincoln, which was fashionable in his age, or Browne's judgment concerning the relative merits of his proofs, we shall hereafter give the reader his reasons in a more convenient place and for the present not to interrupt our main question shall only add the conclusion he draws from them which is this, that seeing the prince cannot make laws contrary to the laws of the Church, but to his own eternal perdition and to the forfeiture of his temporal authority. Raley ought, as well for the King's good as for the discharge of his own conscience, to persuade his Majesty to abrogate as he calls it, iniquitous law.

In answer to this letter, Raley after some ironical slings at the length of it, and at the Bishop's skill in all kinds of laws, intrenchs himself and the practice of the Crown, in the testimony of Richard de Lucy who saith that a bastard placed under the cloak of his parents during the marriage ceremony comes out as true a bastard as when he went in. This Richard de Lucy was an eminent lawyer and justicar of England under Henry II and a great stickler[b] for the articles of Clarendon against St Thomas, in whose honour he nonetheless founded a Church at Westwode in the diocese of Rochester.[c135] But our Prelate asketh what comparison, between the single assertion of Richard de Lucy and the opposite testimonies of the Divine and Canon and Civil Laws? Raley added that this custom was allowed by the Pope, to which the Bishop replieth, that all things allowed by the Pope are not therefore lawfull because his Holiness tolerates many things, as Moses tolerated divorce among the Jews, because of the hardness of men's hearts.

How reasonable soever these remonstrances might be they had little or no effect, and not only the Court persisted to adhere to this Municipal Law, but our Prelate received a particular order from the King and Council injoining him as often as any exceptions of bastardism was put in against

---

[a] Thus were legitimised the sons of Richard I, Duke of Normandy by Gunnor. See, William Genet. Lib. 8, c. 36, Opus Pontoppida, *Hist. Danica*, pp. 330–31, Citus Ducheus, 'Earl of Genet'.

[b] *Dunstable annals*, p. 31.

[c] Randulph Diceto inter X Script, p. 600.

any of his diocescans for being born before the marriage contract to make inquisition in the Court Ecclesiastick whether such persons excepted against were born before or after the contract; and to write back to the King under this form, that such an one was born before the solemn contract of marriage, or that he was born after the said contract.[a] The Bishop of Lincoln however demurred answering an injunction as contrary to his own conviction, as to the Laws of the Church, and was therefore cited to appear in the King's Court to tell the reasons of his demur, the King and Council, having in their summons signified that St Edmund, Archbishop of Canterbury had consented to this form of inquisition and rescript, together with all the bishops, earls and barons of England. The Bishop of Lincoln wrote to his holy and learned Primate desiring him first to let him know whether he had really consented thereto, as was pretended in the royal summons, and if he had, then what he would advise him to do. 'For if I write to the King,' saith he, 'according to the form prescribed, I dread falling into the hands of the living God. And if I refuse to do it, while you acquiesce thereto, then it seems difficult for me to escape falling in to the hands of men. Unless therefore your prudent advice can rescue me from these inconveniences I shall chose without hesitation to fall into the hands of men out of which God can deliver me, rather than into the hands of God out of which there's no one that can deliver.' This letter as appears by the contents was written after the first autumn from his election, consequently either in the end of 1235, or the beginning of 1236.

How the Bishop got out of this slippery step doth not appear. However its very certain the Crown did not rescind the custom in question, of bastardising children, notwithstanding the subsequent marriage of their parents.[b] The prelates sought to get it abolished in the Council of Merton in the beginning of 1236.[136] 'All the earls and barons,' saith the Parliament roll, 'answered with one voice, that they would not change the laws of England which had been hitherto used and approved.' And Sir Thomas More offers that the Spirituality were never able to carry this point tho' they that had all laws on their side,[c] and it must be acknowledged that this ancient Municipal Law of England, tho contrary to the Canon and Civil Law, is well calculated for preserving marriage holy and spotless by punishing its violators with disinherison of the first fruit of their criminal love.[137] This law would be still more perfect and consequent if the punishment reached not only to those born before the contract of marriage but even to those who are evidently conceived before it. For

[a] *Epist. Grosseteste*, 26; et Blackstone, *Law Tract*, vol. 2, p. 84.
[b] Blackstone, *Law Tract*, vol. 2, p. 42; Ex statut Merton, vol. 2, pp. 83–89.
[c] More, *Supplication of Souls*, p. 301.

certainly the prime, nay the only, stain and offence against the sanctity of matrimony is in the illicit generation and conception of such children and not in their birth. Till this law be thus far extended it will be always liable to the objection of inconsequence not to say self contradiction; for if a base birth can render children illegitimate, notwithstanding the subsequent contract of their parents, how much more ought a base conception to have the like effect inspite of a contract, which tho anterior to the harmless birth is posterior to the criminal conception? And if a contract of the parties, subsequent to the criminal conception tho prior to the birth of the offspring, can wipe off the stain of illegitimacy from a base conception why by an exact parity of reason may not a contract posterior to the birth of the child purge away the stain of illegitimacy from a base birth? If the contract hath a retroaction with regard to conception, which is the origin of the stain, why not also with regard to the harmless birth? Whatever advantage therefore the Municipal Law may have in being well calculated for preventing illicit conjunctions by its wholesome severity upon the base offspring, this seems more than sufficiently counterbalanced by the disposition of the Canon and Civil Law, in the double advantage of being firstly more consequent and coherent, and secondly of being better adapted to prevent the mischief of unlawful conjunctions.

In considering this opposition of the Municipal Law to the Canon and general law of the Church, and the seeming advantages of the Church Law over the Municipal, some may be apt to wonder why this Municipal Law, which is owing to our Catholick ancestors, should have been tolerated by the Church, but the wonder will cease if they reflect upon one incontestable principle justified by the constant and universal practice of all ages, viz, that the Church in making general laws of discipline doth not offer to molest but rather leaves particular Churches, in the profession of their ancient and rational, tho opposite, customs. Such assuredly this Municipal Law is, whose severity upon base offspring of unlawful embraces, is a very just preservative of the integrity of matrimony.

The next controversy the Bishop of Lincoln had with the King was not so much against the standing and ancient customs of the Crown, as against the notorious and avowed abuses of the Court-practice, in regard of canonical elections and promotions to benefices. In 1239, the church of Hereford falling vacant by the retreat of its most learned[a] and pious Bishop Ralph [*Robert*] de Maydestone and his entering *among the* Franciscans, the Bishop of Lincoln like a watchful sentinel, and faithfull guardian of the Church, seized this opportunity to write a letter to his Primate St Edmund, concerning the necessity of supporting the freedom

[a] *Chron. Maj.*, p. 354.

of canonical elections and of opposing the encroachments of the Court, whereby not only the Church was enslaved, but the flock either left without pastor or only provided of a nominal one and often of a wolf instead of a pastor. He therefore urges the holy Primate to begin the application of the remedy at the approaching election of a Bishop of Hereford and for this end to write to the Chapter of that church a persuasive letter on the necessity of chosing a proper pastor without fearing any threats that should be made to intimidate them or suffering themselves to be cajoled out of their duty. He presses him at the same time to send his deputies to Hereford to see if all things be done in order, and with the freedom exhibited by the Charter of King John and confirmed by the late Pope Innocent [*III*] of holy memory. To apologise for this writing to his Primate, he concludes by telling him that he hath not done it with a view *to light the sun with his small taper*, but only to applauding him and animating him in his conflicts for the Church. This letter had so far effect that the canons of Hereford seem to have been free in their election of Peter de Egueblank, since Matthew Paris observes that the King, 'admitted his election *without contradiction*', and this prelate became a particular associate to Bishop Grossetete in some zealous acts, tho otherwise no fortunate counsellor to the King.[138]

The year 1241, saw another contest betwixt the King and our Prelate on the same article of canonical promotions. Bishop Grossetete had named Simon de London,[a] penitentiary to the Bishop of Durham, to the rich prebend of Thame in Oxfordshire. Soon after his Majesty by virtue of a papal provision put one of his own chaplains, John Maunsel [*Mansel*] in possession of the said prebend. The King being in Wales, where he had defeated David, son of Lewellen [*Llywelyn*] about the month of August our prelate deputed two of his Archdeacons, the famous John de Basingstoke, Archdeacon of Leicester and William Archdeacon of Huntington, to beg of his Majesty that out of gratitude to God for his victory and for fear God should turn his joy into mourning, he would revoke Maunsel's intrusion into the prebend of Thame. The King's answer was that he had acted by advice of his lawyers and by authority from the Holy See. The deputies replied thereto that their master had an express priviledge from the same Holy See authorising him to reject any papal provision that doth not contain an express derogation to his said priviledge, and there being no such derogation in Maunsel's provisions, the Bishop was not obliged to have any regard to them, especially as he had already precollated to the church of Thame. The deputies added, that even tho their master had no such priviledge it was against reason that any one tho armed with a papal provision should be intruded into any church of his Diocese

[a] *Chron. Maj.*, p. 570; *Dunstable annals*, p. 252.

without his consent, because the Pope always supposes his provisions shall be executed in a canonical way. That there was however no necessity of making a breach, since their master, as well out of respect to his Majesty's recommendations as to Maunsel's personal merit, was ready to name him to an equal, or even to a richer benefice, that should first fall vacant. They concluded by saying that their master begged of his Majesty with all respect and humility not to proceed any otherwise, for that he was ready to fulminate a sentence of excommunication against every invader of the Church's rights and liberties. Thereupon Maunsel offered to quit claim. But the King deferred for the present his final answer. His Majesty returning to London soon after the Bishop went up to town fully determind to excommunicate the intruded Royal Chaplain, and all other infringers of the Church's liberties. Which as soon as Maunsel heard, he ran to the King and begged he might renounce his claim, fearing least the Bishop, who was of a vigorous temper, saith Matthew Paris, and ready to make his threat good should exclude him from all future provision in his diocese, which being at that time the largest in the Kingdom had the most benefices to bestow, and accordingly Maunsel actually quitted his claim and thus, as the *Annals of Dunstable* word it, the Bishop honorably recovered the prebend of Thame. The Bishop of Lincoln being desired shortly after to preach before his Majesty, which his profound science and ready utterance, saith Matthew Paris, enabled him to perform at all times, he took occasion in his sermon to commend his Majesty's, and his Chaplain's, moderation and humility at the same time to give proof of his readiness to oblige his Prince in all that was orderly. He, on his Majesty's intercession, yielded up the Church of Heswele [*Heswell or Ashwell*] to the Abbot of Westminster, with whom he was in contest about the said Church only reserving to himself and to his successors the priviledge of providing for the cure of souls in the nomination of a vicar.[139]

In wrestling with the King, our Prelate was sometimes under, and sometimes over. In 1249, or the beginning of 1250,[a] one Ranulph clergyman in the county of Rutland was convicted of incontinence and deprived of his benefice by our disciplinarian Prelate and on refusing to submit was laid under an excommunication. The delinquent remaining forty days under sentence without suing for pardon, the Bishop pursuant to law, signified to the sheriff to apprehend Ranulph as contumacious. But the Sheriff who was Ranulph's friend, either refused to obey the orders or dallied in the execution. Upon which the vigorous Lincoln laid him under the same censures. The Sheriff applying to the King, and the King to the Pope. His Holiness in a bull addressed to the Abbot of Westminster forbid the Bishop and other prelates to excommunicate any of the King's officers

[a] *Chron. Maj.*, p. 777.

for not answering their summons and for refusing to plead before them in matters belonging to the King's Court, (such as the neglect of a bodily arrest of a spiritual contumacy). This bull, which tied our Prelate's hands, is dated the 9 of March in the 7th year of his Holiness's pontificate i.e. in the beginning of the year 1250.

The Bishop seems to have been more successful in his next controversy with the King. The King having given to the Queen the ward of the minor son of Ralph de Thony [*Richard de Thiony*]. After Easter[a] of the year 1252, her Majesty, by virtue of her wardship, named her own Chaplain, William to the church Flamstede [*Flamstead*] near St Albans, worth a hundred marks.[140] The King disapproving the Queen's nomination, put in one of his own clerks named Haroldus [*Hurtold*], a foreigner and a Burgundian which as soon as the Bishop was apprised of he excommunicated Haroldus for his uncannonical intrusion and laid the church under an interdict.

Another article wherein the Bishop of Lincoln had to deal with the secular power were the *Ecclesiastick Immunities*, which he supported against the encroachments of the Crown. These encroachments were drawing ecclesiastick persons, or causes, into the Lay Court, contrary to the standing and approved laws of the Realm. Some of these infringments of the Church's immunities were in criminal, some in civil matters, of both which our Prelate was a zealous defender.

On St Gregory's day i.e. 12 of March in the end of the year 1237, Cardinal Otho the Pope's Legate being at Osney near Oxford, a quarrel arose betwixt the students and the Legate's officers in which the Legate's Clerk of the Kitchen happened to be killed.[b] On a complaint lodged to the King by his Eminence several of the students were arrested, carried up to London and committed, contrary to their priviledge which was to be judged in the Bishop's Court. Hence in a council held at London[c] about June 1238 the King and Legate being both present, the Bishop of Lincoln stood up for the priviledge of the scholars, without pretending however to justify their violence, and excommunicated in the King and Legate's presence all those who had laid violent hands on the imprisoned clerks whereby he got them released and given up to him. The King and Legate disavowing what had been done as not done by their orders. Six years[d] after this quarrel, happened another in the same place, on the 25 of March 1244, betwixt the students of the University and the Jews of Oxford. The students, on what provocation is not said, broke open the houses of the Jews and carried off their goods in great quantity for

[a] *Chron. Maj.*, p. 839.
[b] *Chron. Maj.*, p. 460; *An. Burt.*, p. 290; *Wykes*, hic.
[c] *Concilia Magne*, B. 1. hic.
[d] *Wykes*, hic.

which several of the scholars were cast into prison, but on our Prelate's interposition they were set at liberty because nobody appeared that could directly convict them of felony. The Bishop's zeal did not rest here, but to secure the clergy from like violence hereafter he engaged Robert de Marisco his official and Archdeacon of Oxford, to make an extract of the clergy's immunities out of the body of the Canon Law wherein were specified the particular cases in which the clergy falls under the secular jurisdiction or are exempt from it. This extract may be seen in the *Annals of Burton*.[a]

Besides these encroachments in criminal cases there were others of the civil kind such as putting Ecclesiasticks or religious men into secular offices which rendered them accountable to the Lay Court. These our strenuous Prelate opposed because of a double inconvenience, as being not only contrary to the immunities of the Church but still more to the character of ecclesiasticks or religious men. By a brief of the 4 of May 1236, King Henry appointed the Benedictine Abbot of Ramsey, one of his justices for the Counties of Bedford and Bucks, in conjunction with Robert de Lexinton [*Lexington*], Oliver de Vallibus, and John de Hulecot[*e*].[141] The Abbot of Ramsey being our Prelate's diocesan, the Bishop wrote immediately to his Primate St Edmund, to get this commission reversed as contrary to the canons, to the immunities of the Church and, above all, to the monastick profession and to the Holy Scriptures which forbid persons devoted to the service of God to engage in secular business.[b] And lest the King should insist upon his commission once given out, our Prelate desires his Metropolitan's advice, what he is to do and whether he ought not to restrain the Justice-Abbot by laying him under censures? 'For if here we do not oppose ourselves,' saith he.

> By thus restraining the Abbot from executing the said office, we shall beyond all doubt incur the reproach of the prophet Ezechiel, 'You have not gone up to face the enemy neither have you set up a wall for the house of Israel to stand in battle in the day of the Lord.'[c] As also that other reproach of the Canon Law. 'An error that is not resisted is approved.' On the other hand, if we do oppose ourselves thereto then the Royal officers will perhaps invade and pillage our temporalities, and no such opposition having been hitherto made in these parts we shall become the scorn and fable of the wise ones of the world. On both sides then we are threatened with dangers, here with temporal there with eternal. But as no temporal danger, how great soever, can bear any proportion with the least part of an eternal one, but is rather a mere nothing in the comparison, it shames me to have asked counsel since this is only necessary in doubtfull cases, and to have said there's danger on

---

[a] *An. Burt.*, p. 398.
[b] *Epist. Grosseteste*, 27.
[c] Ezk. 13:5.

> both sides, since what is here called temporal danger is in reality no danger at all but rather an advantage to him who forgets what is behind him, and only stretches himself forward to the things which are before. We therefore conjure you with all humility and affection to give us your command in this point, that foregoing all dangers and losses for the liberty of the Church and for the rescuing of souls from eternal fire, we may thro God's assistance, oppose ourselves with all our little might against the abuse in question. For even my pusillanimity, when armed with the orders of your prudence and fortitude, will be able thro the divine help to stand in your strength against every assault of malice. But without such a support it will be easily overthrown by the opposition of the wicked.

This opposition[a] of the Bishop of Lincoln, was resented by the King as an attack upon his crown and royalty and occasioned his giving out great threats. And therefore by the advice of wise and discreet counsellors, St Edmund wrote back to him, advising him to dissemble for a while till a council was held which then approached. But the intrepid Lincoln, whose courage instead of falling rather rose at the sight of dangers wherever the good of souls was interested, wrote immediately to his Primate and desired his categorical answer, whether abbots acting as justices, or clerks answering personal actions in the lay court, sinned or not? And whether their prelates permitting them to go on till further remedy was sought in council were not by such toleration guilty of violating the canons? For in this last case he was ready to sacrifice all considerations to that of duty, if in so doing they do not sin then we may tolerate patiently what they do.

> But if they sin, then how can your Grace and I, who are obliged to sacrifice ourselves for them, be guiltless unless we endeavour out of hand to prevent their sinning? Or can we let them tumble into the precipice of sin in order to draw them out with more deliberation? Far be this from bishops and pastors of souls who as you know well, and have often divinely taught, ought to sacrifice all temporal things and undergo the most cruel and ignominious of death, even a thousand times over rather than commit so much as one single sin. Neither can the sin of bishops be light or moderate in the present case, especially if by doing such things or permitting others to do them they run counter to the ordinance of the canons and decretal epistles. Seeing that at their consecration they solemnly promise, and that with oath, to receive, teach and observe the traditions of the orthodox Fathers and the constitutions of the Holy See apostolick.

He therefore concludes, by exhorting the holy Primate to fortitude in confidence that Almighty God hath put him under the special protection of his predecessor the invincible martyr St Thomas. The issue of these zealous efforts doth not appear now. It is however certain the King did not abstain from giving out such commissions to religious men. In 1239 his

---

[a] *Epist. Grosseteste*, 28.

Majesty issued forth one of them to Richard, Abbot of Croyland, another of our Prelate's diocesans.[142] Upon which our Prelate, seeing his former application to St Edmund ineffectual, applied to the Pope's Legate Cardinal Otho, to provide some remedy against this abuse which he stigmatises as an abomination equally contrary to the Divine and Canon Laws, and to very nature of the monastick profession.[a] But whether this application had more effect than the former is not very clear. Clear however it is, that either by this application to the Legate, or by a more immediate one to the Pope himself, he procured a special mandate from Rome, and made it one of his Diocesan Statutes, *forbidding all ecclesiasticks, and all in holy orders, to exercise such secular employment for the future.*

As the Bishop of Lincoln was against those in holy orders meddling with secular offices, so he would not admit to holy orders, or to benefices, such as continued in them.[b] Robert de Passelewe, one of the King's Chaplains, and Justice of the Royal Forests, being presented to the Church of St Peters in Northampton, Bishop Grossetete refused him institution tho recommended, if not presented by the King. Because the said Robert, after several charitable admonitions whether of his own ordinary or of our Prelate, refused to quit his secular employ which engaged him to apprehend, imprison and condemn the delinquents with effusion of blood. Lest however his Majesty should resent his refusal, the Bishop introduces it with a little dissertation on the necessity of union and concurrence between the Empire and the Priesthood, assuring him that far from doing any thing either directly or indirectly to loosen the bond of this union, as some had suggested to his Majesty in his disfavour, he desired nothing so much as to see both powers go hand in hand and all things done by them in an orderly manner. After which he adds this judicious piece of advice, that for compassing so desirable an end, 'Ecclesiastick affairs should be treated by ecclesiasticks and secular affairs by secular persons, as military affairs are by military men. And all corrections and reformation of abuses regarding the state should be effected by secular persons, well skilled and practised in the laws of the Realm.' Whence he concludes, that Robert, refusing to quit his secular office, he was obliged to refuse him institution which he could not grant without transgressing the laws of God and his Church, and prevaricating against the profession he had made at his consecration.

The King in his letter to our Prelate, had put him a question about the meaning of the regal unction and what it added to the regal dignity. To this he answers, that by the sevenfold gifts which that unction signifieth it gives greater grace, and of course brings greater obligation on

---

[a] *Epist. Grosseteste*, 82.

[b] *Epist. Grosseteste*, 124 and 126; *Chron. Maj.*, p. 840 etc.

the anointed. But not any power to do the priestly functions nor any equality with the priestly power, and this he proves from the example of King Ozias, punished for setting his hand to the priestly censer.[143] And from these words of the Patriarch Judas, 'The Lord hath given to me the kingdom, and to Levi the Priesthood, and hath subjected the Empire to the Priesthood. To me he hath entrusted the things of the Earth, but to him the things of heaven.'[144] Browne desires to know where this is written in Scripture and had Browne been as conversant in the Bishop of Lincoln's works, as he is peevish and ready to find faults, even in his heroe, he would have found the saying in the *Testament of Judas* among the *Testaments of the 12 Patriarchs*, which Grossetete had procured and translated from the Greek in 1242. Whence it is plain this letter and the transaction it refers to is posterior to that year. This reply of Bishop Grossetete to the King, whether for refusing his chaplain institution, or for vindicating the Church's immunities, left some little resentment in his Majesty's mind which the Prelate endeavoured to remove in his 125 letter. And there he expresses his hopes of dispersing this cloud in a personal conference, in which he proposed to wait on his Majesty.

In the mean time the official of Canterbury being applied to, either by the presentee, or his presenter, and overawed by threats, wrote to our Prelate that within eight days after the reception of his mandates he *had* to institute the said Robert to the church in question, otherwise he should be obliged to execute the same himself, according to his office. But the Bishop wrote back to the official with equal firmness and affection, giving him the same reasons for his refusal as he had given to the King and letting him know withall that the official's power to correct the suffragans extended only to cases where the suffragans neglected their duty, which blessed be God was not this case. His refusal here being entirely grounded on all laws divine and human. He sent another letter[a] at the same time to Archbishop Boniface, who had succeeded St Edmund anno. 1243 conjuring him not to suffer his official to obstruct his suffragans in the just and conscientious discharge of their duty. The Bishop of Lincoln had so much the more reason to apply to the Archbishop, and the Archbishop to receive his application, as the Archbishop had applied to our Prelate against the said Robert in 1244, when Robert being elected to the see of Chichester for which he was very unfit.[b] The Archbishop and other prelates found no surer means to make his election void than to recommend the examination of his capacity to the Doctor of Lincoln; who accordingly examined him so thoroughly and set forth his ignorance in so clear a light that he was presently declared *incapax*, and another

[a] *Epist. Grosseteste*, 126.
[b] *Chron. Maj*., p. 652.

elected in his place more worthy, viz the illustrious Doctor and Professor of the Pontifical Laws, St Richard de Wiche. There was like reason for not admitting him to the present cure of souls which tho inferior to a Bishoprick, was no less incompatible with his unecclesiastick and secular life. This opposition and letters of our Prelate seems to have had a good effect upon Passelewe, who in 1249 quitted the Court, as Matthew Paris saith, in detestation of its wretched intrigues. About the same time, our Prelate had a little contest with the King's Justices, Robert de Lexinton and others. Henry de Lexinton,[145] Dean of Christianity in Lincoln, having denounced to the said Justices not to try causes of blood on a Sunday, was imprisoned by them contrary to the rights of immunities of the Church. In support of his Dean's religious opposition, the Bishop of Lincoln wrote his 84 letter to the said Justices, and conjured them, if the rumour of this fact were true – for he civilly doubts of it, first to abstain from such unreasonable and unlawful practices on the Lord's day, and second to remember that if the Dean had been as faulty as he was commendable for his opposition, his trial and punishment was out of the boundaries of their jurisdiction. This must have happened either in or before the year 1250,[a] in which Robert de Lexinton, left this world where he had been judge of men, to be judged by the Judge of judges themselves.

In fine, the encroachments of the Court upon the Church's immunities were so many and so heavy at this time that the Bishop of Lincoln drew up a general list of them, related by the Burton Annalist under the year 1258,[b] when they were renewed in the national Council of Merton. These complaints are to the number 18, the substance whereof is that the King tramples upon all the rights and priviledges of the clergy by hauling them to his tribunal in cases excepted therefrom, as well by the laws of the Realm, as by the canons. That Episcopal sees and religious houses falling when vacant under the royal custody, the King contrary to the end of the said custody, which is to guard and protect them, enormously diminishes their revenues, and racks the poor tenants with intolerable burthens. That whereas the bishops and archdeacons cannot perform their respective visitations nor take sufficient information, whether concerning persons or causes, without the tender of an oath, the King forbids the bishops and archdeacons to tender and the laity to make the requisite oath to the total hinderance of the pastoral charge, and to the ruin of many souls under their care. That in presenting and collating to benefices with cure of souls, which ought to be levelled at their eternal welfare, the King by prayers and entreaties, equivalent to commands made sword in hand, forces both the presenters and collators, the one to present the other to

---

[a] *Chron. Maj.*, p. 786.
[b] *An. Burt.*, p. 396.

accept such persons whose ignorance, sloth or disorderly manners render them incapable of the office. And thereby his Majesty loads himself with the guilt of three spiritual murders. First of his own soul, second of those he thus recommends, third of the poor flock who have the misfortune to fall under such wretched pastors. That altho it belongs only to bishops to institute or destitute parochial rectors, the King, Ozias-like puts his hand to the censer and gets up and takes down, whom he pleases. That in his progress thro the realm he takes up his abode in religious houses and lives upon them, he and his retinue, to their grevious prejudice. For which it is no excuse to say, it is at the petition of the said houses, because such petitions are not free but sollicited and extorted by fear. That when the bishops call in the assistance of the secular arm and the King issueth forth his writs to the sherriffs, to be aiding and assisting in the apprehension of contumacious excommunicates. The said sheriffs for the most part dissemble such orders, to the utter overthrow of Church discipline. In fine, that whereas it is the King's glory and prerogative to rule his subjects with lenity and justice, that so they may lead a quiet and undisturbed life according to the charters established for that purpose, his Majesty scarce observes any one article of the said charters. The date of these complaints is not fixed, but they are probably of the end of his episcopacy as they seem consequent to his many particular fruitless oppositions against the like abuses. A like list of complaints had been put up to the King by the Lords Spiritual and Temporal in a council held at London within the octave of the Epiphany of the year 1240,[a] accusing his Majesty of oppressing the Church, especially in keeping churches a long while vacant and infringing the liberty of canonical election. But then these, as Matthew Paris writes, were about 30 in number and probably the same as the 24 greviances[b] which the clergy presented to the Pope's Legate in 1238, with an earnest petition that he would sollicit a redress from the King. Whereas those of our Prelate are only to the number of 18, and by their *heaviness* of the complaint seem a general repetition of what had been already done in several particulars without success.

In fine, a last article of contest between the strenuous and patriot Lincoln and his Prince was the delicate article of subsidies, in which his opposition was so much the more honourable as it regarded not only the ecclesiastick body but the body politick of the nation and people of England.

In the year 1244[c] King Henry demanded a subsidy for defraying his late expedition into Gascony, and an intended one against the Scots.

---

[a] *Chron. Maj.*, p. 523.
[b] *An. Burt.*, p. 290.
[c] *Chron. Maj.*, p. 639.

The Lords Spiritual and Temporal then assembled in the refectory of Westminster Abbey, referred the demand to a committee consisting of 12 members of their own body, four of which were bishops and one of the bishops our zealous Lincoln. The committee, of which our Prelate was the soul, was for an absolute refusal of the subsidy till such time as the King should redress several grievances of the Church and State; especially the neglect to execute the Charter of Liberties and the ill employment of subsidies already granted. The King's main aim was to win over the clergy and therefore he produced the Pope's letter to them for assisting his Majesty. But the Temporal Lords, without whose consent nothing was to be concluded, having withdrawn from Parliament the bishops delayed giving in their final answer. Upon which the King sent his deputies to them and at length came himself begging, blustering and swearing, as his custom was. Some were for returning his Majesty a more favourable answer than that already given but stout Lincoln cried out! 'Let us not be divided in counsel, since it is written, "that if we are divided, we are lost."' This vigour struck spirit into the whole body and the final answer to the King and Pope's demand was put off as the temporality had desired, till three weeks after Candlemas and so the convocation broke up. Nor did they grant the subsidy at their next meeting; but on certain conditions and especially that his Majesty, who had so often promised and so often broke his promise, should give his solemn royal word, faithfully to observe the charters.

In 1252,[a] on the feast of St Edward's translation i.e. the 13 of October, the King in a parliament then sitting at London demanded in virtue of a papal mandate, a tenth of all ecclesiastick revenues for the space of three years and this not according to the ancient evaluation, but according to a new one to be made by the King's officers. When the King's deputies came to the bishops with their demand they began by exacting two years payment out of hand, and the third before the King's departure for the Holy Land, slily [*slyly*] supposing the consent of the House to the grant itself. But the Bishop of Lincoln, who had not forgot his logick, cried out, 'By Our Lady, what is this? You go upon premises ungranted? Think you we shall ever acquiesce to this wretched exaction? God forbid we should thus bend the knee to Baal?' 'Father,' said the young Bishop of Wincester to our Prelate. 'How shall we be able to stand our ground, against both the King and the Pope since one pushes and the other hauleth? The French have consented to a like subvention for their King on his departure for the East. Now they are stronger than we, and more accustomed to resist. How then can we hope to make an effectual opposition?' 'For this very reason,' said Lincoln. 'We aught to oppose it

[a] *Chron. Maj.*, p. 849 et *Annal Burton*, p. 322.

because the French have complied, for two acts form a custom and make a precendent. Besides we see clearer than the day, and to our sorrow, the fatal issue of this contribution extorted from the French (it being given to the enemy for the French King's ransom).[a] Let then their example rather deter us than excite us to follow it. Wherefore lest the King and we should incurr therein the displeasure of God, I frankly declare for myself, that I protest against this injurious contribution.' This protest was forthwith adhered to by almost all the prelates, especially by St Richard Bishop of Chichester and thereupon our Prelate moved that they should all put up an humble petition to his Majesty to beg of him that out of regard to his own salvation he would forbear this rash imposition. This vigorous and spirited opposition obliged the King to speak no longer in the commanding strain,[b] either in his own or the Pope's name, but to beg the subvention in a suppliant manner. This gentleness softened the prelates, who after remonstrating on past grievences, promised to grant a supply providing also that the King would promise on his part a faithfull observance of the charters, as he had swore at this coronation, and by a fresh charter acknowledge that the present grant should not be made a precedent to exact another, and that the money granted should be employed to the ends for which it was raised. This resolution being carried to the King he began to hector and swear in a horrible manner, that he would not be thus shackled and made a slave (by being tied forsooth to conditions tho most equitable and just). He therefore desired an absolute answer, to which the bishops not to exasperate him by a flat denial, replied that their two Primates being absent they could not return a definitive answer without first consulting them. In revenge the King instead of redressing greviences, renewed soon after one of the worst and most complained of, which was that of giving away livings or the revenues of vacant benefices to illiterate and worthless foreigners, and namely to one Geoffrey a scurrilous buffoon clerk of court.

The King and Pope thus continuing to oppress the English Church and drew[c] so much ill will upon themselves that such as were not afraid to utter their minds called them the 'Disturbers of Mankind.' 'As if,' saith Matthew Paris, (observe his words almost prophetick). 'As if that of the Apostle were now fulfilling. "Unless the separation first come, the Son of Iniquity shall not be revealed." For now is evidently coming on, or rather already come, the separation and division if not of bodies and persons, at least of hearts with a general hatred of the Roman Church, and the very last spark of devotion (thereto) is now extinguished.' Matthew's

---

[a] *Chron. Maj.*, p. 851.
[b] *Chron. Maj.*, p. 850.
[c] *Chron. Maj.*, p. 852.

meaning is not to style the King and Pope Antichrists, but that their joint oppressions were the secretly brooding cause of that separation and defection which is to be one of the forerunners and signs of the Antichrist's coming. As in effect these exactions, if we may speak the truth as a warning to others, were one great occasion of the lamentable defection the Church afterwards suffered in Germany etc. As the wise Cardinal Legate Julian[a] foretold in his letter to Pope Eugenius IV.[146] As for England at the period we are speaking of, the avarice[b] of Pope Innocent the IV's officers was now risen to such a pitch that our Prelate with all his respect for the Holy See, and as we shall see hereafter a wonderfull condescendence for that Pope's neccessitious circumstances, could not help taking a list of all the revenues possessed by foreigners in England. Found upon an average his present Holiness Innocent IV, was found to have impoverished the English Church more than all his predecessors put together. The yearly revenue of foreigners promoted by him in England amounting to no less than 70,000 marks, i.e. adds Matthew, above two thirds more than the real revenue of the Crown.

In April 1253,[c] during the fifteen days of Easter which had been fixed for a new debate of the tenth above demanded by the King, the parliament met again at London. The King repeated his demand of a large subsidy for his expedition to the Holy Land. The Prelates, by their deputies, begged of his Majesty that he would permit the Church to enjoy her liberties, especially that main one of canonical elections, for that now all cathedral and coventual churches were given to none but the King's creatures to the joint damnation of the intruded and their subjects and to the notorious prejudice of the Church. This motion was probably owing to our Prelate of Lincoln, who had wrote an excellent letter[d] on that subject to his guardian Primate St Edmund and was now present in Parliament. The King's answer to the deputies hath something very remarkable for its ingenuity. These deputies were Boniface, Archbishop of Canterbury the Queen's Uncle, William Bishop of Sarum, Sylvester Bishop of Carlisle and Aylmer, Bishop of Winchester the King's half-brother and son of the Queen Doweger, Isabel by her seemed husband Hugh, Earl of March.[147] And they were all four of the King's promotion, to whom he therefore made his sarcastick reply:

> I am exceeding sorry my Lords, for all these transgressions, I shall take care to correct what is past and avoid the like for the future and herein I beg your concurrence, lest such as have been unduly promoted by me, should be damned

---

[a] Bossuet, *Variations*, B. 1, p. 1.
[b] *Chron. Maj*., p. 859.
[c] *Chron. Maj*., p. 865.
[d] *Epist. Grosseteste*, 83.

> together with their flocks. For you all remember it was after this manner that I promoted this Boniface to the see of Canterbury, and you William to that of Salisbury, after raising you from the lowest degree to the honour of being my secretary and Chief Justice. And you Sylvester to the Bishoprick of Carlisle, from a little clerk in my Chancery, and that I preferred you to many more respectable divines. And lastly you, my brother Aylmer to the opulent see of Winchester, in spite of the monks and your want both of age and science fit for the office. It is therefore expedient, as well for you as for me, that you lead the way in this redress of grievences by resigning your ill acquired dignities.

To this acute and ingenious sarcasm, which indeed held good against the managers, but not against the cause in hand, the deputies replied as well as they could that their petition regarded the time to come and not the past. Nevertheless their consciousness of having dipped in the complained of abuse probably rendered them more easy and more ready to drop the complaint and to satisfy the King's demands. At length after much altercation the prelates, not to frustrate the King's religious design of going to the Holy Land, granted the demanded tenth and the King promised faithfully to observe the charters and all the other articles required of him. But as King John his Majesty's father, and his Majesty himself, had often broke through their oath and promise the bishops in order to work a stronger impression on the King's mind thought proper to pronounce a most solemn sentence of excommunication against all infringers of the charters, and the King himself bound in the awfull ceremony. The form thereof is singular and worth transcribing.[a] 'By the authority of the Almighty Father, Son and Holy Ghost. Of the glorious and ever Virgin Mother of God. Of the Blessed Apostles SS. Peter and Paul and all the Apostles. Of St Thomas the martyr and Archbishop of Canterbury and all the martyrs. Of St Edward the Confessor, King of England and all the holy Confessors and Virgins. Lastly by the authority of all the saints, we excommunicate, anathematise and cast out of the Church, all such as knowingly and wittingly shall deprive the Church of her rights and liberties, or attempt the same, whether privately or publickly whether by act, word, or advice.' At the end of the sentence, when the bishops threw down their extinguished and smoking tapers with this execration, thus may all that incurr this sentence be extinguished and shut in Hell, the King himself subjoined, 'So help me God, I will keep all these things inviolate, as I am a man, as I am a Christian, as I am a knight, and as I am a King crowned and anointed.' This sentence was pronounced in Westminster Hall, on the 13 of May according to the Burton Annalist, but according to Matthew Paris, on the 3rd of May, 1253.The year following it was confirmed by the Pope, at the petition

---

[a] [*Perry's footnote is missing*]

of the clergy and with the King's consent.[a] And in 1255 it was published throughout the whole realm.

Our Prelate of Lincoln, who had been the chief deviser of the sentence did not stay so long before he published it. He caused it to be forthwith promulgated in all the parish churches of his large diocese against all violators of the Church's liberties, but especially against such priests, as conspired to the oppression of their own order.[b] ^Nay according to some authors, whose authority is not however irrefragable, he went still further. Matthew Paris's continuator[c] writes, that the Bishop of Lincoln was *said* to have extorted Simon Monfort the famous Earl of Leicester to defend the liberties of the Church by the ege of the Sword.^ The *Chronicle of Mailros*[d] affirmeth the same absolutely and both agree in saying the Bishop injoined it him by way of penance.[148] ^Such an exhortation seems little consistent with our holy Prelate's pacifick character, with his several protestations of fidelity to his Prince and with his advice to the same Earl. On another occasion the Earl of Leicester having received some hard words and usage from King Henry, our prelate who was his director, exhorted him to overlook the affront in consideration of the many favours the King had conferred upon him, and still more in consideration of Christian humility and charity, and by following this pacifick advice and standing faithful to Henry, though tempted with course offers from the French, the Earl recovered his Prince's favour.[e]^ Now besides that the Barons' War did not happen till 9 or 10 years after our Prelate's death, let the Reader be judge of the credit of an uncertain rumour advanced barely upon hearsay, or affirmed only by a writer whom Gale justly styles insipid and careless, and who appears otherwise so bigotted to the party of the Barons that he makes Simon a saint and attributes several miracles to his relicks.[149] The sole character of our pacifick Prelate and his most sincere protestations of fidelity to his Prince are a more than sufficient refutation of such doubtful authorities. Our patriot Prelate's known zeal for the liberties of the Church and State, manifested in his frequent remonstrances, and opposition of grievances seems indeed to have afforded occasion to some evil minded counsellors to accuse him of leaning toward disaffection to the Crown. But then he himself denies and wipes off the aspersions as a malicious surmise of the evil minded;[f] and from such evil minded surmises, the two writers above may in all probability have taken up their heresay story. The bottom and truth of

---

[a] *An. Burt.*, pp. 330 and 333; *Wilkins*, B. 1, p. 703.

[b] *Chron. Maj.*, p. 867.

[c] *Chron. Maj.*, p. 998.

[d] *Chron. Mailros*, p. 231.

[e] *Chron. Maj.*, p. 879; *Epist. Grosseteste*, 75.

[f] *Epist. Grosseteste*, 124.

the story seems to be this, that our godly Prelate predicted the quarrel of the barons with the King, and that Simon and his sons should perish in it, for this much is expressly asserted by Matthew Paris. But this was no more advising and encouraging the war than Elisha's foretelling to Hazael, or discovering to him his secret intentions to kill his master King Benedad and seize his crown, was exciting and exhorting him to the fact.[150] Our Prelate's exhorting Simon to the war and declaring martyrs such as should perish in it, is only advanced by Matthew's continuator on *heresay*. '*They* say' saith he, 'that the Bishop of Lincoln, once laying his hand on Simon's eldest son's head, said to him, "My dear child, thou and thy father shall die both in one day and the same death, but for the cause of truth and justice..."'

The Bishop of Lincoln's predicting the insurrection of Simon and the barons, and the death of Simon and his sons, or at least of the latter, seems an undoubted fact, as appears from the reproach we have seen he made their mother, but his exhorting them to it and canonising them as martyrs of justice and truth seems only a favourable consequence drawn from the prediction by Simon and his party, and circulated by them in order to give a sanction to their enterprise from the authority of so wise and so venerable a prelate whom the people venerated as a saint together with St Thomas, St Edmund and St Richard. Had Simon and his party really received any such encouragement from our Prelate they would not have failed to have made the most of it in their publick manifestos. Neither would the King have omitted taking publick notice thereof in his answers. Yet nothing of this appears in the publick records of the Crown, and the grounds of the story is only heresay of one author, and credulous and bigotted affirmation of another. The vanity of this tale will appear more clear from what we are going to observe in the next chapter.

Chapter III

NOTHWITHSTANDING HIS CONTEST WITH THE CROWN, BISHOP GROSSETETE PRESERVES THE KING'S ESTEEM AND FAVOUR

The many oppositions our prelate was obliged to make against the measures of the Court were so just as to their object, and so tempered with prudence and respect for those in dignity, that he always maintained himself in the King's favour and esteem. And the King shewd on many occasions how much he was convinced of the uprightness of his intentions and how great confidence he had in his virtue and abilities, above all the other prelates in his kingdom. He used to write to him to enquire about his health and inform him of his own and his royal family's estate. And consulted him at all difficult occasions. Once the Bishop's infirmities and a multiplicity of affairs having hindered him from going to court as often as the King desired his Majesty wrote to him a letter full of affection and tender complaints for his Lordship's not enquiring after his or his family's situation, either personally or by proxy. To which the Bishop returned this polite, philosophic and Christian answer.[a]

> Our most hearty and affectionate thanks to your Majesty for his kind information concerning his own, the Queen's and the Royal family's estate, as also for his sollicitous enquiry after ours. As to what your Majesty is pleased to add, that if we had the same concern for you as you have for us we should not have failed to enquire, either by ourselves or some others, about your royal estate; we answer with the Philosopher, that the character of true love, which is full of concern and inquisitiveness after the wellbeing of those it loves, consists in this; that the sincere lover doth not frequent his friend in his prosperity, unless he be expressly called upon. But if he hears of his being in adversity and distress, then he doth not stay till he is called, but of his own accord flys to his assistance, and sacrifices both his goods and his person for his relief and comfort. Hence the true friend is not discovered in time of prosperity because prosperity, which appears ambitious only of applause, finds more of this in the flatterer, than in the true friend. And this is one great advantage of adversity among a number of others, that it serves by the sign just specified to distinguish the real lover from the flatterer. Thus

[a] *Epist. Grosseteste*, 101.

> Job's three friends did not frequent him while prosperous on the throne; but when struck with a leprosy he lay upon the dunghill deprived of all human felicity, then uncalled they came to visit and console him. If then we have not personally waited on your Majesty during the prosperity, which blessed be God! you enjoy, and which we are well informed of from certain enquiries after it tho these not trumpeted abroad, which is no part of friendship. This cannot be imputed to us as want of affection and concern for your Majesty, but if nicely sifted is perhaps rather an argument of the contrary. For true friendship doth not seek so much to please as to benefit one's friend, neither doth it abound in protestations of love, which are as common to the false as to the true lover. But it may be objected to us, that altho the laws of love and friendship do not exact personal attendance, yet the laws of duty and allegience due to superiors may command it. To this we answer, agreeing with your Majesty, that all honour and reverence is due to our sovereign and Liege-Lord, yet adding, that these have nevertheless their proper times and seasons, as have all things according to Solomon, neither have we to our thinking let slip this proper time. Since, if our bodily infirmity be duly considered and the multiplicity and urgency of ecclesiastick affairs upon our hands, which will not admit of delay and which your royal piety would be sorry to see omitted, it will appear evident that our personal waiting on your Majesty was impossible before the dispatch of these affairs, which by God's blessing will be now very soon. For it's the glory of the princes of the Earth not to suffer the affairs of the King of Heaven to be retarded on their account. And tho it may not be according to the rules of decency to speak in one's commendation, yet with St Paul we are obliged to act foolishly in declaring to your Highness that we have a true and unfeigned solicitude both for your temporal and eternal welfare, and an earnest desire to labour for both in conjunction with your Majesty, not only by good,[a]but by evil fame. Not only by honour but by dishonour; and to comprise all in few words, not by sharing with your Majesty the advantages of your prosperity but by taking part in your adversities for your salvation.

Happy the princes and superiors who have prelates and friends to speak to them in this truly affectionate and friendly style! And more happy they that listen to them with as much docility and confidence as their friendly disposition deserves. No doubt but King Henry was perfectly sensible of this happiness, since on other occasions he testified his esteem for his respectful and faithfull monitor.

We have seen above, how he consulted him on the meaning of the regal unction and the frank explanation our Prelate gave him thereof. In 1247, he had another occasion to shew his confidence in our Prelate by consulting him on a difficult and intricate point of theology. The[b] Patriarch of Jerusalem, seeing the dangers to which the holy city was exposed, sent over to England the most divine relick of some of our

---

[a] Corinth. 6:8.

[b] *Chron Maj.*, p. 736 and additament p. 161.

saviour's blood which had been gathered up at the time of his bloody passion and preserved ever since with veneration due to it.[151] The adorable relick, which had been sent to England as to a country whose faith and sanctity would receive it with the greatest reverence, was exposed to publick veneration on the feast of St Edward's translation and an indulgence of *six years* and a 140 days was promulged[152] by the pious Walter de Suthield [*Suffield*], Bishop of Norwich, in the name of all the bishops to all such as should come to venerate the precious memorial of our redemption. Some however of slow, or at least cautious belief asked, how Christ rising again with his whole substance, could leave any drops of his blood behind him on Earth? The learned Prelate and Doctor of Lincoln was therefore called upon by the King to resolve the difficulty, which he did to satisfaction by making a distinction between the essential mass of Christ's blood and the superfluous parts thereof which might be in his mortal body as well as in ours, and were of course separable from the essential mass of blood without any impairment of its integrity.[a153]

The Bishop of Lincoln was in like esteem and request with the princes of the blood[154] and with the nobility, which last had such an idea and veneration for him that as seen above they thought no school equal to his episcopal palace for their sons to be bred up in. Among the former, Richard Earl of Cornwall the King's brother was a great admirer of the Bishop of Lincoln which he testified in several occasions whether during Bishop Grossetete's life or after his death.[155] That Prince having founded the Abbey of Hales [*Hailes*] in Gloucestershire, our Prelate was pitched upon by the Prince to perform the dedication in presence of the King and Queen and all the nobility and prelates of the realm in this ceremony performed the 5 of Nov. 1251. While twelve other prelates said private Masses at the lesser altars our holy Prelate of Lincoln sung the Solemn Mass at the high altar in a very *solemn and glorious* manner.[b] It was in this Abbey the holy relick above mentioned was deposited[c] by Richard's son, Edmund Earl of Cornwall.[d156] This Prince gave a still greater mark of his veneration for the Bishop of Lincoln after his death than while alive, for he made a pilgrimage to his tomb, and was there witness of several miracles with which God himself honoured his virtues.

---

[a] See a similar question betwixt the Fr[*anciscans*] and Dominicans in the life of St James de la Morea [*Marca*] in Butler, November 28.

[b] *Chron. Maj.*, p. 827; *Wykes* and *Annals Waverly* hic.

[c] Collier, *Ecclesiastical History*, B. 2, p. 149.

[d] *Ross*, Warwic. Hist. Reg. Angl. p. 199.

Chapter IV

BISHOP GROSSETETE'S TRANSACTIONS WITH POPES GREGORY THE IX AND INNOCENT IV

We are now entering upon the most remarkable as well as the most delicate, and we may add the most glorious part of the Bishop of Lincoln's life, viz those controversies he had with the head of the Church and wherein like another Paul, he resisted Peter's successor or his officers, in the face in some instances wherein he thought them reprehensible. But then if it was with the zeal and courage of St Paul, it was also with a like humility and respect for his superior. And this his resisting the head of the Church is as awkwardly lugged in by some to prove his renouncing or questioning the pope's supremacy as that of St Paul to discredit the superiority and primacy of St Peter over Paul and the other Apostles. Now as the fault of the Prince of the Apostles and opposition made against it by his inferior and brother apostle Paul have been transmitted by the sacred penmen without any prejudice either to the sanctity of the opposer or to the authority of the opposed, so after their example, and we hope with the same spirit, we shall not scruple to lay open the like controversies betwixt the Holy Father and our Prelate of Lincoln without fearing the imputation of disrespect to the Supreme Pastor, or exposing our heroe's virtue to a trial it cannot bear. But they who confine Bishop Grossetete's transactions with the Holy See to this one article of his oppositions are not only faithless historians and suppressors of the truth, but leave out a curious and edifying part of his history, which would present the true clue to the sense and meaning of his oppositions and reflect a new lustre both upon his sanctity and orthodoxy by shewing that as he never lost his respect for the persons whose measures he opposed, so he never forfeited their esteem and confidence, tho in the first moments of surprise he might be the object of their displeasure and would to God all opposers of abuses, whether in Church or State, had known how to have managed their zeal with the like prudence! How many schisms in the Church, and how many rebellions in the State, would have been spared? Had all the English prelates united their zealous efforts with this most zealous and primitive Bishop in weeding out abuses with a vigorous and prudent hand, perhaps others more rash would not have been exposed to the temptation of plucking up indiscriminately the good corn with the tares!

Bishop Grossetete flourished, or rather ruled the see of Lincoln, under two Popes, Gregory the IX, and Innocent the IV.[157] And as by all we have hitherto said, it appears he was no ways inclined to flatter, we may safely trust to the truth of the characters he hath drawn of them and their counsellors. Our Prelate was no sooner raised to the see of Lincoln but he wrote a letter[a] to his Holiness, Pope Gregory IX expressing a wonderfull respect for his great virtues and his own readiness to undergo any labours his Holiness should please to lay upon him. This short letter containing that Pope's character, and our Prelate's idea of the power of the See of Rome, we shall present the Reader with it and leave him to form of it what judgement he thinks proper, after the perusal.

> Altho the general tye of subjection, which binds the whole Christian people, and even the whole race of men, and without which none can attain to salvation, laith me in your regard most Holy Father and excellent Lord, under the debt of an entire obedience, reverence, honour, and fear. Yet the singular eminence, and lustre of your virtues is a sweet incentive, a powerful spur, or rather a violent impulse to the devotion of your humble servant to pay to your Holiness, as well these four as other duties, in a good and full, pressed down and heaped and overflowing measure. For where, I pray, is the man whose mind would not be rapt in admiration, whose heart would not be catcht with an invincible flame of love in considering your Holiness's most ardent zeal of souls, his superabundent profusion of alms, his supereminent charity and affection for all that serve God, his most anxious care and solicitude, not only for all the churches but for all kingdoms over which you are constituted like Jeremy [*Jeremiah*], to pluck up and destroy, to disperse and dissipate, as also to build and plant? This lustre of your sanctity's virtues, whose rays pierce even the eyes of the blind obliges me with all the devotion I can, tho not with so much as I would, first to make you upon my knees the fervent tender of my spirit, i.e. my ardent desires paying your Holiness that obedience and honour which I owe to you as my most Holy Father, together with the reverence and fear which is due to you as my most excellent Lord. And both in the perfect manner above specified, if my strength and abilities are equal to my will. For seeing the sovereign authority stands thus adorned with the sovereign brightness of birth, it doth not become us to honour it with that submission only, which is rigorously due, but to add willingly thereunto the honours of supererogation,[158] tho what I call honour of supererogation might with greater propriety be styled an homage due to so venerable and so excellent a Pontiff. But because in our present state of pilgrimage the inward affections of the Spirit are only manifested by outward acts of the body, therefore to prevent the foregoing oblation of my heart to your sanctity from remaining always secret and inactive, I now offer myself with all readiness to undergo according to my poor capacity any labours it shall please your Holiness to lay upon me. Neither shall my weakness, great as it is, be disheartened by the greatness of the task, having your sanctity to command me and the Holy

---

[a] *Epist. Grosseteste*, 35.

> Ghost to direct and assist me. Seeing the Apostle saith, I can do all things in him that strengthen me. Moreover, the force of friendship, tho much inferior to that of obedience, renders possible, as the wordly wise assent, even things impossible. And St Benedict writes in his rule, 'If any thing hard or impossible be enjoined to any of the brethren let him receive the command of his superior with all meekness and submission, and if the prior persist in his injunction let the inferior believe it is for his good, and obey with charity, confiding in the Divine assistance for its execution.' If then things impossible are to be attempted by religious with courage and confidence, when injoined by their Prior, how much more when injoined by him who is seated not in the degree of Prior but on the very pinnacle of power, viz in the Seat of Peter, Prince of the Apostles and of the whole world? But because no opportunity has yet offered itself of testifying my obedience to your Holiness either in the acceptance of his commissions or in their execution, I have sent you Holy Father, as some earnest of my devotion to your orders, a small present which tho the least of men I presume to offer to the greatest, from a full pursausion that your Holiness's superlative charity doth not weigh the gift by its bulk but by the sincere affection of the giver, altho to so sovereign a potentate, I do not think it possible to give any thing which doth not belong to him, but only to offer what is already his own.

These professions of an entire obedience to his Holiness, and looking upon all he possessed as at his disposal are not to be esteemed as mere highstrained compliments, but as the firm and standing convictions of his most sincere heart, which he never changed as long as he lived. He had the same deference for his Holiness's representatives. ^The Legate Otho had collated one Atto or Acton,[159] his secretary, to a vacancy in the Cathedral of Lincoln but the Bishop, having precollated to the same before the reception of his Eminence's letter, would not admit the Legat's collation and even complained of his offering to collate in his church without requiring his consent as the canons direct. Nothing can be more generous and at the same time more modest than our Prelate's answer. 'I will not conceal from your sanctity,' saith he to the Legate Otho.[a]

> That I am so firmly riveted in my obedience to the Roman Church and that not thro fear, but willingly and affectionately that neither tribulation, nor anguish, nor persecution, nor any of these temptations enumerated by the Apostle, shal ever, Christ assisting, separate me from her. Moreover, I call him to witness who is the searcher of hearts, that if either our Lord the Pope, or you his representative, should order me to the remotest part of the Saracens' country for planting the faith of Christ and his charity among them, and even to water the same with my blood, I would, weak as I am in body, undertake the mission both willingly and cheerfully. Neither can any burthen be laid upon me by so high an authority for the interests of faith and charity, which I would not carry as long and for as far as I were able.^

[a] *Epist. Grosseteste*, 49.

The Legate cancelled his collation. Sometime after he desired the Bishop to give him another prebend, but this time having a cure of souls and Acton having already one living with a cure, and no dispensation for the second, our zealous observer of the canons demurred upon his recommendation and chose to leave the collation to the Legate's own conscience *pro hac vice* [*on this occasion*]. In short, the impartial Bishop of Lincoln not only refused unfit subjects when presented by ecclesiastical persons, but even by the nobility and the King.

On the second head of the Pope's authority over all the temporalities of the Church, the Bishop adds in the same letter to Otho, 'I know, and I know it for a truth, that our Lord the Pope and the holy Roman Church hath authority to dispose freely of all ecclesiastical benefices.' So that the Doctor of Lincoln allows the head of the Church what few even rigorous Catholicks will allow him, a sovereign power to dispose of all Church livings, providing it be done to edification and according to the canons of the Church.

The Bishop of Lincoln doth not confine the power of the Pope to the spiritual kingdom of Christ and its temporalities but extends it to all temporal kingdoms asserting the Church to be not only their directress in spirituals; but their mistress and sovereign, from whom princes derive their authority, or rather the wise exercise of the authority, the dignity and origine of which he vesteth in the Church and its supreme Pastor. So that if they once abuse it to the prejudice of Christ's spiritual kingdom the Church or its head may, according to him, take the sword out of their hand and put it into others, tho she cannot weild it immediately with her own hand or that of her supreme Pastor. We have already observed, that Browne, the editor of his letters, assures us that for this sentiment our Doctor of Lincoln saith more than all that have come after him, and we there promised to give the Reader a specimen of his reasoning without adopting his sentiment, which is now grown out of fashion, and thereby betrays itself to have been only a school opinion and as such we shall here offer it to the Reader's curiosity.

> Whatever[a] portion secular princes possess of that power and dignity, which is ordained by God, that they receive from the Church.[b160] Whereas the princes of the Church receive not part of their Ecclesiastick dignity and authority from secular princes, but immediately from God. Neither can he who receives power from another rebel against him he receives it from, by abusing what he hath received; any otherwise, than if the axe should glory against him that cuts with it, or the saw against him who saws therewith, or the rod or staff

---

[a] *Epist. Grosseteste*, 23.

[b] See the same sentiment in John of Salisbury, Bishop of Chartres in *Polycratio*, B. 4 cc. 1, 2, 3; Collier, [*Eccles. Hist.*], B. 23, p. 273: and in his 210 epist. apud Collier p. 277, where John approves the deprivation of Frederick Barbarossa by Alex[*ander*] III.

rise up against him who lifts it up. Moreover secular princes are to remember that both swords belong to Peter, the material as well as the spiritual, with this difference that the princes of the Church who sit in the chair and office of Peter, wield the spiritual sword by themselves but the material one by the hand and ministry of secular princes who are to unsheath or sheath the sword they carry at the beck and direction of the princes of the Church. For as Paul saith, the secular prince doth not wear the sword in vain, and he adds the reason, because he is the minister of God, an avenger to execute wrath upon him who doth evil. Secular princes therefore bear the sword as ministers of God, to execute his vengeance upon evil-doers in like manner both *Peaces and both Laws* are entrusted with Peter, and Peter's lieutenants with the like difference that Peter and his vicegerents administer by the hands of secular princes that temporal peace and that temporal law, which have been ordained for the good order of society and for our undisturbed passage thro this temporal life. Whereas they exercise by their own proper ministry that spiritual Peace which unites the faithfull in one heart and mind towards God and that Spiritual Law which promotes this spiritual peace. Hence, as secular princes in bearing the sword as avengers of the evil-doer, are thereby ministers of God and consequently of the Church the spouse of Christ; so in holding and exercising the administration of the *temporal Peace and Law* they are also ministers of God, and consequently of his Church. Hence also the laws, which are framed to preserve the peace of our temporal life cannot in any-wise contradict the Laws of God or his Church, since no minister ought to lift up his heel against him whose minister he is.

Now that both the swords, both the Peaces and both Laws are primarily and originally lodged in the princes of the Church appears not only from the expositions of the holy books, but from the divinely disposed examples of the chiefs of the ancient people of God. Moses the divinely appointed chief of the people of Israel, and the perfect type of the presidents of the Church, administered by himself both swords and ruled the people committed to his care by both Peaces and by both Laws. For as the Scripture asserts,[a] he presided over the people in the things which belonged to God, and restrained those who transgressed his Laws, the due observance whereof constitutes the tranquillity of the spiritual Peace. And besides this, he girded his sword upon his thigh and passing thro the camp from one gate to the other, he chastised the disturbers of the civil peace. And these disturbers, whether of the spiritual or temporal peace, he judged and punished by laws proper to each … but when our Lord Jesus Christ appeared upon Earth, then he who is the true God and most meek Lamb would have meekness and contemplation of heavenly things to shine principally in the princes of his Church, and therefore lest this preheminent meekness and application to things above should be eclypsed under the exercise of severity and the application to secular affairs the *actual exercise* of the material sword, which flashes with the terror tho of just severity, and the administration of the temporal Law which is clouded with the darkness of Earthly tho lawfull occupations, are put into the hands of secular princes, the

[a] Exod. 18:19.

power thereof still remaining in the hands of the princes of the Church. Now that the *exercise* of the two Swords, and of the two Laws, is divided between the secular princes and the princes of the Church, the power of both always remaining in the latter, seems to have been signified and ordained by Christ himself, when knowing that those he had fed with five loaves and two fishes were coming by force to make him king, he fled into the mountain.[a] And again,[b] when one of the crowd saying to him, 'Master speak to my brother, that he divide the inheritance with me.' He replied, 'O man! Who had made me Judge and Divider over you?' For there he only renounced the act of reigning and judging in temporals, not the royal and judicious power itself seeing he was truly and by nature King and Judge of all Creatures whether in Heaven, or in Hell, or on Earth. And herein Christ signified, that in the Law of Grace the princes of his Church ought not actually to exercise any judgements of severity in temporal concerns, tho the power and authority thereof he vested in them and from their power do secular princes derive the exercise of such judgements. The Laws therefore of temporal princes ought never to go against the Divine or Ecclesiatick Laws. And if in the framing of Laws, or in the use of the Sword, the secular prince resist Christ or his Church, then he's convicted of disobedience to his father Christ Jesus who hath begotten him by the word of his truth; and to his mother the Church, who hath brought him forth by the sacred fountain of baptism. Consequently, according to the Ecclesiasticus, he is infamous because he hath deserted his Father, and he is accursed of God because he has exasperated his Mother and his very foundations shall be rooted up.[c] According to what is written in the same book, the mother's curse rooteth up the foundation.[d] If then secular princes and judges would escape this malediction let them acquiesce to the wisdom of Solomon, where he saith. 'My son, listen to the instruction of thy father, and forsake not the law of thy mother; that grace may be added to thy head, and a chain of gold to thy neck.'[e] Now whose instruction doth he so carefully injoin us to hear, and whose law doth he bid us beware of forsaking, but those of God our Father and of the Church our Mother? For how can he injoin us not to forsake the law of our carnal mothers seeing these latter, tho empresses and queens, have no power to make Laws?

It being therefore evident from so many testimonies that secular princes and judges can neither frame laws contrary to the Law of God or the ordinances of the Church, nor execute those already framed against them without rebelling against God their father and their holy Mother the Church, to their own eternal damnation and to the forteiture of their temporal administration, it behoves you who are admitted to the king's familiarity to share his judicious power, as you tender the king's eternal salvation and your own obedience and union with the holy Roman and Catholick Church, to labour by all possible means to reform upon the model of the Divine and Ecclesiastick Law, all the

---

a Jn. 6:12.
b Lk. 12:13.
c Eccles. 3:18.
d Eccles. 3:11.
e Prov. 1:8.

> laws contrary thereto which have hitherto prevailed in the king's court, to the dishonour and injury of the Eternal King. And to resolve for the future, manfully to oppose the making, or use of all such so to rescue our Lord the King, yourself and other secular judges of the Realm from the burnings of eternal fire.[161]

They who believe the powers of the church, whether directive or coercive, to be purely spiritual, will not easily admit our Prelate's opinion concerning the temporal powers being derived from and revocable by the Church, yet even these must confess that what he advances of the necessary subordination and conformity of all temporal laws to those of God and his Church, and of their authors being liable to Spiritual censures when they run counter to either, is ingeniously set forth and so solidly proved. As is also the necessary separation of the acts and exercises of the two powers, and indeed this is all the Bishop proves here, for as to the derivation of the temporal power from the princes of the Church, and its revocability by them when abused this he rather supposed as an opinion then allowed from the two powers vested in Moses and natural to the Son of God, than he offers to prove its being transmitted by Christ to his Church. The supposition of the two powers being communicated to the Church rests on the two swords, whose signification of the two *powers* is only supposed as the common opinion, and whose derivation one from the other, is proved from their subordinate use. Since in the opposite supposition of their being both derived immediately from God they ought to be no less subordinate in their exercise and obliged to concur with each other in rooting out evil and encouraging all that is good. Hence it was an ingenious reply of an English Franciscan,[a] who hearing a Benedictine doctor in convocation dilate upon the two swords, as emblems of the two powers vested in Peter, rose up immediately and in the words of Christ bid him put up one of his swords, viz the material one, into his scabbard as not being the sword Christ permitted his vicar to use.

Our Prelate's idea of and respect for the Sacred College was not less in proportion than those he had for his Holiness as he testifieth in several letters addressed either to the cardinals, or other great officers of the pope's Court. In his 36 letter written to the illustrious Spanish Cardinal Giles, Cardinal Deacon of S.S. Cosmas and Damian,[162] a prelate of great integrity with whom he had been in commerce of letters while Archdeacon of Leicester, he calls the College of Cardinals the foundations of the world, and the supports and hinges of the Earth, upon which is firmly fixed the world which shall not be moved and the universal Church, which no commotions can force from the stability of faith. He likewise

---

[a] See, *Biblioth. britannico-hibernica*, 'Marchiley', p. 569; 'Ocham', p. 554.

adds, that as under God and his ministering angels this material world oweth its stability, order and beauty to the visible sun and kings of the world, so doth the spiritual world under God and the celestial hierarchy owe its order, beauty and perpetuity to the sovereign pontiff and to his assisting cardinals.[163] Hence his perpetual attention to recommend the affairs and necessities of his Church of Lincoln, to the most knowing and most virtuous members of the Pope's Court, especially[a] to St Raymond of Pennafort, Confessor to Pope Gregory IX,[b] to brother Arnulphus the same Pope's penitentary,[c] to John de Ferentino, that Pope's Chamberlain and lastly[d] to Cardinal Thomasio, who having been a friend to his predecessor Hugh Wells, he begs of him that as he had shewn favour to Hugh while being here so he will continue the same to him now dead by continuing to protect this Church of Lincoln, over which he saith, 'Hugh still presides from above.' All or most of these recommendations have this remarkable clause; that they would only forward his affairs as far as justice and the good of souls would admit, and would reject whatever their wisdoms found contrary thereto.[164] His letters to the Cardinals were not merely complimental or recommendatory, but full of instructions to honour their high dignity with suitable degrees of virtue. For this freedom his profound learning and equal virtues, and high reputation, authorised him to take with some of them. Nothing in this kind can be more sensible or more episcopal than his 65 letter, addressed to the English Cardinal Robert de Somercote lately made Cardinal Deacon of S. Eustachius by Gregory the IX, and continuing at the same time Rector of Castre [*Caistor*] in our Prelate's diocese.[165] Cardinal Somercote having acquainted his diocesan with his promotion to cardinalship, the Bishop made him this answer.

> We give God thanks for your promotion hoping it will turn out a living promotion and not a dead one. Now I call it a living promotion when the dignity which passes away with time is animated with an elevation of the soul to that which never passes away. When by how much more the person promoted is raised above his former state by the accession of his new dignity and power, by so much and incomparably more his soul is elevated above its former self by a more fervent love of eternity, by a clearer apprehension of heavenly things, by a greater contempt of whatever is earthly, and lastly by an unfeigned humiliation of Spirit, from the dangers lying round so high a station, where falls are more easy and withall more fatal. Since there, as the thundering threats of those in power, the thunderbolts of anger, and the storms of every temptation raged with greater frequency and violence, so

[a] *Epist. Grosseteste*, 37.
[b] *Epist. Grosseteste*, 38 and 42.
[c] *Epist. Grosseteste*, 43.
[d] *Epist. Grosseteste*, 44 and 68.

> the ground is more soft and slippery from the affluent dirt of riches. And the only security possible is never to be secure, but in imitation of Job, to fear and tremble at every step.

The new Cardinal having in his letter professed a great zeal for the beauty of the house of God, the Bishop tells him frank and plain, that his repairing and adorning his church of Castre will best prove the sincerity of his profession. This Cardinal was of such eminent merit that on the death of Gregory IX in 1240 he was thought on as subject fit for the popedom but he died the year following.[a]

The Bishop of Lincoln's warm protestations of obedience to the Pope and his representatives, were not empty words but verified by his constant and uninterupted practice; he never undertook any business of importance without first consulting either his Holiness or his legates, nor without strengthening his ordinary authority with an extraordinary delegateion of the Holy See. We have seen instances of this already while he was Archdeacon and when Bishop in his visitation of the Chapter and in his statutes, many of which he got inforced by particular sanctions from the Pope. We shall see more hereafter and shall only add one more instance here. In 1237 Cardinal Otho the Pope's Legate held a national Council at London on the 18 of November, wherein issued many wise regulations.[b] The first decreed that all cathedral, conventual and parochial churches (whose consecration was not well ascertained) should be consecrated within two years. Our Prelate was the first to execute this decree, the same year he dedicated the Church of Peterborough and the year following two other noble churches in the fenny parts of his diocese, viz Ramsey and Sauterie [*Sawtry*].[c] He was so exact in the execution of this necessary statute, that he suspended the Earl of Warren's chaplain for having said mass in the said Lord's Hall at Grantham in Lincolnshire because not consecrated, as the statute required.[d] In his 63 letter to the Abbot of Ramsey, concerning the preparation necessary for the dedication of his Church, he gives this anecdote of the old English ceremonial on these occasions that according to the general and appointed custom, 'every thing is to be taken out of the Church which doth not make a part of it, even the bodies of the Saints. That these last are to be removed the evening before the dedication and watched during the whole night with great devotion, and that after the dedication, they are to be replaced in the church after the same manner. But because,' saith he. 'The shrines of the saints are to be handled with great reverence, devotion and purity

---

[a] *Chron. Maj*., pp. 524, 527, 542 and 576; Robert de Faversham, *Peterborough Chronicles*, p. 117; *Epist. Grosseteste*, 65 and 87; *Biblioth. britannico-hibernica*, 'Sommercote and Hymo'.
[b] *Chron. Maj*., p. 449.
[c] *Chron. Maj*., p. 481; *Epist. Grosseteste*, 50 and 63.
[d] *Epist. Grosseteste*, 56.

of heart, we therefore exhort you in the Lord, before you attempt the removal of the holy bodies, to purify yourselves by previous fasting, watching, prayer, and liberal alms, thereby to obtain the comfortable assistance of the said saints.'

If our obsequious Prelate knew how to obey in all things that were for edification, he knew also how to withhold his submission in matters of a contrary tendency and to distinguish betwixt assent blind and a rational enlightened obedience. 'There's no burden can be laid upon me by so high an authority,' saith he speaking to the legate Otho,

> for the interests of faith and charity, which I would not bear as long and as far as I were able; but whatever tends to the ruin of charity, that is a burden I cannot bear tamely and since I am obliged to follow the Gospel, which commands me to fear him only who can cast soul and body into hell, no fear of your power shall ever hinder me from speaking the truth which the fire of charity urges me to declare. I know and acknowledge it for a certain truth that our Lord the Pope and the holy Roman Church have authority to dispose freely of all ecclesiastical benefices, but I also know that whoever abuses this authority edifieth for the fire of hell. And I know moreover, that he abuses this authority, who doth not make use of it for promoting Faith and Charity. I know moreover that when Church livings are conferred by plentitude of authority without first consulting the patron, especially when this may be easily done, it's an odious thing and occasions confusion to the pastors, an insulting joy to their enemies, and gives scandal to the good. This is not the way to edify the Church, but to destroy it, neither are faith and charity promoted thereby, but threatened, and the command of the Apostle transgressed, which forbids the pastors to Lord it over the flock. Permit me therefore to say that your wisdom ought not to have covered your humble servant with confusion by conferring a prebend in my church without my consent, more especially as I have always had, and shall have, a most ready desire to gratify any of yours with this or a better prebend, providing it be done not with force and to mine church's confusion but spontaneously and to the edification.

The chief objects of our Prelate's oppositions at this time were some heavy exactions of the Roman officers and the oppressive provisions of foreigners in English benefices. But eer we can enter upon this subject, it will be necessary in order to have a true notion of these grievences, and why they were more heavy in the English than in other Churches, to trace up the effects to their original causes.

These causes were more than one; and the first I take to be King John's resigning his Crown into the hands of the Pope, and his consenting to hold it as a fee of the Roman See.[a166] There's no necessity here of entering

[a] This resignation seems ancienter than King John, if King Henry II speaks his own sentiments in a letter written in his name to Alex[*ander*] III, 'animo me vestris advolvo genibus consilium … armis non utitur, patrimonium Beati Petri, spirituali gladio tueatur'. Bles: Epist 136.

into the particulars of this famous resignation; which may be seen in all our historians, especially in Matthew Paris and Thomas Wikes,[a] all that concerns our present design is the fact and its consequences. King John by his oppressions of the clergy and nobility, having drawn upon himself from Pope Innocent III a triple sentence of interdict, excommunication and deposition, and the joint armies of some of his barons and those of the French King, as executors of the Pope's sentence, found no other means of redeeming himself from his hazardous situation than to make an hommage of his Realms of England and Ireland to the Pope's hand. By this hommage he consented to hold the kingdom as secondary and feudatory to the Pope, and in acknowledgement thereof to pay him an annual tribute of a thousand marks. To this he bound not only himself but his heirs. Accordingly King John dying in this juncture his son and heir King Henry III, who owed the preservation of his right to the Pope's Legate Gualo for rescuing him from the attempts of Prince Lewis of France and his abetters, acknowledged his dependence on the See of Rome, on the double title of his father's hommage and his own particular obligations.[167] Hence when the Emperor Frederick exhorted him to turn the Pope's Legate Otho out his kingdom on account of some heavy exaction, Henry answered that, 'he was more obliged to obey the Pope than other princes, as being his feudatory and because the Pope by his Legate Gualo, had kept the Crown upon his head when his enemies had conspired to snatch it from him.'[b168] Henry indeed learnt better afterwards, as we shall see, but for the present he allowed the title and he was of age, even 33 years old. Hitherto the See of Rome had received the Peter's pence and other temporary gratuities of the English, but after this act it seemed to have a kind of human and allowed right on the King's part as other princes have in similar cases, to treat the English as tributaries. And as right and prerogative are frequently upon the stretch, the exaction of the tribute of a thousand marks yearly ushered in others of larger size, according to the several exigencies the Holy See happened to labour under. Now tho I do not so much as pretend to justify King John for making a present of his kingdom to the Pope; yet I may venture to express my firm belief that few pontiffs of any Church, or potentates of any state, would refuse the present when offered them, and that there are still fewer who having once received it would refuse turning it to their own advantage. Whether our Holy Father will ever be under the necessity of resigning St Peter's patrimony into the hands of the head of the English Church I cannot foretell, but I can give a shrewd conjecture that should the case

---

[a] *Chron. Maj.*, p. 237; *Wykes*, ad an. 1213.

[b] *Chron. Maj.*, p. 524; see also *Epist. Grosseteste*, 117 et Hearne's notes on Gul Newland: p. 811 ex Chronico Bartholemei Cotton.

ever happen, the head of the English Church, whether his Majesty or my Lord of Canterbury, would make as little scruple of receiving it from the Pope as the Pope did from King John, and of making use of it somewhat in the same manner were it only by way of retaliation.

A second cause, or occasion of the grievances in question was the incursion of the Saracens upon the Holy Land and the crusades undertaken and encouraged by the popes, for the relief of the Christians there suffering and for the general interests of Christianity. An Enterprise necessarily attended with immense expenses and whither should the promoter of it apply for the necessary funds, but to those he found most capable and most obliged to contribute thereto, viz to his good feudatory the kings of England!

A third cause, were the contests of the popes and the Emperor Frederick, whom Gregory the IX had not only excommunicated but deposed from the Empire, agreeably to the opinion of several eminent divines of the age and among others of our Doctor of Lincoln, who as we have seen not long since held that altho the material sword be not to be wielded by the hand of the prince of the Church but by that of the secular prince, yet that the secular Prince ought to use it according the direction of the ecclesiastick princes and that if he use it contrary to the just directions of the Ecclesiastical or Divine Laws, as Frederick did, that then in his opinion he forfeited his authority. To support this act of the spiritual sword against the material sword and numerous troops of Frederick, many troops were raised and many alliances formed which were a new and inexhaustible source of taxes upon the different parts of the Church, and nowhere more than in the then acknowledged feudatory kingdom of England. The progress of this contest under Innocent the IV, and his expulsion out of Italy under all the distresses of want both in himself and his court, were a fourth and not the least cause of heavy subventions being raised here to relieve them.

These I take to be four Principal causes of the heavy contributions raised by the popes under our Prelate's episcopate, all as we see more resolvable into their necessitious circumstances than into the virtuousness of their characters. Accordingly we shall see presently that tho our Prelate opposed several of these exactions upon the temporalities of the Church, yet he was wise and considerate enough to take in the mollifying circumstances thereof, and that his most vigorous oppositions regarded some greviances of another more spiritual and more weighty nature. However what happened commonly on these occasions happened then, that these contributions tho heavy enough of themselves were rendered heavier and more odious by the avarice of some of the collectors. It may also be very naturally presumed that the weight of these burdens falling chiefly on the clergy and religious the greviances wherewith they were galled made them sometimes cry louder than was necessary in the historical relation of them. Besides this, particulars being divided between the Pope and Emperor some were but too liable to imbibe and let themselves be imposed upon by the calumnies of the latter against the former, and to aggravate above measure what they found already grevious enough in itself. For this last must not be denied the very facts, and sums specified in the bills of taxation and testified by our best ancient historians are but too clear evidences of the oppressive measures which the necessitous circumstances of the popes in question threw them into against their natural inclinations.

Hence we are not to be surprised that Gregory the IX, tho otherwise a pontiff of great and known virtue should raise so many subsidies upon the English Church, which he found with the rest of the nation in a feudatory state of subjection to his See. Now these being but an incidental part of Bishop Grossetete's life we shall confine ourselves to those which happened under his episcopate and wherein he had an acting part. In a convocation where all the bishops met at London the last of July 1239, the Legate Otho added to his former heavy subsidies a new demand of legatine dues for the support of his office while here.[a] But the bishops answered, that the importunity of the Romans had so drained the revenues of the English churches that they were no longer able to bear the intolerable burthen, and that he who had called him over, viz the King, might defray his expenses. And so the assembly broke up *re infecta* [*business unfinished*].

Another grievance was that of thrusting in foreigners into English benefices. Hence this same year 1239, the temporality by their Deputy Sir Robert Twinge[b] sent to the Pope a very eloquent letter with heavy complaints that by the greediness of his officers the advowsons, which by their foundation belonged to the laity, were wrested out of their hands.[169] Whereupon his Holiness dispatched letters of redress signifying that his mandates for providing and collating to such churches had been granted without knowing they were of lay patronage. But these letters of redress only regarded the liberties of the lay patrons and the yoke of foreign provisions still continued on the necks of the clergy and religious as Mathew Paris complains. It's true that by a prior bull of 1231[c] his Holiness had left the bishops power to confer their respective livings freely and will not have them obliged to admit his provisions unless there be an express derogation from that priviledge; but then this bull was evaded if not then at least soon after, by frequent derogations and especially in 1240 when Gregory IX,[d] being soreley pressed by his enemy the Emperor

---

[a] *Chron. Maj.*, p. 498; *Wykes*, ad an. 1240.
[b] *Chron. Maj.*, pp. 512 and 515.
[c] *Wilkins*, B. 1, p. 629.
[d] *Chron. Maj.*, p. 532.

Frederick, promised to, or as was said, made a compact,[a] with the Roman people the better to retain them in his interest to confer on their sons all the vacant benefices in England, those especially which depended on the monasteries. This the Pope did so much more securely as he had the King on his side.[b] For Henry, like all his predecessors of the Norman line, being enclined to rule his English subjects with the same arbitrary sway as his Norman vassals, thereby disgusted the ancient English nobility who had inherited from their Saxon ancestors the old spirit of liberty which was interwoven in the mild, paternal and common government of the Saxon princes who did nothing but in conjunction with the nobility and clergy. This old spirit therefore sticking close to the hearts of the old English barons and even of the Normans who had breathed the free air of England, occasioned in them frequent remonstrances and oppositions to the arbitrary measures of the Crown, and frequent petitions for the restoration of the mild Saxon Laws and government. This made Henry glad to see foreigners promoted in the Church, as well as in the State, because their quality of foreigness rendered them as more hateful to the natives, so more attached to the Court, tho by this ill timed temporary policy he was continually formenting and ripening the seed of jealousy and discontent betwixt himself and his natural born subjects. Now as this disposition of the Court was a lucky juncture for the hungry foreigners, so the necessitous circumstances of the popes engaged in the crusades and in wars with the Empire, was a no less lucky conjuncture for humouring the turn of the English Court and for supplying them in abundence with the foreign commodity they so much delighted in.

Hence soon after the compact above mentioned, betwixt Gregory IX and the Roman people, a mandate came over to England addressed to St Edmund Archbishop of Canterbury and to our Prelate of Lincoln, with the Bishop of Sarum, as conservators and executors of the same, injoining them to provide no less than[c] three hundred Romans with the first vacant benefices in England under pain of losing their right of collation till all these were provided for. This mandate came attended with another tax upon all the spirituality, in compliance with which every bishop gave for himself, leaving their clergy to give also for themselves. But our generous Prelate of Lincoln paid for himself and his clergy the sum of six hundred marks.[d] But all or most of these contributions, being carried off the same year 1240 by the Legate Otho, fell into the hands of the Emperor Frederick together with the said eminence.

---

[a] *Chron. Maj.*, p. 540.
[b] *Chron. Maj.*, p. 542.
[c] *Chron. Maj.*, p. 658.
[d] *Dunstable annals*, p. 245 and 248.

These and other greviances of the two Courts of Rome and England[a] wrought so deeply on the spirit of St Edmund that rather than see the Church thus given up to the rapine of foreigners, and that with the King's connivance and encouragement, he went into voluntary banishment about All Saints of the year 1240,[170] and died at Soisy [*Soisy-Bouy*] the 16 of November following.[b] This step, or retreat was conformable to St Edmund's quiet and contemplative temper, to which these vexations were a perpetual distraction. But our penetrating Prelate, whose characteristic virtue was an undejected zeal and fortitude, even in the very torrent of trials, thought it more prudent and more necessary to stand his ground and to endeavour to save a part at least from ruin. Twas probably in allusion to these two different dispositions and opposite conduct of two such holy and venerable prelates that God, as Matthew Paris writes, was pleased to reveal to a certain holy man[c] that he had loved the Blessed Edmund in odour of benignity and sweetness and the Blessed Robert in odour of fidelity and fortitude, a virtue which shines through the whole of life of Bishop Grossetete in large characters, more especially in the article under consideration here. The Bishop of Lincoln made it his great study to countermine this promotion of foreigners, which was a discouragement to studies and virtue at home, by promoting in all occasions such of his countrymen as were men of parts and merit. It was the very next year after this transaction that he procured the promotion of the great Doctor Nicholas de Farnham to the See of Durham conjuring him by the blood of Christ to accept of it for fear the King should thrust in some foreigner. Soon after this he stood by the translation of William Raley from Norwich to Winchester for the like reason, because the King wanted to intrude some foreign subject. We have seen above many other illustrious subjects whom he laboured with all his might to provide such as Dr William de Shirewood, Dr Roger Wesham, Dr Thomas Walleys,[171] Dr John de Offington, Doctor Richard of Cornwall, whom Leland honours with the title of Peers of the English School.

The obligation our Prelate was under of providing his share in the 300 Romans, by the bull of Gregory the IX, was no doubt disagreable to one of his patriotic disposition, but he was eased of it before it could be any ways tolerably executed. For in 1241, the year after the bull was sent over, that Pope died in the 30 of September, or according to Matthew Paris the 22 of August.[d] On this occasion the holy Bishop of Lincoln shewd the ardour and perfection of his zeal by extending it to the whole Church, in labouring for the election of a worthy successor

---

[a] *Chron. Maj.*, p. 532.
[b] *Wykes*.
[c] *Chron. Maj.*, p. 903.
[d] *Chron. Maj.*, p. 574.

after the most Christian and godly manner, whether by writing or by praying or by fasting for that end. In a meeting of the bishops[a] held at Oxford on St Andrew's day 1241,[b] the Bishop of Lincoln in conjunction with Walter Gray Archbishop of York, with William [*de Raley*] Bishop of Norwich and Walter [*Mauclerk*] Bishop of Carlisle, appointed publick prayers and a general fast throughout the Realm for the happy election of a new Pope, and because the greatest opposition was likely to come from the Emperor Frederick they sent their deputies to him with letters conjuring him not to oppose but rather to forward the election. The zeal of our Prelate and his collegues was not blessed with so speedy a success as it deserved. Celestin IV, a prelate commendable for his piety and learning was indeed elected 30 days after the decease of Gregory but he only survived eighteen days and his successor was not elected till midsummer 1243.

During the interval the indefatigable Bishop of Lincoln employed his learned pen in enriching the Church with the translations of a book, till this time little known in the west.[c] Having been informed by his Archdeacon of Leicester the celebrated John de Basing, that in his learned travels to Athens he had there seen a book unknown to the Latins entitled, *The Testament of the 12 Patriarchs*, and containing several prophecies relating to the Messiah. Our most zealous Doctor of Lincoln sent quite into Greece for a copy of the book and in 1242, translated it from the Greek into Latin with the assistance of Nicholas the Grecian, subdean of Lincoln. Our Prelate's view in translating this book, which he looked upon as an appendix of the Scriptures suppressed by the Jews, was to furnish the Latin Church with new arms against those infidels whose conversion he sought by the evangelical means of preaching and writing and not by compulsion, having expressly wrote against compulsive methods in a letter addressed to the Earl of Winchester, *de non molestandis Judaeis*.[172]

As soon as the new Pope was chosen, under the name of Innocent the IV, the good Bishop of Lincoln full of joy for the Church's good, wrote to his Holiness a letter of congratulations, wherein he returns God thanks, for bestowing on his Church in the midst of her tribulations such and so great a spouse.[d] This Pope was a noble Genoese of the house of the Counts of Frieschi; and before his elevation was styled Cardinal Sinibald. The Bishop of Lincoln's rejoicing at his exaltation is a presumption much more in favour of his moral character than that drawn by exasperated writers from the grievences, which his hard circumstances occasioned him or his officers to commit especially on the English. This

---

[a] *Dunstable annals*, p. 251.
[b] *Chron. Maj*., p. 577.
[c] *Chron. Maj*., p. 597 and 835.
[d] *Epist. Grosseteste*, 111.

Pope's misfortune was to have succeeded to all the engagements which forced his predecessor upon like harsh measures, viz his trials with the Emperor Frederick and the crusades for the recovery of the Holy Land.[a]

The Bishop of Lincoln not only wrote to congratulate with the new Pope, but his Holiness being obliged to leave Italy and reside at Lions, the Bishop crossed over to that city towards the end of 1244, tho so far advanced in years that at his setting off his two particular friends Walter de Cantilupe, Bishop of Worcester and William de Raley Bishop of Winchester, could not help weeping for fear they should never see him return; and our grateful Prelate was so sensible of their affection that as soon as he arrived at Lions, he wrote to them to express his gratitude for their affectionate tears and to acquaint them that he had been honourably received by the Pope, and for his sake by the cardinals and that he was now prosecuting the affairs of his Church. His stay at Lions being long (viz from November 1244 till about Michaelmas of the following year) and his pastoral heart being always with his flock he wrote his 122 excellent letter to all his archdeacons exciting them to a greater vigilance during his absence, lest the underservants of the family, as usually happeneth, should grow remiss in the absence of their master and give themselves up to all those vices of which idleness is the fruitful mother. He urges them to labour strenuously in the great work of the salvation of souls, by their prayers and instructions, by correcting and chastising the disobedient and to deal out justice gratis. To these duties the Bishop presses them by the joint consideration of the reward promised to the faithfull servant, and of the punishment reserved to the negligent, and by the great and moving example of the Son of God who lived in labour and died in torment for the salvation of every particular soul. Saith he, 'tho all do not receive the effect and benefit of his passion, but only such who truly believe in him, and believing love him.' For this reason he concludes by animating them to finish the work of the salvation of their respective flocks, by inspiring them with the faith and charity necessary for that end.

During this absence of Bishop Grossetete from his flock, Martin the new Pope's Nuncio made a demand of ten thousand marks on the clergy.[173] But they answered that their Archbishop with the Bishops of Lincoln and Durham being abroad they could not do any thing. The Bishop of Lincoln, being as it were the soul, director and oracle of the Convocation, and with this negative answer the Nuncio was forced to be content. However he got from the Religious, what he could not from the clergy.[b]

[a] *Dunstable annals*, p. 260.
[b] *Dunstable annals*, p. 268.

The reason of our Prelate's long stay at Lions was the assisting at the Council of Lion, which was called soon[a] after his arrival there but did not assemble till about midsummer 1245, and several weighty affairs there transacted either in the Council or after it whether with regard to the universal Church, or to the Church of England, or to his particular Church of Lincoln. The first thing there transacted was the excommunication and deposition of the Emperor Frederick,[b] pronounced by the Pope and confirmed by all the prelates holding lighted torches in their hands.[c] The sentence being committed to writing was subscribed by all the bishops and sealed with their seals.[d] The second general transaction of the Council was a crusade decreed for the relief of the Christians suffering under the yoke of the Saracens in Palestine and these regarded the general cause of Christianity.

The chief article urged in this Council, in regard of the English Church and nation, were the complaints of the King, Lords and Commons of England against the grievances of the Roman Court upon the English Church, and the Pope's manner in answering them. The Deputies of the Lords and Commons, headed by their Speaker, Master William de Powerick,[e] exhibited to his Holiness several articles of complaint against the exorbitant exactions of his legatees and nuncios in England especially of the late Nuncio Martin who for a demand of fees had been lately dismissed the kingdom without them,[f] as also against the promotion of Italians to English benefices, whose yearly revenues were computed to exceed the value of sixty thousand marks, which was more than the yearly revenue of the Crown.[174] The Pope delaid answering these complaints because the fundamental causes which had obliged him thereto still subsisted viz his quarrel with the Empire, and the most expensive crusades, which had already involved the Holy See in a debt of a hundred and fifty thousand pounds.[g] Hence the deputies receiving no satisfactory answer and despairing of redress, withdrew in great wrath swearing in the most horrible manner that they would no longer suffer the Roman avarice to exact any tribute from the nation, or to squeeze the churches out of their revenues, especially such as were of the patronage of the nobility. This vigour moved his Holiness, either then or soon after to issue forth several bulls, which both promised and gave some redress.[h]

---

[a] *Chron. Maj.*, p. 656 and 663.
[b] *Chron. Maj*, pp. 668–72.
[c] *Chron. Maj.*, p. 679.
[d] *Chron. Maj.*, p. 681.
[e] *Chron. Maj.*, p. 666.
[f] *Dunstable annals*, p. 269.
[g] *Chron. Maj.*, p. 662.
[h] *Chron. Maj.*, pp. 696 and 706.

However the root which produced these bitter fruits he saved and secured by the prelates, while the Royal deputies opposed this receiving of the desired fruits. His Holiness sent a strict order to all the English bishops then at Lions, to come and set their seals to the charter of resignation, whereby King John of 'deplorable memory', saith Matthew Paris, had unfortunately bound himself and his heirs to pay the Pope an yearly tribute as an acknowledgment of his holding the Crown of him. Innocent's view in exacting the episcopal signatures to King John's Charter seems to have been either to strengthen his title to the annual tribute, whereof the deputies threatened a denial, or else to secure the Charter itself by an authentick copy drawn up and sealed in form, because the original was said to have been destroyed in a late fire which had consumed the Pope's wardrobe and all the papers lodged in it.[a] Be this as it may the English bishops, and among them our Prelate, all signed the Charter and that as should seem without any great reluctance, it being observed of Fulk the Stout Bishop of London,[175] of him alone, that he stood off for a long while. The Bishop of Lincoln had so much the less scruple to give his signature as it was his avowed and reasoned principle that all secular princes hold their kingdoms, or the exercise of their temporal jurisdiction of the Church and are consequently liable to pay tribute to her, as to their Principal and Paramount.[b] When King Henry heard of this great service of complaisance in his bishops, he swore in great anger that altho the prelates had bowed the knee to the Pope he should always stand up for the liberty and independency of his crown, and that as long as he had breath in his body he would never consent to the payment of any subsidy to the Pope under the odious title of tribute.[c] This his Majesty also repeated to our Prelate immediately after his return from the Council, as we shall see presently. As to Bishop Grossetete's particular affairs relating to his own Church of Lincoln we have already seen that he gained his cause against his Chapter of Lincoln in the cause of the visitation.[d] He also laboured with the other English prelates, and pleaded hard before the Pope to have the Cistercians subjected to their ordinaries, but in this he did[e] not succeed. He at the same time procured Roger Wesham, his Dean of Lincoln, to be made Bishop of Lichfield and profited of this vacancy to detach from the deanery the rich prebend of Aylesbury.[176] Besides this he was honoured by the Pope with several commissions to the King of England and some of the prelates.

---

[a] *Chron. Maj.*, p. 658.

[b] *Epist. Grosseteste*, 23 and 86.

[c] *Dunstable annals*, pp. 269 and 272.

[d] *Chron. Maj.*, p. 688.

[e] *Chroniconica de Henrici Knighton*, p. 2443.

The Bishop of Lincoln having dispatched all his affairs, left Lions to return home with his two companions, the *illustrated* Franciscan Doctor Adam de Marisco and brother John his associate. But in passing thro Paris, where he himself had been formerly professor, he had like to have lost Adam. Alexander Hales, an English Franciscan Doctor and John de la Rochelle, a French Doctor of the same order,[a] and both celebrated Professors of Theology in the University of Paris being lately deceased, Adam was greatly desired and sollicited to fill their place, for which reason the Bishop hastened out of Paris for fear of being deprived of a religious auxiliary, who was his chief comfort and support. On the other hand, he was also in danger of losing John or rather actually lost him for the present. For John falling sick of a quartan aigue, Adam attended him down the Seine as far as Mante [*Mantes-la-Jolie*], but there he refused to leave him till he had committed him into safe hands. In the mean time the Bishop, who had gone forward appointed Adam to meet him at the seaside, whether at Rouen or Dieppe or Havre, but not finding him arrived he wrote over to the minister provincial of the Franciscans in England, William of Nottingham, to send some brother to take care of John, and withall brother Peter of Tewkesbury, to be his companion with Adam instead of the said John, and he desires Peter before he crosseth the sea may meet him at Witland i.e. the Isle of Wight, where he intends, God willing, to be on Saturday after St Dennis. This shews the time of our Prelate's return to have been about Michaelmas.

As soon as the Bishop of Lincoln was arrived in England, he set himself to execute the several commissions he had received from his Holiness at Lions. The first was to recommend to the charity of the Archbishop of York the business of the Bishop of Cervia banished with all his relations,[b] I suppose by the Emperor Frederick, for his adhering to the Pope against the said Emperor.[177] The Bishop recommends him as a prelate venerable for his grey years, and for the goodness of his character. The second commission[c] from the Pope was to strengthen King Henry in his attachment to the Holy See. The King returning out of Wales, about the feast of SS. Simon and Jude, the Bishop of Lincoln just arrived from abroad went to meet his Majesty and in a private conference had with him exhorted him to be steady and firm in his adherence to his present Holiness and the See of Rome, the more as some were now seeking, tho in vain to disturb their tranquillity. Thereupon the King returned him this vigorous answer with regards to the prelates signing King John's charter of resignation of his Kingdom to the Pope; an answer which at

---

[a] *Epist. Grosseteste*, 114.
[b] *Epist. Grosseteste*, 116.
[c] *Epist. Grosseteste*, 117.

once contains an explicit profession of the Crown's independency on the Pope as to temporals, and of its entire dependence thereon in spirituals. 'My Lord,' said the King,

> We intend, as in duty bound to preserve the priviledges of our Crown and Royalty untouched. And in this we desire our Lord the Pope and his cardinals to be our assistants. And you may fully assure yourself we shall always pay an entire obedience, fidelity and devotion to our Lord the Pope as to our Spiritual Father and to the holy Roman Church, as our mother and shall always adhere to both with fidelity and constancy, no less in their adversity than in their prosperity. And if ever we fail in this duty the same day we will give our eyes to be plucked out, nay and our very head to be taken off. God forbid, that either life or death, or any other accident whatsoever, should ever separate us from the respect we owe our Spiritual Father and Mother. For besides the general ties which bind all Christian princes to the Church we have others peculiar to us, which knit us more closely to her than other princes. Since, while we were orphans and minors and our subjects not only averse to us but actually up in arms against us, our holy Mother the Roman Church did by her Cardinal Gualo, then Legate in England, bring back the said subjects to their duty and did both anoint and crown us king and place us on the throne.

This answer, different from that he had made five years before to the Emperor Frederick which grounded his peculiar obligation to the Holy See, not only upon the personal benefits he had received from it but upon his father's feudal resignation, which is here omitted. This answer I say the Bishop of Lincoln wrote strait to the Pope to let him know the King's disposition in his regard and what kind of submission he meant to pay his Holiness. We are going to see how the King endeavoured to execute this resolution.

The third commission, wherewith the Bishop of Lincoln was charged, was the raising a subsidy for his Holiness in his present great necessities. The commission was directed not only to our Prelate, but to the Bishops of Wincester, Norwich, Worcester, London, and Coventry, and perhaps to all the English bishops who had assisted at the late Council and the subsidy required was six thousand marks. The Pope was obliged to repeat his demand the year following probably because of the opposition which the levying of it met with from the King, whose profession of spiritual obedience no ways bound him to pay what was exacted as a tribute and acknowledgment of his being feudatory to the Holy See of Rome. The King therefore forbid the bishops to raise the same and this by special briefs directed to each of them. But our Prelate, as zealous for the Pope in what was for edification and of necessity as he was against him in cases of an opposite nature, wrote back to the King in favour of the subsidy and strenuously defended the necessity of it in his 119 letter which is worth hearing as being short it contains the reasons he went upon expressed with no less respect than firmness.

> Your sacred Majesty writes to us that you are surprised, and not a little moved, that of our own head we propose to assess the clergy and religious and to levy the tax for the service of our Lord the Pope. May it therefore please your wisdom to be informed that in this affair we do nothing of ourselves, nor by our own authority, nor alone since our venerable brethren the bishops do the like, or rather have already done it according to the form presented by his Holiness's Nuncio, while in these parts. And both we and they are compelled thereto, by the authority of the sovereign Pontiff, *whom not to obey is as the sin of witchcraft and not to acquiesce to, is as the Crime of Idolatry* [*1 Sam. 15:23*]. It ought not therefore to appear matter of surprise that our fellow bishops and we do this. It would rather be matter of great surprise, and even of indignation, if we did not do something of this kind and even something more, tho unasked and uncommanded. Since we see our Spiritual Father and our Spiritual Mother, to whom we owe incomparably more honour and relief in their distress than to our corporeal parents, banished their own country, pressed on all sides by persecutions and tribulations, stripped of their estates, and not having whereon to subsist with decency. Now if under this deplorable situation we refuse to relieve them it is very certain we transgress the commandment of God, which injoins the honour of parents and consequently we can neither hope to be long lived upon earth nor to enjoy comfort in our children, nor to be heard in the day of prayer. But we cast off the fear of God, we refuse his blessing, we weaken the houses of our children, we disgrace ourselves, and heap up infamy and malediction upon our own heads, as is evident from the testimony of holy writ. For which reason your Royal clemency, which establishes the throne of kings, will not forbid, nor hinder children from honouring their father and mother when they desire to comply with their duty, but will rather encourage and promote their laudable intentions as becomes your Royal magnificence. Your Majesty may be well assured, that such as give you contrary advice are no friend to your Majesty's honour and reputation.

It is highly probable this sensible letter of Lincoln wrought upon the King's mind and inclined him to pass over the odious circumstances of the subsidy being exacted by way of tribute, in consideration of the Holy Father's necessitous situation, for Matthew Paris observes that the King, after some struggles against this *tributary subsidy* yielded at length to it, overcome partly by his brother Richard, Earl of Cornwall partly by the entreaties of some of the bishops who had received powers to interdict the Realm, in case of refusal, and partly by the threats of the Pope who said Henry began to 'Frederickise', and added broad hints of his resolution to treat him in the same manner as he had done Frederick. 'And so vanished,' saith Matthew Paris. 'All hope of seeing the Kingdom freed from the disgracefull tribute.'[a]

What rendered this exaction more odious was its being accompanied with another in favour of Boniface, Archbishop of Canterbury who was

---

[a] *Chron. Maj.*, p. 709.

the Queen's uncle, and this made the subject of a fourth commission which our Prelate of Lincoln received from the Pope while at Lions. By a mandate dated the 27 of August 1245, the Bishop of Lincoln, the Bishop of Hereford and the Bishop of Chichester Elect, i.e. St Richard de Wiche,[a] were enjoined and inpowered to raise for the relief of the See of Canterbury the first year's revenue of all the vacant benefices within that province that should fall within seven years, or till such time as the sum of ten thousand marks should be raised. The Bishop of Lincoln being a leading man among his brethren and of such authority for his understanding and zeal that the rest were disposed to come unto any measure he thought fit to countenance. The Archbishop desired him first to set his seal to the letter, which he and his fellow Commisioners had wrote pursuant to the Pope's injunction to all his suffragans, and then to add thereto another letter to the same suffragans to beg and press them to the execution of the Pope's bull. The Bishop who had undertaken the commission joyfully as to himself, but reluctantly as to others, answered his supplicating Primate that he durst not write the letter he had desired for fear of rendering himself odious to his fellow bishops and to the clergy. Especially as they were already saddled with a double subsidy, one for the King the other for the Pope. For which reason he humbly begged to be excused writing, as desired, and *apposing* his seal to the mandate. The same reasons which hindered the Bishop of Lincoln from taking the step of complaisance for his Primate obliged also the other bishops to suspend their grant of the subsidy. But for this they were all suspended in 1247,[b] nor could they get their necks out of the suspension but by complying with the demand. As to the Bishop of Lincoln, who felt the grievance more than others, he seemed of himself disposed to comply in order to win the new Primate and encourage him to his duty, for he was ready to make a sacrifice of all other considerations that were but merely temporal, providing he could but thereby promote the spiritual good of souls. With this view he had begged of his Holiness while at Lions, and afterwards repeated this petition in his letter[c] to Hugh Cardinal of St Sabina that his Holiness would take care to give the said Archbishop, who was but moderately learned, *good and strong sides* to support him, i.e. wise and godly councillors, not only versed in Canon and Civil Laws but well skilled in the Law of God, and such as have the Holy Scriptures, not in their minds only, but in their hearts and in their actions, which he saith, can be only found in the two orders of the friars (the Franciscans and the Dominicans). What was the effect of this

---

[a] *Epist. Grosseteste*, 89.
[b] *Chron. Maj.*, pp. 692, 702 and 732.
[c] *Epist. Grosseteste*, 115.

most godly and zealous petition doth not appear at present; but from his being obliged to repeat it, it should seem as if other more urgent affairs had obliged this to give way. But how, rationally, piety alone and true zeal are capable of judging.

The Bishop of Lincoln had scarce executed these commissions when the year 1247 beheld new exactions, which rose so high that the clergy and Commons, put up a new list of grievances to the Pope and cardinals and sued for redress.[a] But the distressed Innocent only changed his battery, and in lieu of legates and nuncios now become odious. He sent the same year[b] two English Franciscans, John surnamed Anglicus and provincial of his order in Saxony,[c] and Alexander to make a collection, not by way of demand and injunction, but of a charitable contribution and under this plausible colour they procured the King's licence for making a tour thro all the monasteries and bishopricks of the Realm. When they arrived at Lincoln our holy Prelate, tho greatly affectioned to their order, was exceedingly scandalised at their extravagant dress and equipage, and still more at their extravagant petition, which was no less than six thousand marks for his diocese alone. So that, with all his deference and respect for his Holiness, he declared the petition to be an intolerable exaction and wisely eluded the satisfying it by saying that the affair regarding the whole Kingdom, he could do nothing without first consulting the Lords and Commons and the effect of this consultation, which was held at Oxford the Eve of Low Sunday, was to grant, and this with much adoe, the sum of eleven thousand marks for the whole spirituality. This opposition of our Prelate to the exorbitant demands of these begging nuncios did not make him forfeit his Holiness's esteem, nor hinder the Pope from supporting him in the godly work of reforming his diocese. Hence in 1249,[d] as above related, he obtained of his Holiness a bull for recovering all such churches and tithes as were claimed by certain regulars without a sufficient title. It has been there observed that in consequence of this bull he had assembled all the regulars concerned in it, in the beginnings of 1250, in order to hear and comply with the contents of the bull, but that some had eluded his pastoral vigilance by appealing to the Pope as exemptor these were chiefly the Knights Templars and Hospitaliers, the Norbetines [*sic*], Cistercians, and Gilbertines. The appelants passing over to the Pope at Lions, our indefatigable tho, almost octogenary, Prelate followed them about mid-lent the same year 1250.[e] The Albanian monastick historiographer saith, that by their

[a] *Chron. Maj.*, p. 720.
[b] *Chron. Maj.*, p. [*missing*], 722, 728, 730.
[c] *Collectanea Anglo-Minoritica*, p. 32 and 33.
[d] *Chron. Maj.*, p. 772 and 773.
[e] *Dunstable annals*, p. 287.

presents the appellants found means to escape his pursuits and that our disappointed Prelate made this complaint to his Holiness. 'Holy Father, trusting in your letters and promises, I had hopes of subduing these rebellious children; but I have now the confusion to fail in my expectations and to see them retire free and triumphant.' To which Innocent is said to have returned this unsatisfactory answer, 'Brother of Lincoln, what is this to you? You have delivered your own soul. What if I have a mind to be gracious? Must your eye be evil because I am good?' At which our godly Prelate replied with a deep sigh to himself yet loud enough be heard by his Holiness, 'O money, O money, how great is thy sway, even in the Roman Court!' To which Matthew Paris makes the Pope cry out; 'O wretched English! How do you study to tear and impoverish one another! And you brother of Lincoln, how many religious houses of your diocese which were given to prayer and hospitality have you depressed by your tyrannick and avaricious temper, or to enrich others and perhaps those strangers?' A reproach void of all foundation as to our Prelate, yet so true in regard to him that made it, that either our Albanian censor must have been drowsy when he put this speech in Innocent's mouth or Innocent, if the real author, must have done it with the same view as dishonest women fling dirt at their honest neighbours to make themselves look cleaner. However this be, our Prelate retired hugely mortified and hissed out of the Pope's presence, as a pest old Prelate. The *Annals of Lanercost*[a] add that he resigned his Pastoral Staff, nor would offer any thing for its restitution, for which some avaricious officers of the Court called him the *Sturdy Englishman*. The same annals suppose his resignation was not accepted, as doth the sequel of his history, so great was the Pope's conviction of his zeal being sincere and commendable tho contrary to himself!

After this unsuccessful effort to reduce his refractory children, the Bishop of Lincoln, not to appear to have lost his labours, saith Matthew Paris,[b] applied himself to other business. Hence while several of the prelates and nobility who had crossed the seas with him returned back to England about the rogation-days, or three days before the Ascension, our Prelate staid behind to compass the business in question. The business here hinted, but not specified by Matthew, seems to have been two vigorous remonstrances put up to Innocent the IV, one against the abuses of his Holiness's own court, especially the promotions of evil pastors by his excessive provisions and the excessive exemptions granted to some religious houses. The other against his Primate, the Archbishop of

[a] *Anglia Sacra*, B. 2, p. 341.
[b] *Chron. Maj*., p. 773.

Canterbury, concerning the article of archiepiscopal visitations and the exorbitant fees claimed by him.

The first of these, occasioned as should seem by his disappointment in the attempt to reduce the exempt religious above mentioned, is a memorial couched with all the zeal, understanding, and respect of a St Bernard, of a Cardinal Julian[178] and other select cardinals who, jealous of the honour and priority of the first see, had from time to time put up the like complaint to the popes and expressed the like desires for a reformation of his own particular clergy and Church, which being the head and mistress of all the Churches ought likewise to be their model as she cannot be wanting therein but to their great detriment. Neither is the Court of Rome, like other courts displeased, or apt to resent such zealous remonstrances, when put up with that respectfull and modest tho vigorous zeal, which is due to all superiors and which our Prelate, no less famed for his civility than zeal, observed with all the decorum imaginable, whether in the manner of presenting it or in the terms wherein it is couched. Nay this is the glory of the See of Rome and the effect of that special providence which watches over and preserves the faith of Peter indefectible in his successors, that she not only doth not resent but by her gentleness in the reception encourages such remonstrances of inferior prelates which in the hands of Christ are the means to open the eyes and quicken the vigilance of Peter's successors as were those of Paul in regard of St Peter himself. After this observation, necessary for preventing scandal in the weak, and false constructions in the malicious, we should here give the whole remonstrance verbatim were there any danger of its being lost, but as no such danger is to be apprehended, as long as the Church and her head have enemies ready to store up any thing that can be misconstrued to her disadvantage we shall be content to give a faithfull extract of it without omitting any thing that is material and without fearing any consequences that can be justly drawn from it, either against the authority of the Holy See or against the sanctity, prudence and orthodoxy of him who presented it. Nay so far are we from any such fear that we desire no more authentick testimony of our Prelate's acknowledgement of and respect for the See of St Peter than this very remonstrance, since it must be obvious to the most common Readers that while he crieth out against abuses he leaves the authority of the Holy See not only untouched, but asserted and defended in the most ample and evident manner. All that can be inferred from this remonstrance is that the Court of Innocent the IV had its corruptions and abuses. And what court, I pray, is without them? What wonder there should be abuses where there's a multitude of great officers and especially in the circumstances this Pope was in, who being expelled his see and state was liable like David in his flight from Saul, to have such assemble about him as were hungry votaries of fortune, and at the same time was under the disagreeable necessity of making use of their service for want of better.[a]

This remonstrating memorial was presented to the Pope in a private consistory of select cardinals on the 13 of May and our Prelate who presented it had no other attendant with him in the consistory besides Richard de Mepham, his Archdeacon of Oxford,[179] tho his Archdeacon of Bedford[b] was then at Lions, as were also the Bishops of London and Worcester. The Bishop had drawn up four copies, the first of which he presented to his Holiness. The second to the pious William, Cardinal Bishop of Sabina.[180] The third, to the zealous Hugh Cardinal Priest of St Sabina. The fourth, to John, Cardinal Deacon of St Nicola in Carcere Tulliano,[181] who read the same before the Pope and cardinals. In the beginning of the memorial the Bishop of Lincoln, having premised how Christ, his Apostles and their first successors had planted the Church throughout the world by their labours and blood and had with their authority transmitted the like obligation to the pope as Chief Representative of Christ, to the cardinals as representing the Apostles, and to the other prelates as successors of the primitive bishops. Then he laments the Church's extent being diminished, partly by infidelity, partly by schism and partly by heresy; and the remainder being devoured by all the seven capital sins. Hence descending to the causes of this contraction and misfortune of the Church he attributes so great and terrible a change to two main and general causes, the multiplying of evil pastors and the immoderate restraint put upon the ordinaries, whose business it is to correct such evil pastors. On the first article, after drawing from the prophets a horrible but true picture of such pastors he probes the sore to the bottom and thrusts his spiritual *launcette* in the first and principal cause of the evil. 'And what,' saith he.

> Is the prime and original spring of all these direfull evils? I am sore afraid, and tremble to say it, yet dare I not withhold the truth, for fear of that reproachfull curse of the prophet, 'Woe to me for holding my peace, because I am a man of polluted lips.' [*Is. 6:5*] The original fountain of this evil is this very Court not only by neglecting to purge away these abominations, she *who alone hath the principal authority and a sovereign obligation to do it*, but because by her dispensations, provisions and collations she herself sets up such pastors, or rather destroyers of the flock, and to provide for the temporal convenience of one person, delivers up to all the beasts of the field thousands of souls for the reviving of which the Son of God suffered the most disgracefull of deaths. For he who in the midst of devouring wolves, bears and lions, commits the flock to a shepherd who is either unable or ignorant, or unwilling, or negligent to lead the sheep into proper pastures, or to bring back the strays to the fold, or

---

[a] *Dunstable annals*, p. 266.
[b] *Chron. Maj.*, p. 773.

> refuses to expose himself eer so little to the fury of the devouring beasts for the safety of his flock, he I say, who commits the flock to such a shepherd merely that he may enjoy the milk and the fleece, doth he not give 'em up to be slaughtered and devoured? And is he not guilty of their death, tho some one perchance escape? He who on a stormy and rocky sea gives the helm of the ship full of passengers either to a paralytick or to one ignorant of navigation, or unexperienced, or negligent or unwilling to take upon him the trouble of the steerage, he who confides the ship to such a pilot merely to enrich him with the freight of the passengers doth not he expose the ship and all in it to destruction and is he not guilty of their loss, tho some one perhaps may escape in the wreck? And he, who doth not oppose the flock and the ship's being entrusted with such governors and even hinder the same when it is in his powers and a part of his duty, such one no doubt becomes partaker of the guilt. Wherefore the sheep are to be provided of a careful shepherd and the passengers of a skillfull and able pilot, neither ought either to be exposed to eternal ruin for the temporal convenience of any man whatever. Far be this, even immensely far, from him to whom the charge of the salvation of souls is *immediately* and *principally* committed, and who is the *Chief Representative* of him who hath said by his prophet, 'I will give you pastors according to my own heart, who shall feed you with knowledge and with doctrine.' [*Jer. 3:15*] And by another prophet, 'I will feed my sheep … that which was lost I will seek, and that which was strayed, I will bring back.' [*Ezk. 34:15–16*].

After this, our most zealous and charitable Prelate goeth on shewing the guilt of such a conduct, from the infinite disproportion betwixt the low temporal views on which such collations of evil pastors proceed, and those more sublime and divine ones, on which they ought to be founded. The sole true end of collating any one to the Pastoral charge being the eternal salvation and happiness of the flock, whereas the drift of these irregular collations is only some carnal or temporal motive, and as this disproportion betwixt the two ends, so also the disorder of it is infinitely black. Then he subjoins.

> None in his wits, entrust the care even of an irrational flock but with one who understands the office, and is both able and willing to perform it. If therefore he entrusts the care of a rational and spiritual flock to one who hath neither knowledge, nor capacity, nor willingness to execute the charge, is it not more clear than the Sun that he is more concerned for brute beasts than for rational creatures, more for what is corporeal than for what is spiritual, more for transitory than for eternal things, more for triffles of little or no value, than for souls bought with an inestimable price even with the precious blood and death of the Son of God? O Sovereign ingratitude! … Herod in the massacre of the Innocents sought but one whom he deemed a child and this thro fear of losing an earthly Kingdom, the crucifiers of Jesus, tho most impious only imagined they persecuted a man tho of wonderfull works and contrary to their ways. For had they known him, they never would have crucified the Lord of Glory.[182] But he, who entrusts the care of the flock or the ship of Peter in the manner above specified persecutes Christ in his members, and delivers

> him to destruction whom he believes to be God, the King of all creatures in heaven and earth, his very Creator and Redeemer, his future accuser and judge. Now which of these two persecutions think ye is most contrary to reason and sense? Which of the two is attended with the most atrocious cruelty, and the most rash presumption?

After this the Bishop adds, that this conduct is not only very highly reprehensible in itself but more so in its consequences. 'For this court,' saith he. 'Being the book in which others read the rule of their conduct excites of course all other pastors of churches to follow this pernicious example in presenting unfit persons to the benefices of their nomination and to let themselves be guided therein only by wordly and reproveable views. Then the Bishop refutes the pretences made use of to palliate this abuse, viz that it was for the common utility of the Church. To which he rejoins that our forefathers sought the utility of the Church by suffering evil themselves, but not by doing it. Another excuse was that the persons thus charged with the flock had their substitutes. 'But,' resumes the Bishop,

> Besides that such substitutes are for the most part mercenaries, the pastoral charge doth not barely consist in the administration of the sacraments and saying the canonical hours and Mass, which these hirelings seldom perform as they ought; but in a zealous preaching of the word of God, in a vehement reproving of vice, in correcting it where necessary with vigour and authority, and chastising it with severity. All which tho mercenaries may know, which is rarely the case, they have not courage to perform. It consists moreover, in giving food to the hungry and drink to the thirsty and clothes to the naked and harbour to the stranger, in visiting the sick and imprisoned, and all this chiefly toward their parisioners by whose liberality they subsist. Now all this is not in the power of these substitutes who have scarce a competent maintenance for themselves and yet this evil, how great soever and worthy to be deplored with floods of tears, is tolerable in comparison of the other when the churches in question are conferred on seculars tho negligent etc. There's hopes of their being one day succeeded by good ones, but when the parishes are appropriated to religious houses then the evil is rivetted forever (because then these needy substitutes, and their inability to comply with the various branches of the pastoral office above specified, become perpetual).[a]

After deploring this evil, the Bishop compares the charge given to the Holy See by Christ to that given by God to Moses for building the tabernacle, and saith that the Church militant signified by the Jewish tabernacle is to be formed upon the model of the Church triumphant, whereof the model shewed to Moses on the Mount was a type. On which he runs this beautifull and mystical comparison between the two Churches of Heaven and Earth, where if in one place he seems to admit no more

[a] See in the *Annals of Burton* ad an. 1259 p. 440, the like complaint of the nobility to Alexander IV and that Pope's answer.

exemptions in the Church Militant than in the Triumphant, this must be understood of exemptions against order and their excessive number, for our Prelate was too wise not to see the difference betwixt the order of the Church Triumphant, where every subordinate hierarchist or minister being perfect there can be no room for exemptions, and the Church Militant where inferior prelates, being liable to abuse their power over their subjects, leave room of course and necessity for the Prime Pastor to restrain them and to exempt upon just motives some from their ordering jurisdiction, as far as is consistant with the correction of manners. 'In the structure of the tabernacle,' saith our Doctor of Lincoln, now speaking as a mystick *Theologian*.

> Moses was commanded to consider well and to frame all things in it, according to the original shewn him on the Mount. Now it's most evident this order is chiefly directed to them who preside over this Holy See, whom it highly behoves as it is their strict and bounden duty to see that all things be done to the edification of the Church Militant after the example of the Church triumphant. Now in this latter every hierarchist according to his rank, science, operation and natural capacity is assimilated to the form of God, is brought by divine illuminations to an imitation of and union with God, and is divinely perfected and deified with him. And then thro the love and desire he has to communicate to his inferiors what he hath received from above he intends and with all his might operates the purification, illumination, and perfection of his said inferiors. And according to each one's capacity for receiving his influx, he assimilates and unites them to God and communicates to them according to their respective dignities a portion of that sacred deification he himself hath received from God. Moreover as help to their capacity of receiving his communications, he conferreth upon them whatever may orderly promote in them that degree of divine assimilation, union and deification which is of their competence. But to no one doth he communicate what in the least may obstruct such attainments. Hence he communicates to no one what is above his capacity or what is any ways incongruous or inconvenient. Neither doth he assist one by hurting another, nor raise one by depressing his neighbour; but by the word inwardly communicated and by his examples, he conveys to him all things that are salutary and nothing prejudicial. On the contrary he restrains, protects and defends them from every thing pernicious or hurtful. There moreover, is no exemption of any inferior from his natural and divinely appointed superior, consequently no subversion or interruption of order, no disposition or administration but what is performed in a holy manner.

The Bishop concludes this article by adding that such builders of this inferior tabernacle of the Church Militant as imitate these orderly practices of the heavenly hierarchists and builders of the Celestial Tabernacle, are faithfull servants in all the houses of God and that such as do not imitate them are disturbers and destroyers.

To set forth the dignity and duties of the first see, he draws this other sublime and fine comparison betwixt her and the Sun. 'This most Holy See,' saith he,

> Is the throne of God and is in his sight, as the Sun of the whole Universe. Now as the illumination, the vegetation and sensitive life, the nourishment, the encrease, the perfection, the beauty, the splendour and charms of the visible world are causally in the sun, which by its influx produces all these effects in the body of the world and thereby preserves the whole in its due perfection, so is it necessary that this most Holy See contain in itself as in their cause all the foresaid properties taken in a spiritual sense, and that by her influence she communicate the same continually to the spiritual world of which she is the spiritual Sun, thereby to save the spiritual world. Otherwise as this sensible and material world must perish if once the Sun lose its causality and influence upon it, so likewise, if the spiritual Sun cease its spiritual causality and influx on the spiritual world the consequence is unavoidable, that the world of which he is the light must perish and that he must be responsible for its destruction especially as the spiritual causality and influx are in his power. But God forbid, this spiritual Sun, which is always enlightened by learning and moved by justice, should be ever turned into darkness or becoming retrograde should return back in its course! They *who preside in the most Holy See, are the principal representatives of Christ among men*, and of course are principally obliged to shew forth the works of Christ and none others which are contrary thereto, that as we are obedient to our Lord Jesus Christ in all things so we may also be to those who preside in the Holy See while they put on Christ and shew forth his Spirit in their injunctions, and do thereby truly preside over his Church. But should any of them, which God forbid, put on sentiments of flesh and blood, or the spirit of the world, or any other spirit than the Spirit of Christ, and should by the same injoin any thing contrary to the will and commands of Christ, then he who obeyeth such injunctions evidently separates himself from Christ and his body which is the Church and even from the President of this See as truly presiding in it and truly representing Christ. And when obedience to such injunctions shall become general then the true and *compleat defection is come*. Then is the manifestation of the Son of Perdition near at hand. But far, far be it from this most Holy See, and them that preside in it whose decrees are generally received, ever to become the cause of a true revolt and defection, by injunctions contrary to the Law of Christ. Far be it from them when they meet with truly faithfull servants of Christ, and such as are fully determined never to go against his ordinances, ever to injoin them any thing contrary to the will of Christ and thereby make themselves the cause of an apparent schism and revolt. Let them not therefore either do, or command others to do, any thing against Christ to whom nothing is more hatefull and abominable than the ruin of souls, nor consequently than giving the charge of them to destroyers instead of pastors as above expressed, but rather let them give their lives for them after his example whose *chief representatives* they are.

After lamenting the multiplication of evil pastors and the causes of it, the Bishop decends to the second article of the restraint put upon the power of the ordinaries, who alone are within reach of correcting the foresaid evil pastors. 'The pastoral authority, which was given to the Apostles, and to their children the bishops, over every devil, and every disease in order to cure them, is now greatly shackled,' saith the Bishop.

> Especially in England. Firstly by exemptions, which are nowhere found in the Church Triumphant in so much that if the exempt come to fall into any sin of fornication or adultery, or other enormous and diabolical sins, even out of the precincts of their own monasteries the bishops or other pastors have no power over the devils which thus totally possess them, but are obliged to see their sheep carried off and devoured by the wolves without being able to oppose their enemy or so much as to cry out against him, because of their exemptions. Now when the supreme Pastor shall demand in his rigorous judgement an account of the sheep lost under their pastors' very eye, how will the pastors excuse themselves, but by throwing the blame upon the authors of these exemptions and priviledges?

This complaint was so just and necessary that the Council of Trent and the popes who presided in it, rectified the abuse and ordered no exemptions to have places where the correction of manners was concerned.[183]

'A second restrant upon the power of the ordinaries,' continues the Bishop,

> Arises from the secular power, which in enquiries made concerning the disorders of the laity, will not suffer the tender of an oath to be made in order for coming at the knowledge of the truth. A third restraint comes from the reception of appeals (*tuitionis appellaciorium*) for when the bishop or other pastor labours to expel the evil spirits of fornication out of their subjects and to heal their spiritual diseases some of the delinquents by the quirks of the lawyers appeal first to this See and then to the archiepiscopal see for the defense and reception of their appeal, *ad tuitionem*. Whereby they rot like beasts on the dunghill of their filthy pleasures at least for a year, and by this occasion frequently forever. A fourth restraint on the pastoral authority are appeals to the metropolitan in whose court the causes are spun out thro all the subtleties and formalities of the Civil Law. In the interim the correction of manners is delayed for a long time, and perhaps for ever, the pastor being almost tired out of his life and his zeal for correction of his sheep, often quite extinguished. For where is the Physician I pray, who seeing his patient repell his medicinal hand and himself restrained by a superior power from reducing him, nay and sometimes persecuted for his charity, doth not at the long run slacken his care and solicitude? The fifth and last restriction is this, that whenever a zealous pastor hath the happiness either to keep out of the fold such evil pastors as above described, or where in to expell them, if the pastor thus kept out or expelled chance to be of the Court, or in any office belonging to the Crown, or to have any friend or relations there, then the bishop is sure forthwith to fall under some intolerable vexations, either as to

> the liberties or temporalties of his church. And if the rejected pastors cannot render the secular power subservient to their desires, then by some trick of the law they obtain of some superior court such judges as they know favourable to their inclinations and thus render their pastor's zeal ineffectual and fruitless … to these and such like abuses, tending to the evident ruin of souls, let this Holy See endeavour to put a stop. She whose office it is to save the whole world … and who is constituted over nations and kingdoms to root up all evil and to plant in its place whatever is right and holy.

After this the Bishop returning to the abuses reigning in the Pope's family, and in those of his cardinals, first the crying *impudicity* [*marginal note: sic Bailey*] of their servants and officers. Secondly their own inconstancy in abrogating by repeating *non-obstantes* their first ordinances. He then adds,

> The world also makes loud complaint, that contrary to the command of Christ to Peter to put up his sword, this court weilds the material sword with her own hand tho such as have any concern for the safety of the Holy See are greatly apprehensive least she fall, which God forbid, under the terrible communication annexed to that command, 'All they that take up the sword, by the sword shall perish.' And whereas Abraham, Moses and Samuel, the types and models of this court, rejected and kept their hands clean from receiving of presents, and whereas God hath forbidden the reception thereof especially to judges, because presents blind the wise, subvert the words of the just and prevent judgement, the world hears with astonishment that this court so famed for holiness and for the equity of its judgement stands impeached of receiving presents.

Then our prelate adds that both the people and clergy of England make bitter outcry against the Roman Court for having granted to the See of Canterbury an exhorbitant subvention upon all the benefices falling vacant within that province. After which he concludes his whole memorial in these words.

> In excuse for the abuses let no-one say, 'the times are evil, and the world seated in wickedness,' and that therefore many things are to be winked at for the common good of the Church. As if for this reason, the least evil were to be done that good might come on it. Whereas according to the Apostle an everlasting *vae* [*woe*] and just condemnation hangs over the head, not only of such as do these things but of those who justify them. The worse the times are, and the more weakness there is in the world, the more vigorously ought we who are not of the world to decline every evil course and persevere with a firm step in the paths of virtue, as where the weight of the battle falls heaviest there resistence ought to be more manful and desertion and cowardice more guarded against. The more eagerly we desire to avoid any suffering and either to retain or acquire any good, the more courageously and prudently we ought to stand fast against every evil action. Since by a just judgement of God evidenced in Holy Scripture, he who doth evil to eschew suffering and to obtain or preserve any good, necessarily falls into the evil. He fears and loses the good he lusteth after. Hence it is hugely to be feared or rather

it ought to be held for a certain truth by this Holy See, that the distress and want of conveniences she now groans under, is all owing to the forementioned and to other such like abuses. And that unless she correct the same, she will soon be deprived of (all) good and while she is crying out peace and security, will feel eternal death rush upon her and find herself subjected to those severe and lamentable woes which God the Father hath pronounced by the mouth of his only begotten, and by that of his Son's beloved disciple, as also by the mouth of the Lawgiver (Moses) and all his holy prophets from the beginning.

These few remonstrances have I presented to your Holiness, full of fear and trembling, but overcome by the more powerfull fear of that *vae* which terrified Isaiah, and by the ardent desire of seeing the evils complained of corrected. Wherefore with all humility and devotion, with a heart big with sorrow and bleeding with tears, I conjure your fatherly goodness not to ascribe to presumption what nothing but the fear of God, and zeal for the purity of his house, hath extorted from the *last* of sinners.

What particular effect, or impressions this generous remonstrance had upon the Pope and his consistory is not specified in history; this we are sure of by the sequel, that it had no bad effects with regard to our Prelate. Nor is such the method of that wise and refined Court, which either profits of just and necessary remonstrances, to remedy the complained of abuses, or winks at them and conceals her resentment, as knowing that such resentments only *exasperate* the evil and cover the resenters with new odium. Of this wisdom in the Pope's Court we have an instance in one of the four cardinals to which our Prelate presented his memorial. This Cardinal, which was Hugh, Cardinal Priest of Sabina[a] preaching before the Pope, and his Court, and the whole city of Lions the year following, gave a much more satyrical stroke at one of the abuses complained of by the Bishop of Lincoln, viz the impudicity of the domestick officers attending the Pope's Court. Now as this satyr, tho very biting and publick, drew no disgrace upon its author, much less did our Prelate's more guarded, tho more universal remonstrance, which was presented not in a publick sermon as was the Cardinal Hugh's sarcasm, but in a private consistory and with all the temper that could render it profitable to the parties concerned. Accordingly we are going to see that the Bishop of Lincoln, so far from incurring his Holiness's displeasure, was but the more respected and employed by him in several weighty commissions. Even three months after this remonstrance, and before he quitted Lions, he obtained of the Pope a bull dated the 25 of September in the eighth year of his Pontificate i.e. 1250 for the augmentation of poor vicarages, as we have seen above. And he obtained another the year following for another purpose of ^reducing and^ fixing the taxation of archiepiscopal fees and visitations, as we are going to mention.

---

[a] *Chron. Maj.*, p. 819.

The same 13 of May, on which he presented the foregoing memorial to the Pope, he exhibited another against the Archbishop of Canterbury his metropolitan. This princely Primate, who was uncle to the Queen, seeing the Bishop of Lincoln's successful victory over his Chapter in the cause of the visitation, set about an archiepiscopal visitation of his suffragans.[a] But his views being rather to pick up the fees than to reform the abuses. Our intrepid Prelate, who gave no quarter to abuses whether at home or abroad, pressed his Primate not so much in the office of visitation as in the collection of the visitatorial fees. We have but a part of this memorial which seems levelled not only at the Archbishop of Canterbury, but likewise at his own successors. Therein the Bishop of Lincoln declares that, 'After the example of his predecessors he had visited the religious houses of his diocese, and in consequence thereof had received of them the customary fees.' Then fearing the ill consequences thereof he adds,

> Neither did it then enter my thoughts that my visitation would be made a precedent for aggrieving the subjects. But now from many things I see doing, I am firmly persuaded that unless this Holy See apply some remedy, my successors will extort new and extraordinary fees for their visitation to the great aggrievance and scandal of the souls under their charge. If it be objected that without these dues the work of the visitation will go forward but lamely, my answer is that interested and mercenary visitors will be totally occupied in gathering the fees to the neglect of the visitation and will become farmers out of sins, while the same covetousness will make them take bribes from those they find living in sin, and so let them continue in them without control. Now as much as I, Bishop of Lincoln, am more pastor of the souls of my diocese than our Lord the Archbishop of Canterbury, who in the opinions of many is not their proper pastor, and as much as the said Primate is more able (by his own revenues) to perform the archiepiscopal office than I to perform the office of a bishop, so much the more cogent are the reasons alledged above and so much the more conclusive against his receiving extraordinary fees (for his visitations).[b]

The Archbishop for the present found means to ward off the effect of this remonstrance but in the beginning of the year following the week before Ash Wednesday,[c] our Prelate being on his episcopal visitation at Dunstable, was there met by the Bishops of London, Salisbury and Norwich in person and by the other bishops in their deputies, where they promised by an instrument in writing and under their seals to stand by each other against the Archbishop's visitation, and for this end taxed themselves and their clergy with a little subsidy of two pence in the mark, whereby they sent two deputies to the See Apostolick, one for

---

[a] *Chron Maj.*, p. 802.
[b] *Anglia Sacra*, B. 2, pp. 345–47.
[c] *Dunstable annals*, p. 288.

the bishops and their cathedral chapters, the other for the inferior clergy. And the effect of this league and deputation was a bull addressed to our Prelate empowering him to reduce the exorbitant dues of archiepiscopal, episcopal and archidiaconal visitations, and to proportion them to the revenues of each church and to the taxation fixed by the late Council of Lateran, which was sent over together with the bull and executory letters addressed to the Bishops of London and Welles. This bull is dated from Peruggia, the 10 of July the 9th Year of Innocent IV pontificate, i.e. 1251, which the Burton Annalist places in 1252 because he erroneously places the Pope's accession to the year 1244, instead of 1243. This bull, granted by the Pope after he had quitted Lions is a second evidence that our Prelate's remonstrance above mentioned had been taken otherwise than well. In thanks for this moderating decree the clergy and religious agreed to make his Holiness a present of a twentieth.[a]

---

[a] *Dunstable annals*, p. 296.

Chapter V

THE BISHOP OF LINCOLN'S LAST CONTROVERSY WITH AN OPPOSITION TO POPE INNOCENT. WHETHER HE WAS EXCOMMUNICATED BY THAT POPE FOR HIS LAST LETTER TO HIM

The Bishop of Lincoln who returned from Lions about Michaelmas 1250,[a] seeing the little effect of his zeal, whether for reducing his refactory children or for the general correction of abuses, as also the general confusion which threatened the Church, whether in the broils between the Pontificate and the Empire or the incursions of the Saracens on the Holy Land, he resolved within himself to imitate his most pious and learned friend, Dr Nicholas de Farnham Bishop of Durham, who but two years before had resigned his bishoprick and bid farewell to this world, the better to prepare himself for the next. Nevertheless, as our Prelate's zeal was no less considerate than it was ardent, he could not help reflecting on the bad consequences of his friend's resignation which was a long vacancy of that important see and therefore fearfull of the like fate for his own Church, or that the King would intrude upon it some worthless creature of his own, he wisely kept his counsel to himself and suspended the execution till a more favourable opportunity offered for doing it with safety. Preferring the publick good of his Church to his own private satisfaction which he promised himself in a more quiet course of prayer, contemplation and study.

To enjoy some part of his projected abdication of the episcopacy he discharged himself of the most distracting part of his office upon Dr Robert de Marisco his official and since Archdeacon of Oxford and Dean of Lincoln. He was however far from being idle himself. He continued with his usual ardour to oppose and root out abuses, whether from the particular field of his own diocese, or from the general one of the whole English Church. In the beginning of 1251[b] he made a general visitation of all his clergy and religious of both sexes, and in spite of his great age and infirmities continued to preach frequently to his people and clergy.

---

[a] *Chron. Maj.*, p. 802.

[b] *Chron Maj.*, p. 815.

All that he found living contrary to the canons, especially in the article of chastity, he chastised according to the same canons, without distinction of clergy or religious, natives or foreigners, English or Romans.[a] Such of these last as were not edifying in their lives, he rejected tho armed with papal provisions and abhorred them as so many venimous and destroying serpents. And on these occasions it was a usual saying with him that if he admitted such to the cure of souls he should be guilty of 'Satanising'. For which reason, adds Matthew Paris, he *frequently* stood off, and rejected the Pope's letters and bulls for that effect. But it was not always with impunity. Matthew Paris under the year 1251 writes that in the Lent following viz 1252,[b] Bishop Grossetete was suspended from his episcopal functions for refusing a fat benefice with cure of souls to a certain Italian who did not know a word of English and was unfit of course for the functions annexed to the benefice. Matthew doth not specify, by whom the Bishop was suspended. The *Chronicle of John, Abbot of Peterborough*,[c] observes of the Venerable Sewal, Archbishop of York and a favourite disciple of St Edmund's Archbishop of Canterbury, that soon after his consecration he was suspended by one of the Pope's clerks, and so continued till the day of his death. The Pope knowing nothing of the matter, '[*Consecratus est*] *Magister Sewaldus* [*in archiepiscopum Ebroracensem, et*] *suspensus est statim ab officis suo per clericum domini Papae usque ad mortem; et hoc Papa ignoravit*.'[d]

In all appearance, it was by some such a judge that the just and zealous Lincoln was suspended, as he had been formerly by the assuming Chapter of Canterbury. However whether this suspension came from the Pope or from some inferior clerk it was either revoked immediately or neglected, as evidently unjust, and *ipso facto* void, since we find our Prelate immediately going on with his functions and in full communion with his fellow bishops, and namely with St Richard, Bishop of Chichester, nay and with the Pope and cardinals. Sometime after Easter of the year 1252, which succeeded his said suspension in the foregoing Lent, he himself excommunicated one Hurtoldus [*Hurtold*] a foreigner, whom the King had intruded into the Church of Flamstede [*Flamstead*] near St Albans, in prejudice to the Queen's Chaplain William canonically precollated thereto.[e] The 13 of October, the same year 1252, when the King by virtue of a papal mandate demanded a tenth of all Eccesiastical [*illegible*] for three years, the Bishop of Lincoln was then in Parliament with the rest

---

[a] *Chron. Maj.*, p. 825.
[b] *Chron. Maj.*, p. 816.
[c] *Peterborough Chronicles*, p. 113.
[d] *Master Sewald [was consecrated as Archbishop of York, and] was instantly suspended from his office by the clerk of the Lord Pope until his death; and of this the Pope was not aware.*
[e] *Chron. Maj.*, p. 839.

of Lord's Spiritual and entered a protest against this royal and papal exaction and his protest was immediately embraced by all the prelates, and in particular by the most holy and illustrious St Richard de Wiche, Bishop of Chichester.[a]In April next year 1253, when a new debate of the forsaid tenth came on, and the tenth finally granted on condition of the King's renewing the charters, backed with a most solemn sentence of excommunication as before seen our Prelate was one of the pronouncers of this sentence.[b]

The Bishop of Lincoln was no less in communion with the Pope himself. For soon after the just mentioned parliament and about August 1253, Pope Innocent surprised by false representations, and repeated importunities of his hungry coutiers and relations, directed to our Prelate as he had already often done both to him and to other certain provisional letters which the Burton Annalist styles, 'hateful to God and men'.[c] Whereby the Bishop of Lincoln was enjoined to provide one Frederick de Lavinia [*Lavagna*], his Holiness's nephew and secretary, with the first benefices that should fall in his diocese. But the contents appearing contrary to justice and reason, our zealous observer of the canons, Divine as well as Ecclesiatick, not only demurred executing the letter in question but the more inveterate the abuse and the nearer he approached the dread tribunal of Christ, was the louder he cried out against it and wrote thereupon his famous letter, so often cried up by those who spiderly delight in weaving cobwebs with the filth of the Roman Court. And which Browne no less weakly than insincerely calls his renouncing of obedience to the Pope's authority. Tho nothing can be more evident both from the whole tenor of the letter, which we shall here subjoin that the Reader may judge for himself, and from the reception it met with at Rome, than that while the Bishop of Lincoln crieth out against abuses, he crieth no less loud for the supremecy of the Roman See in its fullest extent. ^And in this reproof our vigorous Prelate hath the example of the inspired writers, who with modest freedom condemn the conduct of the ancient Pontiffs, Aaron, Heli, Alcimus etc.[184] and of the first Pontiff Peter, without any prejudice to their authority, and are therefore the justification of those who gave the like reproof with the spirit of modest and generous zeal.^ Grossetete derives the atrociousness of the guilt in the present case from the super-eminency of the power and to obligations the First See lieth under. The censures threatened against all that opposed the Pope's *provisory* letters, did not frighten our enlightened Prelate who knew the wide difference betwixt just censures annexed to a real violation of duty, and those wicked

---

[a] *Chron. Maj.*, p. 849 etc.
[b] *Chron. Maj.*, p. 856; *An. Burt.*, p. 323.
[c] *An. Burt.*, p. 405.

ones that are *prised* from superiors by selfish and carnal men against an apparent violation, but in reality against a true and real accomplishment of necessary duties. He not only courageously and piously opposed their execution, but in justification of his opposition wrote back the following letter addressed to N. Archdeacon of Canterbury,[185] and to Innocent the Pope's secretary, who had forwarded to him the provisional letters in question. Matthew Paris places this about the Feast of Our Lady in 1253.

> Robert by divine permission Bishop of Lincoln, to the Archdeacon of Canterbury and to Master Innocent the Pope's secretary, greeting and blessing.[a] I hear you have received letters under this form, *Innocent etc*, wherefore be it known unto your wisdoms that with a filial devotion, I embrace and obey all such mandates, as are truly apostolick. But all such as are of a contrary tendency I withstand and oppose out of zeal for the honour of our Holy Father. To both these steps I am equally bound by the law of God. Now no mandates either are in themselves or can be deemed Apostolick, but in as much as they are agreeable to the doctrine of the Apostles and of our Lord Jesus Christ of *whose person and authority our Lord the Pope is the Chief Representative in the Ecclesiastick Hierarchy; Cujus Typum et personam maxime gerit Dominus Papa*. Christ hath said, 'He that is not with me, is against me.' But against Christ, the most divine sanctity of [*the*] See Apostolick neither is nor can be. Yet the tenor of this mandate is so far from being agreeable to the apostolick sanctity that scarce anything can be more opposite to it, first because the accumulated *non obstantes* of this and such like letters, crowded one upon another without any view to inforce the Law of nature do (by contradicting and annulling each other) let in a deludge of inconstancy, audaciousness, shameless lies and deceits, diffidence in believing any one with other numberless sins, to the scandal of Christianity and disturbance of civil society. Secondly because after the sin of Lucifer and Antichrist, whom in the latter times our Lord Jesus Christ is to exterminate by the breath of his mouth, there neither is nor can be any kind of sin so diametrically opposite to the doctrine of the Apostles and of the Gospels. Nor so hatefull and abominable to Christ, nor so destructive to the faithfull, as the sin which destroys the souls of men by depriving them of that pastoral care, which alone can forward and effectuate their salvation. Now of this crying sin the Scriptures evidently convict all such as, vested with pastoral authority, pamper their carnal passions with the milk and wool of the sheep, but take no care to feed them and provide for their eternal welfare by a just discharge of the pastoral functions. Since according to the Sacred Writings, not to feed, and govern the flock is to kill and destroy it. That these two kinds of sin are tho in different degrees, exceedingly enormous, and incomparably blacker than all other kinds of sin, is evident from their opposition to two things which of all others are the most excellent. For the measure of wickedness is taken from its opposition to good. The first (by opening a door to evil) is opposite to, and as much as in it lieth, destructive of the essential goodness of the Deity. The second (by

[a] *Chron. Maj.*, p. 870; *An. Burt.*, p. 326.

destroying the life of grace in the souls of the flock) is no less destructive of the divine Deification or participation of the Divine nature in the soul, but then as in good the cause is reputed better than the effect, so also in evil the cause must be esteemed worse than the evil it produces. Hence the consequence is most clear, that they who let loose such murderers of souls upon the flock of Christ are themselves more wicked than those very murderers, and more nearly allied to Lucifer and to Antichrist. And this in proportion as their *station is more eminent*[a] *and as their greater and diviner power, which they have received from God for edification and not for destruction*,[186] laith them under more strict obligation of banishing and rooting out such most wicked destroyers from the flock of Christ. Hence the most Holy See Apostolick, to *which our Lord Jesus Christ* the holy of holies hath *delivered all kind of power potestas omnimoda*, for edification, as the Apostle saith. And not for the destruction, cannot either injoin or attempt to injoin anything which tends to a crime so hateful to Christ, and so pernicious to his flock. For this would be a glaring apostacy, and an evident abuse and corruption of its *most holy* and *plenary* authority, *potestatis sanctissimae et plenissimae*. This would be descending from the glorious throne of Christ and ascending the Chair of Pestilence, which teaches the road to hell, and there seating herself near the two forementioned Princes of Darkness. Nor can any one who professes a sincere obedience to the Holy See and is not retrenched from it, and from the body of Christ, by schism, obey such injunctions from whence soever they are issued forth, tho from the supreme order of angels above; rather he is obliged to contradict, and *rebel* against them.

Wherefore reverend Sirs, out of the filial obedience *I owe to the See Apostolick*, and from the ardent desire I have of being united with her in Christ's body, I do, I say from filial love and obedience, disobey, contradict and rebel against the contents of the foresaid letters as evidently paving the way to the sins above specified, so hatefull to Jesus Christ, so prejudicial to the society, so derogatory to the See Apostolick and to the canons of the Church. Neither can your Reverences decree any thing against me on this account, seeing my words and actions herein are in truth neither contradiction nor rebellion, but a filial obedience to the Law of God and a dutiful regard to my mother (the Church) and to my father (the Pope). Now therefore to resume in few words what I have exposed at length, the holy Apostolick See can do nothing but for the edification, for this is the plentitude and perfection of her authority, to be able to do all things for edification. But these provisions as they are termed are not for edification but for manifest destruction. Ergo they cannot be issued out, nor injoined by the blessed See Apostolick but flesh and blood, which cannot inherit the Kingdom of God, has inspired them and not the Father of our Lord Jesus Christ, who is in heaven.

On the first reception of this vigorous yet respectful letter, which was transmitted to the Pope by his secretary, his Holiness waxed angry and if

---

[a] *Quanto magis superexcellentes, qui ex majore et diviniore potestate sibi … divinitus tradita* etc. 2 Cor. 10:8.

we believe Matthew Paris he treated the author of it with the appellations of a deaf and doating old fellow, swearing by Saints Peter and Paul that but for his own good nature he would make him the fable and scorn of the whole world, and asking if the King of England were not his vassal ready at his beck to imprison and disgrace him? But the same author[a] adds that several of the Sacred College, especially Giles [*de Torres*] the Spanish Cardinal of near 100 years of age[b] and of prudence and integrity equal to his years, endeavoured to pacify his Holiness saying to him, 'Most Holy Father it would be no ways expedient to decree any thing against this Bishop. For to be plain with your Holiness, he hath written nothing but the truth, nor is he liable to censure. He is a Catholick and moreover a most holy Prelate, by far more religious than us, and of such eminent life that he is thought not to have his superior, or even his equal in the whole episcopal body. This is a point notorious to all the French and English clergy. Neither could our opposing him be to any purpose. The truth contained in *this letter, and probably made known to many, would only* raise us a multitude of enemies. For this Prelate has the reputation of being a great philosopher, an able linguist perfectly skilled in Latin and Greek, a zealous assertor of justice, a Professor of School Theology, a preacher and instructor of the people, a lover of chastity, a persecutor of simonists.' Cardinal Giles therefore, and the other cardinals with him, concluded that their advice was that his Holiness should wink at the letter and say no more about it for fear of greater disturbance, especially as it *was well known that the separation must one day come.*

His Holiness seems to have followed this Christian and judicious advice of the Spanish and the other cardinals since this same year and very soon after this letter and as the Burton Annalist[c] assures us in consequence of our Prelate's zealous remonstrance, the Pope sent over to all the English prelates a bull in the most ample form, in which he excuses his being imposed on in the above and such like cases by the importunity of petitioners and expresseth his gladness that such extorted provisions are rejected.

This is the matter of fact as related by Matthew Paris a contemporary and by the Burton Annalist from the original bulls. Hence appears the little stress that is to be laid on [*Henry*] Knighton and John of Tinmouth who, 150 years after, wrote that for his letter the Bishop of Lincoln was excommunicated. Knighton, who seems to have led the other into mistake and is in general a confused writer, here evidently confounds two or three facts in one.[187] In the first place he marks this letter wherein the

[a] *Chron. Maj.*, p. 872.
[b] *Chron. Maj.*, p. 916.
[c] *An. Burt.*, p. 328.

Pope's nephew is rejected at 1253, the same as his memorial presented to the Pope at Lions in 1250, as appears by his citing the beginning of it. Secondly on this rejection of the Pope's nephew, Knighton sends the Rejector to Rome and there laith him under an excommunication, whereas the Bishop's last journey to the Pope was in 1250 and at the writing of this letter 1253 which was about the Assumption, the Bishop of Lincoln was then in his last sickness which seized him in the dogdays. The origin of Knighton's error seems to have been this; he had read that our Prelate was suspended by the Lord knows who for rejecting unfit Italians for English benefices but did not reflect, or at least did not remember, that this event as Matthew Paris writes happened in Lent in the beginning of 1252, and a whole year before the particular rejection of the Pope's nephew. And therefore, what Matthew assigns to the year 1252 and to the Bishop of Lincoln's rejecting Italians in general unnamed, Knighton misapplieth to the year 1253 and to the particular case of his Holiness's nephew. Now I ask those who profess candour, what stress can be laid on so distant, so confused, and so contradictory a witness? Especially in opposition to two contemporary writers? Matthew Paris who was the Bishop of Lincoln's diocesan, contemporary and admirer, who spares no opportunity of lashing any exorbitance of this Pope, and who mentions the Bishop of Lincoln's suspension the year before this, doth not so much as give the least hint that he was excommunicated on that occasion, but rather hints quite the contrary and that on the remonstrance of the cardinals the Pope repressed his resentment. If after this testimony from Matthew Paris's silence any doubt still remain of the Pope's equitable disposition in regard of our Prelate's letter and opposition this is quite taken away by the Pope's excusatory bull, which the Burton Annalist expressly declares to have been issued forth in consequence of the Bishop of Lincoln's complaint, and whereby it's evident that his Holiness endeavoured to redress the grievance so far from punishing the generous remonstrator. Now as the whole clearing of this affair rested chiefly on this excusatory bull we shall here lay it before the Reader, translated verbatim from the *Annals of Burton*, after adding that as it is an open refutation of the pretended excommunication asserted by Knighton, so it is of those two idle reports, which are relaid by Matthew Paris viz that Innocent IV on hearing of the deaths of the Bishop of Lincoln and of Conrad, King of Sicily should rejoice for that now God had delivered him from two of his greatest enemies. And that as to the Bishop of Lincoln, he intended to have his bones exhumed but was prevented therein by the Bishop's appearing to him in sleep and giving him a mortal stroke with his injured crozier. For these two reports seem no less inconsistent with this authentick bull, than Knighton's excommunication.

Innocent Bishop etc.[a] to our venerable brethren, the archbishops and bishops, and to our beloved sons the abbots, priors, provosts, deans, archdeacons, archpriests and to other prelates of churches, whether cathedral, conventual or collegial, as well exempt as non-exempt, and to all the pastors of churches, whether of the clergy or laity, who shall inspect these present letters, greetings and apostolick benediction. Ever since the divine mercy has set us, tho unworthy, at the head of the universal Church we have always had at heart to keep order and decorum in all things and to observe such a method in our provisions to churches, monasteries, and other religious places as might be for the honour and advantage of the same. If the contrary be known to have happened as well by the malice of the times as by the importune demands of petitions this has been to our great grief and sorrow of heart, especially when after many denials and studied resistances we have been forced against our will to make out provisions which it would have been our satisfaction and great joy to have been able to decline. For which reason, after long casting about for some proper remedy to this evil, we have thought fit for peace of our own mind and for the good of the churches, monasteries and other formentioned places to make the following decree viz, that in regard of canonries, prebends, benefices of parsonages and dignities either with or without cure, as also in regard of revenues and pensions of your election, presentation or collation but now possessed by foreigners, whether abiding with the Holy See or elsewhere, each of you having the fear of God before his eyes shall be henceforward at liberty to collate the same to fit subjects, or to elect and confirm those elected thereto, or to present and admit such [*as*] are presented to them, notwithstanding any contradiction or appeal to the contrary. And that from thereforward the said persons shall acquire a full and uncontestable right to the said canonries, prebends and benefices or dignities and parsonages, revenues and pensions provided nevertheless that the said persons, shall not enter upon the said places before they become vacant. Tho upon a vacancy they may immediately and of right obtain them and have full power and license to enter upon and retain the same without requiring the consent of any one. Provided also, that such as are at present seized of the same shall till their demise or cession retain them quietly and of full right, nor suffer any prejudice therein under any pretext of the present statute. Nevertheless, if in expectancy of prebends in such churches where the foresaid foreigners shall have been provided, any have been received before them, or have impetrated[188] apostolick letters for their provision, then it is our will that these last, who have been first as to their reception or impetration shall be preferred to the others in the acquisition of the prebend etc. And if any of those persons who shall have been provided by virtue of the present statute, or shall happen hereafter of your free favour to be provided in the manner as hereafter specified, shall in the interim decease or cede his place then it shall be lawfull for you to substitute another fit person in his place and to do the same successively.

---

[a] *An. Burt.*, p. 328.

After a clause to prevent any fraud or violence being used against the present incumbents the bull continues.

> But as it may be very inconvenient for the said persons to wait a long while for the vacancy of canonries etc, it is our intention that in regard of canons, etc of your collation, election or presentation, which besides this your provision shall at this present or shall happen to be vacant, it shall be free for you where no other has a prior right to provide the aforesaid applicants with them and afterwards to substitute immediately other fit persons (to the prebends expected by the former). For this end we will that the foresaid regulation made of our own proper motion, for good and salutary reasons shall, tho contrary to (strict) law, obtain its full force unviolable. Yet so as not to be extended to all other collations, elections and presentations that may happen, nor to be made for the time to come a precedent prejudicial to general sanctions of the canons. Moreover, no privileges, indulgences, or letters either of the See Apostolick, or its legates, shall be deemed any obstacle to the execution of the foresaid statute seeing that by the collation, election or presentation in question the subjects aquire a full and entire right which cannot be taken from them without an offence to the Divine name and a manifest injury to the See Apostolick. And therefore whatever shall be attempted contrary thereto, we not only declare it void and of none effect but lay the attempters under the Divine and Apostolick malediction. And it shall be lawfull for all singular persons as our ministers in this article to tear either ours or our legate's letters, that shall be offered to you contrary to the present statute and in the interim, it shall be free for the subjects in question to enter upon and keep possession of the foresaid canonaries, prebends and benefices etc any such letters notwithstanding. Now it is our will that this statute be extended to the bishopricks, abbies, and other regular dignities. Dated from the Lateran Palace, the third of November in the eleventh year of our Pontificate.

This moderating bull of which 30 copies were sent in due form to the English prelates was the happy fruit from of [*sic*] our vigorous Prelate's letter and shews how far the Pope was from the censures and sayings some attribute to him. But ere this the good Bishop of Lincoln was gone to receive in the Church triumphant above the reward of that zeal he had so gloriously exerted in the Church Militant here below, and perhaps this redress might have been not only one reward of his zeal but the effect of his holy prayers. Had the bull been given before his death his soul would have quitted the Earth which he never loved with greater comfort, but he should have been deprived of one other instance of his ardent and instructive zeal, as we are going to see in this next short chapter of this essay.

Chapter VI

BISHOP GROSSETETE'S LAST SICKNESS AND DEATH, HIS MIRACLES AND THE OPINION OF HIS SANCTITY, HIS CANONISATION PETITIONED FOR AND WHY NOT EFFECTED

Not long after writing of the foresaid letter to his Holiness, the Bishop of Lincoln, wore down with labours, age and infirmities, fell dangerously sick during the dogdays of the same year 1253.[a] He was then at Bugden [*Buckden*], a manor belonging to his see in Huntingtonshire [*Huntingdonshire*]. The horror he had of risking the salvation of his flock by setting unworthy pastors over them never appeared stronger than in his dying moments and when within sight of the dread tribunal of his Judge. He publically begged forgiveness of Christ for the faults he might have committed in collating to churches purchased by his blood, yet he called his Judge to witness that tho as fallible man he might have conferred them upon the unworthy thro mistake, yet his intentions nevertheless had been always upright and pure.[b]

This indeed appeared throughout his whole life by his nice examination of those he promoted and by the frequent oppositions he undauntedly made against the highest powers when intruding upon him subjects that were unfit. And these admirable instances of his zeal during life he crowned by another at his death which sent his holy soul to God, purified in the burning furnance of his own love and zeal both for Christ and his flock.

The Bishop finding himself grown worse, called for the Dominican Doctor John of St Giles, equally skilled in Physick and Theology, in order to receive from him both corporal and spiritual comfort. 'For now,' saith Matthew Paris. 'He began to feel in his mind the great tribulation which threatened the Church, and which we did not foresee.' With this view, he renewed his command to all the priests of his diocese to repeat continually in all their congregations the sentence of excommunication fulminated against all infringers of the liberties of the Church. The Bishop had ever expressed a singular esteem and affection for the two orders

---

[a] *Chron. Maj.*, p. 874.
[b] *Annal. Lanercost.*

of St Dominick and St Francis, nevertheless in this last conference with John of St Giles, he accused both him and his brother Dominicans, as also the Franciscans, of manifest abetting of heresy in not reproving the sins of the prelates, and namely of the Pope. So much the more as by their profession of voluntary poverty they were enabled to do it with less fear or danger. 'For what is heresy?' saith he.

> Heresy is a human opinion embraced contrary to Scripture, openly taught and obstinately defended. But to give the care of souls to children, without either science or virtue to comply therewith, is the sentiment of a certain prelate embraced on worldly and carnal motives. This sentiment is contrary to Scripture which forbids making pastors of such as cannot repell the wolf. It is openly taught because brought over in bulls signed and sealed in due form it is likewise obstinately defended, since if any one gainsay it he is presently suspended and excommunicated and war is sanctified against him; now he to whom agrees the definition of heresy, is a heretick.
>
> Again all the faithfull are obliged to oppose hereticks with all their might. He therefore who is able to oppose them but doth it not sinneth and becomes an abettor of heresy, according to that of St Gregory.[189] 'He who doth not resist an open and manifest crime is justly suspected of acquiescing to it in his heart.' The Friars Minors, and Preachers are in a peculiar manner obliged to such opposition as being on one hand entrusted with the talent of the word and on the other enabled by their poverty to deliver it with freedom and intrepidity. Wherefore in not making head against heresy they not only sin but are guilty of abetting it, according to that of the Apostle, they are worthy of death, not only who do such things, but who are consenting thereto. Whence the conclusion must be unavoidable that unless the Pope desist from his sin, and the said friars be zealous to oppose him, they are both worthy of death, even of death everlasting. And hence the decretals declare that in such cases as heresy, the Pope may and ought to be impeached.

Three days before the feast of St Dennis, the dying Prelate repeated the like complaint to some of his clergy who were assembled to spend with him part of the night, now become tediously long as well on account of the season which was October, and still more on account of his illness. Grieved to the heart, for the loss of souls occasioned by the avarice of the Roman officers he fetched a deep sigh and said.

> Christ came into the world in order to save souls. He then who destroys them, is he not justly styled Antichrist? God spent only six days in creating man, but to repair and redeem him he spent thirty years, and those in hard labour. He therefore who labours at their destruction, is he not an enemy to God and Christ Jesus? The present Pope, by his *non obstantes* annuls in a shamless manner all the ordinances of the holy popes his predecessors, which cannot be done but with the manifest contempt of their memory and to the great prejudice of the Church … who then will hereafter observe his decrees and statutes?

> To support this conduct the Pope argues thus. 'Equals have no authority over equals. Ergo the popes my predecessors cannot bind me their successor to this.' I answer that he who is sailing on a dangerous sea and he who is arrived at the port, seem by no means upon a par. Let us but suppose that some of his predecessors are saved, a supposition which God forbid any one should call in question; now Christ declares that he who is the least in the Kingdom of God is greater than the holy Baptist, than whom a greater prophet was never born of woman. Is not then a holy pope, who granted or confirmed these regulations, greater than the present who annuls them? Surely, to me he seems greater. Then he has power over him that is less. Doth not the Pope, speaking of his predecessors say, 'Such an one our predecessor of holy memory.' And often thus, 'We walking in the footsteps of our holy predecessors etc.' Why then doth he their successor dig up the foundation laid by them? An ordinance once piously granted by the See Apostolick hath been often confirmed by several succeeding popes. And are not several, whom the Divine Grace has already saved, greater than one yet in jeopardy of his salvation … tho many of our apostolick Fathers have burthened the Church none ever did it with that heavy hand, and with that multitude of exactions, as his present Holiness.

Then having given a list an abstract of several grievences laid upon the English Church by the King and the Pope and some particular facts, which seem rather the amplifications of the historian than of the dying Robert, the Bishop added, 'The Church shall not be delivered from this Egyptian slavery but by the edge of the sword. Yet these grievances are but light in comparison of those which will ensue within these three years.' After these words, which Matthew Paris calls prophetick, and which hinted at new exactions and perhaps at the Pope's sorrowful death and the insurrections of the barons, words which he the Bishop could scarce pronounce for sobbing and weeping, his speech failed him and soon after his holy spirit passed from the world he had never loved, saith Matthew, to that better world he had always aspired after and had merited by his holy labours. Such was the glorious end of this zealous and primitive Bishop who sacrificed his last breath to the defense of the souls committed to his charge and expired protesting against abuses so highly prejudicial to them.

This venerable Prelate died at Bugden, the night of St Dennis' Feast, saith Matthew Paris, i.e. the 9th of October 1253, but after the second vespers, in the night betwixt the 9th and 10th of October. Hence John Schaldby,[a] Canon of Lincoln and Registrary to Bishop Sutton in the beginning of the next century, and author of a martyrology of the Church

---

[a] *Biblioth. britannico-hibernica*, 'Grossetete.'

of Lincoln,[190] places our Prelate's death on the 10 of October which must have been in the night between Thursday and Friday.[a]

God, as Matthew Paris relates, gave immediate testimony of his having accepted his holy and charitable zeal, and the entire sacrifice of his holy life. John de Crachale, Canon of St Pauls, then chaplain to Fulk Bishop of London, and since Archdeacon of Bedford and Treasurer of the Exchequer, a scholar in high esteem with the whole episcopal order assured Matthew Paris, as Matthew himself declares, that the same night our holy Bishop went to God his master Fulk, being near Bugden, said suddenly to those about him, 'Do you hear what I hear?' They asked, what? 'A sound,' said Fulk. 'As of some conventual bell, but more than human, exceedingly harmoniously, and high up in the air.' His companions declaring they heard nothing the Bishop added, 'By the faith I owe St Paul, I verily believe our beloved father, brother, and master, the venerable Bishop of Lincoln, has just left the world and is now ascending up to heaven, for here is no convent hereabouts.' On further enquiry they found the Bishop of Lincoln had expired that same moment – the same night. Adds Matthew Paris,[b] two Franciscans coming towards Bugden and being lost in one of the King's woods called Wanberge, heard a like harmonious and celestial sound and found in the morning that it had happened the same hour in which our venerable Prelate's soul left his body. Nor will any one that reflects a little be surprised at the manner in which God declared his servant's happiness. We are taught from the example of Lazarus how the souls of the just are carried by angels to the seat of bliss. Christ himself assures us that these happy spirits rejoice over sinners that repent. How much more over such, who having escaped all dangers, arrive safe at their happy mansions and society? What wonder then that Almighty God, to support the spirit of his elect still remaining in the combat should manifest this charitable joy of our blessed guardian spirits by some outward and sensible sign? And what sign so analogous, and so proper to express this joy of the angels conducting their pupil's spirits to bliss, as an heavenly and supernatural harmony, the daughter of joyfulness? God was also pleased to approve his faithfull servant by other more general testimonies, which followed his inferior and mortal part. His body was conveyed from Bugden to Lincoln and there buried the 13 of October by Boniface Archbishop of Canterbury. This Primate had been on visitation at Lincoln, and was got back as far as Newark upon Trent, when hearing of the venerable Bishop's death he returned to Lincoln and performed the funeral ceremony to his deceased suffragan, attended by Fulk, Bishop of London, who seems to have accompanied

---

[a] *Annal. Dunst*, p. 300.

[b] *Chron. Maj*., p. 877.

the corpse from Bugden to Lincoln, and by Walter de Cantelupe Bishop of Worcester and our holy Prelate's intimate friend, and by many abbots and priors with an almost infinite multitude of clergy and people, all assembled to pay this last duty to their holy Pastor; another evident demonstration that he died under no censures!

Bishop Grossteste's buriel place, according to Leland, was in the upper south aisle of his Cathedral, under a goodly tomb of brass with his image upon it.[a] Browne adds that it was under the south wall, where in our fathers' days saith he writing in 1690, was a sepulchral marble with a brass plate, inscribed with his name and titles.[b] These devouring time has now eaten away,[191] but his virtues and learning have erected him another in the place, more durable than either marble or brass and which ages have not been able to hurt, but on the contrary have rendered more solid and indestructible his having been supported by the hand of God himself. Before the year of his death was out, Matthew Paris, his diocesan and contemporary, assures us that his tomb at Lincoln was honoured with frequent miracles.[c] The same author, the *Annals of Burton*, John of Tinmouth and Richard of Bardney testify that in 1255, two years after his holy death, these miracles were repeated with such frequency in presence of Prince Richard, Earl of Cornwall, then on pilgrimage to the Venerable Robert's tomb, that no less than twenty were verified in an evident manner before most creditable witnesses assembled in the Chapter House of Lincoln. At the same time, saith many, various manifest and well approved miracles were wrought in the Church of Lincoln. Moreover those holy ancient confessors St Remigius and St Hugh to congratulate as it were with *Saint* Robert who was lately gone to God, vied with each other in inparting miraculous favours to the faithfull in honour of the same Robert, whence among many others it would be too long to tell and longer to write. There are now twenty manifest miracles proved in the Chapter of Lincoln before grave and creditable witnesses after diligent examination made by the parties, as being convinced that officious lies are hatefull to God. And now appears evidently verified what was signified to certain credible personnages in a nocturnal tho not fantastic vision four years before the said Bishop's decease, in which he seemed to hear distinctly these words. 'The Lord has loved Edmund in odour of sweetness, and Robert in odour of fidelity.' And it was given him to understand at the same, that this was meant of the blessed Bishops and Confessors, Edmund and Robert.[d] At this time adds Matthew, frequent miracles were wrought in the Churches of Lincoln and Chichester, to the

---

[a] Leland, *Collect*, vol. 8, part 2, p. 36.
[b] *Fasciculus*, p. 407.
[c] *Chron. Maj.*, pp. 880, 903 and 905.
[d] Ibid., p. 905.

glory of God and honour of the saintly Bishops Robert and Richard, in so much that in the Church of Lincoln there have been twenty miracles proved with evidence, and besides these there are numberless others. There are as many, or even more wrought in the Church of Chichester, and they encrease every day. Whereof if any one be curious to see the process and examination let him repair to the Church of St Albans, where he'll find the whole written: 'This year (an. 1255)' saith the Burton annalist, 'Saint Robert Bishop of Lincoln shone with miracles.'[a]

The Almighty not forgetting his servent's virtues, saith the Chapter of St Pauls writing to Pope Clement the V in 1307, wrought by him not only after his death, but even in his lifetime innumerable signs and miracles, as a recompense of his merit, which signs and miracles, are both old among us by custom, and yet new by their continuance and encrease.'[b] Dr Thomas Gascoigne, Chancellor of Oxford in the fifteenth century, and the English Gerson for learning piety, and zeal, testifies that an healing oil issued from the tomb of our venerable Bishop. Richard of Bardney, a Benedictine of Bardney not far from Lincoln, writing in 1505. Testifies the continuation of miracles, at Bishop Grossetete's [*tomb*] even to his days. '*Nunc Deus in mundo miracula multa per ipsum, perficit et praestat, qui dedit omne bonum. Loripides saliunt; mutos facundia laxat. Obtusas aures arcuit iste sacer. Languoris florescit hyems, vesania pacem induit et turgens laxa redire datur. Qui dominum coluit exemplo, dogmate, votis, Laude; relativo gaudet honore coli. Explicit istud opus. Precor, O pater alme Roberte, sis pius omnigenis qui tua dona petunt.*'[c192]

The respect, which our holy Prelate's virtues during life, and his miracles after death, begat for his happy memory have merited him the appellation of Saint from the generality of our most ancient, most authentick, and most Catholick historians who commonly rank him with his two contemporary saints and friends St Edmund Archbishop of Canterbury and St Richard Bishop of Chichester. We have already heard it from the mouth of Matthew Paris and the *Annals of Burton*, and Richard of Bardney. When the disinherited barons, who in 1269 had fled to the Isle of Ely and had been excommunicated, were summoned by the Pope's Legate to surrender and return to the faith and unity of the Church, they made answer that they had no other faith than that they had learned from those holy Bishops, St Robert, St Edmund and St Richard, and other Catholick doctors.[d] The *Chronicle of John*,[e] Abbot of Peterborough speaking under the year 1253, saith, this year died Saint Robert Grossetete Bishop of

---

[a] *An. Burt.*, p. 341.

[b] *Anglia Sacra*, B. 2, p. 343.

[c] Vide, *Anglia Sacra f: ubi supra.*

[d] *Chron. Maj.*, pp. 956, 998, 1003.

[e] *Peterborough Chronicles*.

Lincoln. The *Annals of Burton* and the generality of historians style him Saint Robert ^and commonly rank him with St Thomas and St Edmund, Archbishops of Canterbury and Richard, Bishop of Chichester.^ Thomas Wikes, the judicious black Austin canon of Osney near Oxford, saith under the same year, 'Soon after died St Richard Bishop of Chichester; died also the Venerable Robert Grossetete, worthy to be placed in the Catalogue of the Saints, *Catalogo sanctorum merito numerandus*.[193] The same is testified by the *Annals of Worcester* which terminate in 1308. This year, say the *Annals*, died Richard Bishop of Chichester in whose favour God wrought miracles, as also Saint Robert Grocetete, Bishop of Lincoln. The celebrated Dominican annalist Nicholas Trivet, who concludes his annals in 1307 and died in 1328 doth not indeed give him the name of Saint, but he gives him what is still more valuable, his titles to sanctity, calling him a 'Prelate of excellent wisdom, of most clear and pure doctrines and the pattern of every virtue.' Henry Knighton, the white Austin who wrote about the year 1395, saith under the year 1253, this year died *Saint Robert* surnamed Grossetete, Bishop of Lincoln, excellently skilled in all the Liberal Arts, especialy Logick and Astronomy, on which he wrote several comments. The great and eloquent Carmelite divine Thomas Waldensis[194] in his writings against Wicleff [*John Wyclif*], not only styles Bishop Grossetete that *noble* Philosopher and the *Great* Lincoln, but the venerable and blessed father, and most Sacred Doctor, *Sacrosanctus Doctor*, and numbers of times *Saint Lincoln.*[a] A manuscript history cited by Mr Wharton from the Lambeth Library, saith under the year 1254, which is a mistake for 1253, saith, this year died *Saint* Robert Grosted Bishop of Lincoln, the most learned prelate in all Christendom. In fine the famous poet of St Edmundsbury, John Lydgate[195] hath among his poetical compositions, prayers to St Edmund, to St Robert, and St Thomas of Canterbury.[b]

This general opinion of our venerable Bishop's sanctity and the same of his miracles, on which it was raised as well as on his glorious actions, became so prevalent all over the Realm, that within fifty years after his death his canonisation was solicited no less than four several times. First by the University of Oxford, whereof he was Doctor, Diocesan and Chancellor, in their letter to Pope Clement IV, a copy of which was preserved in the Abbey of Osney when Gascoigne wrote in the Fifteenth Century.[c] Secondly by John Roman, Archbishop in a letter addressed to Pope Honorius the IV preserved in the register of that Archbishop. Fol. 115.[d] A letter so much more remarkable as our Prelate had heretofore

[a] Tho. Wald. B. 2, fol. 140 et fol. 131 et B. 1. pp. 47, 57, 379, 523, 524.

[b] *Biblioth. britannico-hibernica*, 'Lydgate'.

[c] *Biblioth. britannico-hibernica*, in 'Grossetete'. p. 347, col. 2.

[d] *Biblioth. britannico-hibernica*, in 'Grossetete'. p. 347, col. 2.

opposed him while Archdeacon of Richmond as above seen. Thirdly by William Greenfield,[196] Archbishop of the same see in an epistle to Pope Clement the V extant in *Registro* Greenfield p. 1.[a] Fourthly by the Dean and Chapter of St Paul's London in their common letter to the same Pope Clement V, dated the 7 of July 1307, ^alledging for their motives of his canonisation not only his virtues but the numberless miracles wrought by him.[b] Both in his lifetime and after his decease.^ Now all these applications are so much the more weighty as except the University of Oxford, none of them could have any other interest in view but the force of truth.

Notwithstanding these repeated petitions his canonisation was either never taken to heart or at least not brought to bear, ^this may be boldly assured that it was not for any doubt either of his sanctity or his orthodoxy.^ Whether that his being obliged to resist Pope Innocent IV, tho' by duty and with due decorum, rendered the Roman Court backward in the undertaking or that more urgent affairs made this give way, or that his miracles and virtues, tho real and notorious, were not in that number or not verified with that vigorous degree of certitude which the wisdom and circumspection of the Holy See justly requires for proposing any holy person to the publick veneration of the faithfull. The Austin canon of Leicester [*Henry Knighton*] and the Benedictine Prior [*John*] of Tinmouth, pretended that altho St Robert, as the first calls him, shone with evident miracles, he was neither canonised nor his body suffered to be translated by the Roman Court, because of his vigorous opposing Pope Innocent IV. But this suspicion is no ways agreeable to the equity and constant conduct of the Holy See, who canonises St Paul tho he opposed her first supreme Pastor and Bishop St Peter. Nay she canonises St Cyprian and St Firmilian, tho they opposed St Stephen and were even in the wrong, because their virtues and blood effaced their faults.[197] How then should she oppose the canonisation of our Prelate of Lincoln, so visibly right in his opposition that Innocent himself thought it necessary to redress the greviences and abuses he complained of? In these important occasions the Holy See doth not suffer herself to be warped, either by aversions or affections. What more zealous defender of the Holy See, not only in articles of faith but even in favourite opinions, than the most learned and holy Archbishop of Capua, Cardinal Robert Bellermin?[198] His beatification and canonisation have been petitioned for and undertaken and yet are still hanging up in the Roman Court and without going so far abroad, what more zealous executor of the papal decrees than the Blessed Robert de Winchelsee, who died Archbishop of Canterbury in 1313?[199] Who had suffered the loss of all his temporalities for going against a decree of Pope Boniface

---

[a] Ibid., p. 3.

[b] *Anglia Sacra*, B. 2; *Concilia Magnae*.

VIII. He was little or nothing inferior to the Bishop of Lincoln, either for learning, sanctity or miracles. He had been rector of the University of Paris, DD. and Chancellor of Oxford, Archdeacon of Essex, and Divinity lecturer in the Cathedral of St Paul's, and celebrated as a doctor that had enlightened the whole western Church by his doctrine, and no less by his virtues. He was rewarded for his devotion, mortification, watchings, charities, zeal in preaching and reforming his monks and clergy, and so chaste that he seemed not to wear a mortal body. In fine of all the English prelate's none bears so strict a resemblance with Robert Grossetete, as Robert de Winchelsee. Neither kings, nor princes could overawe him. Six years after his most edifying death 16 or 17 miracles were judicially proved by the Bishops of London, Chichester and Rochester commissioned thereto by Archbishop Reynolds,[200] and in consequence thereof, Robert de Winchelsee's canonisation was solicited just as many times as Robert Grossetete's.[a] First by Thomas Earl of Lancastris. Second by the Prior and Chapter of Canterbury. Third by Archbishop Reynolds and all his suffragans importuned, as they declare by the publick voice of the nobility and commons of England. Fourth and lastly by King Edward the III but just with the same effect as the former, tho there was no plea of his having opposed any Pope, to stand in his way.

The fancy then of Bishop Grossetete's canonisation being obstructed for his opposing the Pope, is an idle and groundless surmise. And the suspension of this honour being decreed him, must be ascribed to some other reasons such as have obstructed the canonisation of some of the greatest favourites of the Holy See. And whatever these reasons might be, whether multiplicity of other affairs, or a want of those more than sufficient motives of certitude which the See Apostolick requires on such occasions or whatever other reason might intervene this may be boldly asserted, that it was not for any doubt either of his holiness or orthodoxy, as some would make the world believe. Since, as the whole series of his life is a manifest argument of the former so a short review of what we have entracted from his works or letters and the veneration of the whole English Catholick Church, is a no less ample certificate of the latter.[201]

To demonstrate Bishop Grossetete's strict orthodoxy we need only recollect and recapitulate the principles of doctrine laid down above. There he teaches that the primary object of Christian faith is one God in three persons. That the enjoyment of the Blessed Trinity is the last end of man; that a lively and active faith is the necessary means for attaining that happiness; that this faith engages us to believe not only what is contained in the Holy Scriptures and the Creed, but whatever is delivered by the universal Church. That altho' an explicit knowledge and

---

[a] *Wilkins*, B. 2, p. 486 ad 536.

belief of all articles thus delivered be not necessary to salvation yet is it absolutely necessary to have a virtual and implicit faith of them and that the disbelief of any one article, contrary to the authority or declaration of the Church, is enough to damn such unbeliever. That no commotions can force this Church of Christ from the stability of Faith. That the first and chief representative of Christ in his body which is the Church is the Bishop of Rome, as successor of St Peter the prince of the Apostles. That the faith above required for justification and salvation, is a faith enlivened by charity, and shewing itself in good works. That none of these good works can be performed in a manner available to salvation, without the grace of God thro his only Son Christ Jesus. That the Son of God died for all and for every man, tho all do not receive the fruit of his death. That grace doth not destroy freewill, but supposes, helps and perfects it. That this supernatural assistance of heaven is to be obtained by prayer, whether vocal or mental, and by the conjoint use of those heavenly remedies which Christ has set up and left in those sacred institutions called Sacraments. That these Sacraments of the new Law are seven in number, viz Baptism, Confirmation, Eucharist, Penance, Extreme Unction, Order and Matrimony. That the Sacrament of Penance includes confession of our sins to the ministers of Christ, and is of precept. That the holy Eucharist contains the real presence of Christ's most sacred body and blood. That it is a sacrifice as well as a sacrament. That the priests who offer it are obliged to celibacy *by vows* ^and are not at liberty to marry, and the title given to him by Matthew Paris of 'Persecutor of the incontinent', is chiefly verified with regard to priests trespassing their vows, either by marriage or fornication, as appears from his regulations.^ That prayers and the holy sacrifice of the altar are to be offered, as well for the dead as for the living. That the souls and angels reigning with Christ, aid and assist us, and are to be invoked by us. That the relicks of the saints are to be treated with great honour and respect. That monastic vows and institutes are holy and commendable and that the practice of the evangelical counsels of poverty, chastity and obedience, according to the monastick rules, is the glory and honour of the Christian Church. That tho in his time he preferred the two orders of mendicant friars instituted by St Francis and St Dominick, yet the rule of St Bennet was esteemed by him a rule of supereminent sanctity, and full of the spirit of all the saints, and if he had any quarrels with these or other monks it was because of their not living to their holy institute. But this review of Lincoln's principles and doctrine may appear needless, since Browne makes this frank confession. 'As to the articles of the Eucharist, purgatory, the number of the sacraments, the invocation of saints, merit and satisfaction, the sanctity of the Roman See, the pope's power and perhaps other articles in which I am less versed, he is entirely against us.'[a] As to the particular article of the pope's authority, in which Browne here confesses the Bishop of Lincoln, 'a good Papist', but which in another place he tries to make him renounce in his last opposition of Pope Innocent IV, this may be asserted without fear of contradiction, that if there be any one article of the Catholick faith in which Bishop Grossetete is more explicit than others, it is this very article of the pope's authority, and this not only in his first writings, but in those written in the warmth of opposition even in that last letter which Browne would make the world believe Grossetete's abjuration of the Pope. In his letters to Pope Gregory the IX, and to his Legate the Cardinal Otho, and to other cardinals, he calls the Bishop of Rome, *the Successor of St Peter, Prince of the Apostles and of the whole world.* And saith that *all Christians* are subject to him. That he hath, 'a sovereign power over and a right to dispose of all Church livings, as far as it is for edification'. That even the original property of the temporal and secular power is vested in him and that the use and exercise thereof ought to be subject to his directions. In his remonstrance put up to Innocent IV at Lions, wherein he laith open some abuses in that Pope's Court, he styles the pope the *Chief Representative* and *Vicegerent of Christ*, and his See, *the very throne of God, and the Sun of the Universe*. In his last letter to the same Pope, where he crieth still louder against promoting unfit subjects, he repeats over and over that the pope is the, *Principal Representative of Christ in the Ecclesiastical Hierarchy*. That he has *received from above a greater power* than other pastors. That Christ hath delivered all power to the See Apostolick and most holy and plenary authority. This the Pope's council well understood, when his letter being read they nevertheless declared him, 'a most religious and Catholick prelate'. Nor did the Pope ever so much as signify any suspicion of his opposer's faith in this or any other article. Now to go about making the world believe that a letter containing so ample and clear a profession of the Pope's authority, even in the sense and by the confession of the Pope's own council, is an abjuration of the same authority, must betray either an excessive blindness or great insincerity and a design of imposing upon the Reader. But forsooth, Lincoln's opposing the Pope, is enough with Browne to make him a good Protestant and to purge off all his other dregs of popery, and this one title of the *Hammer of the Romans* is sufficient to make even the rankest popery at least tolerable![b] And this much for the Bishop Lincoln's orthodoxy, Bishop Grossetete's sanctity is no less conspicuous than his orthodoxy and as little questioned by the Pope, or his council, which last declared he hath not his superior

[a] *Fasciculus*, p. 245.
[b] *Fasciculus*, p. 406.

nor scarce his equal in the whole episcopal body. And of this we have seen ample demonstration thro the whole series of this essay. Witness his early preference of wisdom to all corporal satisfaction. His early mortification and subduing of his body by abstinences. His godly and judicious manner of studying the divine books and listening to the illustrious examples he there found, as to so many living monitors and tutors. His great disinterestedness in resigning all his benefices but one. His profound humility, his fear of scandalising the weak, his simplicity and purity of intention in all his actions. Witness again his ardent zeal for instructing and forming his scholars while Professor, his subject clergy while archdeacon, his people and clergy while Bishop. Witness his affable, liberal and hospitable temper both toward rich and poor. His fervent devotion and compunction at the altar. His continual watchings and praying for his flock, his indefatigable diligence in visiting, correcting and reforming his clergy and religious. His unwearied solicitude to promote men of learning and merit and his invincible steadiness in rejecting those of contrary disposition. His burning love for Christ for having shed his blood for him, and his unabated zeal for his glory. Witness in fine that heroick fortitude which in the eyes of weak or ignorant souls seems perhaps a dubious virtue, but which in reality and all circumstances considered is the crown and perfection of all the rest. And in some measure, peculiar to this holy Bishop above all his contemporary saints. To comply with duty where there are no obsticles is a degree of virtue commendable indeed, yet nothing wonderfull. But to pursue the narrow and difficult track of duty in the midst of continual opposition, and those from the highest powers upon Earth. To stand firm when deserted by one part of the world and frowned upon and censured by the other. To embrace duty merely for God's sake and in spite of all inconvenience, this is only the effect of an uncommon and deep rooted virtue which seeks God alone and can be content with the approbation of conscience but is thereby so much the stronger, so much the more perfect, as adhering only to God it has the Almighty on its side, to support and render it victorious over all opposition. This was the true character of the Bishop of Lincoln and this God demonstrated His approving him by miracles after death. Which are a testimony of a perfect virtue, in those in whose brow they are wrought and a very sufficient motive for venerating their memory, tho nothing but the approbation of the Church or the Church's supreme Pastor is a sufficient warrant for exhibiting that veneration in the publick honours decreed to canonised saints. Would to God that this imperfect, tho faithfull history of his life and principles, may any ways contribute to acquire him either of these two kinds of veneration which he no ways wants as being perfectly happy in the reward of his virtues, but we greatly as standing in need of being raised up by new and approved examples of Sanctity!

EDITOR'S NOTES

1 The chapter headings given in Perry's list of contents are not always entirely consistent with those found above the actual chapters.

2 The manuscript mentioned is St Edmund's Hall, Oxford, (8560-98E4) 1.

3 Casimir Oudin (1638–1743) was a French Premonstratensian monk who wrote *Supplementum de Scriptoribus vel scriptis ecclesiastics a Bellarmino omissis* (Paris, 1686), a supplement to Robert Bellarmine's *Ecclesiastical Writers*.

4 This is not quite correct. In 1248 Matthew Paris was an envoy of Louis X to Haakon IV. It was the Norwegian sovereign who asked him to oversee the reform of Nidarholm Abbey near Trondheim. See Björn Weiler, 'Matthew Paris in Norway', *Revue Benedictine* 122.1 (2012), 153–81.

5 Genesis 9:18–27 recounts that when Noah was intoxicated Ham looked upon and mocked his father's nakedness. His brothers walked backwards into the tent in order to cover Noah. For this indiscretion Ham was cursed by his father. Interestingly, this reference is a near quote from the preface to Francis Godwin's *A Catalogue of the Bishops of England* (London, 1601). Though an Anglican bishop, Godwin published his work in part to rehabilitate the reputations of pre-Reformation English bishops who had suffered at the hands of harsher critics. Bishop Godwin's work made considerable space for Grosseteste and it clearly influenced Perry, however he showed no inclination to credit it. Perry uses the Latinised forms of the Hebrew names as they appear in the Vulgate and hence in the Douay Bible.

6 The authorship of *Flores Historiarum* ('Florianus') was misattributed to the non-existent Matthew of Westminster until as late as the nineteenth century. In fact it was the work of Matthew Paris and others. For Trivet, see the biographical appendix.

7 For Leland, see the biographical appendix.

8 Ralph Thoresby (1658–1725) was an antiquarian and topographer. Perry is referring to work by Thoresby which appeared in the *Biographia Britannica* after his death. See P. E. Kell, 'Thoresby, Ralph' in *ODNB*, doi.org/10.1093/ref:odnb/27334.

9 The 'Petitio Paulino' that Perry cites is a petition from the Dean and Chapter of St Paul's Cathedral in London to Pope Clement V for the canonisation of Grosseteste. It is dated 1307 and can be found in *Anglia Sacra*, vol. 2, pp. 343–44.

10 Abbot Joffrid, who was thought to have founded a school of philosophy in a barn at Cambridge in 1112.

11 The source Perry cites is the *Historia monasterri Croylandesis*, which purports to be the eleventh-century chronicle of the Abbot of Crowland.

[12] For William de Sherwood, see the biographical appendix.

[13] Aside from Thomas Tanner, Perry is taking this list from John Leland's *De viris illustribus*, written in 1535–36 but only published in 1709 by Anthony Hall under the title *Commentarii de scriptoribus Britannicis*. See *De viris illustribus/On Famous Men*, edited and translated by James P. Carley with Caroline Brett (Toronto, 2010).

[14] In the vast majority of cases it is possible to identify Grossesteste's work from Perry's descriptions. The book on the Arts is *De artibus liberalibus*; that on the difficulties of natural knowledge is *Difficilia naturalis sciencie*. On truth is *De veritate*; on the truth of propositions, *De veritate proposicionis*. God as the first form of all things is *De forma prima omnium*, in fact addressed to his former pupil, Adam Rufus, rather than to Adam de Marisco (on whom see the biographical appendix). On the state, order and sufficiency of causes is *De statu causarum*. On the impressions of air is *De impressionibus aeris*, and on the generation of sounds *De generacione sonorum*.

[15] On the heat of the sun is *De calore solis*; on the generation of the stars, *De generacione stellarum*; on corporeal motion and light, *De motu corporali et luce*; on the finiteness of motion and time, *De finitate motus et temporis*; on angles and figures, *De lineis, angulis et figuris*; on the nature of place or space, *De natura locorum*; on man's being a little world, *Quod homo sit minor mundus*; on the movement of supercelestial bodies (*De motu supercelestium*), on the disposition of the mover (*De disposicione motoris*) and the body moved in circular motion (*De motu circulari*) are all in fact the same work; so too are on local differences (*De differenciis localibus*) and on the six differences (*De sex differenciis*).

[16] This is *Analytica Posteriora*.

[17] These are the *Physica*, *De sphaera*, and *Compotus correctorius*. Simon Bredon (*c*.1300–72), an English astronomer, physician and mathematician, was one of the Merton Calculators, a group of Oxford scholars whose work applied mathematical methods to questions of natural philosophy. See Edith D. Sylla, *The Oxford Calculators and the Mathematics of Motion, 1320–1350: Physics and Measurement by Latitudes* (New York, 1996).

[18] These are *Commentarii in logicam*; *In predicamenta Aristotelis*; *Commentarius in sophisticos elenchos Aristotelis*; *Regule libri priorum analyticorum Aristotelis*; and *Summa in ethica Nicomachea*.

[19] *De potenciis anime* is actually by Walter Burley. Thomson, *Writings*, p. 259.

[20] The author of *Commentarius in Boecii De consolacione philosophie* is in fact William of Conches. Thomson, *Writings*, p. 243.

[21] *De luce*; *De colore*; *De iride*.

[22] This is in fact *De divisione scienciarum*, by Dominicus Gundissalinus, misascribed to Grosseteste. See Thomson, *Writings*, p. 245.

[23] *Questiones in De celo et mundo Aristotelis*; *Commentarius in De generacione et corrupcione* (Thomson lists this as spuria, *Writings*, p. 258); *Meteorologica*; *De natura luminis et diaphoni*; *De cometis*. The *Theorica planetarum* was a correction of a work originally by Gerard of Cremona (Thomson, *Writings*, p. 238).

[24] *Praxis geometrie* is listed by Bale and Tanner but is now lost. Thomson, *Writing*, p. 271.

[25] There is no evidence of Grosseteste's authorship of *De astrolabio*, although there is much evidence of his expertise on the astrolabe. Thomson, *Writings*, p. 243.

[26] Thomson tells us that neither *De lapide philosophico* nor *De necromancia et goëcia* exists. *Writings*, p. 271.

[27] Thomson characterises *De astrologia* as a doubtful work. *Writings*, p. 235.

[28] *De quadratura circuli*; *De impressionibus aeris*; *De lingua*.

[29] The *Distichs of Cato*, a collection of proverbs written in verse, is probably not the work of Cato the Elder. Nevertheless, it was one of the best known and most appreciated Latin books in the Middle Ages. Grosseteste, however, is not the author of the commentary *In Catonis disticha*, which is pre-Grossetestian. The misidentification can be traced to John Bale. See Thomson, *Writings*, p. 245.

[30] Grosseteste's work on land management became known as *Les reulles Seint Robert*.

[31] The work on manners is *Stans puer ad mensam*.

[32] John of Fordun (died after 1363) was a priest and Scottish chronicler. His work was later incorporated into the *Scotichronicon* of Walter Bower (1440s). See Johannis de Fordun, *Chronica Gentis Scotorum*, edited by W. F. Skene. Translated by F. J. H. Skene (2 vols, Edinburgh, 1871–72).

[33] William de Vere actually died in December 1198. He is buried in Hereford Cathedral where his tomb and effigy remain. See Julia Barrow, 'A Twelfth-Century Bishop and Literary Patron: William de Vere', *Viator* 18 (1987), 175–89.

[34] 'Brecken' is Brecon. Though the canons of St David's elected Gerald as their bishop, this election was never accepted by either the Archbishop of Canterbury or the Pope. On Gerald see Robert Bartlett, *Gerald of Wales: A Voice in the Middle Ages* (Stroud, 2006); also the biographical appendix.

[35] Quintus Aurelius Symmachus (*c*.345–402 CE). A Roman statesman and a man of letters. The reference is to his *Epistulae* II, 29.

[36] This poem, 'Ad magistrum Giraldum', is by Simon de Fresne. It was rediscovered and published by R. W. Hunt, 'English Learning in the Late Twelfth Century', *Transactions of the Royal Historical Society*, fourth series, 19 (1936), 19–42 at 36–37. 'Spring that ceaselessly flows, the clergy's flower, wisdom's gem; whatever honour it has it owes to Wales … Yours alone to the tongue you were born with; England for all its wealth laments that poor Wales is the model of the world. The sun at the antipodes, what rejoices in its light? The sun rejoices anything, she nothing. The sun lights up anew with sap, your light diminishes as

it passes away from you. Flower and honour of the clergy, transfer yourself to our city; where are philosophers, there you will be highest. The city of Hereford is much attuned with you, it is the proper place of the Trivium and Quadrivium. It flourishes still, and especially in this city the honour of the seven arts presides. This city, where so many arts shine out, you will maintain according to law, since you will be the honour of art, to love the place of art …'

37 In fact Grosseteste learned Greek, and is generally thought to have mastered a good level of Hebrew later in life.

38 Eustachius, Abbot of Flay in Normandy and papal emissary to England in the reign of King John; Jacques de Vitry (*c*.1160/70–1240) a noted theologian and chronicler; Stephen Langton (*c*.1150–1228), Archbishop of Canterbury banished by King John after a dispute over his candidature to the English primacy; Roger de Curzon (*c*.1160/70–1219) an English cleric, professor and perhaps Chancellor of the University of Paris, he was later a cardinal. They are credited with preaching against the Caursini, who were moneylenders.

39 For Hearne, see biographical appendix.

40 The 'Life of Wolsey' cited is George Cavendish's *Thomas Wolsey, late Cardinall, his Lyffe and Deathe*. Written in the sixteenth century, it was first published in 1641.

41 For John Ayton, see biographical appendix.

42 This manuscript is Bale's *Index Britanniae scriptorum*, which represent his gargantuan effort to record the title, first lines and location of all learned books by British authors. It remained unpublished until the twentieth century. See *Index Britanniae scriptorium: John Bale's Index of British and Other Writers*, edited by R. Lane Poole, C. Brett and James P. Carley (Woodbridge, 1990). The 'Brinkley' referred to is in fact the Franciscan Richard Brinkley who died in 1375; he was long confused with Walter. See Michael J. Fitzgerald, 'Brinkley, Richard', in *ODNB*, doi.org/10.1093/ref:odnb/53480.

43 'Scoti defensor' meaning a disciple of Duns Scotus.

44 Pico Giovanni della Mirandola (1463–94) was a celebrated Renaissance philosopher.

45 The footnote cites William Woodford (died in or after 1397). Named *Doctor Fortissimus*, Woodford was a Franciscan, an Oxford academic and opponent of John Wyclif. His 'De causis condempnacionis articulorum xviii damnatorum Johannis Wyclif' is contained in Brown's *Fasciculus rerum*, vol. 1, pp. 190–265.

46 *Super prologum Bibliae*; *Hexaëmeron*; *Super divatus*; *Super Iobum* (which Thomson lists among the lost or untraced works. *Writings*, p. 271). '80 or 100 of the Psalms': Grosseteste's commentary on Psalms extends from 1 to 100; it is not known why he left off the work (McEvoy, *Grosseteste*, pp. 99–101). The other works listed in this paragraph are *In threnos Ieremie*; *Super Evangelia* (which Bale and Tanner consider to be the same work as the *Moralitates super Evangelia*); *In Lucam*; *Commentarius in epistolam Pauli ad Galathas*; *De cessacione legalium*; *Epist ad Corinthios* (which Thomas Gascoigne says he saw

in Grosseteste's own hand, but if it existed it is now lost: Pegge, *Grosseteste*, p. 275); *In Apocalypsin Joannis* (misattributed by Bale and Tanner, the actual author being the Franciscan teacher Nicholas de Lyra (*c*.1270–1349): Thomson, *Writings*, p. 241); and *Sentencia scripturarum* (which Thomson lists as spuria. *Writings*, p. 263).

47 *Opera Pseudo-Dionysii* and *Commentarii in opera Pseudo-Dionysii.*

48 *Testamenta XII Patriarcharum*, an apocryphal text purporting to be the testimony of the twelve sons of Jacob. It was translated and first made available to the Latin West by Grosseteste and it was one of his great academic successes. The volume received an early modern revival, being printed three times in the sixteenth century and over twelve more times in the following century. The impact of the work makes Grosseteste's translation one of his most significant contributions to the thought of his age. A more flowing style of Latin than he usually employed makes it clear that he was aiming his translation at a non-academic readership. The work's popularity extended far beyond the universities, and it was even translated into Welsh. Grosseteste believed that it was a genuine prophecy of Christ as the Messiah which the Jews had recognised and deliberately suppressed. This assessment of the text survived until the sixteenth century. At present scholarly opinion is divided over whether it is an ancient Jewish text with Christian interpolations, or a Christian text which incorporates earlier Jewish material. See McEvoy, *Grosseteste*, p. 117.

49 The Suda is a tenth-century Byzantine encyclopaedia cum dictionary attributed to Souidas (which Perry spells 'Suidas'). *De probacione Virginitatis Beate Marie* was one article out of the 71 that Grosseteste translated from his *Lexicon Suida*. Thomson, *Writings*, p. 64.

50 The final works mentioned in this paragraph are *De fide orthodoxa*; *Lexicon Suida* (see previous note); and *Compendium sancti Augustini de Civitate Dei*, which in fact is most likely by Robert Kilwardby. See F. M. Powicke, *The Medieval Books of Merton College* (Oxford, 1931), p. 163.

51 Among the works Perry lists in this paragraph, the 'Summ of Theology' is perhaps *Elementarium dogmatum*; the book on the names of God is *De divinis nominibus*; on the local presence of God, *De locali praesentia Dei*. The book on man, *De homine creato*, is listed as Grosseteste's by Bale and Tanner but is considered a dubious attribution by Thomson (*Writings*, p. 237). The book on Original Sin is *Questio de originali peccato* (listed by Thomson as lost or untraced. *Writings*, p. 272). The book on reparation after the Fall is *De reparacione lapsi*, another title for the *Chasteau d'Amour* (see note 53 below). The book on Grace is *Dicta 134: Gracia est bona*; the book on triple Justification *De triplici gracia*. The two books on free will are *De libero arbitrio I & II*; that on knowledge and will is possibly *Difficilia naturalis sciencie*. The treatise on prophets is *Dicta 113-Prophecia maxime*; that on purgatory, *De poenis purgatorii*; on the resurrection, *De fide resurreccionis*; on marriage, *De conjugio* (which is in fact a section of Hugh of St Victor's *Summa sententiarum*); on the Cross possibly *Dicta 119: Crux domini nostri*. The books on angelic and ecclesiastical hierarchy are *De celesti*

hierarchia and *De ecclesiastica hierarchia* (both contained in the *Commentarii in opera Pseudo-Dionysii*). The discourse on the threefold hierarchy is *Sermo 87: Sermo in hierarchiam triplicem.*

[52] The book in question is *De cessacione legalium*, edited Henry Wharton, London, 1658; *De cessatione legalium*, Auctores Britannici Medii Aevi, VII, edited by Richard C. Dales and Edward B. King (London, 1988).

[53] Grosseteste's *Chasteau d'Amour* is an allegorical poem written in Norman French describing the Creation as well as the Fall and Redemption of humanity.

[54] The *Summa iusticie* is not in fact by Grosseteste (Thomson, *Writings*, pp. 263–64). A number of works entitled *De septem viciis principalibus* or similar have been incorrectly ascribed to Grosseteste by bibliographers (ibid., pp. 267–68). The more likely author of *De (septem) venenis* is Malachias de Hibernia, *c.*1300. *De oculo morali* was ascribed to Grosseteste by English biographers but was almost certainly by Pierre de Limoges, who died in 1306 (ibid., p. 256). *De doctrina cordis* was published by Gerard of Liège (Geraldus Leodiensis) but was probably written by Philip the Chancellor (ibid., p. 248). The *Enchiridion* was misattributed to Grosseteste by an author called 'Boston of Bury', whom Bale makes good use of; Tanner suggested it was the same work as the *Manuel de Peches*, an Anglo-Norman text written by William of Waddington (ibid., pp. 249–50). The book of meditations is *Meditaciones*; that on nocturnal illusions, *De pollutione nocturna*; that on the doctrine on confession is *Sermon 31: Scriptum est de livitis*. Bale lists a tract *Contra luxuriam*, but this is *Sermon 81: Restat agree luxuria*. The book on the humility of Christ is *De humilitate Christi*. *De premiis apostolorum* is listed by Bale and Tanner but is now lost (ibid., p. 271).

[55] The book on the pastoral charge is *Sermon 34: Natis et educatis*. Bale and then others called this *De cura pastorali*, which is the title of a separate text, Letter 127 to the Dean and Chapter of Lincoln Cathedral. The book on the priestly functions is possibly *Dicta 35: Exemplum etso fidelium*. The memorial is *Memoriale*. *The Sting of Conscience* is in fact correctly 'fathered' on Richard Rolle of Hampole, a writer of the fourteenth century (see Luard, *Epist. Grosseteste*, p. xi). The work on penance is perhaps *Perambulavit Iudas*. The penitential is *De modo confitendi*. The treatise on examining the penitent is *Sermon 32: Tractatus quomodo examinandus*, and advice concerning penitents is *Concilium circa poenitentes*. The synodal ordinances are *Constituciones* (Letter 52 to the clergy of Lincoln); a second edition of this has an added paragraph adapting them for archdeacons. The *Epistola monitoria* that Perry cites in relation to the *Constitutiones datae Piori et conventui de Newenham* was a letter of admonition to the prior of Newenham, which Samuel Pegge refers to as Cotton MSS Otho, c. xv. 1, 2 (*The Life of Robert Grosseteste, celebrated Bishop of Lincoln* (1793), p. 140); F. S. Stevenson tells us it is no longer there (*Robert Grosseteste, Bishop of Lincoln* (London, 1899), p. 152). Robert Bloet was Bishop of Lincoln 1093–1123. The rules on land management drawn up during 1240–42 for Countess Margaret of Lincoln, the widow of John de Lacey, are *Regule ad custodiendum terras*.

56 The *Statuta familie* was translated into English and is found in BM Sloane MS 1986, ff. 100a–102a, XVm. For a printed version, see J. S. Brewer, *Monumenta Franciscana* (1885), pp. 582–86. The 'method of visitation' is *De modo visitandi*. 'Lions' is Perry's spelling of Lyon, in France.

57 On the first Sunday of Advent is *Sermon 7: Exiit edictum*; on the Annunciation is *In verba Gabrielis*; on Mary choosing the better part, *Sermon 84: Maria optimam partem elegit*; in praise of religious poverty is *Sermon 1: Sermo ... ad Frates minors*. On the Ladder of Poverty and the sermon beginning 'Blessed are the poor' are both *Sermon 8: Beati pauperes*, referred to by Bale and Tanner as *Tractatus de scala paupertatis*. The widely circulated treatise *Templum Dei* may have been based on a sermon (Thomson, *Writings*, p. 138). 'This day, we sing' is *Sermon 16: Canimus hodie*. The sermon collection *Sermones Elegantes* ascribed to Grosseteste was more probably by Robert Holcot, who died in 1349 (Thomson, *Writings*, p. 263).

58 Those listed are *Dicta 103: Recte judicate filii*; *Dicta 113: Prophecia maxime*; *Dicta 129: Colleccio creditorum*; *Dicta 134: Gracia est bona*; *Dicta 136: Orare est exprimere*; *Dicta 127: Superbia est*; *Dicta 128: De superbia*; *Dicta 141: Humilitas est amor*; *Dicta 18: Paciencia est animi*; and *Dicta 130: In omni operacione*. The 'vesperies' that occasioned *In Vesperiis Ade* was the last disputation of a Bachelor of Divinity before he became a Master; the text is now lost (Thomson, *Writings*, p. 272). The prophecy is *Prophecia domini Roberti de Grostest*.

59 Brown intended to produce a further volume but was prevented by illness and eventually death (see Introduction).

60 Nicholas of Lyra (*c*.1270–1349) was a doctor at the Sorbonne and later head of the Franciscans in France. See Philip D. W. Krey and L. Smith, eds., *Nicholas of Lyra: The Senses of Scripture* (Leiden, 2000).

61 Thomas Pope Blount, *Censura celebriorum auctorum* (London, 1690) is a bibliographical and biographical dictionary of literary and scientific writers; the work it cites is Thomas Fuller's *The History of the Worthies of England*, edited by J. Fuller (London, 1662). Fuller was an Anglican clergyman who gave a fuller treatment of Grosseteste in his earlier *The Church History of Britain from the birth of Jesus Christ, untill the year MDCXLVIII* (London, 1655), where he dedicates twenty-five lines to the bishop. John Williams was Bishop of Lincoln from 1621 to 1641.

62 Richard Poore (died 1237) was Bishop of Salisbury, where he played an important part in the construction of the Cathedral. He was later bishop of Durham. See Philippa Hoskin, 'Poor [Poore], Richard' in *ODNB*, doi.org/10.1093/ref:odnb/22525.

63 In Richard of Bardney's account of Grosseteste's life he describes the bishop's journey to Rome as made in a single night on a miraculous horse.

64 For Ralph of Maidstone, see the biographical appendix.

65 This was, of course, before Galileo's famous demonstration when he dropped two spheres of different mass from the tower of Pisa in order to prove that velocity was not affected by mass. Grosseteste's assumption is based on Aristotelian physics.

66 The relationship between bishops and mendicants was seldom quite so felicitous at this time in history. When the Franciscan Salimbene wrote his *Chronicle* only sixteen bishops were presented favourably, and only two called 'Sanctus'. One of these was Robert Grosseteste. See Mariano d'Alatri, 'Il vescovo nella Cronaca di Salimbene di Parma', *Collectanea Franciscana* 42 (1972), 5–38.

67 For Jordan of Saxony, see the biographical appendix. Elias of Cortona was the third general of the Franciscans (1232–39). See J. R. H. Moorman, *A History of the Franciscan Order from its Origins to the Year 1517* (Oxford, 1968), pp. 96–122.

68 William Whitelock (died 1584) was an antiquarian most famous for his *Chronicon Lichefeldensis ecclesie*. This was a history of Lichfield Cathedral using medieval manuscripts. His manuscript additions to the records of Lichfield were used by Henry Wharton in his *Anglia Sacra*, though Wharton incorrectly ascribed the *Historia ecclesiae Lichfeldensis* to Whitelock. See Ann J. Kettle, 'Whitelocke [Whitlock], William' in *ODNB*, doi.org/10.1093/ref:odnb/29318.

69 This is in fact Abbotsley in Huntingdonshire.

70 This is letter 4 of the collection and was probably written in 1231. See Luard, *Epist. Grosseteste*, pp. 25–33.

71 The *congé d'élire* (leave to elect) is, in the English Church, the formal licence issued from the Crown to the dean and chapter of a cathedral authorising them to proceed with an episcopal election.

72 Thomas de Wykes' thirteenth-century chronicle was written at Osney Abbey near Oxford; it was published in the seventeenth century and Perry makes good use of it (see biographical appendix). The *Annals of Winchester* is a Latin prose text based on the work of Richard of Devizes (*c*.1150–*c*.1200), *De rebus gestis Richardi primi*, as well as the *Hyde Annals*.

73 Michael Beleth was the chief Butler at the marriage of Henry III. *Rotuli Roberti Grosseteste episcopi Lincolniensis* (London, 1913), p. 11.

74 The *Statuta Familie*, BM Sloane MS 1986, ff. 100a–102a, XVm, is an English translation of Grosseteste's original text. See Thomson, *Writings*, pp. 150–51.

75 *Quicunque vult*: an alternative name for the Athanasian Creed, from the Latin opening words, 'Whosoever wish [to be saved]'.

76 *Viaticum*: the Eucharist administered to a dying person as part of the Last Rites, from the Latin for 'provision for a journey'.

77 The Feast of Fools had its origin in a liturgical event that took place on 1 January. It involved the inversion of the social order, the lowest in the social stratum becoming the highest. Abuses, that were on occasion deemed blasphemous, meant that it was the subject of many ecclesiastical prohibitions. See Max Harris, *Sacred Folly: A New History of the Feast of Fools* (Ithaca, 2011).

78 The quotation from *Polychronicon* reads: 'The Danes, by nature ferocious drinkers, have left this eternally to be said about the English, that now the strength of the English when it comes to emptying cups outweighs the whole world.'

79 'Vinegar' here means altar wine that has turned sour.

80 The quotation given in Perry's note reads 'That the archbishop should not set up anchorites in the churches of St Augustine of Canterbury without the consent of the abbot.' It has not been possible to trace the source cited.

81 Mattathias was a priest of Modin who killed a Seleucid officer who had commanded the Jews to offer sacrifice contrary to the Law. On his deathbed he urged his son Judas Maccabee to continue the leadership of the revolt (1 Macc. 1).

82 The *Peterborough Chronicle* (Chronicon Angliae Petriburgense) is the only prose history of England written between 1066 and the late fourteenth century. It was edited and published in 1723 by the antiquarian Joseph Sparke as part of his *Historiae Anglicanae Scriptores varii, e codicibus manuscriptis*.

83 This alarming procedure determined whether the nuns were lactating and had therefore given birth.

84 Fleury Abbey, founded in 640, is one of the most celebrated Benedictine monasteries in the world.

85 The abbot is Alan of Cestreham (Chesham) who was one of at least ten Augustinian Abbots requested to resign by Grosseteste. See J. H. Srawley, 'Grosseteste's Administration of the Diocese of Lincoln', in *Robert Grosseteste: Scholar and Bishop*, edited by D. A. Callus (Oxford, 1955), p. 155.

86 Chetwode Priory was in fact founded by Sir Ralphe de Norwich in 1244, though Grosseteste provided the licence. The 'Church History' that Perry cites is Charles Dodd, *An Apology for the Church History of England from 1500 till 1688* (London, 1738–43), a four-volume Catholic ecclesiastical history of which Perry makes surprisingly little use.

87 The Council is question is the Fourth Lateran Council (1215).

88 Heli (or Eli) indulged his sons Hophni and Phinehas who brought destruction on Israel. He was condemned by the boy Samuel. See 1 Sam. 1–4.

89 Hugh of Pattishall (died 1241) was treasurer of the Royal Exchequer until he was elevated to the see of Coventry and Lichfield in 1240. He died a year later. See M. J. Franklin, 'Pattishall [Pateshull], Hugh of', in *ODNB*, doi.org/10.1093/ref:odnb/21540.

90 Sir Philip (II) of Kyme was a Royal Justice 1227–28. The priory had been established by his grandfather, the first Sir Philip of Kyme. See Paul Dalton, 'Kyme family', in *ODNB*, doi.org/10.1093/ref:odnb/54509.

91 In this letter Grosseteste claims to have quashed 'many elections' of which the King was the patron. However, this seems to have happened only once in the early years of his episcopate, at St Frideswide's Priory Oxford. See *Letters of Robert Grosseteste*, p. 143 note 3; *Rotuli Grosseteste*, p. 446.

[92] Perry makes a common error in confusing Nicholas Grecus with Nicholas of St Albans. Nicholas Grecus was dispatched to Rome after Grosseteste's death in order to procure his canonisation. See Kathleen Major, 'The Familia of Robert Grosseteste', in *Robert Grosseteste, Scholar and Bishop*, edited by D. A. Callus, (Oxford, 1955), p. 229; J. C. Russell, *Dictionary of Writers of Thirteenth Century England* (London, 1936), p. 89.

[93] For William de Sherwood, see the biographical appendix. The Pegge that Perry cites is Samuel Pegge, *Memoirs of the Life of Roger de Weseham, Bishop of Coventry and Lichfield* (London, 1761).

[94] For the *Sentences*, see the Introduction, p. xxx

[95] For Constantina, see the biographical appendix.

[96] The chronicle cited has not been identified. The date is presumably a slip of the pen because it is much too early: Grosseteste was lector to the Franciscans 1231–35. Grosseteste's successor was a secular priest who is often linked with Peter Ramsay, Bishop of Aberdeen (1247–56). See Thomas Eccleston's *Chronicle*, coll. 11.

[97] Thomas Wallensis went on to become the Bishop of St Davids in 1248. See *Rotuli Grosseteste*, pp. 22–86.

[98] 'Mulct' is an archaic term for a fine (from Latin *multa*).

[99] Roger of Wesham (died 1257) was made Dean of Lincoln Cathedral by Grosseteste during his time of dispute with the Chapter. When the papal court eventually found in favour of Grosseteste, Weseham was accused of betraying the Chapter. See *Fasti: Lincoln*, p. 10. The Council of Lyon was an ecumenical council convened by Pope Innocent IV in 1245.

[100] This is in fact another Richard of Cornwall. Richard Rufus (mentioned a little later) is a third person, an eminent Franciscan scholar. *Letters of Robert Grosseteste*, pp. 168–69 note 1. In Letter 34 Grossetetste describes this Richard of Cornulia as 'a subdeacon … who lacks fluency in the English Language.' For the Richard of Cornwall referred to here, see *Fasti: Lincoln*, pp. 86–87.

[101] The reference is to *The Chronicles of Thomas of Otterbourne*, edited by Thomas Hearne (Oxford, 1732); better known as *Duo rerum Anglicarum scriptores veteres*. It is Thomas Hearne's publication of the writings of the fifteenth-century chronicler Thomas of Otterbourne, along with those of John Whethamstede.

[102] See *Letters of Robert Grosseteste*, p. 357. The recipient of Letter 118 is referred to only as 'T'.

[103] There is no 'Thomas' listed among the Archdeacons of Huntingdon. See *Fasti: Lincoln*, pp. 26–30.

[104] *Vesperial encomium*: see note 58.

[105] It is now generally accepted that the *Imitation of Christ* was written by Thomas a Kempis. However, after a discovery in 1605 of a manuscript copy describing it as the work of 'Abbatis Johannis Gersen', it was often attributed to

the semi-mythical Abbot of Vercelli, not to be confused with the French scholar Jean Gerson (1363–1429). Gersen's monastery was in fact St Stephen's and not St Andrew's. For a twentieth-century championing of Gersen's authorship, see D. G. Barron, *Jean Charlier de Gersen: The Author of the De Imitatione Christi* (Edinburgh and London, 1936).

106 For Sewal de Bovill, Archbishop of York 1256–58, see the biographical appendix.

107 St Richard de Wych, Bishop of Chichester 1244–53, was canonised in 1262 by Pope Urban IV.

108 See *The Letters of Adam Marsh*. Edited and translated by C. H.Lawrence. 2 vols (Oxford, 2006), as well as the biographical appendix.

109 Peter of Tewkesbury became the fifth minister of the Franciscans in England and was an intimate of Grosseteste. For his biography, see Andrew G. Little, *The Grey Friars at Oxford* (Oxford, 1892), p. 127.

110 As Perry has previously mentioned, Bacon, like Grosseteste, was rumoured to have in his possession a magical brazen head which would provide answers to its owner's esoteric questions.

111 In the Dominican order, definitors represented the chapters at the general chapter. See G. R. Galbraith, *The Constitutions of the Dominican Order, 1216–1360* (Manchester, 1925).

112 Nicholas of Farnham resigned his see in 1249 because of ill health. An earlier cure procured by drinking water laced with bristles from St Edmund of Abingdon's beard had not lasted. He died in 1257 and was buried in Durham Cathedral. See R. M. Franklin, 'Farnham, Nicholas of', in *ODNB*, doi.org/10.1093/ref:odnb/20089. William de Raleigh had been Bishop of Norwich before his translation to Winchester in 1242. Henry II objected but his appeal to Innocent IV fell on deaf ears. See David Crook, 'Raleigh [Ralegh], William of', in *ODNB*, doi.org/10.1093/ref:odnb/23042.

113 In 1229 Blanche of Castille, Queen Regent of France, sent troops in against rioting students in Paris. This resulted in the 'Great Dispersion' when masters and students quit the city until 1231. See Jack P. Cunningham, 'Lumen de Lumine: Light, God and Creation in the Thought of Robert Grosseteste', in *Bishop Grosseteste and Lincoln Cathedral*, edited by N. Temple, J. S. Hendrix and C. Frost (Aldershot, 2014), p. 90.

114 King Louis IX of France (1214–70) was canonised in 1297 by Pope Boniface VIII. See Donald Attwater, *The Penguin Dictionary of Saints* (Harmondsworth, 1965), pp. 219–20.

115 There seems to be an interesting development in Perry's opinion on Grosseteste's chancellorship. His point about the language of this letter is a good one, however this scepticism is only found in the Valladolid manuscript. In the Scottish version Perry seems more convinced, citing the Oxford University

petition for Grosseteste's canonisation which refers to his Chancellorship. See book IV, chapter VI.

116 Ishmael was the son of Abraham and Hagar. He was expelled from the household after the birth of Isaac (Gen. 21:8–21). Matthew Paris used the name as synonymous with someone who had made themselves unpopular

117 William of Thorney was Dean of Lincoln Cathedral 1223-1239. See *Fasti: Lincoln*, p. 10.

118 Perry is confusing Walter de Hemingburgh (more commonly known as Walter of Guisborough) with William of Hemingborough. Walter was a chronicler and William was a clerk of Grosseteste's household. See Major, 'The Familia of Robert Grosseteste', p. 230. For the former, see H. Rothwell, ed. *The Chronicle of Walter of Guisborough* (London, 1957), p. 89.

119 Samuel Pegge made a good case for this Alan de Beccles being the same person as Alanus Beaucliff. Beccles left Oxford for the University of Paris where he 'greatly improved himself.' He eventually became a public reader in philosophy and according to Pegge, 'much admired by the French'. He left Paris in 1229 after the withdrawal of the scholars in a dispute with the city. *Life of Robert Grosseteste*, pp. 233–35.

120 This is Richard de Kirkham. See letter 96 in which Grosseteste asks Richard's master, Bishop Hugh of Northwold, to lend him his services. See *Letters of Robert Grosseteste*, pp. 315–17.

121 Grosseteste's proctor at the Papal Curia was Simon de Arden. See *Letters of Robert Grosseteste*, letters 42, 43 and 80.

122 The Archdeacon of Worcester was indeed a different person, namely William Scot. See S. F. Stevenson, *Grosseteste*, p. 196.

123 For John of Crakehall, see the biographical appendix.

124 This is probably Nicholas of Waddington, Chancellor of Lincoln Cathedral. See *Fasti: Lincoln*, p. 17. Letter 94 tells us that his offence was that he had appeared before Grosseteste and produced a letter in the name of the Chapter appointing him as their proctor.

125 Richard de Wych (1197–1253) is St Richard of Chichester, whose feast day falls on 3 April. He was a reforming bishop very much from the same mould as his friend Grosseteste. See Attwater, *Dictionary of Saints*, pp. 296–97.

126 Robert 'de Mariscos' is the brother of Adam Marsh who went on to serve as the Dean of Lincoln Cathedral from 1259 until his death in 1262. See Major, 'The Familia of Robert Grosseteste', p. 231.

127 The Abbot of Bardney mentioned is Walter de Beningworth.

128 *a gravamina*: regarding disorders or grievances within the Church.

129 'Richard de Wendover' is Richard Wenden, who was elected bishop by the monks of Rochester in 1235. Edmund of Abingdon, Archbishop of Canterbury,

objected since he insisted that he had the right of nomination. The monks appealed to Rome and the dispute was eventually decided in their favour in 1238. See Nicholas Karn, 'Wenden, Richard of', in *ODNB*, doi.org/10.1093/ref:odnb/95168. The 'Bulaeus' that Perry cites for Wenden's doctorate is César Egasse Du Boulay (died 1678), historian of the University of Paris.

130 Uzzah touched the Ark of the Covenant in order to steady it as it was being carried by oxcart. For this act of sacrilege, he was struck down by Yahweh and killed. 2 Sam. 6:3–8.

131 The 'historians' that Perry cites here, also referring to them as 'Centuriators', are the authors of the *Magdeburg Centuries*, sixteenth-century Lutheran histories of the Church written by a team of scholars working under Matthias Flacius (1520–75). Each volume comprises a century, with the last ending in 1298. See Hans J. Hillerbrand, ed. *The Oxford Encyclopedia of the Reformation* (Oxford, 1996), vol. 2, pp. 110–11.

132 The Common Law in England maintained that only children born in wedlock were legitimate. Canon Law legitimised bastards if their parents subsequently married. These were mantle children, so called because a cloth was laid over them during a service and when they emerged they were legitimate. Grosseteste led the argument that the ecclesiastical law should be adopted, but the barons, concerned about inheritance complications, refused assent. See Richard H. Helmholz, 'Bastardy Litigation in Medieval England', *American Journal of Legal History* 13 (1969), 360–83.

133 The Hebrew names are now more familiar in the transliterations Leah, Tamar, Perez and Zerah. Tamar, after Judah refused to allow her to marry his third son, disguised herself as a prostitute and seduced Judah himself, thus securing her motherhood. Genesis 38:12–23.

134 The 'Opus Pontoppida' cited is Erik Pontoppidan, *Gesta et Vestigia Danorum*, volume 1 (Leipzig and Copenhagen, 1740).

135 For Richard de Lucy see the biographical appendix. The St Thomas mentioned is Thomas Becket. Ralph de Diceto (died *c*.1202) was Dean of St Pauls and a chronicler. He wrote *Abbreviationes chronicorum* and *Ymagines historiarum*. Perry's citation refers to the latter.

136 Perry cites the second volume of Sir William Blackstone's *Law Tracts* (Oxford, 1762), which contains his edition of Magna Carta. The introduction lays out a number of the legal principles at issue in the thirteenth century, including the discrepancy between canon law and common law definitions of illegitimacy. This was among the points discussed in a council held at Merton Priory, Surrey, on 23 January 1236. The Statute of Merton, agreed between Henry III and the barons, is regarded as the first English statute. Chapter 9 deals with illegitimacy, stating 'He is a bastard that is born before the marriage of his parents.'

137 More's *Supplication of Souls* was first published in 1529, but Perry cites the 1557 *Workes of Sir Thomas More*, which includes the *Supplication* on pages 288–339. A modern scholarly edition can be found in *The Yale Edition of the*

Complete Works of St Thomas More. Vol. 7, edited by F. Manley, G. Marc'hadour, C. H. Miller and R. C. Marius (New Haven, 1990), pp. 193–28.

138 Peter de Aigueblanche became involved in Henry III's attempts to raise a loan in order to secure for England the Kingdom of Sicily. For this he was unpopular and even arrested for a period by the barons. See Nicholas Vincent, 'Aigueblanche, Peter d' [Peter de Aqua Blanca]', in *ODNB*, doi.org/10.1093/ref:odnb/22015.

139 The Abbot of Westminster was Richard de Crokesley (died 1258). According to the *Annals of Dunstable* he was one of several people who were rich enough to purchase exemptions from Grosseteste's rulings from the papal court.

140 Richard de Thiony, treasurer of Anjou, died in 1252 holding many livings in France, Scotland and England. The Queen, as guardian of his son, assumed the right to bestow one such living at Flamstead. See Stevenson, *Grosseteste*, p. 302.

141 The only clue to the identity of this Benedictine justice is that a person named Ranulph or Ralph was Abbot between 1231 and 1253. See W. H. Hart and P. A. Lyons, eds. *Cartularium monasterii de Rameseia* (London, 1884–93) vol. 3, pp. 180–81.

142 This is Richard of Bardney, Abbot of Crowland 1236–47. Not to be confused with Grosseteste's sixteenth-century verse biographer.

143 Uzziah (Ozias) was struck with leprosy for burning incense in the Temple, a priestly function (2 Chron. 26:16–21).

144 As Perry goes on to explain, the quotation is from the *Testament of the Twelve Patriarchs* (Judah, 21:2–4).

145 Letter 84 only identifies the dean in question as 'H'. He has been unidentified in modern scholarship, though it is perfectly possible that Perry has other information and is correctly identifying him.

146 Giuliano Cesarini (1398–1444) was a powerful papal diplomat. A strong advocate of papal supremacy over the conciliarists, he nevertheless wrote to Pope Eugene IV from the Council of Basel (1431) warning him that his dissolving the Council would result in schism. See Gerald Christianson, *Cesarini, the Conciliar Cardinal, 1431–1438* (St. Ottilien, 1979). Perry's source is Jacques-Bénigne Bossuet, *The History of the Variations of the Protestant Churches* (Paris, 1718).

147 The bishop of Salisbury was William de York; of Carlisle, Sylvester de Everdon; and of Winchester, Aymer de Valence. Henry III's mother, Isabella of Angoulême (*c*.1188–1246), had been the wife of King John. Perry describes Hugh as her 'seemed' husband because Isabella had married the Count of La March without requesting consent of the King's Council in England; a requirement since she had formerly been Queen. See Nicholas Vincent 'Isabella of Angoulême: John's Jezebel', in *King John: New Interpretations*, edited by S. D. Church (Woodbridge, 1999), pp. 165–220.

148 The Chronicle of Melrose is thought to have been written by the monks of Melrose Abbey in the Scottish borders. It is now housed in the British Library,

Cotton MS Fautina B. See *Chronica de Mailros*, edited by J. Stevenson (Edinburgh, 1835).

149 Thomas Gale (1635/6–1702) was Dean of York Minster and an antiquarian. He included excerpts from a chronicle attributed to John of Wallingford (thought to be Matthew Paris's continuator) in his *Historiae Britannicae, Saxonicae, Anglo-Danicae Scriptores XV* (Oxford, 1691), remarking on the reasons for his excisions in the preface to the volume. On Gale, see Nicholas Doggett, 'Gale, Thomas', in *ODNB*, doi.org/10.1093/ref:odnb/10298.

150 Elisha prophesied that Hazael would assassinate his master King Ben-Hadad (2 Kgs. 8:7–15).

151 The celebrated Templar William of Valences brought a vial of blood from Jerusalem which carried the authentication of the Patriarch of Jerusalem, as well as many bishops and abbots. This is not to be confused with the more famous Holy Blood of Hailes which was purchased later by Richard, Earl of Cornwall, and presented to the abbey in 1270. For the relic see Nicholas Vincent, *The Holy Blood: King Henry III and the Westminster Blood Relic* (Cambridge, 2001).

152 'Promulge' is an archaic form of 'promulgate' (from the Latin *promulgare*, meaning to publish or teach).

153 According to Butler's account of the life of St James of the Marches of Ancona (a Franciscan who died in 1476) in his *Lives of the Fathers, Martyrs and Other Saints*: 'A question was at that time agitated with great warmth, particularly between the Franciscan and Dominican friars, whether the precious blood of Christ, which was separated from the body during his passion, remained always hypostatically united to the divine Word; and St James was accused in the inquisition of having advanced the negative: but was dismissed with honour.'

154 Historically this means a man or woman descended in the male line from a hereditary monarch.

155 Richard of Cornwall (1209–72) was the second son of King John. He was first Earl of Cornwall and in 1256 was elected King of Germany. See Noël Denholm-Young, *Richard of Cornwall* (Oxford, 1947).

156 Jeremy Collier was a nonjuring bishop of the Church of England, whose *Ecclesiastical History of Great Britain* (2 vols, London, 1708–14), here cited, brought on accusations of Roman Catholic sympathies. The other sources cited for this sentence are from John Ross or Rous (1420–92). The first is a history of the Beauchamp family with a focus on Richard Beauchamp, 13th Earl of Warwick. The second is his *Historia regum Angliae* (1486), a general history of England containing many legends and myths.

157 This is not strictly true; Perry is omitting Celestine IV (Goffreda da Castiglione) who reigned from 25 October until 10 November 1241, though he may have died before actually being consecrated. See J. N. D. Kelly, *The Oxford Dictionary of Popes* (Oxford, 1986), pp. 191–92.

158 Supererogation: the act of performing more than one's duty.

[159] This is almost certainly Master Azzo de Palma who was one of the Legate's chaplains.

[160] Perry cites John of Salisbury's *Policraticus*, a modern edition of which is available in the series Cambridge Texts in the History of Political Thought, edited and translated by C. J. Nederman (Cambridge, 1991).

[161] The Old Testament references identified in this letter are Exodus 18:19 (*Now listen to the advice I am going to give you! Your task is to represent the people to God, to lay their cases before God*); Ecclesiasticus 3:18 (*The greater you are, the more humbly you should behave, and then you will find favour with the Lord*); Ecclesiasticus 3:11 (*For a person's honour derives from the respect shown to his father, and a mother held in dishonour is a reproach to her children*); Proverbs 1:8 (*Listen, my child, to your father's instructions, do not reject your mother's teaching*).

[162] For Giles de Torres, Cardinal Deacon of Saints Cosmas and Damian, see the biographical appendix.

[163] Grosseteste's letter 36 provides the following panegyric in praise of the princes of the Church: 'Just as the universe is supported by its cardinal points … and has them to hold it up … so the unshakeable world, that is the universal Church, which no shaking shall dislodge from the steadfastness of faith, rests firmly upon the cardinals of the holy Roman Church … For they are the ones whom the Psalm call "the foundations of the World"' [Ps. 17:16]. See *Letters of Robert Grosseteste*, p. 153.

[164] The members of the papal court listed as among Grosseteste's correspondents include: St Raymond de Peñafort, who eventually became Master General of the Dominicans in 1238, compiled the hugely important Church laws known as the Decretals of Gregory IX and is the patron saint of lawyers (Butler, *Lives of Saints*, vol. I, pp. 92–96); Arnulf, a Franciscan friar and perhaps an Englishman, was a penitentiary of Pope Gregory IX (Thomas Eccleston, *Tractatus de adventu Fratrum Minorum in angliam*, p. 40; Rosalind B. Brooke, *Early Franciscan Government: Ellias to Bonaventure* (Cambridge, 1959, 2004), p. 42); John de Ferentino, Archdeacon of Norwich and friend of Grosseteste (Stevenson, *Grosseteste*, p. 96); Thomas de Capua, Cardinal Priest of Santa Sabina from 1216 until his death in 1239 (Paravicini Bagliani, *Cardinali*, vol. 1, p. 13 and vol. 2, p. 393).

[165] For Robert de Somercote, Cardinal Deacon of San Eustachio, see the biographical appendix.

[166] The excerpt is from Letter 136 of Peter de Blois, written to Pope Alexander III on behalf of Henry II. With the parts omitted the passage runs: 'In my soul I prostrate myself before your knees [seeking salvific] counsel. [The realm of England belongs to your jurisdiction, and as pertains to the obligation of feudal right, I am held and constrained subservient to you only. Let England discover the power of the Roman Pontiff, and,] since he does not use material arms, let the patrimony of Saint Peter be guarded by a spiritual sword.' For Peter de Blois (1130–1211), see the biographical appendix. The letter in question has been printed

in Patrologia Latina 200, *Alexandri III Romani Pontificis Opera Omnia*, edited by J.-P. Migne (Paris, 1855), 1389–90.

167 For the papal legate Guala Bicchieri, see the biographical appendix. 'Prince Lewis' is the future King Louis VIII of France.

168 'Chronico Bartholemei' is *Chronicorum Monasterii Sancti Bartholomei de Carpineto*, an early thirteenth-century chronicle from the Monastery of San Bartolomeo at Carpineto in Abruzzi, Italy. See *Il Chronicon de San Bartolomeo di Carpineto*, edited by E. Fuselli (L'Aquila, 1996).

169 According to Stevenson, Twenge had a rather colourful backstory. On Christmas Day 1231 masked men plundered the barns of Roman ecclesiastics and then either sold the stolen corn at cheap rates or distributed it to the poor. Their organiser was Robert Twenge, who had twice had foreign clergy imposed on livings in his gift. He later went to Rome and made his peace with Gregory IX. Stevenson, *Grosseteste*, p. 96.

170 St Edmund's exile is an interesting fabrication of Matthew Paris. Since nearly all of the saints of England between the thirteenth and fifteenth centuries had been either prelates or great laymen who had opposed royal power, the chronicler of St Albans seems to have invented the dispute as a cause for the Archbishop's retreat to France. See M. Paris 'Vita S. Edmundi', in *St Edmund of Abingdon: A Study in Hagiography and History*, edited by C. H. Lawrence, (Oxford, 1960); A. Vauchez, *Sainthood in the Later Middle Ages* (Cambridge, 1997), p. 170.

171 Dr Thomas Walleys: presumably the Thomas Wallensis formerly referred to as Thomas Welchman.

172 This is the much discussed Letter 5, which is in fact addressed to the Countess of Wincester, Margaret de Quincy. It was written in 1231 when Grosseteste was Archdeacon of Leicester. In that year the Jews had been expelled from the city and they were about to be offered refuge by the Countess: an action that Grosseteste strongly urges her against. Richard Southern is right that the letter does not reflect well on Grosseteste but recent studies have, without attempting to exonerate him, set this letter and Grosseteste's attitude toward Jews in general, in the context of the medieval situation and scholastic thought. See *Letters of Robert Grosseteste*, pp. 65–70. For a discussion of Grosseteste's attitude toward the Jews, see Southern, *Grosseteste*, pp. 244–49; John A. Watt, 'Grosseteste and the Jews: A Commentary on Letter V', in *Robert Grosseteste and the Beginnings of a British Theological Tradition*, edited by M. O'Carroll (Rome, 2003), pp. 201–16; Mark W. Elliott, 'Robert Grosseteste, the Jews, and "De cessatione legalium"', in *Robert Grosseteste: His Thought and Its Impact*, edited by Jack P. Cunningham (Toronto, 2012), pp. 314–26.

173 Master Martin was papal nuncio to England 1244–45. He attempted to confer a benefice in Pinchbeck, Lincolnshire, on a person of his choosing, provoking the local people to violence against his agents. The Catholic chronicler Robert Fabyan (died 1513) wrote *The Newe Chronycles of England* (1516) in which he tells of a Master Martin who was a kinsman of Innocent III. Grosseteste had

cause to complain to the King of him as an example of 'alyant' (alien) clergy. *Chronycle*, sig. ee ii. It was repeated by the famous Tudor historian John Stow (1524/5–1605) in *A Summarie of Englyshe Chronicles* (London, 1565), 87v. See J. Flood and J. McEvoy, '*Romanorum malleus et contemptor*', in *Robert Grosseteste and his Intellectual Milieu*, edited by J. Flood, J. R. Ginther and J. Goering (Toronto, 2013), pp. 319–90, at p. 343.

174 William Powick who served as clerk to Henry III. See F. Maurice Powicke, *King Henry III and the Lord Edward* (Oxford, 1947), pp. 358–59; William E. Lunt, *Financial Relations of the Papacy with England to 1327* (Cambridge, MA, 1939), pp. 206–12.

175 Fulk Basset (died 1259) was elected Bishop of London in 1241. See R. M. Franklin, 'Basset, Fulk', in *ODNB*, doi.org/10.1093/ref:odnb/1638.

176 According to Matthew Paris, Grosseteste had substantially impaired the revenues and therefore power of future deans by alienating Aylesbury from the Deanery of Lincoln (*Chron. Maj.*, iv, pp. 424–26).

177 John Ursola, from 1232 to 1254 suffragan Bishop of Cervia in the diocese of Ravenna, had opposed the Emperor's forces who controlled the area. In exile in 1245 he appealed to Innocent IV, who clearly lighted upon the wealthy Archdiocese of York as an appropriate source of succour.

178 St Bernard of Clairvaux (1090–1153) and Giuliano Cesarini (1398–1444).

179 This was in fact Richard of Gravesend (died 1279) who went on to become Bishop of Lincoln in 1258. A Richard of Mepham (Meopham) became Archdeacon of Oxford, but not until after Grosseteste's death in 1263. He was eventually Dean of Lincoln 1273–74, which may account for the confusion. See *Rotuli Ricardi Gravesend 1258–79*, edited by F. N. Davis. Lincoln Records Society, 20, 1925, p. xxxvi.

180 William of Modena (*c*.1184–1251) was an important papal diplomat. See Anti Selart, 'William of Modena', in *The Crusades: An Encyclopedia*, edited by Allan V. Murray (Santa Barbara, 2006) vol. 4, p. 1280.

181 Giovanni Gaetano Orsini (1225–80) was elected Pope Nicholas III in 1277 and reigned until his death in 1280. See Kelly, *Dictionary of Popes*, pp. 201–02.

182 The point that Grosseteste was making here had much contemporary significance. Other schools of thought at this time maintained a harder line by claiming that the Jews crucified Jesus knowing that he was God. Grosseteste states here that they knew him only as a miracle worker who clashed with their own beliefs and practices. This is important in that it does not accuse them of deicide but rather the lesser crime of homicide, at least in intention. For a full discussion of this, see Watt, 'Grosseteste and the Jews', pp. 201–16.

183 The visitation instructions that emerged from Trent in 1555 decreed that all churches and monasteries be visited, including those which claimed exemption. See W. David Myer, *"Poor Sinning Folk": Confession and Conscience in Counter-Reformation Germany* (Ithaca, 1996), p. 54.

[184] According to the First Book of Maccabees, Alcimus was a descendant of Aaron who was installed as High Priest in Jerusalem. Strongly associated with the Hellenising party he was in bitter conflict with the Maccabees. For Heli, see note 88 above.

[185] The first named recipient of this letter is Stephen de Montival who was Archdeacon of Canterbury *c.*1248–69. See *Fasti Ecclesiae Anglicanae 1066–1300*, vol. 2. *Monastic Cathedrals*, edited by Diana E. Greenway (London, 1971), p. 15. The second is Master Innocenzo, who was a papal scriptor then living in Yorkshire. For the best discussion of this letter, see L. E. Boyle, 'Robert Grosseteste and Pastoral Care', *Medieval and Renaissance Studies* 8 (1979), 3–51.

[186] 2 Cor. 10:8: *How much excellence, from great and divine power God has given him, for building up and not for destruction.*

[187] Knighton has taken the idea of Grosseteste's excommunication from Ranulph Higden's *Polychronicon*. John of Tynemouth wrote his *Historia Aurea* around 1350. It is a history of the world from Creation and it also draws extensively on the *Polychronicon*. See Vivian H. Galbraith, 'The "Historia Aurea" of John, Vicar of Tynemouth and the Sources of the St Albans Chronicle (1327–1377)', in *Essays in History Presented to Reginald Lane Poole*, edited by H. W. C. Davies (Oxford, 1927), pp. 379–95.

[188] Impetrate: An archaic word meaning to obtain by request.

[189] This is the reforming Pope Gregory VII (1073–85). His measures to reform clerical life provoked a storm of opposition in Italy, Germany and France.

[190] For John Schalby (died 1333) see *The Book of John de Schalby, Canon of Lincoln, 1229–1333, Concerning the Bishops of Lincoln and their Acts*, translated by J. H. Srawley (Lincoln, 1949).

[191] It was more than 'time' that devoured what Leland called a 'goodly tumbe of marble and brass'. In fact, Oliver Cromwell's army destroyed it in a fit of iconoclasm in 1644. See Donald A. Stocker, 'The Tomb and Shrine of Robert Grosseteste in Lincoln Cathedral', in *England in the Thirteenth Century: Proceedings of the 1984 Harlaxton Symposium*, edited by W. M. Ormond, (Harlaxton College, 1985), pp. 143–48; James McEvoy, *The Philosophy of Robert Grosseteste* (Oxford, 1982), p. 47; J. W. F. Hill, 'The Tomb of Robert Grosseteste with an Account of its Opening in 1782', in *Robert Grosseteste: Scholar and Bishop*, edited by D. A. Callus (Oxford, 1955), pp. 246–50. The work of Leland's that Perry cites is *De rebus Britannicis Collectanea*, edited by T. Hearne (London, 1715).

[192] In English translation: 'Now God has performed many miracles in the world through this man, and He who has given all that is good still causes this to happen. The lame leap about; he liberates mutes with eloquence. This holy man opens closed-up ears. The winter of illness turns to flourishing, he brings peace into madness, and lets the arrogant return restrained. He who celebrated the Lord with example, teaching, prayers, and praise, rejoices to be celebrated with corresponding honour. Here ends this work. O mild father Robert, I pray that you be benevolent to all who seek your favours.'

[193] Catalogue of the Saints: Thomas de Wykes is probably referring to the Martyrology, the register of official saints and beati. Although the *Martyrologium Romanum* was only official published for the first time in 1584 when Pope Gregory XIII revised the Julian Calendar, before that there were various versions. The most commonly used in the Middle Ages was composed by Usuard, a Benedictine monk of the ninth century. See F. L. Cross and E. A. Livingstone, *The Oxford Dictionary of the Christian Church* (Oxford, 1997), p. 1047.

[194] Thomas of Walden is the Carmelite scholar Thomas Netter (*c*.1375–1430). The work referred to is his *Doctrinale antiquitatum fidei ecclesiae catholicae*, which was presented to the Pope in 1427. See Johan Bergström and A. C. Copsey, *Thomas Netter of Walden: Carmelite, Diplomat and Theologian, c.1372–1430* (Faversham and Rome, 2009).

[195] John Lydgate (*c*.1370–*c*.1451) was a monk and a prodigious poet, once much celebrated but now sadly neglected. However, the prayer in question is to St Robert of Bury, a child martyr who the Jews were accused of murdering during a wave of antisemitism. Lydgate did however translate Grosseteste's poem *Le Château d'amour* into English, 'For him Þat con not i-know nouÞer French ne Latyn.' See Derek A. Pearsall, *John Lydgate* (London, 1970), p. 257.

[196] William Greenfield (*c*.1255–1315), Archbishop of York 1306–15. See Roy Martin Haines, 'Greenfield, William', in *ODNB*, doi.org/10.1093/ref:odnb/11421.

[197] St Cyprian of Carthage (*c*.200–58). Following the Decian persecution Pope Stephen I maintained that converts who had been baptised by schismatics (i.e. Novatians) need not be rebaptised on their return to the Church. St Cyprian argued against him for a much firmer line, and was supported in this by St Firmilian, Bishop of Caesarea Mazaca. For Cyprian, see Butler, *Lives of Saints*, vol. 3, pp. 355–69. For Firmilian, see Cross and Livingstone, *Dictionary of the Church*, p. 613.

[198] St Robert Bellarmine (1542–1621), a great stalwart of the Catholic Reformation, was inexplicably canonised only as late as 1930. He was designated a Doctor of the Church the following year. His feast day is 17 September. See Attwater, *Dictionary of Saints*, pp. 298–99.

[199] For Robert Winchelsee (or Winchelsey), see the biographical appendix.

[200] Walter Reynolds (died 1327), Archbishop of Canterbury 1313–27. See J. Robert Wright, 'Reynolds [Heyne, Heyerne], Walter', in *ODNB*, doi.org/10.1093/ref:odnb/23443.

[201] For an account of efforts made toward the canonisation of Grosseteste, see Eric W. Kemp, 'The Attempted Canonization of Robert Grosseteste', in *Robert Grosseteste: Scholar and Bishop*, edited by D. A. Callus (Oxford, 1955), pp. 241–46.

BIOGRAPHICAL APPENDIX

Adam Marsh (de Marisco) (*c*.1200–59)
A Franciscan friar and devoted friend of Grosseteste from boyhood. He was taught by Grosseteste at Oxford and went on to become a highly respected Biblical scholar. He was buried next to Grosseteste in Lincoln Cathedral. See Adam Marsh, *The Letters of Adam Marsh*, edited and translated by C. H. Lawrence. 2 vols. Oxford Medieval Text (Oxford, 2006).

Alexander Hales (*c*.1185–1245)
A highly important scholastic philosopher of the Franciscan School. John de la Rochelle was his pupil and later collaborator. See Christopher M. Cullen, 'Alexander of Hales' and Gérard Sondag, 'John de la Rochelle', in *Companion to Philosophy in the Middle Ages*, edited by J. E. Gracia and T. B. Noone (Oxford, 2006), pp. 104–08 and pp. 334–35.

Boniface of Savoy (1206/7–70)
The Archbishop of Belley in France before he was given the see of Canterbury. He was also the uncle of Queen Eleanor, wife of Henry III. The King tried to have him elected to the see of Winchester and when this was unsuccessful he was nominated to Canterbury, which the Pope approved in order to placate Henry. He was consecrated at Lyon personally by the Pope in 1245 but he did not take up his position in England until 1249. After his death he was regarded as something of a saint on the continent, in England he was less celebrated, his later reputation resting largely on Matthew Paris's assessment of him as a violent, greedy and neglectful foreigner. See Leland E. Wilshire, 'Boniface of Savoy, Carthusian and Archbishop of Canterbury, 1207–1270', *Analecta Cartusiana* 31 (1977), 4–90.

Constantina
Probably the daughter of Michael Acominatus, Archbishop of Athens. Matthew Paris tells us that John de Basingstoke spoke of a nineteen-year-old girl whose knowledge exceeded that of his own acquired at the University of Paris. It is Basingstoke who made Grosseteste aware of the existence of the *Testimony of the Twelve Patriarchs*. Paris also tells us that he had knowledge of a Greek numbering system based on a system of strokes. See M. de Jonge, 'Robert Grosseteste and the Testament of the Twelve Patriarchs', *Journal of Theological Studies*, New Series 42 (1991), 115–25.

Gerald of Wales (Geraldus Cambrensis) (*c.*1146–1220)
A priest and author, his, *Topographia Hibernica* (1186–87) was an account of his travels in Ireland. It gained for him a substantial contemporary reputation and it is generally considered his most important work. Later in life he removed to Lincoln and, after failing in his main ambition to secure a bishopric, he almost certainly spent the remainder of his days there. See *The History and Topography of Ireland*, translated by J. J. O'Meara (London, 1982).

Giles de Torres, Cardinal Deacon of SS. Cosmas and Damian
Created Cardinal Deacon in 1216, reached over a hundred years of age and became a highly respected Churchman. Four of Grosseteste's collected letters are addressed to him. See A. Paravicini Bagliani, *Cardinali di Curia e 'Familae' Cardinalize* (Padova, 1972), vol. 1, p. 16.

Guala Bicchieri (Cardinal)
Papal legate in England 1216–18. Before the battle of Lincoln, he excommunicated the future King Louis VIII and declared a plenary indulgence for all those who took up the King's cause. After the supporters of the King were victorious, Guala imposed a penance on Louis. In addition, the French clergy who had accompanied him to England were made to do penance, while the English clergy who had supported his cause were deprived of the benefices and punished. See Nicholas Vincent, ed. *The Letters and Charters of Cardinal Guala Bicchieri, Papal Legate in England, 1216–1218* (Woodbridge, 1996).

John Ayton or Acton (died 1350)
Most famous for his *Constitutiones legitime seu legatine regionis Anglicane*, which was a gloss on the constitutions of the two papal legatees, Cardinal Otto and Cardinal Ottobone. It became the primary work of Canon Law in England for a century. See Diana Wood, 'John of Ayton's "Grumbling Gloss" a Northern Churchman's view of Society c. 1100–1700', in *Life and Thought in the Northern Church, c.1100–c.1700: Essays in Honour of Claire Cross*, edited by Diana Wood (Woodbridge, 1999), pp. 37–55.

John of Crakehall (Crachale) (died 1260)
Entered the services of Grosseteste *c.*1234. He accompanied him to Lyon and was present at the moment of his death. It was he who reported the sound of heavenly bells ringing at the moment of the Bishop departing. See Major, 'The Familia of Robert Grosseteste', pp. 216–41.

John of Offington (Uffington)
Served Edmund of Canterbury before becoming a proctor at the Papal Court in 1243 and a chaplain to Innocent IV. It seems likely that Grosseteste met him at Lyon in 1245.

Jordan of Saxony (*c*.1190–1237)
Jordan of Saxony who was immediately elected as Master General of the Order of Preachers in 1222 on the death of St Dominic. Grosseteste heard him preach at Oxford and this seems to have had a profound influence on the course of his life. It was at this time that Grosseteste relinquished the majority of his livings.

Knighton (Knyghton), Henry (died *c*.1396)
Was an Augustinian canon and chronicler at St Mary de Pratis, Leicester. His *Chronicon*, which describes events from the Norman invasion to the fourteenth century survives in two manuscripts in the Cotton Collection in the British Library. See *Knighton's Chronicle, 1337–1396*, edited and translated by G. H. Martin, Oxford Medieval Text (Oxford, 1995).

Leland, John (*c*.1503–52)
Poet and antiquarian. He spent six years travelling in Henrician England and his writings marked the beginning of English topographical study. Indeed, he is often also claimed as the father of English local history. His *De viris illustribus*, a biographical dictionary of British writers in chronological order was unfinished before the onset of insanity. It was only published as late 1709. For a modern translation see *De viris illustribus/On Famous Men*. Edited and translated by James P. Carley with Caroline Brett (Toronto, 2010). In 1715 Thomas Hearne published a work entitled *Johannis Lelandi antiquarii de rebus Britannicis collectanea*, which was a compendium of extracts from classical and medieval texts relating to Britain which he collected from monastic libraries. Both works discuss Grosseteste and are much used by Perry.

Nicholas Trivet (*c*.1257–*c*.1334)
An Oxford academic who in addition to being a Biblical scholar of high repute was also a chronicler. His *Annales sex regum Angliae* offers a laudatory account of Grosseteste. See James G. Clark, 'Trevet [Trivet], Nicholas', in *ODNB*, doi.org/10.1093/ref:odnb/27744.

Oddone di Monterrato
An Italian nobleman, he was sent to England in 1225 as papal nuncio. Later, in 1237, he was sent as Legate when he was involved in a protracted dispute over primacy between York and Canterbury. He eventually

became the Bishop of Porto e Santa Rufina but he went down in English history as Legate Otto.

Peter d'Aigueblanche (de Egueblank) (died 1268)
Bishop of Hereford between 1240 and 1268. See W. N. Yates, 'Bishop Peter de Aquablanca (1240–1268): A Reconsideration', *Journal of Ecclesiastical History* 22 (1971), 303–17.

Peter de Blois (*c.*1125–1203)
A statesman and theologian who taught at Paris. In this work Perry is almost certainly referring to his *Epistolae*, which represents his most important writing. See *Petri Blesensis epistolae*, Patrologia Latina 207 (Paris, 1855).

Ralph de Maidstone (Maydestone) (died 1215)
Taught in Paris until 1229, after which he moved to Oxford. He became the Bishop of Hereford in 1235 but resigned his see four years later in order to enter the Franciscans at Oxford. He would have known Grosseteste at Oxford. Only later did he join their convent at Gloucester where he was buried. See Julia Barrow, 'Maidstone, Ralph of', in *ODNB*, doi.org/10.1093/ref:odnb/23057.

Richard de Lucy (Luci) (1089–1179)
One of Henry II's chief councillors. He was regarded as a principal author of the Constitutions of Clarendon (1164) which established the law that clerics who had been found guilty in an ecclesiastical court should be punished by lay authority. He was twice excommunicated by Becket. Richard founded the Abbey of Lesnes or Westwood in 1178. See Roger de Wendover, *Flores Historiarum* (Rolls Series), vol. I, p. 108.

Robert de Somercote (died 1241)
Was made Cardinal Deacon of St Eustachio in 1238. He was the only Englishman to be elevated to the College of Cardinals by Pope Gregory IX. Robert died during the conclave that elected Celestine IV but there is no reason to accept Matthew Paris's verdict that he was poisoned to prevent him becoming Pope. See Dominic A. Bellenger and Stella Fletcher, *Princes of the Church: A History of the English Cardinals* (Stroud, 2001), p. 173.

Robert Winchelsee (Winchelsey) (*c.*1240–1313)
Archbishop of Canterbury (1293–1313). A pious scholar and hardworking bishop the parallels with Grosseteste's life are numerous. Winchelsey quarrelled with Edward I who took his revenge in 1305 when one of his clerks was elected Pope Clement V. At Edward's bidding Clement

suspended Winchelsey from office and he was forced into an exile which only ended in 1308 after the coronation of Edward II. Attempts to secure his canonisation were unsuccessful. See J. H. Denton, *Robert Winchelsey and the Crown, 1294–1313: A Study in the Defence of Ecclesiastical Liberty* (Cambridge, 1980).

Sewal de Bovill (died 1258)
The King objected to his election as Archbishop on the grounds that he was illegitimate, however the Chapter appealed to Rome and a dispensation was granted. Relations with the papacy soured however when the Pope intruded an Italian into one of his deaneries. When Sewal objected he was suspended and excommunicated. However, it is not true, as Perry suggests, that he remained in this state until his death. The dispute was resolved and the excommunication lifted, though, it might be added that more quarrels were to follow. John Bale told his readers that Sewal took inspiration from Grosseteste as he 'defyied' the pope. See C. L. Kingsford, 'Bovill, Sewal', revised by Philippa Hoskin, in *ODNB*, doi.org/10.1093/ref:odnb/25133.

Thomas de Wykes (1222–1291/3)
A canon of the Augustinian house at Osney outside Oxford. He may well have studied at Oxford from 1238, a little time after Grosseteste. His chronicle survives in one manuscript BL Cotton MS Titus A. xiv. Wykes also continued the *Chronicles of Osney* after he became a canon there in 1282. Wykes' chronicle was first published in 1687 by Thomas Gale as part of his *Historiae Anglicanae scriptores quinque* and it is a source much used by Perry. See N. Denholm-Young, 'Thomas de Wykes and his Chronicle', *English Historical Review* 61 (1946), 157–79.

Thomas Gascoigne (1404–1458)
Chancellor of Oxford University, he admired Grosseteste as the greatest of post-patristic scholars and he was a prodigious collector of his theological writings. Gascoigne's *Dictionarium Theologicum*, written *c*.1434–58, is preserved in two volumes at Oxford, Lincoln College, MSS 117 and 118. He considered the Bishop of Lincoln to be a theologian close in status to Augustine and far above Aquinas. See Richard Southern, *Robert Grosseteste: The Growth of an English Mind in Medieval Europe* (Oxford, 1986), pp. 314–15.

Thomas Hearne (1678–1735)
A High Anglican Nonjuror, a Jacobite and an antiquarian. He was called before the Vice-Chancellor of Oxford University when his edition of William Camden's *Annals* was deemed to betray Catholic sympathies. He is an important source for Perry. See T. H. B. M. Harmsen, *Antiquarianism*

in the Augustan Age: Thomas Hearne, 1678–1735 (Frankfurt am Main, 2000).

Walter de Cantilupe (*c*.1195-1266)
Bishop of Worcester between 1236/7 and 1266, he was also one of the papal judges in the case between Grosseteste and his Chapter. He is generally regarded as one of the greatest ecclesiastical leaders of his age.

Wharton, Henry (1665–95)
A writer and an important antiquarian. His *Anglia Sacra* was published in two volumes and it represents a collection of his own writings and those borrowed from earlier text on the lives of English bishops. It is used extensively by Perry.

William de Sherwood (died *c*.1272)
A logician and ecclesiastic. His *Introductiones in Logicam*, survives in manuscript form in the Bibliothèque Nationale MS Lat. 16617. Leland identified three theological tracts in the sixteenth century as being the works of Sherwood but these, even if genuine,have not survived. See William de Sherwood, *Introduction to Logic*, translated by N. Kretzmann (Minneapolis, 1966).

BIBLIOGRAPHY

Works Cited by Perry

(followed, where possible, by reference to a modern edition)

Printed works

Annales (Chronicon) de Lanercost, *The Chronicle of Lanercost, 1272–1346*. Translated by Herbert Maxwell (Glasgow, 1913).

Annales de Burton, in *The Templars: Selected Sources*. Translated by M. Barber and K. Bate (Manchester, 2002).

Bacon, Roger, *Opera majus*. *The 'Opus maius' of Roger Bacon*. Edited by J. M. Bridges. 2 vols (Cambridge, 2010).

Blackstone, William, *Law Tracts*. 2 vols (Oxford, 1762).

Blount, T. P., *Censura celebriorum auctorum* (London, 1690).

Bossuet, Jacques Bénigne, *The History of the Variations of the Protestant Churches* (Paris, 1718). https://archive.org/details/historyofvariati01boss

Boulay, Caesare E., *Historia universitatis Parisiensis*. 6 vols (Paris, 1665–73). http://www.documentacatholicaomnia.eu/25_90_1601-1678-_Du_Boulay.html

Brown, Edward, *Fasciculus rerum expetendaum ac fugiendarum* (London, 1690).

Butler, Alban, *Lives of the Fathers, Martyrs and other Saints* (London, 1756–59).

Casimir Oudin, *Supplementum de Scriptoribus vel scriptis ecclesiastics a Bellarmino omissis* (Paris, 1686).

Chronicon, sive annals prioratus de Dunstable. Edited by Thomas Hearne (Oxford, 1733). *The Annals of Dunstable Priory*. Edited by H. R. Webster. Translated by D. Preest (Woodbridge, 2018).

Chronicorum Monasterii Sancti Bartholemei de Carpineto. Edited by B. Pio (Rome, 2001).

Collier, Jeremy, *Ecclesiastical History of Great Britain*. 2 vols (London, 1708–14).

Dart, John, *Westmonasterium*. 2 vols (London, 1723). https://hdl.handle.net/2027/mdp.39015026728926

Dodd, Charles, *An Apology for the Church History of England from 1500 till 1688*. 4 vols (London, 1742). https://archive.org/details/doddschurchhist01dodduoft

Eccleston, Thomas, *Tractatus de adventu Fratrum Minorum in angliam* (*c*.1258). Edited by Andrew G. Little (Manchester, 1951).

Fabyan, Robert, *The Newe Chronycles of England and France* (London, 1533).

Fordun, John, *Johannis de Fordun Chronica gentis Scotorum* (*c*.1440). Edited by W. F. Skene; translated by F. J. H. Skene (Edinburgh, 1871–72).

Fuller, Thomas, *The History of the Worthies of England*. Edited by J. Fuller (London, 1642).

Gale, Thomas, *Historiae anglicanae scriptores quinque* (Oxford, 1687).

Gale, Thomas, *Historiae Britannicae, Saxonicae, Anglo-Danicae Scriptores XV* (Oxford, 1691).

Higden, Ranulph, *Polychronicon de Rebus Britannicis & Hibernicis usque ad conquestum* (Oxford, 1691). *Polychronicon Ranulphi Higdeni, monachi Cestrensis: together with the English translation of John Trevisa and of an unknown Writer of the fifteenth Century*. Edited by C. Babington and J. R. Lumby (Cambridge, 2012).

Historia monasterri Croylandesis (*c*.1434–58). *Ingulph's Chronicle of the Abbey of Croyland.* Edited and translated by H. T. Riley (London, 1854). https://web.archive.org/web/20060102051731/http://www.r3.org/bookcase/croyland/croy1.html

John of Salisbury, *Polycratio Polycraticus* (1159). *Policraticus*. Cambridge Texts in the History of Political Thought. Edited and translated by C. J. Nederman (Cambridge, 1991).

Knighton, Henry, *Chronica de eventibus Angliae a tempore Regis Edgari usque mortem Regis Ricardi secondi* (London, 1652). *Knighton's Chronicle, 1337–1396*. Edited and translated by G. H. Martin, Oxford Medieval Text (Oxford, 1995).

Leland, John, *De viris illustribus/On Famous Men.* Edited by A. Hall (Oxford, 1709). Edited and translated by James P. Carley with Caroline Brett (Toronto, 2010).

Leland, John, *De rebus Britannicis Collectanea*. Edited by T. Hearne (Oxford, 1715).

Marsh, Adam, *The Letters of Adam Marsh*. Edited and translated by C. H. Lawrence. 2 vols (Oxford, 2006).

Monastici Anglicani. Edited by William Dugdale (London,1693). https://archive.org/details/monasticonanglic00dugd

More, Thomas, *Supplication of Souls* (1529). *The Yale Edition of the Complete Works of Thomas More*. Vol. 7. Edited by F. Manley, G. Marc'hadour, C. H. Miller and R. C. Marius, (New Haven, 1990), pp. 193–228.

Oldys, W. et al. (eds), *Biographia Britannica or, the Lives of the most Eminent persons who have flourished in Great Britain and Ireland* (London, 1747–66). https://archive.org/details/biographiabritan04adam

Otterbourne, Thomas, *Duo rerum Anglicarum veteres*. Edited by Thomas Hearn (Oxford, 1732).

Paris, Matthew, *Matthaei Parisiensis, monachi S. Albani, Chronica Majora* (London, 1640). *Matthaei Parisiensis Chronica Majora*. 7 vols. Edited by H. R. Luard (Cambridge, 2012).

Paris, Matthew, 'Vita S. Edmundi', *St Edmund of Abingdon: A Study in Hagiography and History*. Edited by C. H. Lawrence (Oxford, 1960).

Parkinson, Anthony, *A Collection of the Antiquities of the English Franciscans* (London, 1726). https://archive.org/details/collectaneaanglo00park

Pegge, Samuel, *Memoirs of the Life of Roger de Weseham, Bishop of Coventry and Lichfield* (London, 1761).

Peter de Blois, *Petri Blesensis epistolae*. Patrologia Latina 207 (Paris, 1855).

Pontoppidan, Eric, *Gesta et Vestigia Danorum*. Vol. 1 (Leipzig and Copenhagen, 1740).

Ralph de Diceto, *Abbreviationes chronicorum* (London, 1652). *The Historical Works of Master Ralph de Diceto, Dean of London*. Vol. I. Edited by W. Stubbs. Rolls, *Rerum Britannicarum Medii Aevi Scriptores* 68 (1876).

Robert de Faversham, '*Chronicon Angliae Petriburgense*', *Historiae Anglicanae Scriptores varii, e codicibus manuscriptis*. Edited by Joseph Sparke (London, 1723). *Chronicon Angliae Petriburense*. Edited by J. A. Giles (London, 1845). https://archive.org/details/chroniconanglia00chrogoog

Roger de Wendover, *Flores Historiarum*. Edited by H. O. Coxe (London, 1841). https://archive.org/details/rogeridewendove03rogegoog.

Rous, John, *Warwick Roll* (1485–90). *The Rous Roll/John Ross*. Edited by C. Ross (Gloucester, 1979).

Rous, John, *Historia regum Angliae*. Edited by T. Hearne (Oxford, 1745).

Sherwood, William de, *Introduction to Logic*. Translated by N. Kretzmann (Minneapolis, 1966).

Stow, John, *A Summarie of Englyshe Chronicles* (London, 1565).

Tanner, Thomas, *Bibliotheca britannico-hibernica, sive de scriptoribus, qui in Anglia, Scotia, et Hiberia ad saeculi XVII initium floruerunt, commentaries*. Edited by David Wilkins (London, 1748). https://archive.org/details/BibliothecaBritannicoHibernicaTanner

Thomas of Walden (Netter), *Doctrinale antiquitatum fidei ecclesiae catholicae*. 2 vols. Edited by F. B. Blanciotti (Venice, 1757–59).

Wadding, Luke, *Annales minorum*. 1625–54. *Luke Waddingus, Annales Minorum* (Florence, 1931).

Walter of Guisborough, *The Chronicle of Walter of Guisborough*. Edited by H. Rothwell (London, 1957).

Wharton, Henry, *Anglia Sacra, sive collectio historiarum antiquitus scriptarum de Archiepiscopus et Episcopis Angilae*. 2 vols (London, 1691). https://archive.org/details/AngliaSacra

Wilkins, David. *Concilia Magnae Britanniae et Hiberniae*. 4 vols (London, 1737). https://archive.org/details/conciliamagnaebr03wilk

Manuscripts

Annals of Lannercost. BL MS Cotton, Claudius D. 7.
Bale, John. *Index Britanniae scriptorium*. MS Bodl. Seld. Sup 64, fol. 166.
Burton Annals. BL, MS Cotton, Vespasian E. 3.
Gascoigne, Thomas. *Dictionarium Theologicum*. *c*.1434–1458. Lincoln College, Oxford, MSS 117 and 118.
Melrose Chronicles. BL MS Cotton, Faustina B. 9.

Other Works Cited in this Edition

Attwater, Donald, *The Penguin Dictionary of Saints* (Harmondsworth, 1965).
Bale, John, *Actes of the Englysh Votaryes* ([Antwerp], 1546).
Bale, John, *The Pageant of Popes contayninge the lyves of all the bishops of Rome, from the beginninge of them to the yeare of grace 1555*. Translated by J. Studley (London, 1574).
Bale, John, *Index Britanniae scriptorium: John Bale's Index of British and Other Writers*. Edited by R. Lane Poole, C. Brett and James P. Carley (Woodbridge, 1990).
Barnett, S. J., 'Where was your Church before Luther? Claims for the Antiquity of Protestantism Examined', *Church History* 68 (1999), 14–41.
Barron, D. G., *Jean Charlier de Gerson: The Author of the De Imitatione Christi* (Edinburgh and London, 1936).
Barrow, Julia, 'A Twelfth-Century Bishop and Literary Patron: William de Vere', *Viator* 18 (1987), 175–89.
Bartlett, Robert, *Gerald of Wales: A Voice in the Middle Ages* (Stroud, 2006).
Bautz, Friedrich Wilhelm, 'Ortwin Gratius (van Graes)', *Biographisch-Bibliographisches Kirchenlexikon*. Edited by Faustus von Mileve and Jeanne d'Arc (Hamm, 1990), vol. 2, pp. 290–91.
Bellenger, Dominic A., and Stella Fletcher, *Princes of the Church: A History of the English Cardinals* (Stroud, 2001).
Bergström, Johan, and Richard Copsey, eds., *Thomas Netter of Walden: Carmelite, Diplomat and Theologian, c.1372–1430* (Faversham and Rome, 2009).
Boyle, L. E., 'Robert Grosseteste and the Pastoral Care', *Medieval and Renaissance Studies 8* (1979), 3–51.
Brent, Allen, 'The Enigma of Ignatius of Antioch', *Journal of Ecclesiastical History* 57.3 (2006), 429–56.

Brooke, Rosalind B., *Early Franciscan Government: Ellias to Bonaventure* (Cambridge, 1959, 2004).
Burton, Edwin H., *The Life and Times of Bishop Challoner*. 2 vols (London, 1909).
Burton, Edwin H., and Edmond Nolan, *The Douay College Diaries: The Seventh Diary, 1715–1778*, Catholic Record Society 28 (1928).
Butler, Charles, *Additions to the Historical Memoirs respecting the English, Irish and Scottish Catholics, from the Reformation to the present time* (London, 1821).
Carrera, A., M. J. Carrera, C. Herrero, P. Garcés, B. Cano, E. González-Cascos, and A. Sáez, *Philip Perry's Sketch of the Ancient British History* (Newcastle, 2009).
Challoner, Richard, *Memoirs of Missionary Priests* (Manchester, 1803).
Christianson, Gerald, *Cesarini, the Conciliar Cardinal, 1431–1438* (St. Ottilien, 1979).
Colley, Linda, *Britons: Forging the Nation, 1707–1837* (New Haven, 2009 revised edition).
Cullen, Christopher M., 'Alexander of Hales', in *A Companion to Philosophy in the Middle Ages*. Edited by J. E. Gracia and T. B. Noone (Oxford, 2006), pp. 104–08.
Cunningham, Jack P., *James Ussher and John Bramhall: The Theology and Politics of Two Irish Ecclesiastics of the Seventeenth Century* (Aldershot, 2007).
Cunningham, Jack P., 'Lumen de Lumine: Light, God and Creation in the Thought of Robert Grosseteste', in *Bishop Grosseteste and Lincoln Cathedral*. Edited by N. Temple, J. S. Hendrix and C. Frost (Aldershot, 2014), pp. 81–98.
D'Alatri, Mariano, 'Il vescovo nella Cronaca da Salimbene di Parma', *Collectanea Franciscana* 42 (1972), 5–38.
Denholm-Young, Noël, 'Thomas de Wykes and his Chronicle', *English Historical Review* 61 (1946), 157–79.
Denholm-Young, Noël, *Richard of Cornwall* (Oxford, 1947).
Denton, J. H., *Robert Winchelsey and the Crown, 1294–1313: A Study in the Defence of Ecclesiastical Liberty* (Cambridge, 1980).
D'Ewes, Simonds, *The Primitive Practise for Preserving the Truth* (London, 1645).
De Quehen, H., 'Politics and Scholarship in the Ignatian Controversy', *The Seventeenth Century* 13.1 (1998), 69–84.
Dixon, W. H., *Fasti Eboracenses: Lives of the Archbishops of York*. Edited by J. Raine (London, 1863).
Duffy, Eamon, ed., *Challoner and His Church* (London, 1981).
Elliott, Mark W., 'Robert Grosseteste, the Jews, and "De cessatione legalium"', in *Robert Grosseteste, His Thought and its Impact*. Edited by J. P. Cunningham (Toronto, 2012), pp. 314–26.

Evans, G. R., *Bernard of Clairvaux* (Oxford, 2000).

Evenden, Elizabeth, and Thomas S. Freeman, *Religion and the Book in Early-Modern England: The Making of John Foxe's 'Book of Martyrs'* (Cambridge, 2011).

Field, Henry, *Of the Church: Fiue Bookes*. Edited by Nathaniel Field, second edition (Oxford, 1628).

Flood, John, and James McEvoy, '*Romanorum malleus et contemptor*: Confessional Identity and the Early Modern Reputation of Robert Grosseteste', in *Robert Grosseteste and His Intellectual Milieu*. Edited by J. Flood, J. R. Ginther, and J. W. Goering (Toronto, 2013), pp. 319–90.

Fuller, Thomas, *The Church History of Britain from the Birth of Jesus Christ, untill the year MDCXLVIII* (London, 1665).

Fuselli, E., *Il Chronicon de San Bartolomeo di Carpineto* (L'Aquila, 1996).

Galbraith, G. R., *The Constitutions of the Dominican Order, 1216–1360* (Manchester, 1925).

Galbraith, Vivian H., 'The "Historia Aurea" of John, Vicar of Tynemouth, and the Sources of the St Albans Chronicle (1327–1377)', in *Essays in History Presented to Reginald Lane Poole*. Edited by H. W. C. Davies (Oxford, 1927), pp. 379–98.

Gerald of Wales, *The History and Topography of Ireland*. Translated by J. J. O'Meara (London, 1982).

Gillow, Joseph, *A Literary and Biographical History, or Bibliographical Dictionary of English Catholics*. 5 vols (London, 1885).

Glickman, Gabriel, *The English Catholic Community, 1688–1745: Politics, Culture and Ideology* (Woodbridge, 2009).

Godwin, Francis. *A Catalogue of the bishops of England, since the first planting of Christian religion in this Island together with a briefe history of their liues and memorable actions, to neere as can be gathered out of antiquity* (London, 1601).

Harmsen, T. H. B. M., *Antiquarianism in the Augustan Age: Thomas Hearne, 1678–1735* (Frankfurt am Main, 2000).

Harris, Max, *Sacred Folly: A New History of the Feast of Fools* (Ithaca, 2011).

Harrison Thomson, S., *The Writings of Robert Grosseteste* (Cambridge, 1940).

Hart, W. H., and P. A. Lyons, eds., *Cartularium monasterii de Rameseia* (London, 1884–93).

Hattersley, Roy, *The Catholics* (London, 2017).

Helmholz, R. H., 'Bastardy Litigation in Medieval England', *American Journal of Legal History* 13 (1969), 360–83.

Higgons, Theophilus, *The First motiue of T.H. Maister of Arts, and lately minister, to suspect the integrity of his Religion ...* (Douai, 1609).

Hill, J. W. F., 'The Tomb of Robert Grosseteste with an Account of its Opening in 1782', in *Robert Grosseteste: Scholar and Bishop*. Edited by D. A. Callus (Oxford, 1955), pp. 246–50.

Hillerbrand, Hans J., ed., *The Oxford Encyclopedia of the Reformation* (Oxford, 1996).

Hilton, J. A., 'The Science of the Saints: The Spirituality of Butler's Lives of Saints', *Recusant History* 15.2 (1979), 189–93.

Hoskin, Philippa M., *Robert Grosseteste as Bishop of Lincoln. The Episcopal Rolls, 1235–1253* (London, 2015).

Hudson, Anne, 'Wyclif and the Grosseteste Legacy at Oxford Greyfriars', in *Robert Grosseteste, His Thought and its Impact*. Edited by J. P. Cunningham (Toronto, 2009), pp. 201–16.

Hunt, R.W., 'English Learning in the Late Twelfth Century', *Transactions of the Royal Historical Society*, fourth series, 19 (1936), 19–42.

Hylson-Smith, Kenneth, *The Churches in England from Elizabeth I to Elizabeth II* (London, 1997).

Jonge, M. de, 'Robert Grosseteste and the Testaments of the Twelve Patriarchs', *Journal of Theological Studies*, New Series 42 (1991), 115–25.

Kelly, J. N. D., *The Oxford Dictionary of Popes* (Oxford, 1986).

Kemp, Eric W., 'The Attempted Canonization of Robert Grosseteste', in *Robert Grosseteste, Scholar and Bishop*. Edited by D. A. Callus (Oxford, 1955), pp. 241–46.

Krey, Philip D. W., and Lesley Smith, eds., *Nicholas of Lyra: The Senses of Scripture* (Leiden, 2000).

Lahey, Stephen, 'Wyclif and Lollardy', in *The Medieval Theologians*. Edited by G. R. Evans (Oxford, 2001), pp. 334–54.

Lawrence, C. H., *St Edmund of Abingdon: A Study in Hagiography and History*. Oxford, 1960.

Lechler, Gotthard V., *John Wycliffe and His English Precursors*. Translated by P. Lorimer (London, 1878).

Leland, John, and John Bale, *The laboryouse Iourney serche of Iohan Leylande…* (London, 1549).

Levy, Fred J., *Tudor Historical Thought* (San Marino, CA, 1967).

Little, Andrew G., *The Grey Friars at Oxford* (Oxford, 1892).

Lombard, Peter, *The Sentences, Books 1–4* (Toronto, 2007–10).

Luard, H. R., *Roberti Grosseteste epistolae episcopi quondam Lincolniensis* (London, 1861; Cambridge, 2012).

Luard, H. R., ed., *Annales Monastici*. Rolls Series, 36. 5 vols (London, 1864–69).

Lunt, William E., *Financial Relations of the Papacy with England to 1327* (Cambridge, MA, 1939).

Major, Kathleen, 'The Familia of Robert Grosseteste', in *Robert Grosseteste, Scholar and Bishop*. Edited by D. A. Callus (Oxford, 1955), pp. 216–41.

Manning, Robert, *The Case stated between the Church of Rome and the Church of England* (London, 1721).

McEvoy, James, *The Philosophy of Robert Grosseteste* (Oxford, 1982).

McEvoy, James, *Robert Grosseteste* (Oxford, 2000).

McEvoy, James, 'Robertus Grossatesta Lincolniensis: An Essay in Historiography, Medieval and Modern', in *Robert Grosseteste and the Beginnings of a British Theological Tradition*. Edited by M. O'Carroll (Rome, 2003), pp. 21–99.

Milner, J., 'The Rt. Rev. John Hornyold', *Laity's Directory* (Dublin, 1818).

Moorman, J. R. H., *A History of the Franciscan Order from its Origins to the Year 1517* (Oxford, 1968).

Myer, W. David, *"Poor Sinning Folk": Confession and Conscience in Counter-Reformation Germany* (Ithaca, NY 1996).

Oldham, James, *English Common Law in the Age of Mansfield* (Chapel Hill, NC, 2004).

Paravicini Bagliani, A., *Cardinali di Curia e 'Familae' Cardinalize. 2 vols* (Padova, 1972).

Pearsall, Derek A., *John Lydgate* (London, 1970).

Pegge, Samuel, *The Life and Writing of Robert Grosseteste, the Celebrated Bishop of Lincoln* (London, 1793).

Pegues, F., 'The "Clericus" in the Legal Administration of Thirteenth-Century England', *The English Historical Review* 281 (1956), 526–59.

Perron, Anthony, 'The Bishops of Rome, 1100–1300', in *The Cambridge History of Christianity*. Edited by M. Rubin and W. Simons. 9 vols (Cambridge, 2009).

Pits, John, *Relationum historicarum de rebus Anglicis*. Edited by W. Bishop (Paris, 1619).

Powicke, F. Maurice, *The Medieval Books of Merton College* (Oxford, 1931).

Powicke, F. Maurice, *King Henry III and the Lord Edward* (Oxford, 1947).

Rose, Jacqueline, *Godly Kingship in Restoration England: The Politics of Royal Supremacy, 1660–1688* (Cambridge, 2011).

Russell, J. C., *Dictionary of Writers of Thirteenth Century England* (London, 1936).

Russell, J. C., 'Richard of Bardney's Account of Robert Grosseteste's Early and Middle Life', *Medievalia et Humanista* 2 (1944), 45–55.

Sáez-Hidalgo, A., and R. F. Yaeger, 'Philip Perry's "Schools" Manuscript and the Invention of the Recusant Middle Ages', *Viator: Medieval and Renaissance Studies* 45.2 (2014), 373–97.

Schalby, John, *The Book of John de Schalby, Canon of Lincoln, 1229–1333, Concerning the Bishops of Lincoln and their Acts*. Translated by J. H. Srawley (Lincoln, 1949).

Selart, Anti, 'William of Modena', in *The Crusades: An Encyclopedia*. Edited by Allan V. Murray (Santa Barbara, 2006), p. 1280.

Sondag, Gérard, 'John de la Rochelle', in *A Companion to Philosophy in the Middle Ages*. Edited by J. E. Gracia and T. B. Noone (Oxford, 2006), pp. 334–35.

Southern, Richard, *Robert Grosseteste: The Growth of an English Mind in Medieval Europe* (Oxford, 1986).

Srawley, J. H., 'Grosseteste's Administration of the Diocese of Lincoln', in *Robert Grosseteste: Scholar and Bishop.* Edited by D. A. Callus (Oxford, 1955), pp. 146–77.

Stevenson, Francis S., *Robert Grosseteste, Bishop of Lincoln* (London, 1899).

Stevenson, J., *Chronica de Mailros* (Edinburgh, 1835).

Stocker, Donald A., 'The Tomb and Shrine of Robert Grosseteste in Lincoln Cathedral', in *England in the Thirteenth Century: Proceedings of the 1984 Harlaxton Symposium*. Edited by W. M. Ormond (Harlaxton College, 1985), pp. 143–48.

Stothert, J. A., *Scotichronicon*. Edited by J. F. Gordon (Glasgow, 1869).

Sylla, Edith D., *The Oxford Calculators and the Mathematics of Motion, 1320–1350: Physics and Measurement by Latitudes* (New York, 1991).

Vauchez, A., *Sainthood in the Later Middle Ages* (Cambridge, 1997).

Vincent, Nicholas, ed., *The Letters and Charters of Cardinal Guala Bicchieri, Papal Legate in England, 1216–1218* (Woodbridge, 1996).

Vincent, Nicholas, 'Isabella of Angoulême: John's Jezebel', in *King John: New Interpretations*. Edited by S. D. Church (Woodbridge, 1999), 165–220.

Vincent, Nicholas, *The Holy Blood: King Henry III and the Westminster Blood Relic* (Cambridge, 2001).

Watt, John A., 'Grosseteste and the Jews: A Commentary on Letter V', in *Robert Grosseteste and the Beginnings of a British Theological Tradition*. Edited by M. O'Carroll (Rome, 2003), pp. 201–16.

Weiler, Björn, 'Matthew Paris in Norway', *Revue Benedictine* 122.1 (2012), 153–81.

White, Reginald J., *The Age of George III* (London, 1968).

Williams, Michael E., 'Philip Perry, Rector of the English College, Valladolid (1768–1774)', *Recusant History* 17.1 (1984), 48–66.

Williams, Michael E., *St Alban's College Valladolid: Four Centuries of English Catholic Presence in Spain* (London, 1986).

Williams, Michael E., 'St Alban's College, Valladolid and the events of 1767', *Recusant History* 20.1 (1990), 223–38.

Wilshire, Leland E., 'Boniface of Savoy, Carthusian and Archbishop of Canterbury, 1207–1270', *Analecta Cartusiana* 31 (1977), 4–90.

Wood, Diana, 'John of Ayton's "Grumbling Gloss": A Northern Churchman's View of Society, c.1100–1700', in *Life and Thought in the Northern Church, c.1100–c.1700: Essays in Honour of Claire Cross.* Edited by Diana Wood (Woodbridge, 1999), pp. 37–55.

Wort, Oliver, *John Bale and Religious Conversion in Reformation England* (London, 2013).
Wyclif, John, *Johannis Wyclif, Tractatus de logica*. Edited by M. Dziewicki. 3 vols (London, 1896. Repr. Frankfurt, 1966).
Yates, W. Nigel, 'Bishop Peter de Aquablanca (1240–1268): A Reconsideration', *Journal of Ecclesiastical History* 22 (1971), 303–17.

Published Manuscripts

Fasti Ecclesiae Anglicanae 1300–1541, vol. I, *Lincoln Diocese*. Edited by H. P. F. King (London, 1962).
Fasti Ecclesiae Anglicanae 1066–1300, vol. 2, *Monastic Cathedrals*. Edited by Diana E. Greenway (London, 1971).
Provincial Assembly of London, *Jus divinum minsterii evangelici. Or the Divine Right of the Gospel-Ministry* (London, 1654).
Rotuli Ricardi Gravesend, 1258–79. Edited by F. N. Davis (London, 1925).
Rotuli Roberti Grosseteste episcopi Lincolniensis. Edited by F. N. Davis (London, 1913).
York Minster Fasti. Edited by C. T. Clay (Leeds, 1959).

Works of Reference

The Oxford Dictionary of the Christian Church. Edited by F. L. Cross and E. A. Livingstone (Oxford, 1997).
Oxford Dictionary of National Biography. Edited by H. C. G. Matthew and B. Harrison (Oxford, 2004).

Websites

The Newman Reader. Available at: http://www.newmanreader.org/works/occasions/sermon10.html
The Unabridged Acts and Monuments Online or *TAMO* (HRI Online Publications, Sheffield, 2011). Available at: https://www.dhi.ac.uk/foxe/

INDEX

In line with common practice in Medieval Studies, medieval figures are indexed by first name (with the exception of Robert Grosseteste himself) and moderns by surname.